The Outcasts' Outcast
A BIOGRAPHY OF
LORD LONGFORD

PETER STANFORD

SUTTON PUBLISHING

First published in the United Kingdom in 2003 by
Sutton Publishing Limited · Phoenix Mill
Thrupp · Stroud · Gloucestershire · GL5 2BU

This paperback edition first published in 2006

British Library Cataloguing in Publication Data
A catalogue record for this book is available from the British Library.

ISBN 0 7509 4497 8

> *To my father,*
> *often in the background*
> *but loved and valued*

Typeset in 11/14.5pt Sabon.
Typesetting and origination by
Sutton Publishing Limited.
Printed and bound in England by
J.H. Haynes & Co. Ltd, Sparkford.

Contents

Note on the photographs

All pictures courtesy of Frank and Elizabeth Longford's literary executor, except numbers 16 and 18.

Preface

In 1994 I published an authorized biography of Frank Longford. Even though one of his friends, Bevis Hillier, remarked in a review that it was 'so well-balanced that it may be little to Longford's taste',[1] the book's appearance and the interest it generated marked the start rather than the end of our friendship. In preparing it, I had worked closely with Frank, though he never wanted to read the manuscript or even the published version. He left that second task, characteristically, to his wife, Elizabeth, who gave it her imprimatur. She was particularly pleased that it corrected the general impression created by his long campaign on behalf of Myra Hindley that he was only interested in visiting infamous prisoners.

It was over prisoners that Frank made his only demand on me regarding the book. Before submitting the manuscript, he invited me to lunch at the House of Lords and ran through a list of the names that I might mention in connection with his prison visiting. With each one, he asked what I had said about them. When I recounted the brief description of their crimes I had included, he put in a plea that I might also mention some of their achievements since being inside – whether as artists, poets or musicians. It was, by conventional standards, an eccentric request but captured well his indifference to what was said about him and his passionate belief in finding the best in everyone else.

It was through Frank that I started visiting prisoners, though intermittently and without his great sense of purpose. We did, however, continue to meet, often over lunch where he would gather an eclectic table that usually included several deserving cases that he wanted me to take up in my journalism or elsewhere. Several have since become good friends. His imperative always to act was passed on in some measure to me.

And so our bond grew and my admiration of him increased. If his achievements as a social reformer were dwarfed by his ambitions, as I had written in my biography, then it was certainly, I came to see ever more clearly, through no lack of courage, tenacity and nobility in their pursuit. He was a man of great intelligence, great moral courage and great wit, though – his Achilles heel – often questionable judgement. As his body slowly packed up, his mind remained razor sharp and forward-looking. He never dwelt on the past but on the here and now. It was his recipe for a long life.

When I got married, he asked if he might be an usher and though his eyesight was failing he did a fine job. Later he asked me if I would edit the prison diary he had been keeping for many years and find it a publisher. I did, and it was to be his last book.[2]

It may sound foolish but when I had to postpone a lunch date with him in July 2001 it never occurred to me that I wouldn't see him again a few weeks later. Yes, he was ninety-five, and even unusually mentioned having a cold, but he had taken on a cloak of invincibility. Certainly that is what he projected. I was on holiday when I learnt of his death in August 2001 and still cannot quite rid myself of the belief that one day my phone will ring at some unearthly hour and he will be on the other end with a new scheme or campaign for which he wants my help.

In the absence of such prompting, I have joined forces with his family, friends and admirers to set up the Frank Longford Charitable Trust which will organize an annual lecture on the issues that he cared about most – social and penal reform – and award a Longford Prize to an individual or group working in that area. There are also plans for scholarships for ex-prisoners. Part of the proceeds from this book will go to fund that work. In July 2001 Cherie Booth QC gave the first Longford Lecture, and Frank would have been delighted at the headlines it generated though he was much missed at the party afterwards.

After his death it was felt that an entirely new version of the biography was needed. Frank's widow, Elizabeth, authorized me to use the mass of papers that he had left in the walk-in safe at his Sussex home, Bernhurst, and the diaries she had kept for almost thirty years. Neither had been available first time round when Frank's life had been very much a work in progress.

To be given such a stash of material and the opportunity to revise and substantially rewrite a biography is, I have come to realize, a great privilege. There is also, I realized, a world of difference between working with a living subject and one who has died. There is the chance to step back, to reassess objectively without fear of causing offence, to include episodes kept out when Frank was alive because he would regard them as too sensitive, and overall to present a fuller and, I hope, more honest picture of an extraordinary, colourful but flawed individual. What follows is therefore based on what has gone before but is substantially different. There are several new chapters, a new epilogue and almost every page has been pored over, amended and refocused. Most of all, this new version goes beyond the public life of Frank Longford to explore in much greater depth his private life as a husband and father, his triumphant lifelong struggle with depression and the truth behind the caricature of an odd-ball puritan that he encouraged in the media.

My affection for him has not, I believe, blunted my critical faculties in this re-evaluation. Some may even feel I have been tougher on him than before but Frank was never, after all, one to avoid saying the unpalatable.

Peter Stanford
London, April 2003

Acknowledgements

Lord Longford's life and achievements sometimes seem to be a subject about which everyone I speak to has an opinion, but special mention should go to the following, who gave generously of their time to share with me their special knowledge and insight: Bronwen Astor, the late David Astor, Rachel Billington, Gyles Brandreth, Lord Carrington, Paul Cavadino of NACRO, Sheila Childs, John Cunningham of the *Guardian*, the late Maureen, Marchioness of Dufferin and Ava, Frank Field MP, Michael Foot, Lady Antonia Fraser, Lord Healey, Sir Nicholas Henderson, the late Myra Hindley, the late Lord Jay, the late Lord Jenkins of Hillhead, Marigold Johnson, Paul Johnson, Rosie Johnston, Judith and Miranda Kazantzis, Anthony Marlowe, Andrew McCooey, Eric McGrath, the late Dr Roger Opie, Kevin, Michael, Patrick, Thomas and Valerie Pakenham, Sarah Sackville-West, Jon Snow, Marina Warner, the late Auberon Waugh and Barbara and Peter Winch.

I am eternally indebted to Mary Craig, who allowed me access to her own past research and to transcripts of interviews with characters in Frank Longford's life who are now beyond the reach of a tape recorder. I hope that I will be as generous to another writer should the opportunity ever arise.

I must thank the late Elizabeth Longford, and Antonia Fraser, her literary executor (also executor of Frank Longford), for entrusting me with her diaries and the papers that Frank left behind and for encouraging me to complete this new version of my biography of him. I was slightly in awe of two such successful biographers but they were ever willing to lend a sympathetic ear. I only wish Elizabeth were still here to see the finished result. I am very grateful to Judith Kazantzis for allowing me to reproduce 'The prince in his sleep', the poem she wrote marking the death of her father. Thanks too are due to my publishers – originally Tom Weldon at Heinemann and now Christopher Feeney at Sutton – to my agent, Derek Johns, to Mike Shaw at Curtis Brown on behalf of the Longford estate, and to my mainstay, my inspiration and my everything, Siobhan.

ONE

The Second Son

Ireland is shaped like a saucer. In the dip where the teacup would stand is a large grey limestone Gothic Revival castle, Tullynally, the family seat of the Longfords. As suggested by its towers and turrets, sticking up like defensive spikes, Tullynally is the home of an essentially military clan, soldiers who served the British Empire at home and abroad. Though not all made quite the impact of their relative by marriage, the Duke of Wellington, the victor of Waterloo – a family joke holds that each of Tullynally's thirty bedrooms could be named after a defeat a Pakenham had suffered on the fields of battle – the Longfords first came to prominence in Ireland with Henry Pakenham, who fought with distinction for Cromwell's forces there in the middle of the seventeenth century. As a reward he was given the land on which Tullynally now stands. He swiftly abandoned the Gaelic name and called his new home Pakenham Hall. His descendants thrived as part of the Ascendancy ruling class of Ireland, colonizers whose role was to keep the locals down and who were characterized by Brendan Behan as 'Protestants with horses'.[1] Several Pakenhams served as Lords Lieutenant in County Longford, though by a curious logic their house is over the border in neighbouring Westmeath.

The Irish countryside runs to castles and when it came to a home that reflected their status as overlords of Catholic Ireland, the Pakenhams, ennobled in 1785 as Earls of Longford, were, like many of their peers, slaves to fashion. When it was the vogue to have a classical house, they employed the architect of Trinity College, Dublin, to give the hall an elegant five-bay façade. Come the nineteenth century, with its passion among the Ascendancy families for what was grandly called Irish baronial, and Pakenham Hall was given battlements and a portcullis. It even boasted Ireland's first central heating system. Their neighbour, Richard Lovell Edgeworth, installed huge underground pipes to warm the front hall and family room, with the redundant fireplace filled by an organ.

The spirit of the age, however, was moving against the superimposed ruling class of Ireland. Following the failure of the invasion by French revolutionary forces in 1798 in support of Wolfe Tone and his independence-seeking United Irishmen, the Act of Union of 1800 removed what was judged to have been an ineffective assembly in Dublin and replaced it with direct rule from Westminster. At a stroke it took away the Ascendancy's power base, leaving the British Parliament in 1829 to give some Irish Catholics the vote and in 1872 the right to a secret ballot. No longer could landlords arrange representation in the Commons, which duly started to enhance the rights of Irish tenants and reduce rents with a series of Land Acts. Over this period the Anglo-Irish families came to see their estates no longer as a prize for loyal service to the Crown but more as a burden. For many, whatever roots they had put down in their adopted country were simply not strong enough to survive these changing times. When the Wyndham Act of 1903 offered them government subsidies to sell to their tenants, many cut their losses at a cost to the Treasury of £12 million. Without the surrounding land and hence the cushion of rent, the maintenance of extravagant, ornate homes with acres of roof in the damp Irish countryside became impractical.

Economic reform in Ireland was taking place against the political backdrop of an ever-growing demand for Home Rule, if not independence. Increasingly the landed class which, by and large, opposed such moves, felt itself under attack on all fronts – harassed by their tenants and abandoned by politicians in London who seemed deaf to their protests. 'In the South, from the Union

2

onwards,' Frank Longford wrote in 1935, 'the Protestant class ranked as Loyalist to England. But most of them stayed Irish in everything but political aspiration.'[2] This dual allegiance – to Britain and Ireland simultaneously – became harder and harder to sustain once the political arrangements that had created it altered. For many, despite having lived in Ireland for many generations, the tie to Britain proved the more enduring. That came as no surprise to Daisy, Countess of Fingall, who wrote unflinchingly of others of her own class at the dawn of the twentieth century in her sprightly memoir *Seventy Years Young*. 'The Irish landlords continued to be colonists. The very building of their houses, the planting of their trees, the making of walls around their estates . . . declared their intention . . . They lived within their demesnes, making a world of their own, with Ireland outside the gates.'[3]

Most of the Anglo-Irish aristocracy would go over to stay in rented houses in London for the Season – May to June, preceded by Dublin's own vice-regal balls in February and March – but the fortunate few had permanent homes in England and even English titles which guaranteed them a seat by right in the House of Lords. (Only twenty-eight representative Irish peers, elected by their fellows, were allowed on its voting benches and after 1922 none at all.) Among this privileged élite were the Longfords, who since 1821 had held the English Barony of Silchester, conferred as one of George IV's coronation honours. Up to and for the decade following his marriage in November 1899, Thomas Pakenham, the 5th Earl of Longford, had a series of rented houses both in central London and in the Buckinghamshire and Oxfordshire countryside from where he could indulge the twin passions in his life – attending the Lords (where he always voted against Home Rule proposals) and riding with the Bicester and Heythrop hunts. Pakenham Hall was somewhere he visited at Easter and in the summer, hunting with the Westmeath Hounds and regarding it, economic considerations to one side, as something more important than a holiday retreat but certainly not as his spiritual home. And so it was that his second son, Francis Aungier Pakenham, was born in the family's rented London house at 7 Great Cumberland Place, not their Irish castle, on 5 December 1905. His brother, Edward, was three and his sister, Pansy, just one.

The name Francis – always abbreviated to Frank – was chosen at the behest of the baby's Great-Aunt Caroline, widow of the diplomat Sir Francis Pakenham. She had no children and travelled up to London to inspect the new-born boy in his cradle. Satisfied by what she saw, she offered to make him the heir to Bernhurst, her 75-acre estate at Hurst Green in Sussex, on condition that he was named after her late husband. As a second son, the young Frank had no other inheritance to look forward to, so his parents gratefully accepted.

Thomas Longford, young Frank's father, had married well by the standards of the time. His wife, Mary Child-Villiers, was a daughter of the Earl of Jersey, the former Governor-General of New South Wales and a man of great wealth and influence with homes at Osterley Park outside London and Middleton Stoney in Oxfordshire, where he kept his prized collection of Van Dycks. His wife, Margaret, Countess of Jersey, was an ambitious political and literary hostess who welcomed men such as Stevenson, Kipling, Gosse, Kitchener and Chamberlain into her salon. Osterley was regularly awash with the great and the good at Lady Jersey's celebrated parties. It was the place to which anyone was glad to be invited, but quite what Thomas Longford was doing there remains a mystery. This was certainly not his natural milieu. A dedicated countryman, following Winchester and Oxford he had joined the Life Guards, after which the army became his absorbing interest. He had ridden just behind the gun carriage at Edward VII's funeral. He was not a party-goer or a member of the smart set in London. Shy and reserved, prone to talking in a mumble, he was often described by his friends as one of the worst-dressed men in town on account of his carelessness over appearance. There is a group photograph in which he appears surrounded by tiers of soldiers in correct uniform while he wears a bowler hat and scruffy overcoat.[4]

The link may have been Walter Rice, Lord Dynevor, who in 1898 married Margaret Child-Villiers, the Jerseys' eldest daughter. Dynevor and Thomas were third cousins, Longford's mother, Selina

Rice-Trevor, having been one of a family of Welsh heiresses from whom the Dynevor peerage and their castle in Carmarthenshire had passed to Dynevor's grandfather. Indeed it was Dynevor who was able to vouch for the bona fides of his 35-year-old cousin after the latter had approached Lord Jersey in 1899 to ask for the hand of his 22-year-old daughter Mary in marriage. The Jerseys had initially worried that their second daughter might be marrying beneath her. They had previously steered her towards Lord Beauchamp as a future spouse, even taking her with them to stay at his moated home, Madresfield Court.

Thomas Longford may have lacked Mary's mother's flamboyance or her father's (often ill-tempered) grandeur; she did not find that enough of a drawback to prevent her, after a brief pause – 'am undecided', she wrote in her diary after recording his proposal[5] – from accepting his offer. The hesitation came, it seems, because his offer came out of the blue as far as she was concerned. She had not thought of him up to that point as a suitor, given the age difference. 'One day in the summer of 1899 when the family were at Osterley,' the couple's daughter Mary later wrote in an unpublished biography of her mother, 'Mama heard Grandpapa remark that he wondered why that bore Longford was coming to lunch again, and she suddenly realised that he was coming because of her.' Once she had had time to get used to the idea, though, her enthusiasm was great and genuine. Indeed, she may have seen the contrast between her future husband and her home life as a blessing, for her parents' concerns were most certainly not hers. If she was close to either of them, it was to her father. She felt eclipsed and irritated by her overbearing mother.

Those who knew the couple spoke of a marriage based on genuine attraction and love, rather than dynastic concerns. The two shared an innocence, a strong sense of duty, a hatred of ostentation and a pleasure in the simple things of life rather than the social whirl. On one of the few occasions that Mary took Thomas to a dinner with her smart friends in London, he fell asleep in the dining room at 10 p.m., as he invariably did, and smashed a vase, to her great embarrassment.[6] Later, if they entertained at all at home, it was usually relations since the gap in their ages meant that the couple had few friends in common. Though Mary was initially the more social, she was a loner at heart, her daughter Mary later reflected. 'Osterley was ideal for her – lots of people but no intimacy.'[7]

The Jerseys were relieved to discover from Dynevor that their future son-in-law was, unlike many Anglo-Irish peers, a man of substantial means. Successive Pakenhams had built up their fortune and estates through advantageous marriages. One such alliance had brought them a thousand acres around Dun Laoghaire – or Kingstown as it was then known – when it was still a small fishing village south of Dublin. From 1815 it developed into Ireland's main port. Hand in hand with such good fortune, the Pakenhams were careful with their spending. The 4th earl, a man of great wealth in the latter part of the nineteenth century, wrote to his wife on one occasion from overseas to say that he had decided against buying a Turkish carpet because it seemed too expensive at £45.[8] The Pakenhams were not at all the sort of extravagant buccaneering gaylords who returned from England to their Irish estates for a spot of shooting and a well-earned rest in the manner of the pre-Revolution Russian aristocracy. In the family records for this period at Tullynally there is little sign of entertaining on a grand scale or even anything as innocently social as going to the races. The visitors' book reveals the Pakenhams as anti-show and anti-snob, much more likely to be holding a tea party for local school-children in the grounds than welcoming empire builders and celebrated politicians and writers. Indeed, when Thomas Longford, at Oxford, had written to his father, mentioning that he had declined an invitation to Osterley, he had received by return a letter applauding his decision. 'You were quite right to refuse Jersey's invitation. The *premier pas* often leads to the *facilis descensus*.'[9]

Soon after their marriage, Thomas Longford took his new countess to see his Irish castle. 'Mrs Duffy, who scrubbed the passages, assured me', their daughter Violet later wrote of that first visit by her mother, 'that the station omnibus, with the horses taken out, had been dragged from a lodge half a mile away with my parents sitting on top. She told me too that she had thought my mother the most beautiful young lady she had ever seen.'[10] Soon after this triumphant arrival, however, Thomas Longford sailed off from Cork to Cape Town to serve in the Boer War. As the couple were being married at St George's, Hanover Square in London, in South Africa Kimberley and Ladysmith were being besieged. By the time he came back permanently in 1902 Mary had returned to England and it was in one of their many rented homes that the first of their six children arrived soon afterwards. 'We were', the fourth of the half-dozen, Mary, was later to write, 'a large family of large children. My mother and the doctor mutually congratulated each other when Frank weighed in at ten pounds, fourteen ounces, but I soon set up a new record with ten pounds, fifteen ounces.'[11] Mary came two years after Frank. Then there was a five year hiatus before Violet in 1912 and Julia in 1913.

In the summer of 1911, the family finally acquired a permanent English base with the purchase of North Aston Hall and its thirty bedrooms and 107 acres. They moved in with a full quota of staff – that is to say a butler, Mr Taylor, three in the nursery, three man-servants, three housemaids, three in the kitchen, a char or two, a lady's maid and a governess. Violet in her autobiography was to damn North Aston as 'a wholesome eighteenth-century building' that had been afflicted by 'an outbreak of nineteenth-century medievalism which had turned it into a mullioned and fancy-chimney-stacked imitation of an Elizabethan mansion'.[12] Mary for her part indicted its bland interior, another sign of her parents' shared lack of enthusiasm for the finer things of life. 'They bought it in affluent days and quickly fitted it out with non-committal store furniture from the most non-committal store in London . . . The ultimate lid was put on our dissatisfaction by finding all the bills and estimates, by that time nearly a quarter of a century old. To our postwar bed-sitting-room minds, they seemed as bad as the extravagances of the Bourbons.'[13] Later a permanent London base in Bryanston Square in Mayfair was bought.

Already thirty-eight when his first child was born, and almost fifty when Julia arrived, Thomas Longford was, unusually, the more approachable of the two parents. He was the one who seemed to delight in his children, dropping in regularly on the nursery floor in his scruffy red coat before he went hunting, taking his brood off on walks to the farm and around the countryside, instructing his sons on how to conceal a battalion in woodland and telling them tales from the battlefield. There were also odd outings. On one occasion he took his four older children to a chair factory in Buckinghamshire and allowed each to choose one. He was for ever giving them presents, Mary recalled.[14] When he was away, he would write them affectionate, child-like letters. 'Frank as a boy idolised my father and so idolised the army,' Mary later said. 'Edward and my father didn't get on, but Frank would listen to all this army talk and it created in him a romantic picture of war as rather like the Battle of Hastings with bows and arrows.'[15] For all his reserve, Thomas Longford could also, in the company of his children, exhibit a sharp line in wit and verbal dexterity. 'He once took us for a walk through the village at North Aston,' Mary remembered, 'and Frank and Pansy were playing a game where you had to make rhyming couplets of poetry. When we said "Dada, it's your turn", he replied, "It really is a waste of time to go on making silly rhyme".'[16] He liked jokes and would hum Gilbert and Sullivan tunes. 'Dada was somehow involved with the ideas of not telling lies and of being brave,' Mary wrote, 'even heroic if necessary.'[17]

Their father's close interest in all his children was in some respects by way of compensation for the lack of attention their mother paid them. She would only be seen in the nursery if there was a crisis. She would preside over her six offspring for luncheon ('lunch', she corrected them, 'is a mid-morning snack') and for half an hour in the evening, always insisting on bed-time prayers, before handing them back to their nannies. While this was by no means an unusual set-up for the children of the aristocracy in Victorian and Edwardian times, Mary Longford was even by the standards of her time standoffish. 'Mama was essentially remote, a tall, pale, grey figure who hurried along in the distance with a walking stick [she developed arthritis at a young age], reclined on a sofa painting flowers or drove out to call with a silver cornetted card-case', Mary wrote in her biography.[18] Their mother carried in her wake an almost icy breeze, according to Violet.

On our way out for our morning walk, we would pause at the dining room to greet my mother . . . washing down cold haddock with stewed tea under the shadow of her family's portraits in oil. The dining room was chilly but at that hour it was positively glacial, for economy and coal shortages dictated that dining-room fires were a luxury reserved for visitors. The table was covered with the iciest of damask and the china was white with a barely visible gold rim.[19]

Any display of affection was frowned upon. On her death bed, when her daughter Mary leant forward to give her a final kiss, Mary Longford pushed her away saying: 'As you remember, I was never very good at kissing.'[20]

Only with her elder son, Edward, did Mary Longford make an exception. Primogeniture and Edward's always delicate health appear to have revealed some otherwise buried maternal streak. With him she was not quite so unbending. He alone, for instance, was allowed to argue with her. Even when he was small, he would answer her back and challenge her views while the others looked on in silence. He was the one who would be taken out on trips with her. He was indulged and, her husband believed, spoilt by his mother. She would even put up with the tantrums that Edward continued to suffer in adult life. On one occasion she paid to have a volume of his undistinguished schoolboy poetry privately published, quite a departure for a parsimonious woman with only moderate interest in literature or the arts. One verse began: 'Night is a sweating negro over London'.[21]

Such encouragement did not, however, extend to Frank or his sisters. Instead, when he was still a child, his mother drilled into Frank that as a second son he would have to make his own way in the world. His inheritance at Bernhurst would not be enough to support him, and anyway, she used to warn him, Great-Aunt Caroline was under no obligation and could take it away at any time. She was, he would admit in old age, 'rather cold to me'.[22] On another occasion, he told the authors of a book called *The Change Makers*: 'The truth is that my mother was not very cordial towards me. My elder brother she adored and always did so. I think I would have to say that I could never have satisfied my mother.'[23]

Early life for the Pakenham children did, however, have its high points and triumphs. There were, for example, their visits to their maternal grandparents' homes. Lady Jersey's garden parties amid the pink walls and blue domes of Osterley offered them a chance to run riot, show off and attract the indulgent adult attention that they craved and otherwise largely missed out on. 'Occasionally,' Mary reported, 'we were rounded up to shake hands with interesting individuals. The interesting individuals generally got the worst of it. Some Indian princes flashed their white teeth at us in embarrassed grins and were asked by Frank if they didn't know that it was very rude to laugh at people.'[24] At another party, Frank, aged just eight, threw a rose into a victoria full of old ladies, much to their delight. Through the Jerseys, the Longford children would be invited to smart tea parties. On one occasion, Frank met Princess Mary, daughter of the king, but was too nervous to ask her to dance.

Then there were their colourful relatives. If the Longford parents were quiet and reserved, there were others in both their families who were eccentric and, to the children, highly amusing and affirming. For Frank in particular there was Great-Aunt Caroline for whom he was the most special boy in the whole world. Visits to Bernhurst, his future home, included such indulgences, unknown at home, as warm water in his bath. For all the children Uncle Edward, better known as 'Bingo', their father's youngest brother, was a constant source of bemusement on account of his oddball behaviour. A real tennis enthusiast, he inhabited only the ground floor of his London house, dressing each night in tail-coat, black waistcoat and black tie, even when he dined alone. Best of all was their Uncle Eddie, Lord Dunsany, husband of their mother's youngest sister, Beatrice. An author and Irish peer, Uncle Eddie used to bring havoc to the well-ordered routine in the nursery at North Aston Hall. 'If he took exception to our clothes,' Mary wrote, 'he would nail them to the floor, or put plasticine on them and throw them to the ceiling so that they stuck there. And when someone asked if the lake was deep, he said "Go in and see" and pushed them in.'[25]

The lake in question was at Pakenham Hall and here, on Easter and summer visits, the children's strict, almost puritanical routine was much relaxed. First there was the journey, by train from London's Euston station on the Irish Mail to Holyhead, then by boat to Dublin (once in the company of Maud Gonne and her two marmosets), followed by the train to Mullingar and finally the last fourteen miles by either pony and trap or in their father's Daimler, reputedly the first in the county. 'We leant out and sniffed the turf smoke of cottages and screamed a welcome to every familiar feature of the road', Mary wrote.[26]

Part of their English routine travelled with them to Ireland. 'Life was still very regimented,' Mary recalled. 'By the time Pansy had reached teenage, she and Edward would have their supper in the drawing room, Frank and I in the schoolroom, and Julia and Violet in the nursery. When Frank had the village boys up for cricket, there was no suggestion that my routine might be changed so that I could join the others. I sat and ate all alone and was miserable'.[27] Their father, though, was more available to them when they were in Ireland, without the distraction of the House of Lords, and as adults many of the children's happiest memories of him were set against the backdrop of Pakenham Hall, increasing the emotional hold the place had on them. 'On my countless walks there with him,' Frank later wrote, 'he was patience and gentleness itself in response to my interminable questionings.'[28]

Pakenham Hall offered much more scope for mischief than the bland North Aston Hall. Its long corridors, maps of the Empire, suits of armour, stone lions and moat – 'the final touch of romance,' according to Mary – entranced them, as did the absence of electric lights. An engraving of Rubens's *Silenius* in the best visitors' bedroom was considered by the children to be the last word in smut. Elizabeth Longford was later to describe her first visit to Pakenham Hall in 1930. 'The glitter will never be effaced,' she wrote, 'but it was the glitter of eccentricity not luxury.'[29] In this spartan but unconventional place the children imagined themselves in a giant playground. Nothing was sacred, or, if it was, only because it was in imminent danger of collapse. 'The tennis lawn was on the lowest of three terraces,' Mary wrote, 'and was guarded by a balustrade whose cement pilasters were said to have been home-made by a gardener on wet days in the potting shed. This was given as the reason for the rule that it was to be neither sat on nor walked along.'[30]

Part of each summer would, in line with their parents' wishes, be given over to duty – 'Her Ladyship's Afternoon Parties' – when first the nuns of St Vincent de Paul from Dublin in their winged white head-dresses would bring a group of handicapped children for tea, and then, on the succeeding days, the pupils of the Catholic and then the much smaller Protestant elementary school in nearby Castlepollard would march up the drive in an uneven crocodile – many of the Catholics bare-footed – to pay their respects to their overlords, then have bread, jam and barm brack in the marquees, and finally compete in races with the Pakenham children. Frank's mother also started a clothing club and inaugurated a district nurse, though not all the locals appreciated her efforts. She once received a letter from an old woman complaining 'it is people like you who fill pauper's [sic] graves and emigrant ships'.[31]

Though she had little affection for Ireland or Pakenham Hall, Mary Longford did not allow the outbreak of the First World War to interrupt the pattern of her visits, and considered the threat of German submarines in the Irish Sea only in so far as she insisted that her four eldest children would travel with her, while the two youngest, Violet and Julia, followed on later with the servants. Her husband for his part once more departed on active service. From Egypt he wrote long letters home to each of his brood, full of observations – that the sun in Egypt set with a pop – and encouragement to take up a sport like tennis – 'such a good game'. On 21 August 1915 Brigadier-General Lord Longford, at the head of the Bucks, Berks and Dorset Yeomanry, was killed at Scimitar Hill, Gallipoli, in an operation Winston Churchill later dismissed as 'fruitless', a remark that Mary Longford never forgave.[32] Sir Roger Keyes, who watched the action from his ship, took a kinder view of the operation. 'The Yeomen were splendid: Lord Longford was killed leading his brigade. I remember how hard and straight he used to go in the Bicester country.'[33] One who observed at close quarters, Fred Cripps, Lord Longford's aide-de-camp, was later to seek out his younger son to pass on his father's last words as they came under fire: 'I wish you would stop ducking, Fred. The men don't like it and it doesn't do any good.'[34]

The loss of his adored father was to have a profound effect on Frank. At an obvious level it removed the most immediate male role model for him, a role model moreover who combined most of the traditional Pakenham virtues of military courage and quiet devotion to duty. There were to be others, however, with whom he sought later to replace that influence. Then there was the manner of his father's death, as a hero, creating a sense of expectation in his son. More damagingly, the loss of Thomas Longford focused Frank and all his siblings ever more acutely on their mother, creating demands that she was ill equipped to answer. For her there was a terrible year of waiting and hoping because her husband's body had not been found. 'Mama went on hoping that Dada was alive long after everyone else knew he must have been killed,' wrote her daughter, Mary, 'and once at North Aston she called me into her sitting-room to write him a letter with the vague idea that a child's letter might get through to the Turkish hospital where he was.'[35] When finally forced to face up to his death, she organized a memorial service at St Mary's Church in Bryanston Square, next to their London house. All her children, except Julia, attended. To the hymn 'Within the churchyard', she added an extra verse: 'And those who die away from home, Their graves we may not see, But we believe God keeps their souls, Where'er their bodies be.'

She then retreated into her grief. At a young age, she had lost the man she adored. In her diary she wrote of what she imagined were his last moments. 'I am sure,' she recorded, 'that the last thing he saw was my face.'[36] Even in less tragic circumstances, Mary Longford would have struggled. She was, it seems, a woman who bore children out of a strong sense of duty. It was simply what you did. (The fact that all of them had such extraordinarily large heads, involving extremely painful labours, could, modern experts might suggest, have dampened whatever maternal bond she felt.) She then worked hard to instil that same sense of duty in her brood with such blunt force that it affected their actions ever after. Her ideas on child-rearing were traditional. Her daughters, for instance, were not expected to go to school, though she was later to relent and allow Violet and Julia that privilege as teenagers after a prolonged campaign.

Widowhood only exacerbated many of her less attractive character traits. The family home became colder and less inviting. On the nursery floor, governesses wore their fur coats all day in winter to keep warm. There were fewer visitors than ever. Even the food on the table was more meagre. So when during the austere years of the First World War, it was suggested that the farms on the Pakenham Hall estate might send butter over to North Aston Hall to circumvent any shortages in England, Mary Longford refused. 'My mother', her daughter Mary wrote, 'was the only person I ever heard about who made a hobby of keeping under rations.'[37] As her daughters grew up into young women, lack of inclination and parsimony meant that their mother denied them anything approaching fashionable clothes. 'My mother', observed Mary, 'had somehow not noticed that children's fashions had changed and as we grew older, we became acutely aware of the eccentricity of our appearance. Our chief grievance was that summer and winter alike we had to wear brown ribbed woollen stockings and brown boots, which were a nuisance all the year round and a trial to the temper in dog-days. But worse still was the shame of them which ate into our very souls.'[38] Their strange dress served only further to isolate the Pakenham children from the outside world and throw them onto each other.

Only on Edward did Mary Longford still manage to smile, forgiving his rages and indulging him at every turn. On his father's death, he had become, at the age of thirteen, the 6th earl. Pansy, when an adult, told her friend Evelyn Waugh of the day her mother came to the nursery and told the children of their father's death. 'Your father has been killed in action and in future, your brother, Silchester, will be addressed as "Edward".' (Silchester was the courtesy title for heirs to the earldom.) That important detail settled, she then left them to their grief.[39]

With Frank, her sin was one of omission. She never made him feel valuable, and the harder he strove to catch her eye, the more firmly she seems to have averted it, the more extrovert he became in his demeanour in an attempt to please her, the more she pushed him away in distaste because that was not how she believed one should behave. She may have seen and disliked in her second son the showiness that ran in her family, but her lack of interest served only to propel Frank further down the road of playing to the gallery. Certainly from an early age, he was able to amuse an audience. With his terrace of curls and winning smile, he was forever in the servants' hall, making them laugh, and in the nursery he quickly eclipsed his siblings in the eyes of their nurse, Mrs Williter, who responded by giving him the reassurance that his mother denied him. When, however, Mary Longford heard of the closeness between her second son and the nurse, she dismissed the woman, depriving Frank of the one person who told him he was special.

When still very young, his sister Mary remembered, Frank developed a trait that was to stay with him all his life – telling funny stories against himself so as to attract attention.

The things that happened to Frank when he was alone were famous. The detail that in actual fact he was always accompanied by the nurse and myself made no difference to him at all. He continued to come out with highly circumstantial accounts of the curious things that had happened to him and, though we knew that he had invented every word of them, damn us if we could prove it. 'I was by myself playing ball in the field,' the great Snake Story began, 'when a snake sprang out of a pond and began to chase me. Quick as lightning I jumped back across the sunk fence, but the snake jumped after me and I raced down the lawn towards the house with the snake not six inches behind. It was neck or nothing. The snake was gaining on me, but I just managed to get home in time and slam the door in his face. But I was not safe yet. The snake sprang in fury against the glass pane, smashed it to smithereens and burst into the house. He fell dead at my feet, cut to bits by the glass.' 'But Frank, why isn't the glass door broken?' 'Oh, Mr Beasley [the carpenter] came and mended it.' 'But, Frank, why aren't there pieces of dead snake about?' 'Oh, a rook came down and ate them up.'[40]

With their father dead and their mother ever more emotionally and physically absent, the Pakenham children got on with life on the nursery floor with gusto. They created their own world, with the two youngest, Julia and Violet, often left to one side while 'us four' precociously battled and tussled and vied to come out on top. Among their favourite pastimes were complex imitations of adult manners. One standard involved arranging books on end along the wall and then each child taking a turn at pretending to be a grown-up in a picture gallery. Frank would hold up an imaginary lorgnette and shriek 'How ingenious!' to cries of laughter from his siblings. Another regular was to make lists of the names of their relatives and give them each marks out of a hundred. What kept the game ever-green, his siblings recalled later, was the unpredictability of Frank's vote. He learnt early the reaction he could provoke by defying conventional wisdom and trying to rehabilitate with lavish praise someone who had previously been regarded as beyond the pale.[41]

Where some of his siblings had more artistic leanings – Edward's plays and acting foreshadowing a lifetime's interest in the theatre – Frank's passions were less cultural. He was, and remained throughout his adult life, tone deaf to music, a failing passed on by his grandmother, Lady Jersey, who once, family legend had it, told a distinguished prima donna that, although not musical, she had a strong sense of rhythm. The prima donna evidently replied wearily that a sense of rhythm was the lowest musical sense of all and that even savages had it.

Where his brothers and sisters were keen on books and literature, even founding their own magazine, politics and games were Frank's twin obsessions. He joined in with the others as the price of persuading them to play along with him, but with little enthusiasm. His mother had to bribe him to read *A Tale of Two Cities* (ten shillings) and *Pickwick Papers* (fifteen). The only books his sister Violet recalled him reading of his own free will were the childish novels of Angela Brazil, and then only on a summer holiday at Pakenham Hall when rain and torpor had ruled out all other options. He learnt passages by heart, she noted, but did not explain why.[42] He could on occasion manage a verse of poetry for the magazine if it would ensure the others joined him at football or fighting. His output was brief and lucid. 'On August the 4th/Britain declared war/A few thought it nice / But most a great bore.'[43]

In both of his passions he was something of a changeling. Only his Jersey grandmother had shown the remotest interest in politics. The highest a Pakenham had risen in political ranks was Frank's grandfather, the 4th earl, who was an Under-Secretary of State at the War Office. Both his parents were staunch, if unthinking, Conservatives. Though they followed the Home Rule debates, and in Thomas Longford's case voted with his class, it was Frank who was obsessed with the detail. Though barely in long trousers, he would follow proceedings in Parliament with the concentration of an elderly clubman in the copy of the *Daily Graphic* that was sent up to the nursery once his mother had finished with it. If he had to do painting and drawing, he would produce neat, graphic reproductions of row after row of MPs decked out in their party colours like members of opposing football teams. Politics and competition were synonymous.

It was, moreover, competitive sports like tennis, cricket and football that appealed to him, rather than the more participatory pursuits of hunting, fishing and shooting that his father had enjoyed. From time to time Mary Longford, no mean handler of a hockey stick or tennis racquet, would deign to join her children for a game, standing in goal with her walking stick in one hand and her hockey stick in the other. 'She was so nearly fun,' her daughter Mary recalled, 'if only she could have unbent to us.'[44] Instead it was only in the company of her younger siblings, her sister, Beatrice, Lady Dunsany, and her brother, Arthur, that she seemed to relax. Frank's enthusiasm for sport, however, was not matched by any great aptitude, his poor eyesight a constant handicap which he refused on grounds of vanity to correct by wearing glasses. Instead he tried to make up for lack of ability with extremes of enthusiasm. The

Pakenhams had a reputation for being rough on the sports field, which further alienated them from other children. One summer at Pakenham Hall, Pansy organized an Anti-Fighting League in an effort to try to calm things down, but to little effect.

It was games that drew Frank to the first of a succession of substitute father figures. Arthur Child-Villiers, his mother's favourite brother, was in his nephew's eyes a sporting hero. Frank may have hoped that by winning Arthur's approval he might also secure that of his mother. His uncle had played cricket for Eton at Lords in the annual match against Harrow (getting out for a duck in both innings, prompting his mother to leave the ground in disgust, though his sister Mary loyally remained in her seat to see him take a vital catch) and had gone on to gain an athletics half-blue while at Oxford. He had a good war, serving in France as a lieutenant in the Queen's Own Oxfordshire Hussars, and then made his mark in the City of London. At this point he was introduced to the Eton Manor Boys' Club in Hackney Wick, a philanthropic sporting club run by wealthy men for young boys from poor homes. It was to become Arthur's chief interest and finally his home. Sport was the gospel at Eton Manor, unlike the Christian inspiration of other such philanthropic ventures in poor areas, and so when Uncle Arthur took young Frank there, it immediately touched a chord. Those visits, he was later fond of saying, were his first introduction to social work. His sister Mary saw it as the first true outlet he found for what she described as 'his interest in doing good – not something any of the rest of us worried about'.[45]

Back around the lunch table at North Aston Hall, the growing Pakenham children began to voice their political convictions. The subject that divided them most was Ireland. Edward and Pansy, inspired by the failed but romantic Easter Rising of 1916 against British rule of Ireland and the Russian Revolution of 1917, railed against the Union and Conservatism. Edward learnt Gaelic and proclaimed himself an Irish patriot. Frank and his sister Mary would rally in response to their mother's side. The political situation in Ireland was changing rapidly. With a quarter of a million Irishmen fighting in the First World War under the British flag in France, the attempt on 24 March 1916 by the Irish Republican Brotherhood, a small group of radical and romantic nationalists led by Padraic Pearse, a poet and pioneer of the Gaelic revival, to seize the General Post Office in the centre of Dublin and declare a republic had failed to ignite the country. The brutality of British troops in putting it down, and the subsequent executions of its leaders, however, did the rebels' work for them. Eamon de Valera, the one surviving commandant from the Rising, exploited native anger at the violence of the British reaction to galvanise Sinn Fein into a powerful force for change.

The wars of 1919–23 – known euphemistically as the troubles (a phrase Mary Longford banned from use) and leading up to the founding of the Irish Free State – brought with them tough times for many Anglo-Irish landowners, especially those whose homes were in isolated country areas. Their mail was disrupted by nationalists, their cars were seized, the railways torn up and communication lines back to Dublin and London broken. Many in this erstwhile garrison class, especially in the West, felt particularly exposed and sold up, often handing over their large houses to Catholic religious orders. About seventy out of an estimated two thousand Ascendancy houses were burnt down during the troubles (another six hundred have been destroyed since).[46] For those who refused to be intimidated, the 1922 treaty which created a semi-free Ireland and maintained through dominion status a link to the Imperial Crown, the old world in which they had been brought up had gone forever, but they kept up appearances. The historian Brian Inglis had described their situation as akin to 'passengers in a ship seized by mutineers. The members of the old Ascendancy families continued to behave as they had always behaved – as if determined to give an example to the lascars who might come up from the bilges to take over the ship and who might otherwise disgrace themselves by panic excesses.'[47] Political power may have gone, the houses were crumbling, but they maintained a show of effortless social superiority.

Such a response seemed entirely appropriate to Mary Longford, even if she was largely an absentee landowner. Pakenham Hall suffered very little in the whole cycle of violence that gave birth to what went on to become an independent Ireland. The worst outrage occurred on 28 May 1923, when Flora McIntrye, the housekeeper at Pakenham Hall, wrote to Mary Longford at North Aston to report that Edward's and Frank's bicycles had been stolen along with whiskey and objects from her sitting room. 'They seem to have spent a lot of time there, also in the housemaids' living room where they had a good meal of cake, milk and eggs; they stole from that room a very nice pair of scissors and case belonging to the Hall.'[48]

Though County Westmeath was not a hot-bed of nationalism, Mary Longford's emphasis on duty and social obligations, coupled with the Pakenhams' long tradition of treating their tenants and local people with consideration, may have contributed to the reluctance to target them or their property. Other local Anglo-Irish suffered more, though hardly grievously. The Longfords' neighbours, the Deases at Turbotston, had the slogan 'Damn your English prejudices. We want our country' daubed on their walls, though the family was later told that the perpetrator had been a Sinn Fein hothead who had come from the West to inspire local resistance. There was one Pakenham uncle who was shot in the face in Dublin trying to put down the 1916 Rising.

The children had been at Pakenham Hall when the Rising broke out. Their mother, characteristically, was determined that her plans would not be disrupted and so set off as she had intended for North Aston since she had to return her two sons to their schools. The girls, however, followed later when calm had returned. 'My mother told me long afterwards', Violet wrote, 'that Edward had written a lively account of crossing Dublin, where fighting had recently ceased, but that Frank had preserved a complete detachment.'[49] The future Irish patriot and nationalist was apparently unmoved by what he saw.

TWO

The Distracted Scholar

For all her rationing of maternal spirit, Mary Longford was a conventional upper-class mother when it came to her sons' schooling. Eton had been the best start in life for her father and brothers. And on the Pakenham side, it had long been held in Anglo-Irish circles that to fail to send your offspring to a major English public school was either to sink to dreary depths of provincialism or worse – for those who preferred a Dublin alternative – to go native. So Edward and Frank were bound from birth for Eton.

The first step, however, was a decent prep school, and their mother chose the highly recommended Furzie Close at Barton-on-Sea in Hampshire. One of those who influenced Mary Longford's decision to opt for this relatively new establishment was an acquaintance, the mother of Alec Spearman, later a Conservative MP.[1] He was four years older than Frank and when young Pakenham arrived, aged nine, Spearman took him under his wing. As a quid pro quo, Frank had to help Alec unstrap his wooden leg at bedtime: a strange task for a young boy on his first night away from home, but one that evidently forged a bond between the two, who remained lifelong friends.

The clever, sporty, extrovert young boy of the nursery floors of Tullynally and North Aston Hall, the darling of most adults save his mother, continued to shine at prep school. He competed ferociously in the classroom and on the sports field at Furzie Close. He was made head boy and his teachers and the headmaster Philip Stubbs liked him. His reports were exemplary. In classics he was 'doing more advanced work than the rest of the form'. The precocious interest in the world of politics that had seen him engrossed in newspaper reports of parliamentary debates on Ireland was maintained, though occasionally he had problems getting his hands on source material. In one letter home to his mother he pleaded: 'Please could you tell me roughly what the German peace proposals are, as I only caught a hasty glimpse of them in Mr Stubbs' paper before he took it away. From what I saw it looked as if they thought they had won the war.'[2] There was only one black spot on his academic record, an area where he had already displayed a marked lack of ability compared with his siblings. His drawings, said the report pithily, 'are remarkably unlike the object'. It added, however, foreshadowing a tenacity in the face of adversity, that 'his interest never flags'.

In sports, he ruled the roost, though he did on one occasion come up against an opponent who managed to dampen his enthusiasm. It was one of his favourite stories later in life and it has come down to us augmented by that gift for embellishment and presenting himself as the comic fool that Mary Clive has already noted. Frank reached the final of the school boxing competition: in the other corner of the ring stood Alan Griffiths, later to achieve an international reputation for saintliness as the saffron-robed Dom Bede Griffiths[3] of the Shantivanam ashram in India, a pioneer in bringing together eastern religions and Christianity. That day, however, Griffiths was in less pacific mood and the two young pugilists slogged it out for several rounds to the delight of the crowd, swollen by soldiers on leave from the local camp. When the bell rang to signal the end of the round, Pakenham retired to his corner covered in blood but he took comfort in the sight of his opponent similarly afflicted. 'It's not going too badly, is it?' he remarked, but, to his horror, his second pointed out that Griffiths was wiping off all the blood which was, in fact, Frank's. At that moment the referee moved over and lifted his opponent's arm in the air to indicate the victor.

At twelve, he sat the entrance examination for Eton and was the youngest boy to be awarded a place that year. It was a time when most parents would have been showering their children with congratulations. Instead he detected a note of disappointment in his mother's reaction. 'I'm sorry I didn't do better,' he wrote to her without indicating – or indeed understanding – where there could be room for improvement; and then added boisterously, 'I'm sending you a photograph which I got out of a paper of an enormous Austrian. Isn't he terrific?' Reflecting on this letter many years later, Elizabeth Longford was in no doubt about her future husband's aim. 'The motive for the photograph was clear, even if it involved a touch of sympathetic magic. For the sight of this "terrific" Austrian sent to Lady Longford by her son might suggest to her a novel association of ideas: that Frank himself was just a little bit "terrific" after all.'[4]

Frank Pakenham joined his brother Edward at Eton under housemaster C.M. Wells, a retired international cricketer, scholar and traditionalist. Both were Oppidans, a less exalted though often grander caste than the Collegers, the seventy or so boys who had won scholarships. Mary Longford's sense of duty and her concern for her own social standing refused to allow her sons to enter for a scholarship when she had ample funds to pay for them. She had no intention of allowing anyone to regard her as the poor widow in need of a helping hand and on her occasional visits would sweep up in her black chauffeur-driven Daimler to take tea with the headmaster, the formidable Dr Cyril Alington, later Dean of Durham Cathedral, in his pink-walled sitting room.[5] On one occasion, her daughter Violet recalled, there was some controversy because the driver appeared to be wearing an Old Etonian tie.[6]

Alington, revered by Frank, was a staunch Christian, fond of preaching moral tales to his charges in the school chapel on Sunday evenings. One in particular stuck in Frank's memory throughout his life and was often referred to. Alington began: 'It was just such an evening as this at Shrewsbury [where he had been head before he got the job at Eton] when a boy went and sat on a seat in the playing field. A lady of the town approached him. "Come home, dearie" she urged him. He replied: "We don't do that sort of thing at Shrewsbury". Curiously enough he had been expelled for doing it that very day. Good night and don't forget to pray for your headmaster.'[7]

23

At first Frank's sainted progress at Furzie Close continued unabated at Eton despite his relative youth. His initial reports were excellent: 'a very clever boy who can talk Latin with some fluency'. Though not blessed with a technical brain, he even came top of the class in science – but was later to dismiss this as a result of the eccentric marking system employed by his teacher, a young John Christie, later the founder of the Glyndebourne Opera.[8] As he moved up the school, however, a rapid decline is charted in Frank's reports. 'His whole life consists in a more or less elaborate pretence,' one teacher wrote cuttingly. 'His written work is indescribably filthy. Considering his obvious abilities his place is discreditable.'[9] It was not, then, that he was thought stupid, simply that he was not trying.

His teenage years were a strange hiatus in a life otherwise marked out by a restlessness and a tremendous capacity for hard work and, when necessary, slog. It may simply have been part of growing up, breaking free of the hermetically sealed North Aston nursery and experiencing the world outside. He may even have calculated that success at school was unlikely to win the praise of his mother, so why bother seeking it? Or perhaps there was simply a certain arrogance in his approach. 'I calculated,' he later wrote of this period, 'not quite correctly as it proved, that the moving staircase which I set foot on at twelve would bring me to the top at eighteen without any exertion of mine.'[10] Another cause could have been the curriculum. Eton rated Classics above every other discipline, but soon its appeal had evaporated for Frank. The only abiding legacy of day after day spent writing out Latin and Greek verse was, he later told his wife Elizabeth, a boundless capacity for composing poems in a matter of minutes.[11]

His schoolboy concerns were more contemporary. If politics had been on the syllabus, he might have stretched himself a little more, though the records of the school's politics society show little evidence of his participation. His only contribution was to ask the rather po-faced but prescient question in 1920 as to whether Winston Churchill had a future. Instead his time was spent on a variety of pursuits. He shocked his siblings who had regarded him in the nursery as a philistine by acting in the school production of

Sheridan's *The Critic*, playing Don Whiskerandos, as his sister Violet reported, 'with small whiskers of his own in addition to a mutton-chop pair provided for his part'.[12]

For the most part, however, he was hanging out in his natural habitat – the sports field. Until the end of his long life, he would tell anyone who asked that his crowning achievement at Eton was leading his house to victory in the final of the Eton Field Game in his last term in 1923. It had been, he would say, his ambition from the first day he arrived there. Again it was a success that rested more on gusto than ability. In addition to shortsightedness and a lack of coordination, he also had to battle with flat feet, cured, he claimed, after 'three years of walking about my bedroom with curled up toes'.[13]

One of the few long-term friends that he made at Eton was Esmond Warner, two years his junior, and the son of the most celebrated English cricketer of the time, Sir Pelham 'Plum' Warner.[14] Because of his background young Esmond's childhood was unusually worldly, his daughter Marina later recalled. 'He knew everybody and moved in very glamorous circles with courtiers at one end and bohemian society at the other.'[15] Frank was, even at this early stage, attracted by that sort of glamour, so different from his parents' world.

It is hard on reading of his years at Eton not to suspect that Frank was at least deflated if not depressed. There was the loss of his father and the coldness of his mother which prompted a lack of confidence in his own worth and an unease with any sort of intimacy. Moreover, if lack of academic enthusiasm is not so unusual in teenagers, what must have been hardest for him to understand was his first taste in the wider world of unpopularity. Mary Longford may have rejected him, but everyone else had usually responded positively to his stories and humour. Crushing then was his failure to get into Pop, the élite group of twenty-five or so schoolboys who, in true *Lord of the Flies* English public school tradition, were elected by their Eton fellows to rule over them, set apart by their resplendent checked trousers, coloured waistcoats, seals on their hats and other such finery. Frank had assumed that he would get elected as Captain of Oppidans, the non-scholars, and that he would therefore get one of the reserved places within Pop which, at that time, boasted Alec Douglas Home, the future Prime Minister, as its president. (Home's younger brother, Henry, was Frank's 'fag' at Eton.)

'It was the last Sunday of the summer "half" of 1923,' Frank wrote later recasting what had been a personal disaster as an amusing anecdote.

My closest friend outside our House, Ronnie Shaw Kennedy, and I were taking our Sunday afternoon stroll round Upper Club. We discussed as always the football season ahead. Then I touched on his chances of Pop. Ronnie, immensely popular among those who knew him well, had incurred the hostility of some of the faster elements by beating a prominent member of his House for smoking. Neither of us was confident that he would be elected, but I tried to be as encouraging as possible. A pause. He definitely did not take his cue or broach my own possibilities. Finally I said, a shade complacently: 'It seems rather unfair, the Captain of Oppidans getting in ex officio.' A further pause and then Ronnie decided that the news must be broken to me. 'Bridge [the Captain of Oppidans] is staying on another year.' 'No, no,' I began to protest, for Bridge was many months older than I; but a horrible calculation told me all too quickly that it could just about be done.[16]

Unable to let the matter drop, but more in hope than expectation, he asked Ronnie about his chances of getting elected in the ordinary way. 'Any previous pause of Ronnie's shrank beside this one. At last, very sadly, he told me: "I think you ought to know that you are the most unpopular boy in the school".'

Even allowing for a little hyperbole, something must have changed. Why did the youngster who held the servants' hall rapt and who had risen effortlessly to the top at Furzie Close end up so marginalized? He did not, it is fair to say, go out of his way to court popularity at Eton. He could be bombastic – forcing his house team to practise relentlessly for the Field Game in all weathers. He was priggish about schoolboy crushes and sexual experimentation. One visit by his mother to Furzie Close remained imprinted on his memory. '[She] told me', he wrote in a newspaper article, 'that my brother had been attacked in a bath at Eton where two boys habitually shared. The boy in question was later expelled. . . . There was plenty of it as I could not help being aware at Eton at that time.'[17] And he was iconoclastic on the props of the Eton system. He would not, as Head of House, for example, allow beating.

However, the true explanation lies in his link with his older brother, Edward, with whom he shared a room. Ronnie Shaw Kennedy's description of Frank as the most unpopular boy in the school better fitted Edward. Sickly, swotty – he twice won the school's highly coveted Wilder Divinity Prize – he was an awkward loner who took great delight in offending others by trumpeting his ardent Irish nationalism. It was a stance guaranteed to cause a stir in this bastion of the English Establishment, particularly since several of his schoolmates' fathers served in the British forces during the Irish wars of 1919–23. They took a very dim view of Edward proclaiming his support for Sinn Fein and signing himself in Gaelic, Eamon de Longphort. They called him a communist and when he responded with 'Up the Republic', he disappeared under a sea of fists.

Though he had never been particularly close to Edward and the two had very different characters, Frank faced a dilemma. Edward's apostasy held no appeal for him. Unionism was the position Frank had advocated across the lunch table at North Aston Hall in opposition to Edward's nationalism. (Some of his siblings believed that Edward's nationalism began as a form of rebellion against his overbearing mother, a view expressed many years later in print by Violet's husband.)[18] So it came down to personal feelings. Frank was torn between his own desire to be liked, and brotherly duty towards a weaker sibling who was under physical assault. After some hesitation, he stood up for his brother and suffered the worst of all worlds. Edward had sensed the hesitation and years later his wife would say, 'Edward never forgave Frank for not flying to his defence when Edward found himself in a minority of one.'[19] Yet in the eyes of his fellow pupils, he had stuck up for Edward and so he travelled some way with him down the road of stigmatization.

Edward, for all their differences, remained as a young adult broadly fond of his younger brother's company. Christine Trew, a clever blue-stocking from Somerset and protégée of Lady Ottoline Morrell,[20] had married Edward in 1925. She described the first time she met her future brother-in-law, a charming seventeen-year-old.

He was described to me by Edward as somebody who was so clever he could make any argument in the family sound ridiculous. I remember him in the family. He was very good at family arguments. One could manage to get a three-cornered argument. Edward and his mother would fight, in a very friendly way, about Conservatism and what we would call communism. It was not so long after 1917. Frank would take a third point of view, whatever it might have been, and would make each side sound ridiculous.[21]

Shunned by Pop, Frank responded by burying himself with renewed vigour in his work, earning a half-compliment from Dr Alington on his final report. 'He is no longer such a contented dweller in Philistia.' He briefly dallied with the idea of staying on for an extra term to outlast Bridge and get into Pop as Captain of Oppidans, but his mother brusquely dismissed any such notions. He left Eton fearing that he would never be popular again but with some reborn confidence in his possession of an intrinsic academic worth that did not need to be fed by hours of study. He took the Oxford entrance exam as a matter of course – as his brother had before him, going up to Christ Church – and, though he failed to win a scholarship, was awarded a place at New College to read history.

He arrived at university at the end of the golden age of Harold Acton and the aesthetes with their Oxford bags, of the social whirl of the Bright Young Things, reacting almost hysterically against the war and their parents' Edwardian attitudes, and of the drunken excesses of the wealthy aristocrats of the Bollinger Club recorded in

Evelyn Waugh's *Decline and Fall*.[22] This generation had its own variation on the rebellious spirit endemic to students that had in the past sparked political revolutions across Europe and would again. Their uprising was instead aimed at brushing away the *fin-de-siècle* cobwebs that they saw as still engulfing the social and intellectual world of Oxford. Hugh Gaitskell,[23] an exact contemporary of Frank's at New College and a lifelong friend, summed up the spirit of the age.

Oxford in the middle twenties was gay, frivolous, stimulating and tremendously alive . . . it was a brief, blessed interval when the lives of the young were neither overshadowed by the consequences of the last war nor dominated by the fear of a future one. Most of us sighed with relief and settled down to the business of enjoying ourselves . . . Politics, to tell the truth, were rather at a discount. We were in revolt all right – against Victorianism, Puritanism, stuffiness of any kind, but most of us weren't sufficiently bitter or perhaps sufficiently serious – to be angry young men . . . [in] the heavenly freedom of Oxford [revolt] took the form of an outburst of scepticism, a mistrust of dogma, a dislike of sentimentality and of over-emotional prejudices or violent crusades . . . We professed the happiness of the individual as the only acceptable social aim.[24]

Another Oxford friend, the future Poet Laureate John Betjeman,[25] described Oxford life at this time in terms of a rivalry between two camps, 'hearties' and 'aesthetes'.

Hearties were good college men who rowed in the college boat, ate in the college hall, and drank beer and shouted. Their regulation uniform was college tie, college pullover, tweed coat and grey flannel trousers. Aesthetes, on the other hand, wore whole suits, silk ties of a single colour, and sometimes – but only for about a week or two while they were fashionable – trousers of cream or strawberry-pink flannel. They let their hair grow long, and never found out, as I never found out, where the college

29

playing fields were or which was the college barge. Aesthetes never dined in hall, but went instead to the George restaurant on the corner of Cornmarket and George Street, where there was a band consisting of three ladies, and where punkahs, suspended from the ceiling, swayed to and fro, dispelling the smoke of Egyptian and Balkan cigarettes. Mr Ehrsam, the perfect Swiss hotelier and his wife kept order, and knew how much credit to allow us. I was an aesthete. The chief Oxford aesthete when I went up in 1925 was Harold Acton.[26]

Betjeman was exaggerating. Very few undergraduates fitted the stereotypes exactly. Many, like Frank Pakenham, flitted between both worlds. The aesthetes' belief in the pursuit of individual freedom and happiness, the discarding of the old conventions and manners, held great appeal for him. It offered an escape from both the regimented life of Eton and the cold puritanism of his home, where his mother remained trapped in pre-war notions of propriety and duty. He sharpened up his wit in the pages of the *Oxford University Review*, an arts and satirical magazine he founded with Robert Henriques with the aesthete leanings if not the cachet of Acton's own *The Oxford Broom*. Contributors to the *Review* included Betjeman and Gaitskell and the targets of its character assassination included the 'luvvies' of the fabled OUDS, the university drama society. On setting up the *Review*, Frank wrote to many famous people asking for messages of support. Among those he approached was his fellow Anglo-Irishman George Bernard Shaw, now in his seventies and at the height of his fame with the opening of *St Joan* in 1924. Shaw sent a terse reply. 'Anyone who fills up his first number with messages that no one wants to read will fail and will deserve to. Even young Oxford should know better than that.' The young publisher turned the rebuff into a publicity coup. He covered the town with posters of Shaw's message in a successful campaign to promote the first issue.

This stroke of genius contributed to a growing reputation among his fellow undergraduates. His sometime tennis partner, Lord David Cecil, three years his senior, subsequently Professor of English

Literature at Oxford,[27] remembered Frank Pakenham above all for his humour. 'He was always telling stories in which he came out rather comically. He was very gay and sociable indeed. I used to have people to lunch in my rooms in Wadham and he was someone it was very good to have. He was so appreciative and quick, and when he was there the conversation flickered to and fro in a special way.'[28] Frank soon found himself accorded the honour of an invitation to another of the focal points for the aesthetes, the salon of Maurice Bowra, the dean of Wadham, a First World War hero and a celebrated scholar.[29] Bowra is best remembered as Oxford's Dorothy Parker, brimming with quotable one-liners, but in his time he assembled around him all the brightest stars of successive Oxford generations. As Betjeman put it, he was:

> certain then,
> As now, that Maurice Bowra's company
> Taught me far more than all my tutors did.[30]

In such gatherings, discussion of politics would be considered dull and a *faux pas*. Douglas Jay was two years behind Frank at New College.[31] It was, he said, a resolutely apolitical world. 'The conventional morality of the intellectuals was violently antipathetic to politics or indeed to serious interest in anything other than philosophy, literature and the arts. We were constantly warned against "careerism" which was regarded as the unforgivable sin.'[32] Jay was admonished by fellow undergraduate Richard Crossman[33] (a whole generation of Labour statesmen was formed at Oxford in this period) that 'anyone who joined the Union, or talked about politics was really falling below the minimum standard expected of an educated man'.[34]

Frank's participation in Oxford Union debates was minimal. He spoke only twice. Of one occasion *Isis* recorded: 'Mr Pakenham rose like a ghost and like a ghost faded into the night.'[35] The only time he got closely involved was when his brother Edward, true to form, found himself the lonely voice of opposition (although Maurice Bowra sided with him) to a motion condemning the murder of Field

Marshal Sir Henry Wilson by Irish nationalists in London. For his pains, a mob seized the 6th Earl of Longford on his way back from the Union building to his college, ducked him in Mercury, the lily pond in the centre of Christ Church's Tom Quad, and proceeded to destroy all the books in his rooms that contained a word of Gaelic. Frank was outraged at such treatment, but Edward took such rough justice in good spirit and made a joke out of it.

That single incident aside, however, Frank's early interest in politics had waned. If the subject came up – as it might on his visits to his Jersey grandmother's salon – his inclination was towards her and his parents' Conservatism and Unionism, as natural a part of his life as the butler who would sharpen his pencils when he was busy writing.

Yet for all his aesthete leanings, Frank stood apart from the core group on several counts. Their world, for instance, was a homoerotic one. Betjeman reputedly had sex with fellow under-graduate W.H. Auden for £5. Evelyn Waugh was observed by Tom Driberg[36] at the all-male Hypocrites' Club 'rolling on a sofa' with another man, their 'tongues licking each other's tonsils'.[37] For some it was a passing phase. Waugh and Betjeman both went on to marry and dismissed such homosexual romps as an aberration. That is how they seemed at the time to Frank. On sexual matters he was a lifelong puritan. Then there was the aesthetes' dress code: Frank never displayed any concern for his appearance. Nor would he have had the money for an endless round of socializing at the George. His mother kept him on a tight budget. More pointedly, he knew where the sports field was. He played soccer and tennis for New College.

From a social perspective, the high point of Frank's time at Oxford came not during evenings with Bowra or Betjeman, but when he was invited to become a member of the Bullingdon, the most exclusive of those dining and hunting societies that thrived in the University. His admittance came through the good offices of his fellow Old Etonian Roger Chetwode (whose sister Penelope was to marry Betjeman) and renewed his contact with other Old Etonians like Esmond Warner, two years below him at Magdalen College. Admittance went some way towards making up for his failure to get into Pop. Like the Eton élite, the Bullingdon had its own extravagant uniform and traditions, detailed and some would say exaggerated by Evelyn Waugh[38] as the 'Bollinger'.

> For two days they had been pouring into Oxford: epileptic royalty from their villas of exile; uncouth peers from crumbling country seats; smooth young men of uncertain tastes from embassies and legations; illiterate lairds from wet granite hovels in the Highlands; ambitious young barristers and Conservative candidates torn from the London season and the indelicate advances of debutantes; all that was most sonorous of name and title was there for the beano.[39]

The high jinks of the Bullingdon/Bollinger after their drunken dinners would include smashing windows – 'the sound of English county families baying for broken glass', as Waugh memorably put it – and picking on would-be aesthetes like the young Tom Driberg who was relieved of his green Oxford bags or unpopular grammar school boys like the anti-hero of *Decline and Fall*, Paul Pennyfeather.

Yet, for all his connections with these rich, titled, well-connected and often child-like young men, Frank had a foot in another camp. His life was made up of a series of often apparently contradictory compartments. He continued to make regular trips to Eton Manor. Douglas Jay accompanied him for a game of soccer in the East End of London.

> We were playing for the Second XI, I think, and Frank asked me if I'd come and play at a boys' club in Hackney. That was the first time I had realised that he had a social conscience. Those were the days, of course, of that brand of paternal conservatism with a social conscience. I remember him about college, very vigorous, very active and I'd been told rather vaguely that he had some claim on an Irish earldom, but I wasn't sure if it was a joke or not. He was known for his extravagant jokes.[40]

Those trips down to Hackney brought the socialite of Oxford into contact with socialism. In the East End, already a solid block of

33

Labour seats, the election of the first Labour Prime Minister, James Ramsay MacDonald, in January 1924 gave a boost to the burgeoning trade union movement. Though Ramsay MacDonald's coalition government collapsed within the year, the growth of the Labour Party and its commitment to a welfare state would ultimately sound the death knell for the Poor Law Boards of Guardians and the sort of philanthropic Conservatism practised by men like Arthur Villiers. In the shorter term the incoming Conservative administration of Stanley Baldwin quickly became involved in a wages dispute with the miners. Declining exports had led the employers, noted for their truculence and shortsightedness, to try to impose reduced pay and longer working days on their employees, who already suffered bad and dangerous conditions. The two sides were at loggerheads when Baldwin intervened to give a government subsidy on wages until a Royal Commission reported on the problem. In effect the Prime Minister only managed to buy time. Eight months later the commission recommended that the subsidy be stopped. On 4 May 1926 the first ever General Strike began.

While Douglas Jay joined the Labour Party as a result of the General Strike and Hugh Gaitskell and John Betjeman both lent practical support to the protesters, Frank, like most of Oxford, slept through the nine-day confrontation. However, the prolonged exposure to life on the other side of the tracks does seem to have planted some seeds of doubt in his mind about the value of his own Conservative inclinations. A further spur was his growing friendship with Evan Durbin, the first out-and-out socialist the earl's son had met.[41] The child of a Nonconformist minister, he had come from humble beginnings in Taunton to win a scholarship to Oxford. In later years he used to describe his first sightings of Frank Pakenham in the Junior Common Room, full of the 'arrogance and stupidity of the privileged classes'. The two of them got into a political argument which ended with Durbin saying: 'Man, have you ever been hungry?' (In retrospect Frank wrote that Durbin himself rather exaggerated the exigencies of his childhood.)[42] After that encounter, they were often to be found debating the relative merits of their political positions on the staircase of New Buildings where they both had rooms. 'He forced me', Frank was later to admit, 'to build up a kind of intellectual defence of Conservatism, to rationalise what I really believed in. From that time on I was never oblivious or ignorant of the Labour case in broad outline.'[43]

After a couple of terms of reading history, he decided it was not the subject for him and obtained permission from his tutors to change course to the new and as yet not quite established school of Modern Greats – subsequently known as PPE: politics, philosophy and economics. One contemporary remarked that at this early stage Modern Greats was regarded as an unknown quantity and an option that 'no gentleman would read'. Frank was beginning to chart his own course free of such constraints. When he took his finals in 1927 he had fewer than two hundred predecessors. 'I originally chose the school', he recalled, 'for the rather degraded reason that, unless I went in for something like Oriental Languages, it was the one chance offered me for making up for nine or ten years of relative slackness and starting level with my contemporaries.'[44]

When he went to see Lionel Robbins,[45] the economics tutor, about some additional reading over the long vacation to catch up on what he had missed, Frank hardly made a good impression. Confronted with an endless list of weighty tomes, he smiled brightly and said, 'They sound rather dull.' Robbins asked him if he disliked dull books and when Frank, the flippant Old Etonian, said that he did, his tutor retorted: 'I should have thought that they would rather have appealed to you.' The sting in the tail obviously had its effect for under Robbins and Harold Salvesen Frank thrived. Hugh Gaitskell was his tutorial partner and in his final year his flatmate at 2 Isis Street near Folly Bridge. 'I think', Frank later reflected, 'that Harold Salvesen always preferred the mind of Hugh to mine. Again and again he advised me to model my literary style on Hugh's which possessed a charm and lucidity I sadly lacked.'[46]

Despite their political differences during these undergraduate days – Gaitskell had already become involved in Labour Party politics – the two had much in common. Both had lost their fathers at an identical stage, Gaitskell's dying from a disease contracted when working for the Indian Civil Service in Burma. Both were second sons who had gone through school, Gaitskell at Winchester, in the shadow of elder brothers who won all the academic prizes. Both had been poor relations in their extended families. Both liked sports and both found their feet in the social and academic world of Oxford. The bond remained strong between them thereafter.

Where Gaitskell chose as his special subject the history of the Labour movement, Frank concentrated on the less charged area of economic theory. This seemed to him to offer a third way between Conservatism and socialism that could reconcile a fairer and juster world with material prosperity. Hard as he worked at the task, however, his tutors couldn't help comparing what he achieved unfavourably with Gaitskell. 'One evening in my second year,' he later wrote, 'Harold Salvesen was so rough with me that I could not help asking him finally: "I suppose you do feel that I can get a First if I really work, which I admit I am not doing at present?" He refused to commit himself and that night a sort of anger took possession of me which spurred me on and did not finally exhaust itself until eighteen months later when, for good or ill, I had done with schools and my fate was settled.'[47]

As he buried himself in books, Frank developed a passion for economic theory which was to stay with him in his immediate post-Oxford years. This was the pre-Keynesian era when many Conservatives were none the less beginning to question the prevailing economic wisdom of laissez-faire and free trade, notably its cost in terms of social deprivation for workers. Moreover there was a growing school of thought that a return to protectionism was needed. In keeping with his own philanthropic background, Frank opposed such a retreat into tariff barriers and held up unfettered private enterprise as the best way to improve the lot of the working classes.

If he was in Gaitskell's shadow in tutorials, and put on the back foot by him politically, Frank also lagged behind him in familiarity with the opposite sex. According to his biographer Philip Williams, 'Gaitskell spent much more time with girls than most undergraduates did.'[48] His natural and easy charm made him something

36

of a lady-killer in the chaste and segregated atmosphere of those times. In his final year Gaitskell's cousin Audrey Townsend came up to Lady Margaret Hall. Through her Gaitskell got to know her fellow 'undergraduette' Elizabeth Harman, the daughter of a well-to-do Harley Street ophthalmic surgeon and a relative on her mother's side of the Chamberlain clan. He introduced her into the almost exclusively male world of the Bowra salon, where she scored a spectacular hit. And, in the celebrations that followed his finals, he invited her to the Magdalen and New College summer balls. In the process he introduced her to Frank. There was an eclipse of the sun that night, but other momentous events were under way. Elizabeth takes up the story at the first of these two grand parties.

About midnight, on my way back from the cloakroom to the dance floor, I was astonished to see a large sleeping figure draped over a garden chair in the middle of a wide canvas corridor. As I approached the figure on tiptoe I saw that it was wearing a Bullingdon uniform, the last word in social glamour: yellow waistcoat and navy blue tail coat with white facings and brass buttons. The face was of monumental beauty, as if some Greco-Roman statue – the Sleeping Student maybe – had been dressed up in modern clothes by some group of jokers. I stood for a moment admiring but puzzled. 'What sort of girl', I asked myself, 'could have allowed such a magnificent partner to spend the best part of the night alone and asleep?'[49]

The sleeping beauty was Gaitskell's friend, Frank Pakenham, who had been abandoned by his partner for the evening, Alice Buchan, daughter of John Buchan[50] the novelist. Elizabeth continues:

After a good day's sleep myself, I awoke refreshed for the New College Ball on the following evening, 28 June 1927. For the first and only time I wore my most poetic dance frock of lavender taffeta printed with bunches of little flowers floating in four petal-shaped panels, with a chiffon underskirt and knickers to match. Next morning I found that I had been literally (but not metaphorically) deflowered: one of the petals had floated away or been torn off . . . Some time after midnight Hugh took me along to the room in Garden Quad that Ken McKinnon, a third-year Australian scholar, had hired for the occasion. At that time 'Provvy', as Jeremy Bentham used to call Providence, began to show her hand. There, extended on Ken's sofa, lay my vision of the night before, again deeply and serenely asleep. This time I did not hesitate. A performance of the Sleeping Beauty act was clearly called for in reverse. Bending over his mop of classical brown curls I kissed him on the forehead. His brown (as I now saw they were) eyes opened wide. 'I'd like to kiss you but I can't'. . .[51]

And Frank Pakenham slumped back, fast asleep.

A few days after the ball, he was staying in London with Alec Spearman when he heard that he had got one of the two best firsts for his year. His anxiety that his illegible handwriting might have let him down proved groundless. For once he had gone one better than his rival Gaitskell, who had to endure a long viva before scraping his first. Mary Longford, travelling up to London by train with her friend Mrs Barry, scanned the results in *The Times*. With characteristic under-expectation, she started with the seconds, worked her way down through the thirds and fourths and then concluded resignedly to her companion, 'Frank must have failed altogether.' Mrs Barry took the copy of *The Times* and began reading from the top. Almost at once she pointed to Frank Pakenham among the firsts. He celebrated with a dinner for a few close friends at the Café Royal in London, followed by an outing to the theatre. And among those he invited was Elizabeth Harman.

THREE

The Party-goer

Elizabeth Harman's awakening of her future husband, like George IV arousing the spirit of Brighton in Rex Whistler's allegorical painting, failed to spark a romance. After the celebratory dinner at the Café Royal in the summer of 1927, the couple scarcely saw each other for three years. Frank had planned to study law in London, reluctantly abandoning economic theory for the practical reason that he felt there was more prospect of a well-paid career as a barrister. At the last moment, however, he changed his mind and opted to do his second degree in Oxford. In his 1953 book, *Born to Believe*, he suggested that this volte-face was a result of his encounter with Elizabeth. 'I fear I never gave my mother or anyone else the real reason for the change and perhaps I hardly admitted it to myself. But as with the lesser things in my life, a good start having been made, I failed to follow my inspiration; indeed I seemed to lose awareness of it, while in fact retaining it below the level of consciousness.'

That passage was written with the glow of hindsight, when the Longfords were already nearing their silver wedding anniversary. It is hard to credit that for the three years from 1927, first in the tight-knit community of Oxford and then in a social world where they had friends in common, even someone so emotionally repressed as Frank carried the seeds of this blossoming romance in his heart without once acting upon them. There were many less prosaic reasons for staying on in Oxford. His success in finals had belatedly convinced the Warden of New College, H.A.L. Fisher,[1] that he had an academic high-flyer on his hands. Fisher began to dangle the prospect of a fellowship at All Souls. Oxford, moreover, was a place where Frank had grown to feel comfortable, accepted, and even admired.

And even if his explanation about wanting, subconsciously, to stay close to Elizabeth were accepted, Frank certainly did not let this buried desire cramp his style. With Hugh Gaitskell gone, first to the heart of the Nottinghamshire coalfield for a year to teach in an adult education centre before taking up a post at University College, London, and Evan Durbin away pursuing his ambition to become a Labour MP, Frank managed to put to one side any uncomfortable political and social questions they had forced him to consider, and to throw himself into the world of the 'bright young things', rich, titled and every one of them Conservative. In *Vile Bodies*, his novel chronicling the antics of this set, Evelyn Waugh ran through their diaries.

> Masked parties, Savage parties, Victorian parties, Greek parties, Wild West parties, Russian parties, Circus parties, parties where one had to dress as someone else, almost naked parties at St John's Wood, parties in flats and studios and hotels and night clubs, in windmills and swimming baths, tea-parties at school where one ate muffins and meringues and tinned crab, parties at Oxford where one drank brown sherry and smoked Turkish cigarettes, dull dances in London and comic dances in Scotland and disgusting dances in Paris – all that succession and repetition of massed humanity . . .[2]

At the heart of all this activity was Frank Pakenham. Nancy Mitford has left a particularly comic picture of him at the fancy-dress pageant in Hyde Park, 'one of the highlights of the Season'. 'Stephen Tennant as Shelley was very beautiful, Lord Furneaux was a modern "young-man-about-town" & Frank Packenham [*sic*] in a sailor suit rode on one of those enormous bicycles.'[3] Furneaux,[4] who had taken over the editorship of the *Oxford University Review*, was the son and heir to the Earl of Birkenhead, who as F. E. Smith had risen from middle-class origins on Merseyside to be Lord Chancellor and one of the most formidable characters in the Conservative Party. In these post-graduate days in Oxford Frank struck up a strong friendship with first Furneaux and then his family. His glittering first, his Bullingdon connections and his growing reputation as a wit had made Frank quite a star on the Oxford stage and drew in younger students like Furneaux and Basil Dufferin.[5]

Dufferin was also Anglo-Irish, his family seat being at Clandeboye in County Down, a house every bit as eccentric in its own Victorian way as Tullynally. Dufferin's daughter, Lady Caroline Blackwood, painted a thinly veiled portrait of Clandeboye in her novel *Great Granny Webster*, evoking the damp-infested library, the idiosyncratic plumbing – 'it was considered a luxury if anyone managed to get a peat-brown trickle of a bath' – and the leaking roof which necessitated a stream of buckets and jugs when it rained.[6] The 1920s and 1930s were a golden age for the house party, when the aristocracy would organize weekends and sojourns of hunting, eating, drinking and conversation at their country estates for friends and colleagues. Frank was a regular visitor to Clandeboye, along with other Oxford friends of Dufferin such as John Betjeman, who in a letter of September 1928 recalled trying – unsuccessfully – to learn the Charleston in its parquet-floored salon amid stuffed rhinoceroses, walruses and bears, collected by Basil's father on his journey home from India.[7] Betjeman later immortalized the Byronesque Dufferin as 'the dark, heavy-lidded companion' in his poem 'Brackenbury Scholar of Balliol'. Elizabeth Longford, who got to know Basil Dufferin well in the 1930s when he was a rising young minister in Conservative governments, described him as 'brilliantly clever, extremely handsome and very athletic',[8] all three qualities acting as a magnet on her future husband. Certainly from university days until his death at the end of the Second World War in Burma, Dufferin and his wife Maureen, a member of the wealthy Guinness clan whom he married in 1930,[9] remained close friends of Frank, part of the grand social world in which he and later Elizabeth moved in the London of the 1930s. In old age Maureen Dufferin recalled the young Frank Pakenham above all for his humour. 'He wasn't madly good looking. And I don't remember him as especially eccentric at that point. He never had the right clothes and was always borrowing black-tie and jacket. But it was his wit and his stories. He and my husband were both very funny and very clever.'[10]

More immediately significant in affecting Frank's political opinions, however, was Furneaux. 'Freddy and his family soon came to occupy a place apart in my eyes,' Frank wrote. 'Through them and their expanding circle I was initiated into Conservative politics at their most romantic: at the point, that is, where they made contact with the more intellectual side of London society.'[11] There was already a family connection between the Longfords and the Smiths. F.E. had served in the Oxfordshire Yeomanry under Frank's father and Charlton, his beloved country seat, was only eight miles from North Aston Hall. The contrast between the two places could not have been greater, though, the one solemn, enclosed, hostile to visitors, as if eternally in mourning and uncomfortable with Frank's exuberance, the other dynamic, bursting with life and well-connected callers, 'an adult culture', as Frank was later to describe it, though its antics could be very child-like.

I easily recall my nervousness as I approached the house for my first visit, on an April evening in 1928. Margaret Birkenhead gave me that wonderful sparkling welcome of hers. 'You know my daughters,' she said, pointing to a sofa where Eleanor, already grown up, and Pam, a child of fourteen, sat with their backs to me. Both subsequently melted towards me. But that evening neither Eleanor nor Pam was interested in the stranger. Eleanor, without turning her head, stretched her hand and arm over the back of the sofa and Pam, after a furtive glance sideways, copied her elder sister precisely. Totally nonplussed, I grasped Eleanor's hand in one of mine and Pam's in the other and stood there gaping while Margaret Birkenhead burst into laughter.[12]

Frank's embarrassment was saved – temporarily as it turned out – by the arrival of the man of the house. F.E. Smith had made his name as an eloquent barrister, entering the Commons in time to play an outspoken part in the opposition to Lloyd George's 'People's Budget' and in the 1909–11 crisis that surrounded House of Lords attempts to block it. Smith was a throughgoing Unionist who had become one of the most persuasive advocates of the Ulster Protestants in the pre-war Home Rule crisis. He despised Irish nationalists and in 1916 successfully and flamboyantly led the prosecution of Roger Casement, who was convicted of planning a republican rising in Ireland with German help and hanged. From 1919 to 1922 he sat on the Woolsack and returned for a second spell in the cabinet from 1924 to 1928 as Secretary of State for India. George Dangerfield, admittedly a partisan observer, summed up in *The Strange Death of Liberal England* the reputation F.E. enjoyed at the time Frank first met him on that April evening. 'Many people loved him, most distrusted him, some despised him, and he despised almost everybody. In his later career as Earl of Birkenhead he served himself more faithfully than God or his country . . . he was without question the most fascinating creature of his times.'[13]

Birkenhead rescued the young visitor from his daughters that evening by suggesting they went for a ride. Still ill at ease with young women, Frank was so relieved that he failed to reveal that his expertise on a horse was limited to hunting on ponies on the farm at Tullynally. He duly disgraced himself on the ride by losing control of his steed, in the process frightening his host's horse.

We jogged back in silence. When we reached the house Lord Birkenhead turned to me. 'We have survived,' he said, 'though you will not, I feel sure, claim an undue share of the credit for that achievement. We have preserved our skins, if not our dignity. In reciting these events to the ladies it would be unwise and, indeed, injudicious to depress their spirits and our own prestige with too slavish an adherence to the literal facts as they may have appeared at the moment of their occurrence.' He shot me the rich, warm, illuminating smile of partnership that I came to know so well, and went in to pitch some tremendous yarn in which he and I won infinite glory and saved each other's lives.[14]

Out of that shared delight in spinning a tale grew a strong friendship. F.E.'s politics and convictions mirrored those Frank had been raised on, and injected some new vigour and life into a viewpoint that had begun to feel threadbare as Gaitskell and Durbin picked away at it. However, it was not politics particularly that each admired in the other. It was the same combination that drew Frank to Basil Dufferin – a common passion for sport and a brilliant, showy cleverness. A weekend at Charlton revolved around physical exertion with F.E. at the centre of events – golf before lunch, tennis all afternoon – and throughout the proceedings conversation where the mental gymnastics were as impressive as anything seen on the playing field. Frank was able to sparkle. By matching his host's enthusiasms and his humour, he was appreciated and encouraged. Birkenhead was, if anything, more competitive than Frank. He certainly confirmed that tendency in him. A weekend at Charlton was virtually dedicated to the cult of virility. Everyone present had to compete to be the fastest, the sharpest, the wittiest.

Birkenhead's independent views and outspokenness increasingly led to him being shunned by former colleagues in his last years – he died in 1930 at the age of fifty-eight. Plagued by financial worries that threatened to force the sale of Charlton, he preferred the company and adulation of his children's friends. Oswald Mosley wrote of his 'Pied Piper appeal to the young'. 'He was a tremendously amusing, funny, glamorous man,' Frank later reflected, adding with hindsight: 'It was the listening to him that I enjoyed, not so much his views.'[15] He became for Frank the latest of a series of substitute fathers to whom he was drawn as a young man, though ironically few of these figures had much in common with the reserved, taciturn, apolitical 5th earl. 'Frank believed that there were kings of the world,' Lord David Cecil once noted, 'and that they could come from anywhere at all. He was always searching for people he could admire.'[16]

If there was a more lasting effect of Birkenhead friendship, it was to encourage Frank to take an independent stance. The older man was seemingly endlessly willing to go against his party on points of principle even if it cost him friends and influence. He was detached in his thinking, casting a critical eye and tongue over the Establishment from within.

Another with a similar status in Frank's life at this stage, and someone who taught him the same values of free thought, was Lord Waldorf Astor. Their friendship had its origins – like so much else in Frank's life at this time – in the Bullingdon. Unperturbed by his equestrian failure on his first visit to Charlton, he and his friend from Eton days, Roger Chetwode, were among the organizers of a Bullingdon point-to-point in the spring of 1928. After a good deal of practising in secret, Frank turned up on the day in his pale mauve jockey's outfit, riding a trusty but plodding horse called Bosun. Among the guest riders who had been invited to take part was Bill Astor,[17] heir to Cliveden and son of Lord Astor and his formidable wife Nancy. Bosun threw Frank off at the first fence, but his competitive urge soon had him back in the saddle and chasing the field. Disaster struck at the final fence of the first round. 'I only remember hitting it very hard, breast high it seemed; then oblivion. I awoke to find myself lying on the ground with the horse plucking idly at the fence.' Frank again remounted but, severely concussed and a little confused, set off in the wrong direction and came face to face with Bill Astor. 'He was coming at me full tilt and gesticulating, as well he might, like a madman. "That's the way," he shouted, pointing over my shoulder. "That's the way," I retorted, pointing over his and we zigzagged this way and that while he strove to save his victory from what seemed to him my crazy antics. Finally he gave us the slip and I was led away by the spectators.'[18]

Bill Astor had, before this confrontation on the course, invited Frank to dine with his family that evening at Cliveden, Charles Barry's classical palazzo on the Thames at Taplow. His father, owner of the *Observer* and *The Times*, wanted to meet some of the brightest young men of that generation at Oxford. Concussion rendered Frank unable to string a sentence together, much less produce the sort of sparkling repartee for which he was well known in the university's smart set. Lord Astor plied him with endless questions on every political topic of the day and received only a melancholy series of grunts in return. (Bill Astor much later told his wife Bronwen that Frank's taciturn performance that evening had placed a question mark in his father's mind over his eldest son's judgement and may have cost him the editorship of the *Observer*.)[19]

Despite such an inauspicious start, Waldorf Astor must have spotted something of interest in his guest, for afterwards Frank was to be a regular visitor at Cliveden, where his burgeoning reputation for eccentricity only served to inflate his reputation. There was always a stud missing in his collar, a tear in his clothing, the wrong laces in his shoes, or an ill-matched combination of garments held up by a safety pin. Bill, a contemporary, and his brother David,[20] seven years younger than Frank, became lifelong friends. To David, who was to take over the editorship of the *Observer*, Frank became 'a funny sort of godfather. I was just leaving school and was a very idealistic youth. He encouraged me. Frank and my father were very alike in some ways, in their dedication, their sense of service, their courage in standing up for what they believed to be right in the face of any opposition. I think to some extent Frank modelled himself on my father.'[21]

When Waldorf Astor had to give up his Plymouth Sutton seat in 1919 on inheriting his father's peerage, the new Conservative candidate was Nancy, his wife. Her victory led to her becoming, on 2 December 1919, the first woman to take her seat in the House of Commons. (The first woman MP, Sinn Feiner, Countess Markievicz, never attended Westminster.) The daughter of a Virginia planter, Nancy was, like Birkenhead, a larger-than-life character with independent views and no qualms about expressing them in colourful language. In the male bastion of the Commons she found 'all the ingenuous shyness of boys at their first dance'. Her debating style so needled Aneurin Bevan that he once remarked while she was speaking: 'It really is intolerable when this old gas-bag gets up and gabbles away.'[22] At Cliveden, less than an hour from London, Nancy Astor and her husband gathered around them people they found interesting. It would never be just a straightforward 'political' weekend, though the leading statesmen of the day were often on the guest list. The Astors did not harbour ambitions for high office, so their guests tended to be judged not on their political credentials but on whether or not they had something to say – a trait designed to appeal to Frank. Thus a typical house party would include the occasional world leader or royalty. Gandhi sat turning his wheel in the drawing room while the future Edward VIII popped in for a round of golf. There would be writers like George Bernard Shaw, whom Frank once heard recite 'The Applecart' to the other assembled guests 'nearly falling off his chair with amusement over his own jokes', and Hilaire Belloc.[23] Making up the numbers would be members of the far-flung Astor clan and their friends and various 'lost causes' that Nancy's Christian Scientist missionary spirit prompted her to take in.

Frank was one of her favourite guests, falling into the category of 'extended family'. In the discussions and debates that would often go on into the night at Cliveden among the guests, David Astor recalled that Frank was never in awe of the company or frightened to challenge even the most eminent man or woman if he disagreed with them. 'He and my mother were devoted to each other,' according to Astor. 'He loved that courageous outspoken part of her and she regarded him as a very close relative.'[24] Frank went on to campaign for Lady Astor in Plymouth during the 1929 general election. Her sort of independent Conservatism was what he then aspired to.

By the time of the poll, however, for all his powerful friends, Frank was effectively at a loose end, his once-promising academic career in tatters. His law studies had come to a rather abrupt end after the incident at the point-to-point. A doctor diagnosed a severe case of concussion and recommended prolonged rest and categorically ruled out the prospect of taking the law exam that was looming at the end of the Trinity term in 1928. Illness also put an end to his hopes of All Souls. When he took the examination, Frank was ill prepared, flummoxed by a question on 'The Limits of Loyalty' and failed to gain admittance to the academic inner sanctum of the university, performing with distinction only in his economics papers.

He recuperated at his mother's home at North Aston over that summer, spending a good deal of time escaping her irritation with him at the Birkenheads' and popping down to Cliveden and London for parties and dinners with Oxford friends. For all his talents, he had no clear idea of what he wanted to do. The prospect of spending another year waiting to resit the law examination did not appeal to him. His Jersey grandmother and her friends in Conservative circles floated the idea of finding him a safe Tory seat, but those doubts sown in undergraduate days just wouldn't go away and so Frank remained indecisive. At a crossroads, he was, for the one and only time in his life, bitten by the travel bug – and even then in a fairly half-hearted fashion. He decided that he needed to learn German so set off for Austria, but failed to discover either the joys of being in foreign parts or any hidden talent as a linguist. The sole achievement of this brief sojourn in the autumn of 1928 was getting through three rounds of the Lower Austria Tennis Championships.

Spring of the next year found him following Arthur Villiers into the City and, thanks to Alec Spearman's good offices, briefly dallying with a career as a stockbroker, a suitable profession for a gentleman and one where Frank hoped that his background in economics might be put to good use. His timing was appalling. Within a few months of him joining Buckmaster and Moore, Wall Street collapsed, taking the world markets with it. As well as closing off a career avenue, it cost him a large chunk of what capital he had. Inspired by his new job, he had bought shares in Radio Corporation at 109, only to see them slide to just 5. His one hope of turning this interlude in the City to good effect evaporated when he sought out the rising star of economists, Maynard Keynes,[25] and at a meeting in a stockbroker's office asked if he could go and work with him at Cambridge. 'I am afraid', said Keynes, 'that I cannot see inside your head. I simply can't tell whether you could be any good to us.' He turned him down flat. It was a crushing blow.

If Frank was seeing everything crumble to dust, the country was in little better condition. Labour had been returned as a minority government in the spring of 1929, promising peace, full employment and slum clearances – 'a wonderful, almost miraculous victory', according to Hugh Gaitskell.[26] The Stock Market crash and ensuing depression threw the government into chaos. At the start of 1930 there were 1.5 million unemployed. By December that figure had almost doubled to 2.5 million. Ramsay MacDonald's attempts to deal with the crisis split his party and in 1931 he and two senior Labour colleagues joined with Conservatives and Liberals to form a National Government with the express intention of saving the pound. He promptly abandoned the gold standard, cut unemployment benefit and went to the country. The Labour Party saw MacDonald as a traitor to the working class, a tool in the hands of the bankers, and campaigned against him. In the election of 1931 Labour was reduced to a rump of fifty MPs, led by the Christian pacifist George Lansbury,[27] and condemned to opposition until after the Second World War.

The Stock Market crash and ensuing depression cast its shadow even over the carefree world of the Bright Young Things. As Elizabeth Longford wrote: 'the ivory tower of aestheticism could not stand up to the buffets of the economic blizzard which began to blow in 1929. As my older contemporaries left and the younger generation came up, politics began to oust poetry. If I had had to take a refresher course to qualify for elite male society, it would have been on Karl Marx not Oscar Wilde.'[28]

For Frank there was no hiding place from the events that were changing the world. He was still going to Hackney Wick and there he saw at first hand the unemployment and deprivation caused by the financial crisis. It may have been those times spent at the Eton Manor Boys' Club in the midst of the financial melt-down that made him susceptible to a quite unusual offer of work that came in the autumn of 1929. Sandy Lindsay, the Master of Balliol, suggested that he become a lecturer in the Workers' Educational Association in Stoke-on-Trent. From an office in Oxford, run by Stuart Cartwright, young graduates were sent out by the WEA to spread their learning among those who had not enjoyed their educational privileges but who wanted to tackle such subjects as economics and politics. Gaitskell and Durbin had both joined fellow Oxford socialists as WEA lecturers, but it was rare for someone with Frank's Conservative background to sign up. The WEA – with its motto 'learn as you teach' – was for its participants a two-way process, the academic prowess of its lecturers exchanged for the worldly wisdom of their pupils.

The influence of Lindsay was significant. He was another of the older men Frank looked up to, but unlike Birkenhead or the Astors he was a committed socialist, the product, he said, of his Christian beliefs. It was a phrase Frank was later to employ of himself. Lindsay had been one of Longford's examiners in Modern Greats and had spotted a young man questioning his inherited notions and searching for something to believe in. The 'learn-while-you-teach' ethos of the WEA would, he calculated, give his former student a different perspective.

In Stoke-on-Trent Frank lectured in economics and politics in the evening and supplemented this by teaching during the day, first in a primary and then a secondary school. To his pupils, Frank was just another lecturer who thought he knew it all because he had been to Oxford. They, trade unionists and socialists to a man despite the supposedly apolitical status of the WEA, set out at once to relieve him of his pretensions. Ultimately it was their judgement that mattered, for, at the end of the year, the class had to say whether or not their lecturer was worth his pay and should be kept on. Frank found their trenchant views and appetite for debate enjoyable. 'I was young and when you're young you don't mind a challenge. You're not set in your ways.'[29] He did, however, go to some lengths to keep secret his courtesy title – the Honourable Frank Pakenham – for fear of the ammunition it might give his charges.

He lodged with a local railway foreman and his family in Longdon. Two-up, two-down was a far cry from weekends at Cliveden with its forty-six bedrooms and uniformed domestic staff. 'Frank was used to extremes of grandeur or informality,' Elizabeth Longford commented.[30] He may have enjoyed his forays into the servants' hall, but this was the first time Frank had lived among those at the other end of the social spectrum.

Despite this prolonged exposure to the poverty and despair brought by the slump, Frank, buttressed by occasional weekend breaks with his Conservative friends who regarded his WEA exploits with amusement, continued to cling to the notion that some sort of synthesis could be made between Toryism and an articulate working class demanding equality, a twentieth-century variation on Disraeli's 'one nation' ideals. It was, he could see, an increasingly tenuous hope and rested, in Frank's mind, on finding a moral basis for Conservatism. How could he justify a system where his landlords in Longdon laboured all the hours God sent for very little while the people he mixed with at weekend parties had every material comfort through inheritance? His heart was attracted to the socialist cause but his head, dominated as it was then by economics, told him that the Labour programme of state control and nationalization to bring prosperity would never work.

From the day Gaitskell and Durbin had first challenged him to justify his inbred Conservatism, he had been struggling. His time living and working in Stoke was another stage in a drift leftwards as 1929 turned into 1930. He may have completed his journey to Labour much sooner had he not been snatched away from the Potteries by an invitation to join the newly formed Conservative Research Department under Neville Chamberlain. Based in central London at Old Queen Street, overlooking St James's Park, the Research Department, which was ultimately to grow into Conservative Central Office, was set up in an attempt to promote fresh economic thinking in a Tory Party that had seen many of its cherished icons destroyed by the 1929 crash. It was a pioneering venture, very much a personal initiative of Chamberlain's, and had little support in the rest of the party. When Chamberlain went to the Treasury as part of the Conservative-dominated coalition that took power after the 1931 election, the Research Department lost its patron and was eclipsed, but for a brief spell in 1930 and 1931 its small team of researchers was buzzing with ideas. Henry Brooke,[31] a future Home Secretary under Harold Macmillan, worked alongside Frank. Both had served as WEA lecturers and both were wrestling with the problem of reconciling Conservatism and its dogmas with the conditions they had witnessed in working-class areas.

A leader that appeared in *The Times* at this period gave Frank and Henry Brooke particular heart. It seemed to advocate the combination of practical economic wisdom and moral conscience to which both subscribed at that time and which held Frank back from socialism. While he believed in the equality of humankind, his economic training led him to conclude that it was, in practical terms, a Utopian dream. Socialism's economic programme could never achieve the goal that it had set itself. 'The article said that unfortunately wealth is like heat. It is only when it is unequally distributed that it performs what the physicists call work; in other words that is the doctrine of inequality of wealth as against equality of wealth.'[32]

Much of his energy at the Research Department was spent on Chamberlain's pet scheme – to introduce protectionist tariffs on imported goods as a means of generating domestic demand and assuaging the worst effects of the Depression. The work done at Old Queen Street was the basis for legislation introduced when Chamberlain became Chancellor of the Exchequer. The tariff question to one side, however, Frank was continually frustrated at how little impact the Research Department had on party policy. The Tory grandees seemed to see Chamberlain's team as little better than administrative assistants. During the 1931 general election, for example, Frank was assigned the mundane task of monitoring Liberal Party publications.

By the time of that poll events in his personal life had moved at such a pace that any professional disappointment had to take second place to thoughts of Elizabeth Harman. Just as he started to question whether there was something more substantial to strive for beyond the social success he had enjoyed at Charlton, Cliveden and Clandeboye and went off to Stoke, Frank also remembered the attraction he had felt for Elizabeth Harman. It was as if in looking beyond the fashionable salons in a political sense, he also wanted to court someone with wider horizons than the beautiful, aristocratic women among the Bright Young Things. Previously, it had been from this group that Frank had expected to find a wife. The Birkenhead girls, Eleanor and Pamela Smith, and their friends Zita and Teresa 'Baby' Jungmann, were at the epicentre of the set. Eleanor, a budding romantic novelist, and Baby in particular were shining stars, the latter counting Evelyn Waugh and Lord David Cecil, as well as Frank, among her admirers.

Frank had met Baby at Charlton in the spring of 1928. Her father was a Dutch artist whom her mother had left, later marrying one of the Guinness clan. Baby's background did not seem to stop her being much in demand with some of London's grandest hostesses. Frank later remembered that he was convinced they would marry, though he had never even kissed her.[33] Her mother – known to some of the Bright Young Things as 'Gloomy' – certainly had other ideas. She was a dab hand at scaring off or intimidating potential suitors, of whom Baby was never short, like the oft-engaged Nina Blount in Waugh's *Vile Bodies*.

Nothing had been said between the two when, in June 1930, Frank, during a visit to old friends in Oxford, had a dream about the girl – quite unlike these society belles – who had kissed him as he slept at New College Ball. The next day he sought her out in her lodgings in Chadlington Road in North Oxford where she was preparing for finals. Elizabeth opened the door and was greeted by Frank Pakenham. 'My first impression was repeated, of an extraordinary pink and white complexion combined with classical curls, Greco-Roman features and a far from classically tailored suit of untidy clothes. A taxi was ticking over at the garden gate. He must have kept it ticking there for at least 20 minutes, a habit I was soon to discover could be extended to last if necessary for an hour.'[34]

They agreed to meet the following week. Anxious to make up for lost time, Frank then invited her to a house party at Pakenham Hall in August. He also suggested that she might like to join him before then as one of the tutors at a WEA summer school in Oxford. Faced with this onslaught on her diary, Elizabeth felt 'an overpowering but inexplicable conviction that something unalterable had been mapped for the future'.[35] Since their first meeting back in the summer of 1927, Elizabeth Harman's social and intellectual success had been on a scale to eclipse Frank's. *Isis*, the university magazine, chose her as one of the first undergraduates to be honoured as an '*Isis* Idol'. Its eulogy described her as 'artistic, beautiful, cultured, decorative, enigmatic, fashionable, even headstrong. If in full womanhood she fulfils the wide promise of her brilliant maidenhood then she will take her place in the honoured band of female worthies.' She came from a family where women were not used to confining their attention to keeping house, looking attractive and having children. Her mother had been one of the first women to train as a doctor and her grandmother had been one of the first of her sex to go on to higher education.

At Oxford, Elizabeth used her wit, beauty and charm to cross what had hitherto been a great gulf between the women's colleges and the rest of the all-male university. Maurice Bowra welcomed her into his salon – and later proposed. Hugh Gaitskell was another who was captivated by her. He too proposed and was likewise rejected. 'There was not an undergraduate', Quintin Hogg[36] later wrote, 'who would not have considered it a privilege to hold an umbrella over her.'[37] Isaiah Berlin,[38] the philosopher, later told her that he had avoided getting to know her at Oxford 'for fear of you taking precedence over my work'.[39] And in a copy of *Oxford Today* in 1990, Justin Evans, who had been at University College between 1926 and 1929, wrote on behalf of 'many of my fellow students reading Mods and Greats in the late twenties – Quintin Hogg, Dick Crossman, Louis MacNeice, Noel Huitton, D.L. Page and R.O. Wilberforce'. There were, Evans said, 'very few women students [who] attended Mods and Greats lectures in those years, but when Greats followed Mods a most glamorous scholar from LMH suddenly appeared at Professor Joseph's philosophy lectures. None of the men students seemed to know who she was and, in the light of her beauty, christened her Daphne. Later they discovered she was Betty Harman.'[40]

Though Elizabeth's degree had been in Classics (she abandoned the more traditionally female English after a year), Frank decided that his new recruit should teach economics at the WEA summer school. Over a lunch with Evan Durbin, by now a tutor at the London School of Economics, he tried to cram her with enough information to enable her to get by. In the end Elizabeth spent the week with a North Staffordshire schoolteacher, trying to unravel Rousseau's *Social Contract* and its implications for the Potteries.

The WEA gave Elizabeth a new perspective. Though her family background was political – her mother's uncle was Joseph

Chamberlain – she had shown little interest in such matters when at Oxford. The golden age of the aesthetes had become rather tarnished by economic adversity by the time she took her finals in the summer of 1930, but her university circle remained largely self-consciously literary, introspective and slow to come to terms with the financial forces that were shaking the world outside. It was something of a rude awakening, then, for her to attend a WEA summer school at Balliol College with out-of-work coal miners from North Staffordshire, men and women passionately seeking the education she had taken for granted. Yet she found them politically conscious and often sardonic.

She did not approach the WEA with any of the political baggage of Frank. She knew little of economics and therefore shared few of his reservations about social parity on that front. She was quick to realize that she could not remain indifferent to what she saw and heard. Education seemed the key to emancipating the working classes and achieving social equality. So she decided to become a full-time WEA tutor but first was persuaded by Evan Durbin to get some economic qualifications herself by attending the LSE.

Before that, however, there was the trip to Ireland. Mary Longford had no patience at all with her second son's attempts to bring friends home to North Aston Hall. Where they found him amusing and entertaining, she was merely cross and resented his attempts to impose on her solitude with loud youngsters. Fortunately for Frank, his brother Edward was more accommodating with Pakenham Hall (though he was later to empty the top floor to prevent invasions by his married siblings and their children). Edward had taken over the Irish house in 1925 upon his marriage and with his wife Christine had removed much of the heavy Victorian furniture, painting the entrance hall flaming red and littering the rooms with the Japanese and Chinese vases that Christine had been collecting as a hobby since her undergraduate days at Oxford. Mary Longford disapproved and told the couple they were turning Pakenham Hall into 'a third rate cinema'.[41]

Other guests that summer included Frank's friend from undergraduate days, John Betjeman, and Evelyn Waugh, whom he had got to know well through the author's friendship with his oldest sister Pansy. Several of the Pakenham girls were there. Already a published novelist (*The Old Expedient*), 24-year-old Pansy, who was close to the Bloomsbury set and to Dora Carrington[42] in particular, had caused something of a stir two years earlier by marrying the divorced artist Henry Lamb, twenty-two years her senior. Only Frank and Mary had attended the registry office ceremony. Violet was eighteen and Julia still a schoolgirl. Betjeman arrived before the other guests. His hosts were not quite sure who or what to expect. With a disregard for detail that used to drive his mother mad, Frank had sent a note warning of Betjeman's plans, but his handwriting, erratic and illegible, had defeated Edward and Christine.

Even when he arrived, Frank almost immediately left his guests in the capable hands of his brother while he hurried off to the Cavan Tennis Tournament for his daily dose of 'ekker' (as he used to call exercise). When they were not exploring Pakenham Hall and its grounds, Edward would evangelize on behalf of Ireland by piling his visitors into his car and taking them on a tour of local Celtic ruins. An alternative was to play republican songs on the gramophone – or better still to sing them. However, there was no sharp political edge to discussions. The atmosphere was decidedly relaxed. 'I have seen at Pakenham what I have seen nowhere else,' Waugh later wrote, 'an entirely sober host literally rolling about the carpet with merriment.'[43]

The guests hit it off well. Betjeman and Waugh were to return several times to stay with Edward and Christine Longford. Betjeman shared Edward's High Church Anglicanism – the pair would indulge in bouts of hymn-singing after dinner – while he described his wife, on the publication of her novel *Making Conversation* in 1931, as 'the funniest woman I ever knew'. Elizabeth Harman was a hit with everybody – except Evelyn Waugh, who told mutual friends for years to come that Frank had married beneath himself. He used to annoy Elizabeth by always greeting her with 'How's hockey?' as if she was a hearty schoolgirl.[44]

In that summer of 1930 Waugh's first marriage to Pansy's erstwhile flatmate Evelyn Gardiner had broken up and he was in a dark mood throughout the holiday. Occasionally it lifted to reveal his mischievous side, as on the last night when, after dinner, as the guests trooped upstairs to bed, he seized Elizabeth's arm. 'Go after Frank,' he whispered. 'Go up with him. Follow him. Go on.' Taking his advice, Elizabeth sprinted up the staircase and joined her future husband in his bedroom. 'There was a double bed but I didn't get into it, just sat on the edge, while we conducted an ardent but chaste and anxious conversation about ourselves far into the night. I can remember only one of the nice things he said: "Why doesn't your face fall to pieces at night like other people's?"'[45]

Frank was smitten, and the romance of Pakenham Hall had worked its spell on Elizabeth. On their return to London – he at the Conservative Research Department and she at the LSE – they saw each other a great deal. His devotion was so marked that he even overcame his usual lack of interest in clothes to buy a new hat simply because the shop selling it was called Harmans (no relation) and he told Elizabeth he liked having her name on the hat band next to his head.

While economics did not prove nearly so interesting as Elizabeth had hoped (she abandoned her course after a year), the couple were travelling up to the Potteries each week on WEA work. Frank had continued to give economics lectures and his new belle was to teach literature. They managed to schedule their classes at the same time so they could catch the last train back to London together. Frank soon found that his previously apolitical protégée was fast being swept past him by their experiences in the Potteries, hurried on through conversations with Hugh Gaitskell, her old beau. If it was Frank who had introduced Elizabeth to the WEA, she was the one to start attending the local Labour Party meetings. For a while there was talk of her standing in the 1931 election as the Labour candidate for the local constituency of Stone.

If their reactions to Stoke were different, the late-night train journey back to London allowed them time on their own to put such matters to one side. Neither had any great experience of physical intimacy with the opposite sex. 'One of the principals at LMH used to think I was fast,' Elizabeth recalled. 'She once called me into her study and said she had heard a lot of unpleasant noise when I came home one evening. She didn't like this sort of thing, she said, and began looking very serious. I couldn't think what she was talking about but it dawned on me in the end. She thought I was misbehaving with men in the street outside the college and that I was probably drunk too. Quite untrue.'[46]

However, it was Frank whose greater inhibition began to make Elizabeth doubt his professions of love. Frank's emotional repression was such that he found it very hard even to kiss the woman he said he loved. It took Elizabeth a good few weeks to melt away his shyness. 'Frank's happiest moments', she reflected in her auto-biography, 'seemed to be tinged with melancholy, while this state of never more than half-happiness seemed to be accepted by him without regret; rather with a kind of acquiescence.'[47]

On the night of 21 November, the couple waited, as usual, in the lounge of the North Stafford Hotel. 'Suddenly,' Elizabeth wrote, 'the hotel manager arrived to put out the lights. "Here you can't do that there, not in my hotel you can't." Driven out on to the windy platform like Adam and Eve, but conscious of a glow rather than a guilt, we were still warm enough when the train came in to continue our conversation. Frank showed himself "capable of endearments", contrary to his own analysis, and at 2.15 a.m. proposed that we should get married.'[48]

Elizabeth accepted and soon afterwards Frank went to her father's consulting rooms in Harley Street to ask for her hand. All did not go according to plan, but through no fault of the prospective bride's father. Frank was struck down by what he later called indecision, but which was also associated with that 'tinge of melancholy' that Elizabeth had already noted and attributed to being starved of maternal affection. The depressive side of Frank's nature, seen at Eton, was resurfacing. Elizabeth was at first puzzled by his introspection, suggesting he seek medical treatment, and then she began to despair. Slowly she encouraged Frank to unburden himself to her and out came all the anxieties and unhappinesses that he had stored up from boyhood – that he was unlovable, unworthy of affection, that as a second son he would not be able to support her or any children. Subconsciously he had made a decision – like many younger sons of aristocratic families at that time – that if he did marry it would have to be when he was older and had carved out a career in the City or politics and with it an income for himself. His ancestor Kitty Pakenham had turned down the proposal of the future Duke of Wellington on the grounds that he was a poor second son of an Anglo-Irish aristocratic family (their castle was at Trim, close to Tullynally). It was only when he had proved himself in India and earned the rank of major-general that she consented to marry him.

If Frank had intended to put off marriage until he had established himself (or at least until Great-Aunt Caroline died and he became the master of Bernhurst), then his love for Elizabeth had thrown such plans into chaos. Emotionally he was paralysed. On 5 December 1930, the occasion of his twenty-fifth birthday and a couple of weeks after the débâcle at Harley Street, he wrote to her of his fears and confusion. He ended his letter on a thoroughly low note: 'What a way to write. As though a false step would be fatal and a step in any direction likely to be a false one.' By Christmas things were not much better. On the card he attached to her present – a pearl bar brooch – he wrote: 'Elizabeth from Frank. Love, kisses and tears.'[49] He was having what later would plausibly have been called a nervous breakdown.

Elizabeth was understandably bemused by this and occasionally irritated. In January 1931, she tried spending more time in Stoke to try to shake Frank out of his lethargy, but separation only seemed to make her unhappier. Already, the pattern of their relationship was being established. It was Elizabeth who was the strong one, who patiently endured this and subsequent crises, postponed the wedding, quelled his fears, brought him out of introspection, unravelled his tangled emotions. Her love was enough, she convinced him, to make up for all that he felt he had been denied in the past. Her love and her strength became in that moment the means by which he held the gloomy side within him at bay.

After Christmas they paid a return visit to Pakenham Hall – again with Betjeman – and this seemed to raise Frank's spirits. Between them the couple began to deal with the perceived barriers to their marriage. From a practical point of view each had a private income of around £300 per year. He earned £500 with the Conservatives and another £100 with the WEA. Elizabeth was getting £85 from the same source. They decided that just over £1,000 would see them through if they were careful.

The one obstacle left between them lay in their political differences. Elizabeth's growing commitment to Stoke and the community in which she was spending more and more time sparked off a lively debate between them over economic policy, currently top of the agenda at the Conservative Research Department. 'Frank and I did not see eye to eye on the causes of the slump,' recalled Elizabeth. 'Their word was "over-production", ours in Stoke was "under-consumption". That put the difference in a nutshell. But it did not get us any nearer to solving the country's problems or our own problem either.'[50]

While Elizabeth was being courted as possible Labour candidate in the 1931 election for Stone, Frank was still considering whether he should yield to pressure from friends and family and stand for the Tories, despite his dwindling faith in their policies. His continued attendance at the parties of the grand and good strained Elizabeth's patience. 'I learned to speak their language – "pith" for everything good and nice, "path" for everything nasty.' In February 1931, Frank wrote to her with a mild rebuke. 'I can't find fault in you, except your attitude to my attitude to the kind of parties I like. I think you are rather hard on me.'[51]

If neither actually appeared on the list of candidates in the 1931 poll, it was down in part to a wish not to antagonize the other. Their doctrinal arguments were conducted by letter from positions that were as far apart geographically – London and Stoke – as they were politically. The gap between Elizabeth's faith in democracy and the equality of all and Frank's agonized and dwindling trust in the sort of paternal philanthropy characterized by his uncle Arthur Villiers came through in his defence of the principle of rulers and ruled.

You seem to me [he wrote] not to realise the importance of rule in life. I look upon it as a fortunate accident that men living in society require co-ordination . . . correction and guidance. The accident is fortunate in that it gives the opportunity for rulers to arise. If all men were perfect, it would be very difficult for the 'men born to be kings', even minor kings, to serve a useful purpose and their special talents would be lost to the world.[52]

When the logic of Elizabeth's arguments touched a nerve, he would lapse into a rather romantic and patronizing notion about how the couple would divide their life into separate but complementary spheres. In exchange for a free hand in literature and painting, Elizabeth would give up her political notions: 'What you don't realise is that I know a great deal about politics. My views may be terribly dull and even inconsistent, but if one treated English politics in its widest aspects as a technical subject, I have the wide knowledge that one would expect of an experienced, if stupid, technician.'[53]

This line did not cut much ice with a woman who had deliberately turned her back on 'female' subjects while at Oxford. Nor was invoking a spirit of pragmatism much of an answer to the strong emotions prompted by the privations suffered by the people of Stoke. On 8 March a truce was temporarily called. Frank went down with bronchial pneumonia and pleurisy. Since Eton he had been prone to nervous exhaustion, the physical expression of his inner anxieties. His mother – true to form – refused to let him convalesce at her new home, Peverel Court, near Aylesbury (she had sold North Aston Hall in 1929), so instead Elizabeth rushed to his bedside at his sister Mary's lodgings in Halsey Street in Chelsea, where she read to him from 'The Lady of Shalott'. Two weeks later Mary Longford finally relented and took him in. (Once she moved to Peverel, she insisted that Frank, when he visited, should make an appointment and sign the visitors' book.)

Frank's slow recovery took the steam out of their political differences and left a little space for romance. One evening that stuck in Elizabeth's memory was a visit to the White Tower restaurant. Many years later the couple went again. 'I reckoned', she wrote in her diary, 'we were at the same historic table where Frank recited "Now sleeps the crimson petal, now the white" when we were first engaged and after I said teasingly "do you know who wrote it?", replied "I did".'[54] In June they went to Oxford to attend the Balliol Commem. Ball and, in that same world where first they had caught sight of each other, the cloud finally lifted entirely and they announced their engagement. In an inadvertent attempt to reproduce those original circumstances as accurately as possible, by midnight Frank was dead to the world. Feeling that she could not abandon her fiancé on such a night, Elizabeth found them an empty bed in one of the students' rooms where they both fell asleep at once, a pillow between them, their virtue intact. Nancy Astor's quip to Frank on hearing of the engagement, 'It's only her body you want', was as yet wide of the mark.

The wedding date was set for 27 October, but it had to be put off for a week because it clashed with the 1931 general election. Frank took leave of absence from his job to campaign for Lady Astor in Plymouth. Elizabeth spoke in King's Norton in Birmingham alongside Hugh Gaitskell in support of the Labour candidate, Dick Mitchison, husband of her friend, the novelist Naomi Mitchison.[55] He was defeated – as were all but fifty Labour candidates.

Such differences and disappointments were put behind them the following week. The wedding on 3 November was a grand affair. Elizabeth wore cream satin with a wreath of orange blossom and a Brussels lace veil that had been in the Pakenham family for many years. She was attended by twelve bridesmaids who each wore different-coloured velvet jackets over their white satin dresses. Frank had chosen Freddy Birkenhead (who had succeeded to the title on his father's death the previous year) as his best man. The church was St Margaret's, Westminster, next door to Westminster Abbey and the scene earlier that year of Basil Dufferin's marriage to Maureen Guinness. Displaying that eccentric charm that was becoming more prominent in his character, Frank arrived at the Abbey by mistake. He was a little despondent to find that there were no guests. Freddy tried to console him. 'People don't go to weddings nowadays.' Finally they realized their mistake. After a reception at the Grosvenor, the newly-weds set off for their honeymoon in the land that always inspired them to romance, Ireland.

FOUR

The Irish Socialist

The honeymoon got off to a rough start. The Irish Sea did not afford a placid welcome to the newly-weds and the couple's journey over to the west coast of Ireland had to be broken at an empty and cold Pakenham Hall where they picked up Edward's car and his chauffeur, Mr White. 'Nor was sex the elixir and panacea it was to become,' Elizabeth wrote, 'despite the fact that Dr Helena Wright – a world famous gynaecologist who lived well into her nineties – had prepared both Frank and me for our first experience.' Things began to look up, however, when they finally arrived in Connemara, where they stayed at the Renvyle Hotel, run by the Irish wit Oliver St John Gogarty,[1] the model for Buck Mulligan in James Joyce's *Ulysses*. The trip was rounded off by a few days with Frank's eccentric Uncle Eddie and Aunt Beatrice, his mother's favourite sister, at their home, Dunsany Castle in County Meath.

Back in England, the newly-weds made their home in the village of Stone in Buckinghamshire, in an outsized cottage on the small Peverel estate where Frank's mother had moved after selling North Aston Hall. Originally two workers' dwellings, the cottage had been knocked into one but still retained both its original staircases and was, for that reason, christened Stairways. Mary Longford got on well with Elizabeth, while Frank, blissfully happy in his marriage, was now able to relax more in his mother's company. He grew to admire her quiet courage in battling with her crippling arthritis. Often unable to take more than a few steps at a time, she would tour her estate in the Baby Austin she had taught herself to drive.

Married life quickly fell into a pattern. For Elizabeth, as she was to write later in her diary, Frank's virtues were 'his wit, gaiety, never a dull moment'.[2] Politics was their shared passion, though they were in different parties. Each had their own enthusiasms. Elizabeth had very little interest, for example, in sport, regarding it as a very male thing, while Frank had almost no curiosity about visiting foreign parts, one of Elizabeth's great joys. He was not one of life's great travellers, his passport lying unused for years on end. But such differences mattered little. From the start, despite their inexperience, this was a great love affair and a very romantic one too. The couple would write to each other when they were apart in almost rhapsodic terms. 'My darling sweetheart,' Elizabeth started a letter during one of her jaunts, 'I began this as a note but it has now become a letter, but containing none of the adoration or longing I feel. Here it all is, my darling, darling beloved Frank, interspersed with wonderings about what you are doing. As it is 10.45am here on Sunday, it will be 5 o'clock in the morning with you, so I hope you are fast asleep, after a lovely match on Saturday. All my love and kisses and longing for your arms. My beloved angel.'[3]

And while Elizabeth was away, Frank would pine. During one of her absences, he felt inspired – perhaps prompted by a hint from his wife – to read Shakespeare's love sonnets and for her return produced his own variation on the theme.

> Your beauty is the beauty of a star.
> You come to earth in answer to our call.
> Your brilliant light to ours superior far,
> If such comparison makes sense at all.
>
> Your courage is the courage of a lion,
> Or lioness, if the word's preferred.
> Behind your gentleness a hint of iron.
> By no-one and by nothing you're deterred.

Your goodness is a goodness all your own.
Your virtue is a flame so quick to burn.
Your love is spread to all of us on loan.
You never think to ask for its return.

Your beauty, courage, goodness I proclaim,
And still fall short of justice to your fame.[4]

During the week, when they were together in London, the couple rented a one-room flat on the Embankment but it was at Stairways, at weekends, that they would welcome their friends and repay past hospitality. The style was modest in comparison to Cliveden, Clandeboye and Charlton – though they did employ a married couple to cook, clean and drive the car since neither of them possessed a licence. Kitty Harman, Elizabeth's younger sister, was the first name in the visitors' book. Frank's two young sisters were also regulars. It was through the newly-weds that Violet was introduced to her future husband, Frank's Eton contemporary but Elizabeth's friend, the novelist Anthony Powell.[5]

Some guests were not impressed by the accommodation. Arthur Villiers, Frank's philanthropic uncle, compared the cottage to a battered HQ behind the lines in war-torn Flanders. Yet neither his own humble abode nor marriage to a self-avowed and unrepentant socialist appeared to diminish Frank Pakenham's *élan* as a weekend guest at the various great houses where he was still regarded as a rising Conservative political star, though with rather eccentric interests in the WEA. These were viewed, however, more with amusement than as a sign of any serious intention, a process to which Frank would contribute by making everything about himself into a joke at his own expense. There were the occasional asides. When Elizabeth was photographed outside Buckingham Palace, complying with her mother-in-law's wishes to present herself at court after marriage, the cutting was captioned by Uncle Arthur 'socialette at play'.

It was at Hatfield, home of the Tory grandees Lord and Lady Salisbury, parents of Lord David Cecil, that Stanley Baldwin, three times prime minister and the most influential politician of the period, requested Frank's company on a Sunday afternoon constitutional. It was tantamount to a summons but once striding across the great park the young man could not think of anything to say to impress Baldwin. He fell back on talking about the Workers' Educational Association and the poverty he had seen in the Potteries, hardly a subject designed to impress and win preferment.

The thirties, Quentin Bell wrote, was a decade of 'mounting despair . . . unable to shake the complacency of a torpid nation, we saw the champions of war, tyranny and racial persecution winning . . . it was bloody to be alive and to be young was very hell'.[6] As economic recession fast became depression and unemployment soared, the mainstream political parties struggled to come up with a response. Their inability to provide answers gave rise to radical alternatives with ready solutions to grip the popular imagination. Most notorious was Oswald Mosley,[7] a Labour cabinet minister in the 1929 government, who set up his New Party of black-shirted Fascists in 1931 and stormed up and down the country preaching an anti-Semitic, anti-Establishment gospel that dwelt on the shining example of Hitler's Germany.

Frank's faith in Conservatism had been all but demolished; he dismantled it logically, brick by brick, though he continued to work – albeit with ebbing enthusiasm and growing doubts – at the Conservative Research Department. Its founder, Elizabeth's first cousin Neville Chamberlain,[8] had declined his invitation to the wedding, although his daughter, Dorothy, was one of the brides-maids. Elizabeth suspected that he had heard the rumour that young Pakenham was flirting with socialism and therefore 'thought it best not to embroil himself too deeply with a man of such curious fancies'.[9] Finally in the spring of 1932 Frank resigned. It was to be the end of his formal attachment to Conservatism.

Despite the imminent arrival of his first child, the summer of 1932 found Frank once again drifting without any particular career direction. He dabbled briefly in journalism, but showed little of the talent that was later in the decade to make his sister Mary – who in 1940 married Herefordshire landowner and Grenadier Guard

Meysey Clive – a star turn in Lord Beaverbrook's *Evening Standard*. Frank was taken on as a stand-in for Peter Fleming as literary editor at the *Spectator* while Fleming went off on a holiday to the Amazon. The editor, Wilson Harris, sensing Frank's lack of interest in books, sent him off to Eton to follow up a report in the *News of the World* on drunkenness among pupils there. His old headmaster, Dr Alington, was not to be soothed into making any revelations, and sent him away without the hoped-for scoop. When Fleming returned, Frank moved on to the *Daily Mail* as a leader writer. Again his Conservative pedigree got him the job. He was greeted on his first day by H.W. Wilson, who had been the paper's sole leader writer for a good many years and whose tactlessness can perhaps be explained by the fact that he would have viewed the interloper with some suspicion. 'I am glad to have you to help us,' he told Frank, no doubt fully aware of his Anglo-Irish background. 'You will find our policy easy enough to understand. I regard the Germans as the cruellest people in the world, except the Chinese – and of course the Irish.'[10] The new recruit was given to writing 'leaderettes', frothy shorts to slot in if there was space below the main editorials. Many carefully crafted pieces of Frank's wit landed on the spike. Others that did appear hardly used his talents to the full. 'The hobble is here again', began his warning on the vogue for tight-fitting narrow skirts, which continued with the practical but not exactly germane thought that women might find it hard to walk as quickly as they might want in such garments.[11]

Antonia was born on 27 August 1932, ten months after the wedding. The father – uncommonly for the time – was present at the bedside throughout a long labour which was not helped by the fact that London was in the midst of a heatwave. It was not an experience he particularly enjoyed: 'I didn't want to see any more babies born after that. I was always in the house when the others were born – except for Michael when I had to be away – but I didn't watch them being born.'[12]

Mary Clive was the first visitor to the nursery and named the baby Gandhi because she was suffering from a mild dose of jaundice. Frank was momentarily keen on Winnie, after a favourite maid from his childhood at Pakenham Hall, but in the end the couple decided on Antonia after Willa Cather's novel, *My Antonia*. Maureen Dufferin was among the godparents. Frank did not instantly take to fatherhood. He developed at this stage and retained a horror of holding babies, and was never much interested in them. It was only when they grew into children able to express opinions that he started to listen and pay attention. Even then their achievements rather more than their characters were what interested him, if only as a yardstick to measure their progress. But such was Elizabeth's enthralment with infants – what she used to call the baby itch – that, ever devoted, he tried to think himself into her way of looking at things. A decade later, soon after his third daughter Rachel was born, he wrote to Elizabeth – he was away in London at the time – to announce unconvincingly but with an evident desire to please that he had a new-found interest in babies. He ascribed this change of heart to a variety of reasons. 'Partly perhaps because I am fundamentally much more interested in children of all ages than I was – no doubt through having studied and loved ours. When Antonia was a baby, I was hardly interested in children at all, but that is quite changed now.'[13] The truth of that admission can be judged against the occasion when Frank went to collect Antonia, then aged fifteen months, from a children's party at the Dufferins. Catching sight of a little mass of curls and frills among the other guests, he turned to Maureen Dufferin and remarked, 'That's a jolly little child.' 'Yes, it's your daughter,' the hostess replied.[14]

Frank was the first to admit that he found being a father to small children a trying and uneasy role. 'I would say that I was an alpha beta/beta alpha father. I would play games with the children and unlike many fathers I came home most nights – except when I was in London during the war.'[15] Like many men of his generation, he tended to leave the task of child-rearing to his wife. Even in old age, he would admit that he found the idea of a man pushing a pram ludicrous. In this very traditional division of responsibilities, fatherhood did increase the burden on him to 'settle down' as the family's main breadwinner. The careful financial calculations made at the time of their marriage had not allowed much for bringing up children and it was only a matter of months after Antonia's birth that Elizabeth found herself pregnant again.

The anti-Irish sentiments Frank had encountered at the *Daily Mail* coincided with a growing political interest in his homeland. Previously his ties with Ireland had been more romantic and sentimental. Politically he was still poles apart from his brother Edward's nationalism. However events in Dublin began to concentrate his mind for the first time on the nature of his own Anglo-Irish identity. The Irish Free State, set up in 1921 to run its own affairs but bound to the British in matters of defence and foreign policy, was pushing for full independence under its new leader, Eamon de Valera.

After the rebellion and civil disorder that followed the First World War and British mishandling of the aftermath of the Easter Rising, a peace treaty had been agreed between Lloyd George and the Irish leaders Arthur Griffith and Michael Collins in 1921, partitioning off the north-east corner of Ulster, which remained part of the United Kingdom, and giving the rest of Ireland semi-independent dominion status under the Imperial Crown. The treaty split Ireland. The pro faction – led by Griffith and Collins – and the anti forces – headed by the charismatic figure of de Valera – fought out a bloody civil war. The majority of the population was in favour of the treaty, for all its shortcomings, and the pro forces triumphed with William Cosgrave ruling the Free State for a decade (Collins had been murdered in the civil war and Griffith died in 1922, a broken man). In February 1932, however, de Valera, the sole survivor of the leaders of the 1916 Rising and the leading opponent of the treaty, defeated Cosgrave at the polls.

In the Conservative circles in which Frank moved, de Valera was demonized and regarded as beyond the pale. It was a sign of Frank's growing independence of thought that such vilification only made him more interested in meeting Dev, as he was known. When he managed, through friends in Dublin, to get to see him in the spring of 1932, he fell, as he put it himself, 'an instant victim to his charm and the more I studied it, as I began to do with real earnestness, to his case'.[16] It would be simple-minded to say that de Valera led

Frank to discover he was an Irishman. Frank would not have sought him out in the first place if he had not had a powerful interest in Ireland. De Valera did, however, bring it to the front of his consciousness and his political life.

Yet again Frank had fallen for a glamorous, larger-than-life character who defied easy categorization. De Valera was a single-minded patriot whom Frank saw as being prepared to put principles before party. It was another case of hero-worship. Thomas Pakenham, Frank's eldest son who later got to know de Valera well, saw them as an odd pair. 'De Valera was a puritan – more puritanical even than my father. He was also a violent Irish nationalist – more fanatical than my father. In fact many of de Valera's qualities were the very reverse of what was considered Irish. He wasn't good company. He didn't like conversation. He didn't like discussing things with people. He was a very alien figure to my father who always loved talking and discussing things.'[17] The bond forged in 1932 was nevertheless to endure throughout de Valera's long life until his death in 1975.

Not long after their meeting, Frank was roped in as a speaker after the invited guest dropped out at the last minute at Chatham House, the Royal Institute for International Affairs, founded in 1923 and one of Waldorf Astor's pet projects. Frank surprised some of those who thought they knew his concerns by picking Ireland as his theme. John Betjeman was later to paint an idealized picture of the scene. 'Obviously this was no practised or accomplished speaker, but as he went on the strange, hurried young man began to make an impression.'[18] The truth was somewhat harsher. Frank wore his new-found pro-Ireland sympathies on his sleeve, to the annoyance of many of the audience, who were backing the British government in its tough stance against de Valera. 'You can tell the Irish farmer doesn't know which side his bread is buttered,' one heckler in the audience called out.

Frank was to date his public sympathy with the Irish cause from that Chatham House lecture, but also argued that there was a pre-existing private bond. 'Irish nationalism had begun to stir me emotionally, but it was all on an imaginative, almost poetic plane.

Yeats' poems and autobiographies jostled for pride of place with Roger Casement's speech from the dock. "Loyalty is a sentiment not a law. It rests on love not restraint."[19]

Despite this new-found passion, however, his employment prospects were still a cause for concern. In the spring of 1932, he was snatched away from writing about fashion on the *Daily Mail* by the offer of a part-time lectureship at the London School of Economics, teaching alongside Evan Durbin and under the director-ship of Sir William Beveridge.[20] It was the first step on the ladder of academia. Frank found it a world where his brilliant, showy cleverness was more thoroughly appreciated than anywhere else hitherto, and in the autumn of the same year he was appointed to a lectureship in politics at Christ Church, his brother's old college and scene of his famous ducking. His choice of politics over economics showed how far he had travelled from undergraduate days. Much later one of his sons was to ask Elizabeth 'why Frank and I had not gone out to train our children to have a money sense. I said I was interested in money but did not understand it and Dada understood it but was not interested.'[21]

The academic world and a don's salary and perks allowed Frank the freedom to pursue his growing interest in Ireland. Chance again played a part when, staying with friends in Ireland, he was presented with a unique set of papers dealing with the 1921 treaty. He and Elizabeth were guests at the home of Robert Barton at Glendalough House in the wilds of the Wicklow Mountains. Barton, like Frank, was Anglo-Irish and had served under Collins and Griffith in the Irish delegation at the London peace conference in 1921. Until the last moment he had been torn between Collins's pragmatic acceptance of the terms Lloyd George had put on the table and de Valera's insistence, back in Dublin, that Ireland had to achieve a greater measure of independence than the halfway house of dominion status under the British Crown. Barton had in fact signed the treaty but later repudiated his action and sided with de Valera. He suffered for this change of heart less than his first cousin Erskine Childers, author of the classic detective novel, *The Riddle of the Sands*. Another Anglo-

Irish member of the Collins delegation, Childers had opposed the treaty all along and had been seized at Glendalough House in 1922 by pro-treaty forces. He was tried on a trumped-up charge of possessing an illegal firearm and died at the hands of a Free State firing squad. (Ironically the gun in question had been given to him by Michael Collins.) Childers's American widow, Mollie, continued to live with the Bartons.

Robert Barton took to Frank, recognizing in the young man's background elements of his own upbringing. Moreover, he saw in Frank someone who might be in a position to appreciate both sides of a contentious story. Though he was by now close to de Valera, Frank also had, through his pro-treaty brother, Edward, ready access to the leading lights among the Free Staters, notably Desmond Fitzgerald.[22] Barton was equally impressed by Frank's connections with many of the principal players on the Imperial side in the 1921 negotiations. Austen Chamberlain,[23] a relation of Elizabeth's, and F.E. Smith had worked alongside Lloyd George. On the stairwell at Charlton hung a portrait of Collins, whom Birkenhead had grown to admire.

And so Barton entrusted, to a young man with no track record as a writer or a historian and fairly untested credentials as an Irish patriot, his papers from 1921 covering that crucial period of negotiation between 11 October and 6 December when the fateful deal was signed. 'I have been exceptionally fortunate in my material,' Frank acknowledged, with a heavy dose of understatement, in the preface to the original 1935 edition. *Peace by Ordeal* was widely acclaimed for its detail and balance by both factions. Serialized on publication in the *Irish Independent*, it remained for the rest of the century the standard book on that crucial turning-point in Anglo-Irish relations, a remarkable achievement for one so young and inexperienced as a writer. It was reprinted four times up to 1992.

The book begins with the historical background of the Home Rule movement. It shows how in 1921, in the heat of the moment with the threat of civil war throughout Ireland, the concessions made to the Ulster Protestants were seen as a way of ensuring peace.

Indeed, writing in 1935, Frank seemed confident of an eventual reuniting of the whole of Ireland. In the book he praises the Dublin government for 'the justice it has provided for minorities' and expresses his hope, while acknowledging the bitterness felt in the north, that de Valera's policy of non-coercion of the Orangemen might one day heal the divide.

The British Establishment – whose members like Lloyd George and Austen Chamberlain had helped Frank with his research on the book – are criticized in the text, but so too are the Irish. Referring to the bloody civil unrest that led up to the 1921 peace talks, Frank writes:

The British showed scant respect for the rules of the Hague Convention. They carried hostages on lorries, they terrorised the civil population, they destroyed the property of civilians when no military necessity dictated. But on the other hand the Irish forces seldom wore uniform or distinctive badges, and they could hardly expect much encouragement from an appeal to any generally recognised code. Each side in fact made its own precedents and used all methods judged essential for victory, in so far as seemed expedient in view of world opinion and in so far as its own humanity permitted.

The book's balance was much admired by reviewers. Even in dealing with characters for whom he personally had the greatest of admiration, Frank does not fail to see them from the other side. His hero, Lord Birkenhead, is described through Irish eyes.

Carson's galloper in 1914, he had more recently been foremost in the public reiteration that the [Irish] rebels must be crushed by force. The South thought of him as a materialist, with what political altruism he possessed used up in fierce allegiance to the British Crown; full of contempt for what was small, and callousness towards what was suffering; as one likely to pay scant attention to the plea for special treatment of what he probably regarded as a disloyal and treacherous sect.

For all its even-handedness, though, *Peace by Ordeal* proclaimed Frank's fundamental Irish nationalism. Despite this, several commentators in Ireland were less impressed. They were dismayed that Frank had not been tougher on de Valera and in particular probed why it was that Dev had not gone to the peace talks himself but had left Collins and Griffith to carry the burden. The text accepts at face value de Valera's explanation that as President of Ireland he needed to stay above the fray. 'The strategy was understandable enough. As long as de Valera was in reserve the Irish delegates could avoid being rushed into any hasty decisions.' Those who saw de Valera's refusal to endorse the treaty as a betrayal of Collins and Griffith, however, found such an explanation less than convincing. Desmond Fitzgerald, Edward Longford's friend and a pro-treaty man, criticized *Peace by Ordeal* on this account, as did Moya Llewelyn Davies, another intimate of Collins who had helped Frank in his research. (In a new introduction to the 1992 edition, the Irish historian Tim Pat Coogan, Collins's biographer, attacked Frank's homage to de Valera. The president, according to Coogan, brooked no rivals to his throne and avoided going to London in 1921 not because he was prepared to trust his colleagues and sometime rivals for power, but rather because he wanted to 'distance himself from the harsh realities of a debate which he knew was bound to involve compromise'. He thus 'managed to wriggle out of entering the lion's den'.)

The most immediate effect of publication, however, was to add weight to Frank's academic reputation. Michael Foot, who was a student at Wadham in the mid-1930s and President of the Oxford Union, subsequently said that it was when he read *Peace by Ordeal* that he became aware of Frank Pakenham as one of the leading lights among the university teaching staff.[24] Christ Church duly promoted him to a full-time teaching post, with a salary of £1,000 a year, double his previous wage. In choosing Frank, the college turned down the philosopher Freddie Ayer. 'I decided,' he wrote, 'I had to leave the Carlton Club because *Peace by Ordeal* was pro-de Valera. I told the chairman of the club while he was having port with some other members. I perched nervously on the edge of the armchair and told him about the book, said that I thought it might cause trouble and said I would leave the club. He told me not to be so silly, that if everyone who had written a book resigned, there would be no members.' Frank was temporarily deflected but he returned to the subject several months later when Elizabeth decided to stand as the Labour candidate at Cheltenham in the November 1935 general election. 'Even then the club secretary took me to one side and said that if I was ever in trouble overseas . . . He obviously thought I would have to leave the country.' After bidding the secretary goodbye, Frank had also to take leave of the Carlton's barber, where he had been a regular customer. He had planned to lay in a substantial stock of the barber's hair oil, but was advised not to buy too much. 'You'll be bald in three years whatever you do,' he was told, and it proved an accurate prediction.[25]

It was finally the unremitting and, from Frank's point of view, illogical hostility towards de Valera that broke any lingering hold the Conservative Party still exerted on him. De Valera's moves to reduce the role of the British Governor-General in Dublin, to drop the oath of allegiance to the Crown from the constitution, and to cancel land annuity payments, the mortgages to the British Treasury paid by Irish farmers so that they could become owners of the land they worked – all to Frank's mind practical and justifiable policies – were met by Stanley Baldwin and his ministers with economic sanctions. 'I had always assumed till then that whatever the theoretical arguments either way,' he wrote, 'the best Conservatives would approach a particular problem of statesmanship without distorting prejudice; that they would meet argument with argument; that whether I agreed with them or not they would always be able to convince me that they were acting on a plausible principle.'[26]

He had not, however, joined the Labour Party at once, but his stance over Ireland did narrow the continuing political divide with Elizabeth. 'Ireland', she wrote, 'was the only political problem – or rather, political answer – on which I accepted without question the judgement of Frank's head and heart. At the same time, it was a minority cause and perceptibly drew him nearer to my way of thinking on English politics.'[27] For in siding with the Irish against the British, Frank was not only turning his back on the traditions of his Ascendancy ancestors; he was also taking the part of the underdogs. It was a significant moment, according to his friend David Astor. 'You could see Frank's life as a long search to be on the side of the people. That's why he became a socialist. On this occasion over Ireland, he wanted to be with the people.'[28]

Frank's interest in Ireland caused something of a *rapprochement* with Edward Longford, though Edward did occasionally complain that 'my brother lives in England and has become a pillar of the British establishment, but is seen over here as an Irish patriot. I, on the other hand, live here, and have given what talent I possess to the Irish language, Irish literature and especially the Irish theatre, but I'm still regarded as a West Briton.'[29] Where once he had been embarrassed by his elder brother and hesitant to defend him, Frank would not now suffer any insult on Edward's behalf, even when it came from one of Frank's close friends. At a smart dinner party Randolph Churchill[30] goaded Frank, 'Your brother's a Sinn Feiner, a traitor to his country.' After trying politely but firmly to change the subject, Frank finally unleashed a fine-tuned sharp tongue and disarmed his tormentor by asking, 'Randolph, what did your grandfather die of?' Randolph crumpled. It was not well known in those days that Lord Randolph Churchill had died of syphilis.

When Elizabeth had accepted the nomination to stand for Labour in the no-hope Conservative seat of Cheltenham, her husband had given her enthusiastic, if qualified, backing. He spoke for her once on a public platform – stressing, unsurprisingly, his personal esteem for her, praising her attachment to the League of Nations (at that time the cornerstone of Labour foreign policy as a block on Hitler's ambitions and as an alternative to the need to rearm) and then, to the confusion of the audience, referring to his own Conservatism. Elizabeth's worst moment during canvassing, however, came when she was introduced, wearing her red rosette, to a group of Catholic nuns. Noting the candidate's surname, they launched into a eulogy of Blessed Mary Pakenham, the male founder of the Passionist Order in Ireland who, as was the Catholic tradition, had taken on the name of the Virgin. Elizabeth had heard much of previous generations of Pakenham generals, but had not been made aware by her in-laws of this ancestor or his sex, and so parried the nuns' praises by expressing her own view that Blessed Mary was a fine woman. Despite this slip, Elizabeth did a creditable job, increasing the Labour vote and cutting the Conservative majority of the incumbent, Sir Walter Preston, in a town then renowned for its retired colonels.

Aside from his foray to Cheltenham, Frank spent the 1935 election in a non-party-political capacity as agent to Alan Herbert,[31] who stood as an Independent in one of the Oxford University seats. Herbert was persuaded by Frank to run against the Conservatives on a ticket of defending academic freedom. Herbert cut a dash next to his Tory rival, the bumbling Hertford College don C.M. Cruttwell – much despised by Evelyn Waugh, who introduced a villainous character with the same name into his novels. Frank's campaign organization was widely praised, building on his successful undergraduate experience of promoting the *Oxford University Review*.

Siding with Herbert against the Tories was a clear indication of his switch from right to left, but a decidedly personal factor should not be overlooked. Frank's Christ Church colleague and friend from days at Charlton, Professor Lindemann,[32] had been passed over – unjustly, Frank felt – for the Conservative nomination in favour of Cruttwell. Furthermore, Herbert's liberal views on morality – notably his tireless work towards easing the restrictions on divorce – found no great favour with his agent. His early years as an Oxford don saw Frank keeping up many of his Conservative associations. In the spring of 1933 the Oxford Union held its landmark debate on whether it would take up arms for King and Country. In the wake of the national outcry at the refusal of the cream of the generation to put national defence before self, the Conservative Randolph Churchill, then an undergraduate at Oxford, tried to get the motion overturned. Frank was at his side, his own family's military traditions no doubt in the front of his mind. The anti-war stance of Labour under its pacifist leader George Lansbury was another aspect of party policy that he could not stomach. Churchill was heckled, booed, shouted down and showered with stink bombs. There was something in his manner, Frank later concluded, reflecting on the incident, that provoked strangers. On that particular evening, so provoked did the crowd become that the two of them had to make a hasty exit, mission unaccomplished, to cries of 'To the Cherwell with both of them!' An icy stare from Churchill managed to disarm his accusers and the students restrained themselves from attacking one of their dons.

Churchill was soon afterwards to offer Frank the post of secretary to the India Defence Committee, a group which he chaired with Lord Lloyd whose purpose was to defeat the India reforms proposed by the Baldwin government. The committee suspected that the reforms were aimed at paving the way for eventual Indian independence. If Randolph Churchill was officially at the head of this group, it was his father Winston who was the leading light. Frank went to one of the meetings of the committee, with Winston Churchill in attendance, but it was not a crusade the younger man had any interest in (indeed, in its keep-the-Empire-together-at-any-cost message, it ran counter to all his views on Ireland), and he politely but firmly declined. Even if he had wanted to take up the job offer, it would have been difficult for him to do so without earning the enmity of his mother. Mary Longford, shortly before her death, on hearing that her son had even considered such a post, told him: 'You would never have been able to look me in the face if you had accepted a position under Winston Churchill.'[33] She held Churchill responsible for her husband's death at Gallipoli and by association for all her own sufferings thereafter. Churchill, as First Lord of the Admiralty and then Chancellor of the Duchy of Lancaster in the wartime cabinets of first Asquith and then Lloyd George, was credited with ordering the assault on Gallipoli. He added insult to injury in Mary Longford's eyes when he wrote of the ill-fated campaign in his book, *World Crisis*: 'On that battlefield of fog and flame fell Brigadier General The Earl of Longford . . . and other Paladins.'

When Frank had been appointed to the full-time fellowship at Christ Church in 1934, he and Elizabeth had decided to move their burgeoning family to Oxford. Thomas was born on 14 August 1933, thirteen days before Antonia's first birthday and just in time for Mary Longford to see him christened in Hartwell Church. Given her predisposition for sons and heirs, she may have viewed Thomas with a benign smile. Edward and Christine Longford were by this time despairing of ever having children. Old enmities remained, however. Elizabeth wrote that she 'always felt that she [Mary Longford] wished and wished that Thomas was Edward's son and not Frank's'.[34] Mary Longford died shortly afterwards of cancer at the age of fifty-six. Since diagnosis she had made it plain that she did not wish to speak of her illness and handled her own death with the same lonely aloofness that had characterized her long widowhood. Still her younger son wept at the news of his mother's death. She was buried in the churchyard at Middleton among her Villiers relations. By the age of twenty-eight, he had lost both parents.

With his mother's death, Stairways had to be vacated. The new family home was at Singletree in Rose Hill, east of the city centre between the village of Iffley and the industrial suburb of Cowley. Designed by an Oxford chemist to match the grand architectural style of the university's academic buildings, it abounded with carved oak mantels, parquet floors and even an odd bow window in the drawing room. Within months of the Pakenhams' arrival, its countryside views were marred by the building of the Florence Park estate nearby, not that the couple, with their social consciences, could complain.

At Christ Church Frank was respected by colleagues and regarded with affection by students who, he liked to boast, began in the 1930s with Michael Berry, later Lord Hartwell, owner of the *Telegraph* titles and husband of F.E. Smith's daughter, Pamela, and ended two decades later with Nigel Lawson, subsequently Chancellor of the Exchequer. Among those whom Frank taught in between was Philip Toynbee, the writer and a life-long friend.[35] 'He was popular with undergraduates,' Toynbee recalled, 'slightly laughed at, but I think he was good at his job. We used to call him Polkinghorn. No sexual application, just a kind of joke name, old Frankie Polkinghorn. Because he was clumsy and odd-looking, though actually he was quite dexterous with his tongue. He was perfectly capable of looking after himself if attacked.' Frank never played the distant, detached tutor with his undergraduates. He was always happy to sit down with them over a tumbler of sherry – an enduring predilection – and talk about anything but work. 'He was always asking about my girlfriends,' said Toynbee. 'He was fascinated by my goings-on.' The two also played tennis. Again there was a mixture of respect and ridicule between tutor and student. Toynbee recalled that Frank 'played in a ludicrously clumsy way', but usually won.[36]

Restored to the academic world of Oxford, the Pakenhams were an instant social success. Elizabeth's old friend Maurice Bowra featured large in their circuit. Frank was very influenced, Philip Toynbee later suggested, by Bowra and the rather malicious style of wit then popular at Oxford, where cruel stories were told about anyone and everyone. 'There was an old don at Christ Church who died and Bowra said to Frank, and I happened to be there, "Well, what's the reaction at the House [Christ Church] to the death?" And Frank said, "Oh, immense relief." It was a typical Bowra remark, but not a typical Frank remark. But Frank was under his thumb. He was even a bit sycophantic to Maurice Bowra.'[37]

Through Elizabeth, who had become an active member of the Oxford Labour Party, holding fetes for the Cowley branch in the garden at Singletree, the couple also moved increasingly in socialist circles. Patrick Gordon Walker, the Labour candidate for Oxford, was a Christ Church colleague and became a great friend,[38] as did Dick Crossman, then a don at New College, a Labour councillor. The Oxford City Labour Party in the 1930s was the incubator for a future generation of Labour cabinet ministers of the 1960s. As a branch it had a radical, questioning environment with a heavy over-representation of dons and a corresponding lack of the union figures who are usually the backbone of many a local Labour Party. In this atmosphere, Oxford's academic socialists moved to the left wing of a national party that was deeply divided in its reaction to Ramsay MacDonald's defection to the Conservatives in 1931 and over the rising threat of Fascism on the continent. At the heart of the dispute

at a national level was the party's emotionally rooted commitment
to pacifism. In the iconography of the Labour Party, war was seen as
a matter of worker fighting worker on behalf of the capitalists and
imperialists. Pacifism was therefore the logical response, an
international workers' solidarity against such exploitation. On the
reformist wing of Labour, men like Hugh Dalton[39] sought to temper
their party's instinctive opposition to the growing cries for rearmament against Hitler with a more positive commitment to meet
the threat through collective security under the banner of the League
of Nations – a prominent plank of Elizabeth's campaign in
Cheltenham. The left wing, though, saw the League as a capitalists'
organization, the tool, as Sir Stafford Cripps,[40] another of the
prominent pacifists in the leadership, put it, of the haves against the
have-nots, the 'International Burglars' Union'.

The disagreement came to a head in October 1935 at the Labour
Party conference which coincided with Mussolini's invasion of
Abyssinia. The left opposed a motion calling for concerted League
of Nations action and sanctions. George Lansbury, the leader of the
Parliamentary Labour Party, made a highly emotional speech
emphasizing his own Christian pacifism and calling for the motion
to be rejected. Those who lived by the sword, he warned, died by
the sword, but he was defeated in the vote after a decisive
intervention by Ernest Bevin,[41] and replaced by Clement Attlee, who
was in favour of collective security under the auspices of an anti-
Fascist (not pro-capitalist as the left claimed in its rhetoric) League
of Nations.

Under Attlee and Bevin, there was a crackdown on those in the
party who were influenced by communism, but it was far from
effective. The Oxford City branch was on the left of the party and
had a strong contingent of communist fellow-travellers who looked
to figures such as Stafford Cripps in the national hierarchy to move
Labour leftwards. Frank, as part of working through a process of
logic from right to left, decided to read Marx but was not convinced
by his thinking. 'In his "Labour Theory of Value" and his "Surplus
Value" I still found', he wrote, 'a stimulating though inadequate
effort to provide an economic justification for his sense of moral

indignation; and I had a similar opinion of the other main feature of his economics – his claim that capitalism inevitably breaks down owing to its inherent tendency to produce more than it can consume.'[42]

Though more and more drawn to the Labour Party on moral and ethical grounds, and almost inevitably attracted by the maverick Cripps, Frank balked at the Marxist bent of the local Oxford Party, which only served to exacerbate what he saw as the lack of a logical economic basis for socialism. His instinct was that inequality was inevitable, that there was no quick fix. He may have yearned for a redistribution of wealth, but he was far from sure whether it could be made to happen or that it would bring with it practical benefits. Perhaps if he had lived somewhere other than Oxford, he might have found a local party more amenable, less strident and less idealistic. The party's national 1935 manifesto after all did promise measures such as bank nationalization, but nowhere was there a hint of trying to bring a Soviet-style, centrally controlled economy to Britain.

So he remained on the outside looking in. It took a bump on the head to sort things out. Oswald Mosley had made great capital out of Britain's economic distress in the first half of the 1930s, contrasting it unfavourably with what was happening in Germany and Italy under Fascist rule. A handsome, moustachioed figure, clad all in black and surrounded by henchmen in similar attire, Mosley was a polished speaker with a provocative line in argument. Booking the Carfax Assembly Rooms in central Oxford on 14 May 1936 was a typical gesture. His aim was to goad the academic establishment and the university's radical socialists in particular. They responded as he had expected, and packed out the hall. The Pakenhams were there, as were most of their circle – Crossman, Toynbee, Gordon Walker. But Mosley also had a wider pull. There was a large contingent of bus drivers, staunch Labour members who had come to give Mosley a rough ride.

In this tense atmosphere, with Mosley in mid-flow, someone stood up and shouted 'Red Front!' and gave the clenched-fist salute. The speaker responded at once to this act of provocation. 'The next man who shouts "Red Front" goes out.' Several others defied him but he made a show of ignoring them, at the same time beckoning his Blackshirts, complete with their rubber truncheons, up the aisles. And then up stood the somewhat incongruous figure of Basil Murray, Philip Toynbee's uncle, who had been chatting with Frank outside the hall, to repeat the blasphemy. Mosley's massed supporters pounced on Murray and within minutes the room was one big scuffle. The busmen took the lead in responding to the fascists' aggression. Heavy buckled belts met with steel chairs. Frank, who had been sitting in the row behind Murray, dived into the fray. 'I can remember struggling with a little team of fascists, all much shorter than I, but each one, I expect, at least as good as I was in the rough and tumble.'[43] His opponents soon had Frank on the floor and were kicking him in the kidneys with their jack-boots. He was saved by a timely intervention from the police. Philip Toynbee, blood streaming down his face, greeted his tutor as a fellow revolutionary.

Elizabeth, who had been separated from her husband in the mêlée, returned home to find him already in bed, with a doctor in attendance. He diagnosed concussion, two black eyes and minor injuries to the kidneys, and ordered complete rest. Never a man to stay still for very long, Frank's frustration at being laid up only added to his anger at what he had witnessed. When the police announced they were to prosecute Basil Murray, his disgust was total. Several weeks later, when the local magistrates fined Murray £2, Frank rose to his feet in the public gallery and shouted, 'I'd like to tell those buggers on the bench what I think of them.'[44] Instead he obtained an interview with the Home Secretary to lodge his protest. Sir John Simon,[45] a friend of Basil Murray's parents, listened politely but declined to take any further action.

Any residual faith Frank had in the political establishment evaporated at that point. The authorities were refusing to take what had happened seriously and to face up to Mosley. Official indifference was for Frank a moral abdication, a tacit approval of Mosley's methods. In a highly emotional state and still nursing his injuries, he abandoned the torturous logical path he had been on and saw the issue crystallize into terms of child-like simplicity. He was either on one team or the other. As his friend Lord David Cecil remarked, 'Frank was always a great partisan. He saw things in terms of one side against another. It's a sort of sporting view.'[46] Any previous doubts and equivocations over economic policy disappeared. His careful academic weighing of Labour's claims gave way to a determination to nail his colours to the mast. 'In that room I could see only two sides. The solid citizens of north Oxford and the busmen. And there was only one side for me. My life at Oxford at that time had been one of entering into the lives of the working classes. I was enthusiastic about the spirit I found in Cowley on our doorstep.'[47]

Two more events hastened his decision to commit to Labour. In 1936 the Spanish Civil War had broken out. It was a seminal event for many in his generation. Again Frank did not dwell on the nuances of the situation. His instinct was against Franco and the fascists and in favour of the democratically elected socialist government of Spain. Those around him encouraged such a stance. His friend Basil Murray, for example, joined up and was to die in the struggle against Franco.

Owing to her prominence in Labour politics in Oxford and the good show she had put up in Cheltenham, in August 1936 Elizabeth was invited to take over from the husband of her friend Naomi Mitchison as candidate for the eminently winnable Birmingham seat of King's Norton. Frank was right behind her decision to accept the challenge of winning the seat, in the Chamberlain heartland, from the incumbent Conservative, Ronald Cartland, brother of Barbara, the bestselling romantic novelist.

Frank's political passion was great enough to overcome his dislike of travel and, in September, he went to Berlin with Elizabeth for a conference on peace and democracy with European academics. The couple were initially reluctant to go to Hitler's Germany but the trip was to prove the final push into the arms of Labour. Though little that was dramatic happened when they were in Germany, on their return he joined the Cowley and Iffley Labour Party.

It was an emotional response, almost a lunge. At the moment when he was at the height of his academic powers, widely admired for his book *Peace by Ordeal* and regarded by his colleagues as a clever man able to grasp and convey to students the intricacies of political thought and debate, Frank chose to act in a linear fashion, rejecting intellectual subtleties in favour of a passionate determination and blinkered faith in one view of the situation. His heart was ruling his head.

FIVE

The Radical Don

With his decision to join the Labour Party, Frank embarked on one of the most frenetic periods of his life. In addition to his teaching duties and the usual round of sporting and social activities, he was at the troubled heart of a particularly volatile local branch of the Labour Party whose divisions reflected those of a national movement unable to agree a common response to the rise of fascism.

Part of his frenzy was undoubtedly the ardour of the new convert, anxious to prove his credentials as a socialist after standing so long outside the movement criticizing it. Part, too, was a conscious effort to bury any lingering intellectual doubts under an orgy of activity, hoping the practical would vanquish the cerebral. Then there was an element of wanting to emerge from Elizabeth's shadow in Labour Party terms. He had noted, if not been stung by, a remark made of them when they were working with the WEA: 'the grey mare is the best horse in the stable'.[1] In a marriage of equals, he wanted to be her equal in what was now their shared political forum. Intensely competitive and intensely loving, the two made for an awkward combination at this time. Another factor in his restlessness and activity was a belief that grew in him through the years that it was only by keeping remorselessly busy that he would prevent himself slipping back into depression. As Samuel Johnson had once advised Boswell: 'If you are idle be not solitary; if you are solitary be not idle.'[2] And the final part was his reaction to the historic events of the time. In March 1936 Hitler marched into the demilitarized zone of the Rhineland; in March 1938 he seized Austria; the following year it was Czechoslovakia. The Nazi menace and the Spanish Civil War combined to define political positions across a whole generation.

In a period of uncertainty and fear, Frank was anxious to act but was unsure quite what to do. There must have been a romantic temptation to join the International Brigades in Spain. He had remained acutely aware since childhood that he came from a military clan. In the battle against Franco his past and his present could be as one. But then there was his career and his family, though in his frenzy he was spending precious little time with the children. He was not the sort of idealist to put them second. Neither was Elizabeth likely to allow him to do so. Instead he had to make do with collecting signatures on petitions and donations for the republican cause in Spain, involving *inter alia* repeated condemnations of the Catholic Church for its part in backing the Franco-ist forces in Spain.

In the autumn of 1937 his increasing involvement in local Labour politics led to his election as councillor for his home ward of Cowley and Iffley. He scored the largest majority ever for a Labour candidate in the city, a sign of the industrial transformation that had overtaken Oxford in the 1930s. In the 1931 local elections, Labour did not even bother to field a candidate in the ward. Yet the growth of Cowley, alongside the Morris car factory where most of its inhabitants worked, was changing the local political map. As a councillor Frank tackled his duties with the sort of extreme, almost fanatical diligence that had been his hallmark of late. It was the first time in his life he had represented a constituency and he thoroughly enjoyed the experience. Meetings with the City Engineer over waste-collection on the Bullingdon Housing Estate or the level of pavements in Fernhill Road, visiting Oxford City Prison on behalf of his constituents, lobbying alongside the pension movement crowded his diary between tutorials, tennis matches with Philip Toynbee and formal hall with his fellow dons in Christ Church. He felt unqualified enthusiasm for Labour's social policy and from the start he focused on these issues with the determination of a social worker to better the lot of the underdogs.

But Frank could take it to extremes. In the first flush of conversion – naïvely, he later conceded – he yearned for the removal of all obstacles that he saw as separating him from his constituents. He wanted none of the deference of Eton Manor or courtesy titles. So when in 1938 he inherited a sizeable sum of money from a relative, an unforeseen windfall, he opted to spend it as soon as possible for the good of the cause. One venture he paid for, in the wake of Hitler's aggression towards Czechoslovakia and Chamberlain's capitulation at Munich, was the digging of trenches by local, unemployed men around the Florence Park Estate that bordered Singletree. The prospect of a German invasion of Oxford was somewhat remote but Frank's eccentric act was born of his anxiety about Britain's ill-preparedness for the onset of war and of his burning desire to redistribute his own wealth. He was putting his own house in order in the light of his socialist beliefs. Unemployment was bad, so he would pay for people not to be unemployed. It was, Elizabeth Longford remarked, with her habitual knack for putting the best possible gloss on her husband's actions:

[a] whimsical gesture. Though he agreed entirely with Labour on the view of the League of Nations and collective security as the best way to prevent a war, he did feel that there was a danger that our theoretical belief had to be shown to be working and that until it could be then people should make efforts towards defence. It only lasted for three days. Even though he knew a great many Cowley workers, he had no idea of what it would cost to pay the wages. It was a thunderbolt for him. He would soon have been bankrupt.[3]

The reality of the social gap between Frank and those whose causes he took up was brought home to him one day at Singletree. He had started to visit prisoners in Oxford Jail in 1936. It began as an effort to help a constituent and then developed into something more. He was so anxious to be of assistance, to prove his credentials, that he was easily roped in to any issue raised by any of the inmates. One of the first was a local lawyer who had been imprisoned for altering the markings on eggs. 'Twenty-four hours ago I was a respected professional man,' he told Frank, protesting his innocence, 'and now this'. Frank took up his case with gusto, only to find that he had eight previous convictions.[4] He had to learn to take care before accepting every sob story, but that to him was not the point. He could be on the side of prisoners without wanting them proved innocent. Their guilt or not was, in his way of looking at things, irrelevant. Other problems, though, could arise further down the line. When one of his charges was released, Frank invited him to Singletree to celebrate. He had laid on a bottle of Liebfraumilch, with tall glasses with long pale-green stems. The visitor and his family were no doubt grateful for the intention but, as Elizabeth noticed, 'did not know what to make of this finicky liquor'.[5]

Oxford proved an irresistible draw to the great and the good of the Labour movement, a stage on which the confusions and contradictions that beset the national party were played out before an audience of socialist academics and ardent activists. It was over the response to fascism at home and on the continent that the divisions were most apparent. Clement Attlee, the party leader, preferred studied moderation and so appeared unable or unwilling to deflect the Prime Minister, Neville Chamberlain, from his appeasement policy. Attlee promoted the League of Nations as a means of restraint, but since the Abyssinia crisis of 1935 few on the Labour left had any faith in its effectiveness. The only force it could envisage standing up to Hitler was Soviet communism. To that end Stafford Cripps was constantly pressing Attlee to endorse an alliance between Labour and the Communist Party in Britain to fight jointly to reverse the policy of appeasement. To Cripps and his supporters such a Popular Front was a means for the workers of Europe to unite against the fascists. To Attlee it was a potential vote-loser, hinting at a Labour return to the revolutionary rhetoric of the early 1930s.

The British communists for their part were trying to infiltrate the Labour movement and the Oxford party could not see the need to prevent them. Some of the incomers kept their real loyalty hidden and, posing as left-wing socialists, managed to gain influence and pull strings behind the scenes. Others were less discreet. When Frank stood for Cowley and Iffley in 1937, he was joined on the Labour ticket by a man he later described as a 'crypto-com'.[6] At the time, however, he welcomed him as a comrade in arms and was convinced of the need to work with the far left against Hitler. He backed the wisdom of a Popular Front and even considered leaving the party in 1939 when Cripps was expelled for his efforts on behalf of such an alliance. (Cripps convinced him of the futility of the gesture.) Frank's tolerance, however, had its limits. He decisively rejected Philip Toynbee's invitation – made in Dublin where they were observing the 1937 Irish general election – to join the Communist Party. Toynbee did not give up, however, and persuaded Frank to accompany him to a 'socialist weekend' outside Oxford. They arrived only to find the whole of the city's Communist Party membership in attendance to hear a speech by their leader, Abe Lazarus, sometimes known as 'Bill Firestone' because of the successful strike he had led at the Firestone tyre factory in London. Abe was in fact a friend of Frank and Elizabeth through his activities with the Morris workers at Cowley and via two of his lieutenants who had managed to rise to be chairman and treasurer of the Oxford City Labour Party. Frank nevertheless beat a hasty retreat. Unlike such communists and his colleagues in the Oxford Labour Party, he was not prepared to overlook the realities of life in Soviet Russia. There had been public protests in the West as early as 1931 about Soviet forced-labour camps. There were also many accounts of the failure of collectivization and the practical evidence of the 1933 famine. Then from 1936 to 1938 Moscow was the stage for show trials of dissidents, events which left the young Alexander Solzhenitsyn 'stunned by their fraudulence'.[7]

Yet in seeking an accommodation of sorts, Frank was going further than some thought wise. His Christ Church colleague, Patrick Gordon Walker, the official Labour candidate for Oxford, was more clear-sighted about the extent to which communists were exploiting a genuine desire for peace to attempt to take over the local group. In his diary, Gordon Walker described a meeting of the Left Book Club with Frank in the chair. 'It is an obvious Communist Party thing – with their usual semi-deceit etc.'[8] Elizabeth was later to suggest that too much had been made of the communist influence on the Oxford party.

> There certainly wasn't any conscious working for the communists. If they turned up supporting the same cause as we were, we would work with them. The same with the Liberals. I know you could say that the communists infiltrated in the sense of working with the Labour Party, but they didn't infiltrate in a really deep, profound and obvious way. In one sense they were infiltrated the other way round. They took the Labour line. Nobody ever looks at it that way. It was both ways round. You can't have infiltration without both sides being influenced.[9]

In June 1938, however, Labour's national agent reported unfavourably on efforts by the Oxford party to establish an *ad hoc* Popular Front against Hitler with local communists and Liberals in the form of the Oxford Coordinating Committee for Peace and Democracy. Transport House gave the constituency party fourteen days to leave the umbrella organization on pain of disaffiliation. Frank and his colleagues agreed to this ultimatum grudgingly, noting 'the discouraging effect on workers in the party' of the national line. Events came to a head in the autumn of 1938. Neville Chamberlain returned from Munich on 30 September, clutching a piece of paper and promising peace in our time. In the Commons Attlee attacked the Prime Minister for betraying Czechoslovakia, and for giving in to Hitler, but the radical elements in the Labour Party wanted more than fine words. Cripps renewed his appeal for a Popular Front, and even extended an invitation to the anti-Chamberlain Tories, led by Winston Churchill and Anthony Eden.[10]

The malcontents, determined to give Chamberlain a bloody nose, turned their attention to a by-election that was pending in Oxford. In August 1938 Captain Bourne, the local Conservative MP, had died. The parliamentary constituency did not yet include the Cowley housing estates where Frank was local councillor, and it seemed unlikely that Labour alone could mount much of a challenge to Bourne's successor, Quintin Hogg, a young Fellow at All Souls and a friend and admirer of Elizabeth's from student days. On 13 September, even before Chamberlain's peace mission, the Liberal candidate, Ivor Davies, had offered to stand down on condition that the Labour candidate, Patrick Gordon Walker, did likewise and that a non-party, anti-Conservative candidate was put up instead. It was an offer that instantly struck a chord with those in the Labour camp who dreamt of a Popular Front. With Chamberlain's return from Munich and the distribution of 84,700 gas masks to the civilian population in Oxford, it seemed to many to be irresistible.

Gordon Walker refused to be part of the scheme but Frank and Dick Crossman nevertheless pushed the idea of an 'Independent Progressive' candidate. (Using the term Popular Front was judged as too provocative.) They hit on the vehemently anti-communist Sandy Lindsay, a former vice-chancellor of the university and Master of Balliol, the man who had first involved Frank in the WEA, as their compromise candidate. At the time Frank believed himself to be driving events, but later he reflected ruefully that 'the coup was engineered by the Oxford communists with the rest of us more or less starry-eyed dupes'.[11] Transport House, of course, was less than enthusiastic, but under public pressure abdicated and left the decision to the local party.

Just as Labour seemed in the bag, the Liberals now began to waver. They were suspicious of Lindsay. As a long-standing member of the Labour Party, they protested, he could hardly be counted as independent. They had also already spent some £300 on their campaign and wanted reimbursing before they would sign up to the joint ticket. It was to be a one-off protest. Frank dug into his own pocket to deal with this obstacle and at the same time convinced them of Lindsay's bona fides by promising that he would not seek re-election. (Hogg was later to claim that this was Frank's great mistake in the by-election campaign. By saying that Lindsay would hold the seat only until the next election, expected in 1940 at the latest, the Popular Front was, Hogg kept repeating in his speeches and propaganda, putting up a lame duck candidate. He even rather mischievously suggested subsequently that Frank had engineered the whole matter for his own benefit at the next general election. 'Was it, as I rather uncharitably was inclined to suspect at the time, a clever ruse by Frank Pakenham himself, hoping once he had got rid of Gordon Walker, to have the revision of the seat himself?')[12]

Once the Liberals were bought out, Labour met on 17 October and voted forty-eight to twelve in favour of backing Lindsay. 'I am not standing down,' Gordon Walker retorted. 'The local Labour Party is withdrawing the Labour candidate.' He took little part in the subsequent campaign and would never entirely forgive Frank. 'It represents the political step which I would most prefer to have back if I could have my time again,' Frank later remarked, but for the moment he was caught up in the fever of the campaign and put personal considerations to one side.[13]

The Oxford by-election marked the debut of the opinion poll, not to mention one of the first outings of the Mass Observation data-collecting initiative started by anthropologist Tom Harrison. With so much attention focused on one result, the campaign took on a broader national significance. It became a mini referendum on Chamberlain. It was, in truth, very much a university affair, with the *Picture Post* reporting that 'an interesting feature of the by-election was the intense interest taken by undergraduates, who had no votes, and the comparative apathy of the townsmen, who had'. The academic community divided over the candidates, with different groups of dons compiling pro or anti manifestos in first the *Oxford Mail* and then *The Times*.

Lindsay was a huge disappointment to his backers. Though he was a commanding figure in the university world, to the voters outside he lacked appeal. He was, Elizabeth later wrote, 'both too amateurish and too lofty to face a political orator like Quintin Hogg. The press was nonplussed by Lindsay's unconventional conferences, conducted in the college kitchen with Lindsay sitting on the kitchen table nonchalantly swinging his long legs.'[14] He was also increasingly unhappy at some of the tactics being employed on his behalf. The slogan 'A vote for Hogg is a vote for Hitler' particularly angered him. Yet he carried with him the hopes of a disparate group of anti-appeasement zealots. Harold Macmillan, a Tory opponent of Chamberlain's policy, spoke for him, reportedly giving Lindsay Churchill's blessing. Those in the Labour Party who hoped to ginger up their leadership into reconsidering a Popular Front staked all on a Lindsay victory. Attlee and his colleagues watched with interest. In the end Lindsay did not fulfil the expectations that had been placed on his candidature. The count on 27 October showed that he had increased by 6 per cent Gordon Walker's share of the vote in 1935 but he was still just under 3,500 behind Hogg, who instantly proclaimed, 'It is not my victory but Mr Chamberlain's.'

The significance of the Oxford by-election in national terms is hard to assess. It certainly focused attention on events in Europe and Britain's state of unpreparedness to fight. For Chamberlain it was a short-lived triumph. At Bridgwater three weeks later in another by-election in a Tory seat, a Liberal candidate running with Labour backing as an Independent Progressive defeated the Conservative challenger.

When the Oxford constituency came to select its candidate for what was assumed would be the 1940 general election, Gordon Walker had already put himself out of the running by attacking the backers of the Independent Progressive candidate in the aftermath of polling day. In a valedictory interview with the *Oxford Mail* he described Lindsay's excursion into politics as 'initiated in middle-class and university circles. There has been no shortage of money in a most lavish campaign. The progress of this Democratic Front to a large extent reflected the views of people who are rich enough to afford the luxury of ignoring everything except foreign policy.' Though the description could have applied to any of Lindsay's backers, Frank felt that its criticism of funders was directed against him personally. If this was the case, Gordon Walker had hit his Achilles' heel: his fervent desire to be a people's politician embracing popular concerns, not a patrician embracing those of an academic and privileged élite. On 2 December 1938, Frank Pakenham was adopted as the official Labour candidate for Oxford, aware that, without the voters of the working-class estates of Cowley and

Headington (at that time lumped together with rural Oxfordshire seats), he stood no chance. That revision was not to come about until the late 1940s.

He had already accepted the candidature for eminently winnable West Birmingham and had been enthusiastically nurturing the seat for months. Yet the pull of Oxford proved too great. He threw over the Birmingham seat. Transport House briefly considered blocking him in Oxford, but that threat soon evaporated after a good-hearted interview at Labour headquarters. 'I was ecstatic,' Elizabeth wrote. 'Already I saw myself entering Westminster along with Frank, architects of the New Jerusalem. I took it for granted that Oxford was more "winnable" than Birmingham. All the more need to nurse King's Norton as effectively as Frank would nurse Oxford.'[15] It was an inspiring dream, typical of the idealism that the couple felt at the time – husband and wife entering the Commons together to start building a new society.

With their dual candidature, well-placed friends and academic credentials, the Pakenhams were fast acquiring a reputation on a national Labour stage. Elizabeth continued to commute between Oxford and her constituency in Birmingham. In the spring of 1939 she rented a house in King's Norton for overnight stays and even removed Antonia and Thomas from their smart prep school in Oxford and enrolled them in the local primary school for a week. They survived with flying colours. Frank wrote to his wife, full of the ardour and naïveté that characterized his politics at the time, 'I am so glad that they enjoy the school – a good omen for their great working-class leadership careers.'[16]

For the time being Elizabeth's dedication to politics and motherhood went hand in hand. She had learnt to drive – Frank never did, preferring to let others drive him – and would travel between home and King's Norton with the children sleeping peacefully on the back seat of the car. And she was still intent on expanding her brood. In an interview with the *Daily Express* many years later, she admitted, 'I really got mad about families. Every time the baby became a toddler I wanted to have another one. It's absolutely addictive.'

Frank continued to play only a supporting role in the upbringing of his young children. In his crowded diary of politics, teaching and sport, something had to give, and often it was family. Antonia's abiding image of her father in this period was of a distant figure, 'occasionally spotted sitting in a deckchair with books and papers'.[17] Whatever his belief in equality and his fervent advocacy in favour of equal rights for men and women, Frank was not one to roll up his sleeves and tackle even the most basic household task. After a weekend staying with the historian Alan Taylor[18] and his wife Eva, Elizabeth recorded in her diary Eva's determined attempt to get Frank to do the washing up. 'He soon drifted away from the sink and let me take his place.'[19]

As Antonia and Thomas grew older, started walking and talking, asking questions, his time for them increased. He wasn't a playing-horses-on-the-floor sort of person but the moment the children reached a point where they could argue with him or discuss or be taken to rugger matches, then he became extremely interested in them and correspondingly popular with them. Elizabeth, by contrast, was often cast as the tough one. 'My original Puritanical Harman instinct was never to praise my children, at least not to their faces,' she wrote in her diary.[20]

Both Antonia and Thomas were certainly precocious in their intellectual development, a facet their mother put down to their father's donnish desire to stir up their minds. His intellect was regarded with awe by his children well into adulthood. 'Antonia and I discussed an apparently favourite subject of hers and Thomas's,' Elizabeth recorded, 'why none of our children was as "clever" as Dada (Antonia very courteously added Mummy). I pointed out there would have been a harvest of firsts if they had wanted them as much as Frank did.'[21]

At a routine check-up in 1936 with her gynaecologist, Dr Helena Wright, Elizabeth was persuaded to take part in a research programme. Dr Wright was convinced that the sex of a baby could be determined by the fact that male sperm preferred an alkaline solution in the uterus while female sperm preferred an acid one. Elizabeth wanted another boy and so followed the steps advocated by Dr Wright – a douche of one dessert-spoon of sodium bicarbonate dissolved in one pint of water, twenty minutes before sex. It worked. Patrick was born on 17 April 1937. His arrival was precipitate, and the doctor didn't arrive in time. Instead their live-in nurse had to deliver the baby, assisted, not altogether ably, by the father. Elizabeth was more concerned that he might injure himself opening the sterilized drum containing bandages, gauze and other essentials than she was with her own pain.

For the parents – especially Elizabeth, who took care of all domestic arrangements – striking a balance between political ambitions and children was a difficult task. Frank's selection as candidate for Oxford at least meant that they were not both in a state of perpetual transit between home and Birmingham. And since Oxford was a relatively small city, his teaching schedule in theory allowed him time to drop in at Singletree at all hours of the day. Even though he continued to be largely an absentee, his new son did catch his eye. Even as a small boy Paddy showed a combination of humour and showmanship that mirrored his father's. He would miss no opportunity to make people laugh.

Frank's outside interests were developing all the time. He attended, for instance, meetings of the XYZ Club, founded in 1932 by Douglas Jay and Evan Durbin, aimed at evolving a sound socialist economic policy with sympathizers in the City. Yet the passion of the Pakenhams' socialism in these years did not inhibit old friendships with those on the other side of the political divide. 'Socialist principles did not require one to diminish the quality of life by giving up one's friends,' Elizabeth wrote firmly.[22] Though the couple never made any attempt to hide their beliefs, their friends noted a certain confusion in Frank. In political terms he may have become a committed socialist, but in many of his social attitudes he had not changed at all. 'At heart he has always remained very conservative,' reported Maureen Dufferin. 'I remember when my daughter Perdita was coming out. Frank was her godfather and wrote to her saying that he hoped the young men at the coming-out dances still wore gloves.'[23]

Cliveden, in particular, was hostile to Frank's anti-Chamberlain sentiments. Waldorf and Nancy Astor were pro-appeasement and their papers, *The Times* and the *Observer*, followed that line. Much has been written about the influence of the 'Cliveden Set' on Chamberlain. The phrase was coined by Claud Cockburn[24] in *This Week* in 1937, but no real lobby has ever been proved conclusively to have existed, as Frank's presence at Cliveden in this period would suggest.

Rather more conducive to his growing enthusiasm for a Popular Front were his visits to Chartwell, home of Winston Churchill. Randolph invited him down to lunch with his father in the autumn of 1935. Conversation inevitably turned to Germany. 'If the Germans are already as strong as you say, what could we do if they landed here?' Frank asked. Churchill, helped no doubt by the copious quantities of alcohol that had been consumed over lunch, replied:

That should not prove an insoluble conundrum. We are here five able-bodied men. The armoury at our disposal is not perhaps very modern but none of us would be without a weapon. We should sally forth. I should venture to assume the responsibilities of command. If the worst came to the worst, we should sell our lives dearly. Whatever the outcome we should, I feel confident, render a good account of ourselves.[25]

It was precisely the sort of fighting talk to inspire Frank to hero-worship (and may even have given him the notion of the Florence Park trenches), as it was later to inspire the nation, but he never imagined that Churchill, whom he regarded at this juncture as something of a relic from the past, would ever hold high office again. The friendship between the two men developed slowly. Elizabeth's parents had a house in Kent, just four miles from Chartwell, and, with their children safely in the hands of their grandparents, the young socialists would visit the brooding reactionary in exile. They would occasionally be joined by Professor Lindemann, Frank's old friend from Charlton days. Lindemann, later Lord Cherwell, was Churchill's scientific adviser, a post he held through the war.

Spending time with friends of differing political opinions did open Frank up to the risk of compromise in the eyes of his electors, and never more so than when the couple visited his old Furzie Close and Eton classmate Alec Spearman, now a Tory MP, at his Essex home. Among other guests was Unity Mitford, who had befriended Adolf Hitler and become a Nazi. On the Sunday evening she was heading back to her parents' home near Oxford and offered Frank, who had an early meeting on the Monday morning, a lift. He had cheerfully accepted before he noticed that her car was flying the swastika. Not wanting to appear rude, he hit on a pragmatic and face-saving compromise. As they approached Oxford, he was dropped on the outskirts and managed to disappear down a side-street before being spotted.

At the start of 1938, Frank's already comfortable financial circumstances changed quite dramatically when his Uncle Bingo died leaving everything to him. It is a mark of how unmaterialistic Frank was that it had never occurred to him such a windfall was a possibility. He had assumed that his elder brother would inherit, but Uncle Bingo had developed a distaste for Edward's nationalism that eclipsed any concerns about his brother's membership of the Labour Party. So it was Frank who became the owner of a furnished house just off Park Lane, which boasted P.G. Wodehouse[26] as a next-door neighbour, plus a collection of his grandmother's jewellery – heavy snake bracelets, some set with amethysts and jet. And in May, Great-Aunt Caroline passed on at the age of ninety-six. Bernhurst, her house and small estate at Hurst Green, passed, as had been arranged at his birth, to her godson Frank. A Georgian house, with Regency additions giving it the look of an elegant rectory, Bernhurst had a five-acre garden with a view of the valley beyond, where the field patterns were little changed from the time of Henry II. It was large enough to accommodate the Pakenhams' growing family, but in the rush of events leading up to the outbreak of war it was hardly used.

The acquisition of such wealth by an accident of birth was a burden and to some extent an embarrassment for Frank: the contradiction between his lifestyle and his creed was once again highlighted. Yet pragmatically his good fortune would enable him to look forward to life as an MP without the attendant worries about providing for his family – at that time the post carried only minimal financial reward. The best way to ease his conscience, he decided, would be to spend some of his fortune on promoting the cause. He duly bought the *Town Crier*, a small and unassuming Labour Party newspaper published in Birmingham. In a keynote leading article, Frank set the radical tone for his paper. It is an uncharacteristically graphic, almost crude, piece of writing whose passion can be understood only in the light of his anxiety to prove his credentials to his new-found party. 'I learnt at first hand the snobbery and corruption that are the lifeblood of the Conservative machine. My stomach turned and reaching for a basin I said "goodbye to all that" . . . I know the whole dirty business from the inside – I shall never hesitate to use that knowledge for the benefit of the working class.'[27]

The new proprietor replaced the incumbent editor, Herbert Green, with his old friend Philip Toynbee, a member of the Communist Party, and drafted in his sister, Pansy, as women's-page editor. Dick Crossman wrote a column on international affairs and W.H. Auden a review.[28] Toynbee took to his task with relish, replacing Green's parish pump approach with the ambition to exceed by far the current circulation of 2,600 and take the nation by storm. After Eden's resignation as Foreign Secretary in February 1938, the *Town Crier* boldly demanded, 'Chamberlain must go. The *Crier* will make Birmingham too hot to hold him.' (Chamberlain represented the Edgbaston division of Birmingham from 1929.)

Another of Great-Aunt Caroline's legacies, her grey Standard car, came in useful in the hands of George Tyler, who became both circulation manager for the *Town Crier* and, briefly, Frank's election agent in West Birmingham. The new team at the paper and its proprietor saw it as in the vanguard of a Labour sweep of Birmingham seats. Protest meetings were organized for *Crier* readers to lambast the government. They were moderately well attended, but circulation plummeted. As a financial venture the *Town Crier* was about as successful as Frank's sally into the world of stocks and shares in 1929. With his nomination as Labour candidate for

Oxford in 1939, he became less willing to shoulder the heavy losses for the good of Labour in Birmingham and reluctantly sold the *Town Crier* at a huge loss. The new proprietor replaced Toynbee with Green and the paper returned to worthy but dull accounts of local meetings.

When he had joined Labour in 1936 Frank had announced, 'I am socialist because I am a Christian.' It was a fairly loose claim, simply referring to their common principle of fundamental equality for all. As a child he had been brought up to say his night and morning prayers and, when in Ireland, to take his place along the Pakenham pew in the Church of Ireland in the neighbouring village of Castlepollard. At North Aston Hall, spiritual solace had been closer at hand. There was an Anglican chapel attached to the house. Furzie Close and Eton had reinforced this dutiful Christianity, inseparable from public service in Frank's mind. His uncle, Arthur Villiers, for example, claimed a Christian basis for his work in Eton Manor.

As a young man, however, Frank had drifted away from any formal practice of religion. In 1925, while still an undergraduate, he had undergone an operation on his knee for the removal of cartilage and during the period of convalescence and forced inactivity, he began to examine his inherited Christian beliefs more closely. He experienced, he later recalled, a burning desire for faith, for something to believe in. He described one summer day in 1925 practising his serve on the tennis court at North Aston Hall and contemplating life without the hope of an after-life. 'Suppose that there is no such person as God? Suppose there is no one and nothing there at all? I was overwhelmed; I was temporarily shattered.'[29] He was inspired to pray for faith, but to no avail. He therefore abandoned his childhood dislike of books and began what became a lifelong addiction, reading works about Christianity like Lowes Dickinson's *The Meaning of Good*. But he also sought out the other position – principally by ploughing through Darwin's *On the Origin of Species*.

From that moment on Frank embarked on an erratic search for a deeper meaning to life and defiantly called himself a Christian. However, he made little attempt to pursue his interest further – by discussing it with priests or theologians, for example, or even by attending church regularly. He did not as yet subject Christianity to the sort of rigorous logical examination that he had undertaken on the claims of socialism. When he married Elizabeth in 1931, he found little encouragement for his desire to investigate Christianity. Her upbringing had been a strictly Protestant one – 'simple in content and serious in tone. No frills like cribs at Christmas.'[30] Though she had married in a church, had her children baptized and subscribed to a strong ethical code, she had little time for organized religion and a particular dislike of the doctrines of Catholicism.

Marriage had hastened his conversion to socialism, and part of the attraction of the Labour Party was the moral basis for its policies of social justice and wealth redistribution. For a while socialism was enough to satisfy his craving for belief, and thoughts of Christianity retreated in his mind. The role of the Catholic Church in the Spanish Civil War, siding with the right-wing forces and the army against the republicans, horrified him. Moreover, the very circles in which he was moving were strongly anti-Christian. Freddie Ayer,[31] who had been elected to a Christ Church Fellowship the year after Frank, had no time at all for Christianity, and the pair of them would have long arguments in the Senior Common Room, with Frank usually coming off worse, Philip Toynbee later recalled. The Oxford academic Establishment at the time was disbelieving, though individual dons were practising Christians.

Frank's discovery, during his research for *Peace by Ordeal*, of Irish nationalism was an ambiguous factor which both drew him towards the Catholic Church and at the same time pushed him away. The Catholic Church epitomized the differences between Ireland and England and was one reason why the Protestant Anglo-Irish like Frank were out of place in their own land. In conversation with his daughter Antonia many years later, he remarked, uncritically, that Catholics regarded Ireland 'as their country'.[32] Though he regarded himself as Irish, he was not Catholic and therefore excluded.

Eamon de Valera, with whom Frank struck up a close friendship in the 1930s, was an ardent Catholic with great faith in the Church's capacity to effect the smooth and just running of society, so much faith in fact that he enshrined a 'special place' for Catholicism in the 1937 constitution that he drew up for Ireland. Yet while ideologically Catholicism would complement Frank's new-found Irish nationalism, it was also rather incongruous with the peculiar circumstances of his own childhood there. 'My father once told me,' Antonia remembered, 'when we were staying at Tullynally with my brother and we all were going to mass that as a child he had been brought up to think of the Catholic Church as the "dirty church" – exactly those words. In his childhood they had been a true Ascendancy family – the servants were Catholics and the gentry were Protestants.'[33]

It was the decisive influence of Father Martin D'Arcy[34] that turned Frank's conflicting emotions and his sporadic religious search into something much more purposeful. The Jesuit Master of Campion Hall in Oxford (located opposite the main gates of Christ Church) was a well-known figure in university circles. Patrick O'Donovan,[35] the *Observer* journalist and a Christ Church undergraduate in the late 1930s, described D'Arcy as 'the epitome of all that was brilliant or dangerous within the Roman Church, of all that was sensitive or guileful among the Jesuits'.[36] Such a combination of glamour and cleverness inevitably appealed to Frank, though D'Arcy was the first Catholic priest he had ever known. Elizabeth first met D'Arcy when she was an undergraduate. They both attended a lunch party at Balliol. First impressions were clouded by the anti-Catholicism of her Unitarian upbringing. 'His elegant figure, dark wavy hair, aristocratic features and air of subtle sophistication immediately made me think of Mephistopheles – a character who in any case I tended to equate with all but the untidiest priests. But when, at the end of lunch, Father D'Arcy politely offered me my coat back to front so that I could not get into the sleeves, I realised I had got him wrong.'[37]

In 1931 D'Arcy published a book, *The Nature of Belief*, which Frank enjoyed, and the two met occasionally. One day they bumped into each other in the street. 'I had just chaired a meeting for a visiting speaker, the general secretary of the Communist Party, at the

Town Hall,' Frank recalled, 'and I was walking back to my room in Tom Quad when I ran into Father D'Arcy. I felt like St Peter seeing Christ.'[38] He felt moved to outline his confusion to the Jesuit and was invited to visit him in Campion Hall. It was only a short walk, but the decision to go ranks as one of the most significant moments in Frank's life. 'I rang the bell, asked to see the Master and fortunately found him at home. Within half an hour he knew all, and no doubt more than all, that I thought worth telling him about myself.'[39]

Their relationship quickly developed. Frank would visit Campion Hall whenever his already overcrowded schedule allowed. Father D'Arcy would suggest books – starting with St Augustine's *Confessions* – that he should read to move him forward in his search for faith. On Sundays Frank would attend mass at Greyfriars, the Franciscan Church on Iffley Road near Singletree. But he held back from embarking on formal instruction. There was the problem of Rome's stance in the Spanish Civil War but Frank managed, with Father D'Arcy's encouragement, to separate the political acts of particular leaders from questions of faith and morals. Then there was the intellectual way in which Frank insisted on evaluating everything. Just as he had taken socialism to his heart long before he was convinced in his head, he knew quite soon that he wanted to be a Catholic, but he could not make such a leap of faith unless he could convince himself of the logic of the fundamental tenets of Catholicism. The rigid adherence to the Church's rules demanded of all Catholics also proved a stumbling block. To be bound to a set of regulations handed down from on high went against Frank's democratic beliefs.

At Greyfriars, however, Frank grew attached to the Catholic ritual, its mixture of certainty and humility and its ability to draw together the high and the low as equal before God – an achievement that had eluded him in his political activities in Cowley. He began to overcome that indecisiveness that hovered around all the great changes of his life – marriage, joining Labour and now coming over to Rome. In the past his indecisiveness had also been linked to his introspective side, and in religion he saw a way of channelling that introspection by subscribing to a spiritual code that gave a generally positive view of the world and an uplifting explanation for the random blows of fate.

Accepting that Christian ethics – particularly those concerning society – were compatible with his socialist principles was no great problem, but he felt he had to justify any conversion in absolute terms. With Father D'Arcy's help, he began to ask the fundamental questions – does God exist? Was Jesus divine? Much of his reading centred on the resurrection. His approach was characteristically logical. If the tomb could be proved to be empty, if the change in the behaviour of the disciples after they claimed to see the risen Lord could be accepted, then the divinity of Christ, for Frank, followed.

After a few months [of study with Father D'Arcy] I knew in outline the main arguments for and against the existence of God. But I soon saw that some of the deepest philosophical problems centring round God's existence – I mention only the problem of suffering – were not going to decide the issue one way or the other for me. If I could believe in the Son of the Gospels, I could believe in the Father described there.[40]

The challenge then was to take the gospel accounts at face value. Once he had achieved that, all else would follow naturally. As he pondered over this, there remained one huge obstacle to Frank's conversion. His wife had not the least idea why he had been visiting Father D'Arcy nor of what he was contemplating. He knew that she would be horrified both at his betrayal and at his choice. It was to be the gravest crisis in their marriage.

SIX

The Outcast

In early 1939 Winston Churchill paid a visit to the Oxford Union, where six years earlier a motion in favour of fighting for 'King and Country' had been voted down. It was symbolic of the changing mood both in the university and the country at large that Churchill's fighting talk about facing up to the Fascist threat was this time round loudly applauded by an audience which reflected all shades of political opinion. In place of the differences that had left Britain divided in the face of Hitler and Mussolini for much of the decade, a consensus was emerging. Frank Pakenham was there to see Churchill responding to his ovation by saying, 'I have not changed but you have trained on.'

Hitler's naked aggression towards Czechoslovakia in the March of 1939 made a mockery of the Munich settlement and hopes for 'peace in our time'. Mussolini's invasion of Albania the following month destroyed Chamberlain's hopes of detaching Italy from Germany and opened up the prospect of further territorial aggrandizement by the Axis powers in the Balkans. Chamberlain's blithe statement a week before the German takeover of Czechoslovakia that Europe was 'settling down to a period of tranquillity' made him look increasingly foolish and out of touch. Pressed by public opinion, the Labour opposition and his own backbenchers, on 31 March Chamberlain guaranteed Poland's independence and integrity against Germany, in effect marking the end of appeasement. War loomed ever larger.

Even in the face of such military expansionism, some on the left of the Labour Party continued to cling to the hope that peace could be maintained through an alliance with the Soviet Union, but such a dream was effectively dashed when in August 1939 the communists sided with the Fascists in the Molotov–Ribbentrop Pact. Those like Gaitskell, who had long warned that Popular Front ideas were not the ready answer they seemed, were unsurprised but for those who had put their trust in a defensive agreement with the Soviets to contain Hitler it was a heavy blow.

After Mussolini's invasion of Albania, Frank had slowly back-pedalled from his Popular Front enthusiasms, ever more convinced that war was inevitable and in such a scenario, given his background and the rose-tinted view of battle that he had cherished since those childhood walks with his father, he would have no truck with those on the pacifist wing.

The divisions in the Labour Party between the left and the national leadership over how to avoid war had started to seem irrelevant. The real question worrying pragmatist minds like Frank's was what role to play in the preparations for the fight. When, as a response to the Italians' takeover of King Zog's realm, Chamberlain introduced conscription – six months for men of twenty – Attlee and his team voted against. Part of their reasoning was that the Tories were breaking a guarantee given only weeks before not to opt for conscription. There were also fears among the union leaders that the measure was a prelude to industrial conscription, forcing workers to labour in the armament factories. Attlee said in effect that his party had no objection to men volunteering, and saw it as a better way to build a strong and motivated defence force. Hugh Dalton reinforced the point in a document he presented to the party conference in Southport in the summer, adding a plea that the hierarchical structure of the military be reviewed in line with democratic principles.

Critics of the Labour stance said that the Party was paying lip service to fighting the Nazi menace without giving the government practical support. Frank, who had attended the Southport conference, swung behind his party leaders and was attracted to the loophole that the Attlee–Dalton line offered to those who wanted to prepare for war in a practical way by volunteering. So while he was attending protest meetings in Oxford's Co-op Hall on behalf of Labour, alongside such youthful communists as Denis Healey,[1] then an undergraduate at Balliol, to condemn the policy of conscription, he had also volunteered for service. Proud of his physical fitness (he reached the semi-finals of the *Oxford Mail* tennis championships in 1939 and ran regularly around Christ Church Meadow, clocking up a five-minute mile), he could not remain idle. The desire to act, to prove he was willing to defend his country, already seen in his commissioning of the Florence Park trenches, led him to break ranks with many erstwhile close comrades in the Labour Party and enlist as a volunteer with the local territorials.

He took it a stage further and complained openly that so few of the young lionhearts in the Labour movement joined him in what he saw as a patriotic gesture. Certainly among his progressively minded intellectual friends, he noticed a marked reluctance to act which he was fond of contrasting with the public-spirited rallying to the flag of what he called 'the more dissolute type of West End club man'. Two conflicting influences were seen in conflict – of an aristocratic background and upbringing which stressed from an early age that a young man's place in times of national trial was at the Front, and of a Labour movement reluctant to get entangled in a capitalists' war as some of the more radical left supporters then regarded it.

Yet for all the Longfords' long history of service on the field of battle, Frank had little, beyond his physical fitness, to offer the territorials as a volunteer. Already in his mid-thirties and suffering the first twinges of rheumatism and lumbago, he had not even been a member of the 'Corps' at Eton. Indeed, his house had taken 'playing soldiers' with a healthy dose of humorous scepticism. 'There was a terrible occasion when our Company turned out on the great day of Inspection in false horn-rimmed spectacles and when called upon to number rapped out very smartly one, two, three, four, five, six, seven, eight, nine, ten, knave, queen, king.'[2] Edward Longford refused to join the Corps on the grounds of his Irish nationalism. For Frank it was a less principled stance. To join would have meant rifle practice. Rifle practice would have meant wearing his glasses and his vanity ruled that out.

At the territorials' barrack square at Cowley in 1938, he cut a rather lonely figure as he was put through his paces by a genial regimental sergeant major. He was similarly ill at ease doing early morning manoeuvres in Port Meadow with the university Officer Training Corps's cavalry section. Hitler, it seemed, was to be rebuffed by Oxford dons and undergraduates on horseback.

In the wake of the Albania episode, he nevertheless made what he described as 'an emotional dash' to volunteer for service in the newly formed Fifth (Territorial) Battalion of the Oxford and Bucks Light Infantry. As a good socialist and mindful of Dalton's demand in Southport that the forces be democratized, he preferred to be a private and not an officer. Enlisting at first demanded little more than his involvement with the territorials. There was drill once a week, the occasional spot of target practice at Bicester, and then a fortnight's camp in August. Yet as a gesture it carried great resonance in the city, especially after pictures of 'Private Pack', cigarette in his hand (the sub-title, 'Have a fag, mate' was a clumsy egalitarian affectation especially since he didn't smoke) appeared in the local paper, the *Oxford Mail*. That knack for what Frank saw as using himself to publicize an important cause, and what his detractors saw as 'ink-hungry' self-publicity, certainly meant that his example was noticed. Here was the progressively minded, some would say communist-influenced, donnish Labour parliamentary candidate for Oxford joining the humble ranks of the territorials to do his patriotic best. Many wrote it off as an election ruse to restore the credibility of a party which overall seemed to be at best equivocal about fighting. Others, watching 'Private Pack' marching up the High Street at the rear of the column, simply put it down to his eccentricity. 'He was a very weird soldier because he was so uncoordinated,' recalled Denis Healey.[3] Left-wing activists in the city took a very dim view indeed of what they saw as Frank's *de facto* desertion of the party line.

The reality of being a private came home to Frank when he attended summer camp in 1939. Since none of his fellow Oxford socialists had joined the ranks, he was deprived of like-minded company. The ritual of preparing his uniform for parade was more than one so shambolic in his dress could manage. He ended up compromising any socialist credentials by paying a kindly sergeant ten bob a go to do it for him. Notwithstanding his attachment to a more equal society where all class barriers were removed, sleeping twelve to a tent was quite beyond him, while the four-letter words that peppered his colleagues' prose left him speechless. He had picked up enough of this badinage, Elizabeth Longford later wrote, to shock the local vicar when they played tennis several weeks later.[4] In his diary for October 1939, Evelyn Waugh, a merciless observer of the contradictions in Frank's behaviour, recorded: 'Frank, full of ambitions to serve in any capacity, civil or military, greatly dismayed by the obscenity of conversations among private soldiers and full of resentment that he was obliged to attend Church of England ceremonies'.[5]

Some of the more staunchly Conservative members of the officer corps regarded having the local Labour candidate in the ranks as a chance to teach him a lesson as to where his real allegiance lay. They had touched a nerve. Frank did not enjoy the endless round of saluting men who made little attempt to disguise their aim of needling him. His dream of military heroism was quickly turning sour. Antonia remembered going with her mother to visit her father at the summer camp. They found him very depressed. 'It was a ghastly experience, a canvas camp with the stink of latrines and Dada looking ludicrous in his uniform like a noble lion.'[6]

A brief respite at Bernhurst was all he managed after a thoroughly disheartening two weeks at camp. It did little to lift the depression that was descending on him. When the family returned to Oxford at the end of August, he was recalled to his unit with the outbreak of war now predicted any day. Elizabeth took the children to stay with friends at Water Eaton Manor to the north of the city. (Idealistically they had handed Singletree over to the council complete with furniture and fittings, for the use of evacuees.) At camp near Banbury Frank heard on the wireless Chamberlain's announcement of war on the morning of 3 September.

The phoney war was a time of contrasting fortunes for the couple. Elizabeth and the children, living in the countryside, found it was almost a rural idyll. For Frank, however, it was abject misery. Two of the props that he had already identified as capable of holding his tendency to depression at bay had been taken away. He was separated from Elizabeth – geographically and by his as yet secret interest in joining the Catholic Church – and he was inactive. With the official declaration of hostilities (and his distaste for life in the ranks) he needed little persuasion to drop his objections to the officer caste and was elevated to second lieutenant. His tormentors no doubt looked on with some satisfaction. His appointed task as an officer at the battalion's base at Banbury was welfare work, his lack of skill with military hardware evidently having already been noted. His job specification included giving French lessons to both officers and NCOs: the defence of France was envisaged as one of the first tasks of the British troops. His WEA training also came in handy when he was called on to give history lectures. 'When I asked them,' he wrote to Elizabeth, '"Hands up those who knew that Austria-Hungary existed before the Great War?" – one hand went up. "What is neutrality?" – half knew.'[7] The image of his father at Gallipoli, in the heart of the battle dying for his country, seemed distant.

His depression lifted briefly in October when he was approached by the Ministry of Information. His reputation as the author of *Peace by Ordeal* and as a friend of the Irish leader de Valera had preceded him. The British government was keen to secure Irish involvement in the war against Hitler and the use of Ireland's ports for the Royal Navy and merchant shipping which was suffering under attacks from U-boats. The fear was that Ireland – which had determined on a neutral position – would be exploited by the Germans as a back-door route to attack Britain and British shipping. Wanting to persuade de Valera to change his mind, the government turned to the person they saw as the one Englishman who had stood up publicly for the Irish leader.

Frank was flattered but felt uneasy in the role. He was in effect, as he later remarked, a 'double agent', ostensibly anxious to promote the British war effort, a parliamentary candidate for an English seat and a member of the British army, yet also an Irish nationalist, an admirer of de Valera and someone who strongly sympathized with his old friend's determination to keep Ireland out of the war. Frank thus approached his task in two minds and had little hope of success – though he was thankful at least to escape camp routine for a week. Just before leaving he was approached in a London restaurant by Winston Churchill, who had heard of his impending mission. 'You can tell your friend, de Valera,' Churchill said (Frank, in telling the story would imitate Churchill's pronunciation 'dee Valera'), 'that he is behaving abominably. He is behaving disgracefully. We treated him with prodigal liberality. With unprecedented generosity. And what did he do? He sinks the *Courageous*, an aircraft carrier, off the south west coast of Ireland.'[8] Frank pointed out that the sinking had been carried out by German guns, but it was to no avail. Churchill's disdain for de Valera was not open to discussion. In a broadcast at the end of the war, he denounced him publicly once again (though later in the 1950s he welcomed him to Downing Street).

It was against such a backdrop that Frank had arranged a meeting with de Valera. Once face to face he could not think how to persuade him. 'Ireland must do what one small country can do to bind the wounds of suffering humanity', Dev told him by way of explaining why he would not waver from his policy of neutrality. 'Dev seemed terribly tired,' Frank wrote that night to Elizabeth. 'It was heroic of him to see me at eight o'clock – but when I repeated Winston Churchill's rude remarks about Ireland's part in the war, he perked up.'[9]

The mission was a failure and Frank was soon back in Banbury where any interest in national and international politics was quickly dispelled by the daily drudgery. There was talk that the battalion would be part of a British expeditionary force to the continent but beyond such a glimmer of what Frank took to be future glory there was only his reading to keep him occupied. Community living was ever more impossible. All the privileges and privacy he took for granted had been replaced by a strict and unbending hierarchy of ranks. Depression took a hold. He sought solitude in a hut on the base and tried to teach himself to admire the qualities that were valued in the army. He swotted up on his military strategy books – anxious in some small way to make good his own deficiencies with his kit and in arms drill. 'And like every other intellectual of my acquaintance,' he admitted in his autobiography, 'I returned to *War and Peace* and said how like the past was the present, and Napoleon's role to Hitler's.'[10]

All of which left little time for the spiritual reading prescribed by Father D'Arcy. War found Frank in a similar prevaricative state about the Catholic Church as he had been about the Labour Party a few years earlier. His old friend Evelyn Waugh was later to attribute this equivocation to Father D'Arcy. 'He likes to keep his converts hovering on the edge of the Church.'[11] But the block was Frank's, not Father D'Arcy's. Emotionally won over, he could not quite accept all the Church's claims on an intellectual level. The logical don in him had been holding him back, but now he found himself transported from the secluded environment of Tom Quad to an army camp with soldiers preparing for combat. Just as the Mosley meeting had dissolved the seemingly intractable intellectual obstacles to his political conversion, so the possibility of front-line service precipitated his religious conversion.

In November Frank received a letter at Banbury from Waugh, asking him to act as godfather to his son Auberon. Waugh had heard, erroneously, that Frank had finally come over to Rome. Writing back to disabuse him, Frank revealed that he was indeed very close to the Church but not quite in the fold (though that did not stop him going on to be godfather, a role in which he served, according to his charge, with distinction, save for one occasion when he sent the teenage Auberon a Nevil Shute novel as a Christmas present, only to be rebuked by his father over its snares for an impressionable mind).[12]

Evelyn Waugh responded to Frank's letter by advising him to cast aside his doubts, his indecision and his reading, act on instinct and take the plunge. 'There is nothing to stop you asking for immediate reception. Discussion can become a pure luxury. This is no time for a soldier to delay.'[13] The battalion, he pointed out, was expected to

113

be sent overseas and there might never be another chance. Frank later enjoyed likening the effect of reading this letter to St Augustine hearing a voice in the garden telling him to pick up the Bible. On absorbing a couple of verses, Augustine wrote: 'No further would I read; nor needed I; for instantly at the end of this sentence by a light as it were of serenity infused into my heart, all the darkness of doubt vanished away.'

Inspired by Waugh's straight talking, Frank sought out his spiritual mentor. Father D'Arcy, however, was away in America (reportedly as an agent of the British government sent to win over the Catholic community there to the war effort, though this was never confirmed). So he turned instead to Father Wulfstan, the Guardian of Greyfriars in Iffley where he had been attending mass for some eighteen months. He asked for formal instruction with a view to joining the Church and, given the imminence of his battalion's departure for the field of battle, was rushed through the various stages. He would get leave to visit Father Wulfstan and was taken through the clauses of the Penny Catechism beginning with 'Do you believe in God?' It was a very different approach from the intellectual subtleties of Father D'Arcy but one well suited to Frank's mood. When he finally embraced socialism he did so in an atmosphere of emotion rather than one of tortuous reason. It was the same with Catholicism. Under stress, believing himself to be facing death, he buried his intellectual doubts and grabbed at a black and white Catholicism that took fundamental doctrines on trust. Sensing failure as a soldier because of his depressed state, he embraced religion in part as one more way of exorcizing his own demons and fulfilling his military duty.

In January news came through that his battalion was being sent to the Isle of Wight. He obtained a night's leave and spent it with the community at Greyfriars. That evening he was received into the Church and took Communion for the first time the next morning. Any joy he may have felt was tempered by the prospect of telling Elizabeth what he had done. His searching for a Christian belief had been undertaken alone. It was the first significant decision during their marriage that they had not shared. While the two of them had, at differing paces, been convinced of the appeal of socialism, Frank's conviction that socialist ideas of the equal worth of human beings led to a Christian belief that we are all children of the one God was his alone. Elizabeth's upbringing had left her with a residual antipathy to organized religion in general and the dogma of Roman Catholicism in particular. She knew her husband had been going to mass, seeing Father D'Arcy, but she was not prepared for the news he brought her that Sunday morning. 'I knew it was going on,' she admitted, 'but we would perform parts. I never once said, "Don't go to mass this morning. Let's have a morning off", or anything like that. But we didn't discuss it.'[14]

It was a colossal betrayal. This was a marriage based on mutual trust and sharing of ideas, thoughts, enthusiasms, politics, friendships – in short everything. Each had their areas of prime responsibility – in Elizabeth's case the home, in Frank's his career as a don – but the idea that he could have gone off and made such a major decision about the future of his life, their life and their children's lives, and on a subject that went to the heart of his view of the world, without first consulting her, would have been a huge blow to Elizabeth, especially given her strong dislike of Catholicism. Had she been a different sort of person, it might have broken their marriage. In her autobiography, written almost thirty years later, there were still clear traces of her anger in an otherwise emollient book. 'We didn't have a bloody row or anything of that sort. Frank said it was better this way, a fait accompli. If I had known I would have felt obliged to do everything I could to stop him. This way there was nothing I could do except leave him and I wasn't going to do that.'[15] The hurt, though, ran very deep. When she was very old, a young visitor told her he was planning to follow Frank's example and join the Catholic Church. 'Go home and tell your wife first,' she advised, and refused to discuss the matter any further until he had done so.[16]

She felt in 1940, she wrote, as if a barrier had been erected between them, a barrier of priests. Part of her phobia about Catholics had centred on the influence of clerics over their flocks. 'A black beetle has got on my tram,' she once wrote as a student to her parents when she spotted a Catholic priest. There were also more recent grounds for her dislike. Spurred on by Dr Helena Wright, her gynaecologist, Elizabeth supported the wider availability of contraception, and had spoken up for the cause in an Oxford Union debate. Her opponent was the formidable D.W.J. O'Donovan, one of the handful of Catholic MPs, who regarded her arguments as tantamount to heresy. It was only in the 1950s that the Pope accepted that women might legitimately space the births of their children, although 'artificial' contraception remains banned.[17]

That Frank could have taken such a decision without consulting her reveals something that marked his character, especially in regard to his dealings with his family. While there can be no doubt at all that he loved Elizabeth profoundly and exclusively, he was at heart an introspective person for whom others' feelings and sensitivities often took second place to what he believed, after long contemplation, to be right. The cause ultimately counted above individuals. It was as if they did not register on the same scale, even when those people were the ones closest to him in life. He was aware of the hurt, but put it second to what for him was a higher ideal.

There was another element that cut across and possibly explained this insensitivity – an inability to confront individuals. He had not wanted to confront Elizabeth, fearing her quick temper and the loss of the love that had sustained and empowered him. If he saw in religion a means of coping with his own tendency to depression, it was Elizabeth above all who had helped him try to conquer it. He knew that she would try to talk him out of conversion, that it was unnecessary, and he did not want to go through what he suspected would be a drawn-out and confrontational process.

Apart from her own feelings of betrayal, Elizabeth worried about the effect their father's decision would have on the children. Would they be expected to convert to Catholicism, and where would that leave her and her relationship with them? It was not something Frank would have thought about, but he assured her he had no plans to force anybody's hand. More practically, she wondered out loud, would Catholicism be a handicap to Frank's career at a time when Catholics in high political office were rare? Nancy Astor, for one, was horrified by his conversion. Though her anti-Catholicism had a fanatical edge on account of her Christian Scientist beliefs, it was not an uncommon attitude among the ruling classes. (David Astor said that his mother's disagreement with Frank over his change of faith did not come between them for long. 'Soon he was teasing her about it. They were both at a Buckingham Palace garden party once when Frank spotted a cardinal. He rushed over to kiss his ring like a good Catholic should. My mother thought he was doing it just to annoy her.')[18]

In the 1930s and 1940s the Catholic Church in England had yet to emerge from internal exile. Its hierarchy had been restored 100 years previously after the persecutions of the post-Reformation period. Civil rights had only been conceded to Catholics the previous century and in the folklore of the Church memories of past injustices remained fresh. It stood, for the most part, separate from national life, acutely aware it was different, outside the Establishment of which Frank had hitherto been a part. This was the era of the 'fortress' Church, as Cardinal Basil Hume[19] was later to describe it, when Catholics huddled together in their schools and parishes and avoided contact with a wider world. Their allegiance to the Pope – a foreign power – and their prayers for the conversion of England – 'Mary's dowry' – made the Catholic community an object of suspicion for many in the governing classes. Catholicism could be a severe handicap for a young man with aspirations to sit in the cabinet.

Elizabeth was not the only one who felt betrayed by Frank's conversion. His brother Edward was furious and it put an end to the *rapprochement*, based on Ireland, between them. Though he had seen nothing illogical in Frank, a self-professed Irish nationalist, signing up for the British army (Christine Longford once remarked that Frank was the only individual she knew who could be an Irish nationalist and English socialist 'in one person'),[20] Edward took great offence at his younger brother joining the Church of Rome. A devout and dutiful High Anglican, whose commitment to Irish nationhood did not preclude membership of the Church of Ireland, which had been a bastion of colonial rule, Edward accused Frank of treating religion as a plaything, to be taken up with enthusiasm and then discarded at will. When Frank wrote trying to explain a deeper and longer-standing commitment, Edward threw the letter away in anger.

The atmosphere at home in Oxford was tense. Antonia described an incident one Sunday morning in the summer of 1940 when their father arrived back from mass. 'My mother said, "Beat the Orange drum, children. Go on, beat the Orange drum!" So I said, "What do you mean?" I'd imagined a very beautiful, enormous orange drum. And she said "Oh well Dada's been to church, beat the Orange drum". Then I think she got quite embarrassed. But it was significant, a very hostile kind of behaviour from my mother who unqualifiedly adored my father.'[21] In the end it was that adoration that saved the day. As Elizabeth herself had admitted, if she wasn't going to leave, she would have to find a way of living with her anger at the betrayal.

Frank headed off to camp on the Isle of Wight on 11 January. His letters home were full of woe. If he had expected conversion and Catholicism to ease the ordeal of being in the army, he was quickly disillusioned. Though he had been out of the familiar, comforting and stimulating Oxford world during the five months he had spent at Banbury, he had at least been within striking distance, able to pop back to talk to old acquaintances, engage in debate and discussion, see his family. On the south coast all ties with kindred spirits were broken. Among his colleagues, Frank just did not fit. Even his choice of daily newspaper for the mess – Labour's *Daily Herald* as an alternative to the *Daily Telegraph* and *The Times* – emphasized that he was the odd one out.

On the Isle of Wight there was no longer time for educational and welfare activities as front-line service loomed. Frank's health had been poor since the summer camp of the previous year. He had suffered a series of colds and attacks of flu which had coincided with his depression and frustration at the inactivity of the phoney war and the philistinism of those around him. Despite his outward physical fitness, he was prone throughout his life to mild attacks of

1 The Gothic castle of Tullynally, the Longford family seat in County Westmeath, described by Elizabeth on her first visit as glittering in its eccentricity.

2 Frank with his Great-Aunt Caroline at Bernhurst. As a second son, Frank could expect no inheritance, but his childless great-aunt made him her heir and left him her country home in Sussex.

3 'Us Four': (*from left*) Pansy, four and a half, Frank, three, Edward, six, and Mary, one and a half. Their nursery was a hothouse of precocious competitiveness, their games a contest to win the attention and affection of their distant mother.

4 A studio portrait of Frank, aged nine, taken around the time that he heard his father had been killed at

5 At the opening of Hurst Green Village Hall in 1927. The tradition of philanthrophy was well established in the Pakenham family. Frank is seated second from the left next to his Great-Aunt Caroline.

6 Bright young things: Frank (*seated*) with, from the left, Evelyn Waugh, Fred Warnes and Maureen, Marchioness of Dufferin and Ava.

7 Frank and Elizabeth's wedding, in 1931, at St Margaret's, Westminster. The groom turned up at the adjacent Westminster Abbey, which was empty. 'People don't go to weddings these days,' his best man consoled him before they realised their mistake.

8 Frank in front of Stairways in Buckinghamshire, where he and Elizabeth moved after their wedding.

9 Edward Longford raising funds for his beloved Gate Theatre on the streets of Dublin. He became chairman in 1930 and exhausted the family fortune through his support of the theatre.

10 Always a keen jogger, Frank as a lecturer in the 1930s at Christ Church, Oxford, leads the field around Christ Church Meadows.

11 'Private Pack' in the Oxford and Bucks Light Infantry in 1939. 'He was a very weird soldier because he was so uncoordinated,' Denis Healey said of Longford.

12 In a refugee bunker in Hanover in June 1947 as Minister for Germany. Never a party politician Longford embarrassed his colleagues in government by telling journalists that conditions in the British zone in Germany were appalling.

13 In Paris in 1948 as Minister of Civil Aviation getting into a tangle with a map. Longford surprised his colleagues – who could not see beyond his donnish, dishevelled appearance – by his inspired stewardship of an essentially technical ministry.

nervous exhaustion. (Evelyn Waugh records in his diary for July 1947 that Frank was suffering from fainting fits.)[22] Usually these could be dealt with by a couple of days of taking it easy, watched over by Elizabeth, but on a wintry Isle of Wight there could be no such respite.

He tried to summon up the enthusiasm to join in with drilling and assault courses in arctic conditions, yet, despite his pride in keeping fit, he was so depressed that he could not find the necessary spark. Far from giving him a new lease of life, as he had fervently hoped it would, faith had only added to his troubles by involving him in an unhappy situation at home with his angry wife. When he crept away to the chapel to pray for strength and endurance, he found little solace. In such a low state of mind, Frank succumbed, after crawling through a wet field on exercises, to a bout of gastric flu.

Less than a week after he had left for the Isle of Wight, news came through to Elizabeth that her husband was in hospital in London. His physical and mental wretchedness did not stop him trying to return to camp several weeks later to do his patriotic duty as generations of Pakenhams had before him, but by March he was back in hospital with a second attack of flu. Army life, even in the relatively gentle atmosphere of a training camp, did not suit him. Regimentation and order broke his spirit. The gap between his romantic ideals and the reality of battalion life was insufferable. Boredom, inactivity and a sense of powerlessness did the rest. Though it was his body that was letting him down, Frank was suffering a mental breakdown.

In March, during that second stay in hospital in London, he received what he described to Elizabeth in a letter as a 'congenial' note from the adjutant in his battalion, 'saying that a Board would be arranged when he applied for it – no hurry suggested'. The Board would probably decide Frank should be invalided out on health grounds. The battalion had clearly decided he was not an asset to the army. Part of him rejoiced. He fervently wanted to be invalided out as a means of escaping the mental torture he had endured. Yet the much more significant part felt abject and humiliated by failure to serve his country and countrymen in their hour of need. His confused reaction became apparent when he was released from hospital in April and spent some time on leave with Elizabeth and the children at Bernhurst. While he would admit to Elizabeth that the Board might be a blessing in disguise, that he indeed might not be suited to army life and could better help the war effort with his mind rather than his body, with Thomas and Antonia he would plan and eventually carry out a mock assault on the house from the woods beyond. In the garage he set up a sand-table, where he showed them how to take advantage of the lie of the land and 'features' in battle strategy.

His family could not distract Frank from an overwhelming sense of wider impotence as Britain finally shook off the lethargy of the phoney war and Churchill took over as Prime Minister. The declaration of war had been followed by the partitioning of Poland between the Germans and Russians. Chamberlain tried to salvage his reputation by including erstwhile opponents of his failed appeasement policies in his war cabinet. Churchill returned as First Lord of the Admiralty and Eden as Dominions Secretary. Labour supported wholeheartedly the war effort and hence the government, though it did not prevent Attlee from pointing up some of the shortcomings in Chamberlain's actions. Why, he asked in March 1940, after six months of war, were there still 1.4 million unemployed when pits, ships and ports were lying idle?

Chamberlain's final downfall came in May. Norway, though officially neutral, had been invaded by Hitler in April. The British troops sent out there were ill equipped and were forced to evacuate on 2 May. In May, just as the Oxford and Bucks was preparing to depart for the Low Countries, Second Lieutenant Francis Pakenham was gazetted as having resigned his commission owing to ill health. He had not applied for release – that would have been to compound what was already almost unbearable – but neither did he protest against the decision which was approved by two medical boards. His battalion went on to serve with honour in France but at the cost of many casualties.

Though not unexpected the Board's verdict once again devastated Frank. For him it was absolute failure. The scar it left never healed.

'I think now', he conceded many years later, 'that my war record was more glorious than if I hadn't tried at all. I try to take a philosophical view, that it was good for me to fail. I was so privileged – a don, an Honourable, at Christ Church. I had a wonderful marriage, children. Everything was going so well. In a practical way I was humiliated. Not to be in uniform when my whole background revolved around whether you had had a good or bad war was a humiliation. Yet to have failed and to be aware of it – for better or worse – means that you can share with people. When I meet people society despises, I know what it is like to be humiliated.'[23]

It was an experience, Elizabeth said, that gave her husband greater understanding of others who had been brought, perhaps not before an army board, but before a magistrates' court and sent, not back to civilian life, but to prison.[24] To cure his own grief he turned it into other people's griefs. In time, as with most of the significant events in his life, Frank managed also to turn his army débâcle into a joke against himself. He wrote an article in *Horizon*, a magazine founded by Cyril Connolly[25] and Stephen Spender,[26] about the pain of being of an age to serve your country when it is at war, but not being able to take the pace. He signed the piece 'Neuro' but made little attempt to hide his identity as the author. Indeed, he often used to sign letters to his old friend David Astor with the same epithet.

The April trip to Bernhurst was to be the last the Pakenhams made for the duration of the war. Four days after their return to Water Eaton Manor on 6 May, Hitler launched his attack on the Benelux countries. As his forces swept away all opposition they rolled into France, pushing the British Expeditionary Force back to Dunkirk. Because of the invasion scare, families living near the south coast – Bernhurst was just thirteen miles from Hastings – were given the choice to evacuate. Frank had been offered his old job back at Christ Church, so the furniture was put in storage and the house was taken over by the government.

Back in Oxford, they began slowly to rebuild their lives after the trauma of Frank's conversion and his failure in the army. Water Eaton Manor had been only a temporary refuge and Elizabeth decided that she had better find a home for her family. The task was all the more urgent since she was pregnant. The house she chose – 8, Chadlington Road in north Oxford – was next door to her student digs, the place where Frank had visited her back in 1930 after his dream. The only drawback was the neighbourhood. It was staunchly Conservative, not the place for the city's Labour candidate, as his colleagues in the party pointed out when they joked about his home in the 'White Highlands'. Judith was born on 14 August 1940, during the Battle of Britain.

Back at Christ Church, Frank found life unchanged by the war. He might almost have forgotten it was happening. There were still students to teach and the only privation the dons had to suffer was a three-course lunch instead of four. A.J.P. Taylor described Oxford as 'a haven of peace' during the war years. On the one occasion that war did intrude, Paddy recalled, his father was oblivious. 'He was sitting in the garden on his deck chair reading when a blazing Lancaster bomber passed no more than 50 yards over his head and then crashed into a barn 300 yards away. In typically donnish fashion, my father looked up, as if momentarily distracted. "What was that, Elizabeth?" he called to my mother.'[27]

The comfortable life at Oxford only made Frank feel worse about what others regarded as his good fortune. Salvation was at hand though, in a scheme Churchill launched in the summer of 1940. While Britain was 'standing alone' after the invasion of France, Churchill backed a plan to raise Local Defence Volunteers but changed the name to the Home Guard. It was a godsend to Frank. He was able to displace a small part of his guilt about not being in France by setting up the South Company of the Oxford City Battalion with his friend Maurice Bowra, the Warden of Wadham and a veteran of the First World War, as his number two. It was, he was later to claim, the keenest company in Britain, eclipsing even that of the fictional Walmington-on-Sea.

Its activities were not, however, without a touch of Dad's Army about them. Frank's war wound was inflicted when one of the privates in the battalion accidentally discharged his gun into the pavement of the Abingdon Road. The bullets ricocheted into the feet of three officers standing nearby. Frank suffered most and was rushed to hospital, where an incompetent doctor managed to sew his wounded foot and his sock together. It began to suppurate and only the speedy intervention of another more skilled medic managed to drain the poison and save the foot. Frank kept the splinters of bullet as a war memorial. On another occasion, Elizabeth woke in the middle of the night to the sound of the church bells ringing. This was the signal for a German invasion. When she tried to rouse her husband, a notoriously heavy sleeper, as she had discovered the first time she met him, he merely turned over and did not wake. Luckily for him it was a false alarm.

Oxford escaped the German bombardment. When other historic towns like Bath were targeted, the people of Oxford held their breath and partied. It was at a Troops-Aid ball at Oxford Town Hall that Frank and Elizabeth introduced her beloved younger brother, John, to his wife Anna. When the bombers did not come, a rumour began to circulate that Hitler wanted Oxford as the capital of the Nazi colony of Britain and was therefore keeping it intact. One malicious tongue even suggested that Frank's old adversary from the 1935 election, Cruttwell, was to be the Germans' cultural attaché. But if Oxford escaped, the war was never very far away. Almost daily news would arrive of another friend lost in action. Ronald Cartland, Elizabeth's Conservative opponent in King's Norton, was killed with the British Expeditionary Force while Aidan Crawley, a fighter pilot and good friend of the couple, was shot down and incarcerated in Germany. Oxford felt just a little bit too safe.

SEVEN

The Postwar Planner

Frank Pakenham's conversion to Catholicism was to have a profound impact on his politics. Catholicism did not eclipse his passion for Labour but it certainly replaced it as the central influence in his life, with socialism playing a complementary, interlocking but increasingly secondary role as the years went by. He did not lose faith in a career in politics, but, in contrast to his enthusiasms of the late 1930s, he grew to see it with more perspective as a means to an end, that end being to put into effect Christian values. While his reading in preparation for reception into the Church had been principally theological, surrounding the nature of the Resurrection and the existence of God, once in the fold he began to range more widely. Catholic social teaching caught his eye. It was his studies in this area that led him to shift his allegiances within the Labour movement from the leftish radicalism of the late 1930s to a more mainstream, even right-wing position by 1945.

This was a period that saw the development of avowedly Catholic parties first in Germany and then Italy. Christian Democrats occupied the centre-right political ground, building up mass movements that united the pulpit and the political platform to counter what they regarded as the atheistic, Marxist-inspired socialism of the Labour movement. Separate Catholic unions were established to run against their secular counterparts. Yet these Catholic parties were not out-and-out conservatives in the British

124

sense. There was also a commitment in their programmes to limited social reform and to state involvement. The landmark papal encyclical *Rerum Novarum* (1891) had at the end of the nineteenth century set Catholicism's face against unbridled capitalism and its social concern had been reiterated in *Quadragesimo Anno* (1931).

The Church for its part regarded socialism as anticlerical and intent on dismantling ecclesiastical influence, especially in schools. To continental Catholics Frank's description of himself as a Catholic socialist would have been untenable. Yet in Britain, he was not so unusual. Although his own constituency party in Oxford held a meeting in the summer of 1940 to discuss their candidate's conversion to Catholicism, few felt that it was anything other than a personal decision. The Labour Party had no denominational bias and believed everyone had a right to any religious faith or none.

English Catholics, making up around 10 per cent. of the population, were in this period mostly of Irish descent and the vast majority were urban, working-class Labour voters. (It was only with the postwar influx of European *émigré* Catholics that the picture began to change significantly.) The English hierarchy had none of its continental cousins' ambitions to set up separate parties or unions, nor did it share their suspicion of socialism. It was content with Catholic caucus groups within the broader union movement, aimed at influencing but not undermining. Under first Cardinal Hinsley[1] and then after 1943 Cardinal Griffin,[2] Catholics were encouraged to venture out of their parishes and get involved in the politics of whatever party they felt best represented Christian ideals (so long as it wasn't with the communists). Men like Frank and his Catholic colleague in Attlee's government, Richard Stokes,[3] were held up as role models of a new more integrated, more assertive Catholicism.

Through his reading of the Catholic social encyclicals, which trod a careful line between right and left in politics, Frank came to realize how seeking the goal of equality, so central to his conversion to socialism, could potentially involve diminishing liberty, how the state, even out of well-intentioned anxiety to improve the lot of the majority, could in the process trample their freedom.

I realised that it was not enough to insist on the preservation of formal democratic rights; freedom of speech and religion and democratic elections. One must ask oneself additionally at every turn whether the extra equality being achieved by a deleterious increase in the role of the State was justified so that the good was outweighed by evil. More fundamentally, I came to realise that it was not enough to preach a Society based on the equal worth of all of us in the sight of God. Such a creed could cover a complete disregard of the dignity and self-respect of the individual by treating each of us as equally valueless.[4]

Any lingering regard Frank may have had for the Soviet system in his pre-war anxiety to forge an effective alliance against Hitler disappeared as he applied the restraining influence of Catholic social teaching to his socialism. 'My shallow revolutionary emotions, a by-product of near-Marxism operating on a somewhat excitable temperament, had lost all intellectual validity.'[5] The Catholic Church's social teaching was often called its 'best-kept secret' and to many in Labour circles Frank's enthusiasm for it would have run counter to their own woeful impression of a Church which had sided against socialism in the Spanish Civil War, which was building anti-socialist parties in postwar Europe, which was thoroughly undemocratic in its organization and whose teaching on sexual morality deprived women of the chance to limit the size of their families. Women in the Labour Party like Elizabeth and Naomi Mitchison attacked the Church for its stance against contraception. 'But in Frank's defence,' Elizabeth later conceded, 'he has never been interested in medical matters and those kind of things. Over our own family he realised perfectly well that those arguments affected me more than him and he never tried to impose a "Catholic" solution. And for him Catholicism has always been more about personal relationships – love your neighbour. It's age-old, that side of Catholicism. After all, Jesus wasn't able to tell us anything about the safe period but He did tell us to love our neighbour.'[6]

Such a view of Catholicism was often described as *à la carte*. Yet it was typical of Frank's way of approaching a broad issue. Where he was enthusiastic, he would be engaged at full throttle. No doubt mindful of a favourite Catholic adage of the period for internal dissenters, 'if you don't like the rules, don't join the club', he would accept less favoured edicts, but was half-hearted in their defence. Thus he would give general backing to papal teaching on contentious issues yet avoid being drawn into lengthy discussion. He would shirk from questioning the Pope's wisdom even when he knew it was not right.

Frank's re-evaluation of his own position within Labour was hastened considerably when, out of the blue, he received an invitation to act as Personal Assistant to Sir William Beveridge. The appointment would contribute enormously to his political reputation. He took over from another young Oxford don, Harold Wilson.[7] His task was to work with Beveridge on two reports commissioned by the wartime coalition government. The first was essentially technical, ordered by Ernest Bevin as Minister of Labour, on 'The Use of Skilled Man-Power in the Services'. The second, commissioned by Arthur Greenwood,[8] the Lord Privy Seal, was destined to become one of the landmarks in British twentieth-century history, on 'Social Insurance and Allied Services'.

Frank had known Beveridge slightly when the latter was Director of the London School of Economics and he had been a part-time lecturer there in the early 1930s. Beveridge had then moved on to become Master of University College, Oxford, where he would have been aware both of Frank's academic reputation and of his political activities. Janet Mair, Beveridge's companion and later his wife, had struck up a friendship with Frank and before his marriage he had been a visitor at the couple's country retreat, Green Street, near Avebury.

At the outbreak of war, Beveridge had placed his formidable skills at the disposal of the government. Throughout the autumn of 1940 he had chaired a secret committee on the allocation of manpower in relation to munitions and other industrial production. After that he had been seconded to the Ministry of Labour under Ernest Bevin. However, Beveridge, despite his distinguished academic and public service record, was not a man for team-work, and his colleagues found him lofty, austere and solitary. Several of the Ministry officials complained to Bevin, himself notorious for his single-mindedness, and it was decided in May 1941 that Beveridge had to be shuffled to one side and set to work on the two reports. When told the news, he is reported to have broken down and wept. Like Frank, he had been frustrated in his determination to aid the war effort. However, whatever his disappointment at not being at the centre of events, he took to his appointed task with gusto and within six months had delivered his report on skilled men in the services. Among its recommendations was the establishment of the Army Corps, later to become the Royal Electrical and Mechanical Engineers.

The report on social security initially filled him with less enthusiasm. He saw planning for the postwar society as a distraction when Britain was facing a Nazi invasion. However, Janet Mair convinced him that it was a heaven-sent opportunity to bring together in a single comprehensive scheme different aspects of work on social security that he had been undertaking for nearly forty years. In the pre-First World War years he had worked with Churchill to set up Labour Exchanges and unemployment insurance and then, in 1924, when Churchill became Chancellor, he had again called on Beveridge to assist him in implementing his promise of old-age pensions.

Beveridge's break-neck pace of working suited Frank well. He would commute up to London from Oxford when he could. 'He was always', Paddy remembered, 'acutely aware of the contrast between the safe world of Oxford and the bombed out sites of London near his office. It added to his agony about his military failure.'[9]

It very soon became apparent that the advisory committee which was to assist Beveridge in drawing up his report was more of a hindrance than a help and it was quietly abandoned. Beveridge, with Frank at his side, would not tolerate any restraints on his field of enquiry and set about assembling the evidence over twelve months that was to lead to his landmark report.

Politically a Liberal, he and his Labour assistant were united in wanting to create a more equal society. For Frank it was a point of Christian principle. For the atheist Beveridge it was a practical dilemma to harness society's wealth in order to eliminate the extremes of poverty. He did not believe, as Frank did, that an imposed redistribution, taking money from the rich to give to the poor, was the answer. Rather he aimed at allowing individuals to provide for themselves. They would set aside earnings when in work to provide for the times when they were out of work (during illness, unemployment or in old age). The pool made from their contributions would be supplemented by funds from state taxation and employers' profits.

Frank's role in the production of the Beveridge Report was essentially that of organizer. He would set up the meetings, travelling around the country with his master as he examined various aspects of employment policy, health and education provision. 'I was like a man's wife,' he once said. 'I was there the whole time, rather like one of those personal assistants that important men have. Because of the war, Beveridge had hardly any staff at all. I would travel with him as he assembled the material. I think he saw my economic training as an advantage because, although he had got a double first at Oxford – in maths and classics – and had been master of the LSE, he wasn't an economist.'[10]

Several of Frank's friends, though, felt that he had, modestly and out of loyalty to Beveridge, played down his own role in the writing of the report. David Astor described his friend's role as more akin to that of co-author.[11] Beveridge certainly grew to depend on his young assistant, but Frank was always emphatic that the main body of the text was all Beveridge's own work, a product of his long experience in the social services. 'He would dictate the report [though for more difficult passages Beveridge, once a leader writer on the *Morning Post*, liked to write out his draft in longhand] and occasionally pause and ask me what I thought.'[12] Frank would concede, however, that his social connections proved useful to Beveridge in opening doors as they conducted the research. He would even admit that Beveridge was difficult and often grumpy to work for. One day, feeling that his ceaseless labours were not receiving quite the recognition that they might, Frank wrote to his wife at home in Oxford: 'No acolyte ever worshipped as Beveridge does at the altar of his own work.'[13]

Janet Mair, later Lady Beveridge, gave perhaps the most credible picture of Frank's role in her memoir – more than a glorified PA but short of a full collaborator in her husband's office in Buckingham Gate during this period of frenetic activity. 'He threw himself into the work, becoming absorbed in the task of the administration of the continuous interviews, consultations and deliberations. He kept at bay the press and the photographers without giving offence, and he coped with a stream of correspondence, both relevant and ir- relevant. He looked after William and the interests of the Report with completely impersonal devotion.'[14] The two became less employer and employee, more mentor and protégé, another in a long line for Frank. He took Beveridge to meet Antonia and Thomas over tea at his house in Oxford.

On a professional level, Frank learnt an invaluable skill from Beveridge: how to commit one's deeply held beliefs to paper in a report with clarity, precision and persuasiveness. As he grew used to Beveridge's unusual ways of working, Frank came to admire him more and more. He shared the independence of mind, the fixed gaze and the touch of vanity that Frank found so attractive and glamorous in men like Birkenhead and de Valera. Beveridge was one of a then rare and subsequently extinct breed of public-spirited pro-consuls, spreading their wisdom in a grave and magisterial way through independent, non-political reports and quangos. He even revealed a dry sense of humour, evident in this interview with an employer over industrial insurance that Frank recounted in a letter to Elizabeth:

Beveridge: There's no real reason, is there, for distinguishing between the man who is run over by a lorry inside the works and the man who is run down outside?
Employer: No reason – from the point of view of the man – no.
Beveridge: Well, we're hardly concerned with the point of view of the lorry, are we – um – um. (No laughter for once from the chairman's sycophantic associates.)[15]

The Beveridge Report was published on 1 December 1942, the greatest civilian event of the war years. Frank had learnt from his

130

master's thoroughness, and when asked to organize the publicity for the launch took to the task with enthusiasm. Granted a report that promised to 'abolish want' did not need a great deal of pushing to make the front pages, but the keen sense of anticipation on the eve of publication, the subsequent interest it generated, its impact on the public imagination and its decisive role in the 1945 general election result were extraordinary.

Having abandoned his committee, Beveridge decided to sign the report himself. He identified five evil giants. 'To get the New Britain of all our desires,' he said at the time of publication, 'we must deal not only with Want but . . . with Disease (that is the purpose of the National Health Service), with Ignorance (dealing with that means more and better schools), with Squalor (curing that means better planning of towns and countryside and more and better houses), with Idleness, that is to say unemployment.' He showed in detail how with the help of the state this could be achieved. In the case of want it was to be a double process of redistribution: by social insurance between times of earning and times of unemployment, sickness and retirement; and by children's allowances between times of large and small family responsibilities. Planning was an essential tenet of his programme. 'Nothing worth having can be had for nothing; every good thing has its price. Maintenance of employment – prevention of mass idleness after the war – is a good thing worth any price, except war or surrender of essential liberties. It can be had without that surrender, but not without giving up something; chiefly we must give up our darling vice of not looking ahead as a nation.'

It was an inspiring message which found a ready echo among British troops as something worth fighting for beyond sheer survival. Its appearance coincided with the culmination of a series of victories – El Alamein, Stalingrad and Guadalcanal. It was, as Beveridge realized when he took responsibility by signing the report, a challenge to the politicians. It struck an immediate chord in a nation that sensed the tide of war was beginning to turn and which saw in Beveridge's vision a peacetime El Dorado where the deprivations of the 1930s would be banished for ever. The newspapers, guided by Frank, who on the eve of publication dined with Lord Rothermere,[16] owner of his erstwhile employer, the *Daily Mail*, took up the report with enthusiasm. 'Freedom from want' was the headline on *The Times*'s leader. 'Beveridge tells how to banish want', trumpeted the *Daily Mirror*. The *Manchester Guardian* heralded a 'big and fine thing'. Frank used to like to tell the tale that on the morning after publication he went to his local newsagent only to find all the papers had been sold. 'You don't think I've got any papers left this morning,' the assistant told him. 'It's that Sir William Beveridge. He's going to abolish want.'[17] Within this nicely rounded anecdote there was no doubt a grain of truth.

Beveridge became a household name overnight. Not everyone was as enthusiastic in their praise as the newspaper editors. Despite all the changes Frank had been through in recent years, some of his old friends in the Conservative Party were surprised to see his name associated with such a radical report. 'Abolishers of want', one remarked, 'should know their subject a bit better at first hand.' His series of rapid about-turns – from Conservative to Labour, Protestant to Catholic, Anglo-Irish to Irish nationalism – had left agog many of the group with whom he had partied at the Bullingdon and weekended at Charlton. 'My childhood', recalled Esmond Warner's daughter, Marina, 'was punctuated by my father exclaiming "look what Frank has done now" at the news of another conversion. His self-shaping was very foreign to my father, and occasionally made him feel envious, but within that he retained this great affection and fascination for Frank all his life. He asked him to be my godfather. And I think Frank for his part managed to play down any disagreements by always playing a kind of holy fool. Whatever my father thought of what Frank had done, he couldn't help but remain very fond of him.'[18]

The image of Frank as a latter-day Don Quixote, romantically, even humorously, tilting at windmills and coming up with idealistic solutions from a position of personal privilege was to stalk him ever after in some minds. More immediately, though, the Church of England was enthusiastic – 'It is the first time that anyone has set out to embody the whole spirit of the Christian ethic in an Act of Parliament,' William Temple, the Archbishop of Canterbury, remarked. Some sections of the Catholic Church, including his mentor Father D'Arcy, gave a less than enthusiastic greeting, to Frank's acute personal distress. 'There is a certain kind of very devout and gifted Catholic to whom not only socialism but what may be called the whole progressive movement of social reform is singularly repugnant,' he concluded sadly afterwards.[19] At his local Catholic church on the Sunday after publication, he sat with barely disguised anger as the priest attacked Beveridge in his sermon from the pulpit. Elizabeth, who had accompanied him on this occasion, was confirmed in her dislike of the 'black beetles'. Changing such negative opinions became a personal crusade for Frank in the aftermath of publication. It was he who responded to the flood of invitations to go and explain the report to groups of servicemen, workers, students and whoever wanted to hear. Beveridge delegated these mundane tasks to his assistant, preferring himself to travel to America to greet supporters of his work.

If the reaction from certain quarters of the Church upset Frank, he was deeply dismayed by the attitude of the government to the report, in particular that of his Labour colleagues in the wartime cabinet. As the finishing touches were being put to the report, Whitehall began to hear disturbing rumours about the nature, extent and detail of Beveridge's plan. What had been intended as a sop to keep a distinguished public servant quietly occupied looked like turning into a major political event. Initially, the Minister of Information, Brendan Bracken,[20] seemed inclined to play down the publication, fearing the 'socialism' of the report. When it became clear that Frank's work in priming the press would make that impossible, Bracken decided to chair the launch conference himself. He pledged abundant goodwill to the plan but was not specific. Beveridge became the name on everyone's lips – eclipsing briefly that of Churchill – and 635,000 copies of the report were sold. A telegram from Buckingham Palace commanded Beveridge's presence the week after publication. Lloyd George travelled up from his country retreat to congratulate the author.

Thereafter the government remained ominously quiet. A fortnight after the report's publication the Archbishop of Canterbury married

Beveridge and Janet Mair, with Frank organizing both the event and the publicity. Churchill sent his own four-volume *Marlborough: His Life and Times*, and inscribed it to Beveridge adding, 'May he bring the magic of averages to the rescue of millions.' Yet the Prime Minister made no attempt to meet Beveridge. It was not until the following February that the government found time to debate the report in the Commons and then under the guise of a bland, non-specific motion of welcome. When it became clear that there was no official intention of taking any steps towards implementing Beveridge, a group of dissident Labour MPs, including Manny Shinwell,[21] put down a motion deploring the lack of action. Though the front bench felt unable to back it out of loyalty to the coalition government, 121 mainly Labour members did, the largest Commons revolt in the war years.

Frank was disappointed by Churchill's negative reaction. In view of his earlier political record in introducing insurance measures, Churchill's disdain for Beveridge puzzled him. He came to see that Churchill was fighting shy of the 'socialism' of the report and did not want to be the Prime Minister to introduce such measures, but Frank never quite forgave Churchill's personal dismissal of Beveridge. His failure even to mention the report in his triumphal *War Memoirs* was 'tepid and crabbed', and the government's refusal to employ Beveridge further for the remaining period of the war 'deplorable'.[22] The Labour Party's equivocation caused him deeper personal distress. Here was a plan that set out the longed-for economic means for putting cherished beliefs into practice, a way of reconciling the emotional pull of socialism with a hard-headed scheme to bring greater equality. Here, Frank was sure, was a potential vote-winner, a blueprint for a postwar Labour government.

Attlee, as he made clear in an interview just before the report came out, saw social security and state planning not as an alternative to socialism but as part of it. Yet he was torn by his desire for Labour to be seen as wholly loyal to the coalition. Given Churchill's implacable opposition to the plan, Attlee did not want to divide the government over it. He was in any case under fierce pressure from Ernest Bevin, who said he would resign if Labour went into the lobby against the government. In the end Attlee managed to force Churchill into the bland compromise motion which the government placed before the Commons, welcoming the plan.

Frank, however, was not prepared to let the matter drop. He was convinced that the Liberal Sir William Beveridge would be a great asset to the Labour Party. All that needed to happen was a little wooing and flattery. He therefore worked out a scheme with Arthur Jenkins,[23] the Parliamentary Private Secretary to Attlee. The two young men would get their bosses together over dinner in the hope that Attlee would persuade Beveridge to sign up for Labour. The dinner took place at the Oxford and Cambridge Club, but the desired alliance did not materialize.

Beveridge [Frank recalled] unwisely laid down the law on many matters involved in the running of the war, with which Attlee, Deputy Prime Minister, was too closely concerned to discuss them. He lapsed into almost total silence. Finally, after dinner, he disappeared into the depths of an armchair and fell asleep. By the time he woke, Beveridge had followed his example, leaving Arthur Jenkins and myself to chatter away as best we could. Soon after, the party broke up. Our masters walked along Pall Mall together, Arthur and I following at a respectful distance. Arthur turned to me and said 'I think it went pretty well, don't you?' Feeling that it could hardly have gone worse, I made no comment.[24]

Soon afterwards Beveridge told his assistant he was to be a parliamentary candidate for the Liberals, the only party which had been united and enthusiastic in backing his plan.

Politics and social life had up to this moment mixed easily in Frank's life, friendship dovetailing into political alliances and vice versa. This, then, was a major reverse. It was followed by another failure. He decided to introduce Beveridge to Evelyn Waugh, one of the vocal Catholic critics of the plan. Beveridge, riding a wave of national adulation, found Waugh somewhat off-hand. 'Tell me, Sir William,' said Waugh, 'how do you get your main pleasure in life?' 'I get it', Beveridge replied, 'by trying to leave the world a little better place than I found it.' 'And I get mine', Waugh retorted, 'in trying to spread alarm and despondency, and I expect I get a great deal more than you do.' Afterwards Beveridge kept shaking his head and asking Frank, 'That fellow Waugh, he was a crackpot, wasn't he?'[25]

The incident not only revealed Frank's continuing political naïveté but symbolized how his life had changed. He had known Evelyn Waugh for fifteen years and still admired his waspish humour as much as he had when he first encountered it, at a time when he was also delighting in the bitchy world of Maurice Bowra. Frank himself remained a witty raconteur and an entertaining after-dinner speaker with a good line in the acid put-down. But his Catholic conscience told him that giving his tongue free rein was sinful and he made a conscious effort to restrain it, especially in the public arena. Moreover the sort of high-mindedness epitomized by Beveridge no longer amused him as much as it still did Waugh. He had come to value it hugely, even if he could still all too readily see some of the absurdities of Sir William himself. 'Frank was a master of the witty phrase,' remarked David Astor, 'and remained so in private when he was relaxed and among friends, but from this time on he developed away from it. He saw it increasingly as an unkind, unchristian thing to do, to dismiss people with a joke.'[26]

Even though the government was not going to give him any more work, Beveridge determined to continue his task of shaping postwar Britain. During his research, he had become convinced of the need to investigate the whole question of full employment, fearing that with peace would come a return to the dole queues of the 1930s. Admirers provided the finance for this new venture and Frank was again at Beveridge's side. They began work in the spring of 1943 and were almost at once made aware of the government's hostility when an order issued from the Chancellor of the Exchequer's office banned all communication between Whitehall and the new Beveridge inquiry. Friends and colleagues from a lifetime of public service were prevented from talking to Beveridge about full employment. Faced by such an obstacle, the new report never quite built up the momentum of its predecessor. Beveridge himself became distracted by Liberal party politics (he was elected to the House of Commons as a Liberal for Berwick-on-Tweed in October 1944) and by the continuing struggle to get his earlier work taken seriously by the government.[27]

On the advice of David Astor, Frank employed Fritz Schumacher,[27] a German exile and economist, to work alongside Beveridge. Another recruit was Barbara (later Baroness) Wootton,[28] whom Frank had first met when he applied to work with the WEA. Wootton had been less than impressed that his application was sent on Carlton Club notepaper. His own involvement with Beveridge's work was then scaled down and in 1944 he returned to academic life at Christ Church, to his constituency and to his family in north Oxford. (Living in London had been hazardous. He began by staying in a hotel whose address, Heartowest, Leicester Square, did not ring any alarm bells in his head but which he discovered after a couple of noisy nights there was in fact a brothel. He then moved to a room in Charlotte Street which narrowly missed being bombed.)

His work with Beveridge did something towards restoring Frank's shattered confidence. It was a halfway decent wartime contribution, he conceded, more in tune with his political and religious convictions than any alternative he had considered – like Randolph Churchill's invitation to became a wartime military spokesman in Cairo. Yet he still craved front-line action. The writer Robert Kee,[29] who was introduced to the Pakenhams in the war years when he was stationed near Oxford with the RAF, went to dinner with them one evening. After he recounted, at their insistence, his experiences of flying bombers over Germany, Frank implored him to try to arrange for him to join one of these missions.

It may have been a substitute, but the Beveridge Report and the acclaim it subsequently received reflected well on Frank and enhanced his political reputation. He had been fortunate in landing a job where his academic skills had been put to good populist effect, and to his credit he had stuck at the task and recognized its potential. If Beveridge himself could not be wooed into Labour, then at least the Party could point to having his number two among its parliamentary candidates.

Yet, for all the kudos that it brought him, Beveridge was never more than second best in Frank's eyes, a distraction from the real business of war, the arena where he had tried but failed to make his mark. Indeed, when faced with some of the Tory opponents of Beveridge's plans, he often found himself in those closing months of the war holding back from winning the political points. Many of them had distinguished military records. His achievement alongside Beveridge, he felt, paled into insignificance. 'As I watched so many Conservative contemporaries – though not of course only Conservatives – making the sacrifice that I had proved incapable of making, the impulse to denounce or expose half the country or even its leaders faded and finally died.'[30] It was a significant diminution in his political passion. While Frank could still have a political argument and come out shining, that sharp and abrasive edge necessary for party knock-abouts eluded him.

Back in Oxford in 1944, there were family decisions to be made – for example which school to send the children to. Given Elizabeth's continuing hostility to his Catholicism, he made no attempt to stake a claim for Catholic education. There was then a straight choice between state and private education. Chadlington Road was a stone's throw from the Dragon School, Alma Mater of Hugh Gaitskell and John Betjeman. It enjoyed an unparalleled academic reputation in the town but was just the sort of bastion of educational privilege that was anathema to the radical left of the Labour Party. Like most of the Labour leadership, however, Frank justified the decision to send Antonia, Thomas, Patrick and later Judith there on the age-old grounds that there was no point depriving them of a good education to prove that he was dedicated to improving the standards in the state system. This, of course, stood in direct contradiction to his belief in the redistribution of wealth. 'In the case of material things a levelling would be certain to contain some element of levelling down for certain people,' he was later to write. 'I myself incidentally would lose by it, but in the case of education you cannot level down without destroying what might never, or not for years, be replaced – the spirit of a noble institution. This conclusion did not make me less a leveller in education, but it made me hostile to any educational reforms that did not consist in preserving the highest levels and extending them widely and rapidly.'[31]

Judith was only one when Elizabeth got her 'baby-itch' again. In May 1942, twenty months after her sister, Rachel arrived, a little too quickly for the doctor and the midwife, and was therefore delivered by the district nurse. By the summer of 1943 Michael was on the way and Elizabeth's constituency party in King's Norton was growing restive about the ever-expanding Pakenham clan and the drain such a large family would place on their candidate. Frank missed Michael's birth in November 1943 – the only time he was away for such an event – because of work with Beveridge in the north of England. His expanding brood could occasionally overwhelm him. Solly Zuckerman recalled visiting the Pakenhams at Chadlington Road soon after Michael's birth, to be greeted by a distracted Frank at the door, surrounded by children, saying, 'Come in quickly or they'll fall out.'[32]

Besides children, the crowded house resounded, Antonia remembered, with her father's students – mostly older men, the younger generation having abandoned their studies in favour of front-line service. And Frank continued his interest in prisoners. Antonia pictured one particular newly released inmate who was invited to tea. 'I remember having arson explained to me because this person had committed arson. I was amazed because it seemed like such a strange thing to do. And I remember thinking that it was very odd that, since this person had done it, my father should invite them home for tea. I thought perhaps I hadn't quite got the point of the crime.'[33]

King's Norton Constituency Labour Party was having a turbulent war. Frank may have moved towards the middle ground in Labour terms but Elizabeth remained on the left, siding with her local party when it was expelled by the national leadership in 1941 for arguing that, despite the restrictions placed on it by membership of a wartime coalition, Labour should be working harder to promote its distinctive programme in preparation for peacetime. In January 1944, however, after much agonizing, she resigned as candidate. There had been rumblings in the constituency about how the mother to so many children could manage to find time to be a decent MP. Some suggested she should give an undertaking not to have any more, an imposition which she rejected out of hand. At a crisis meeting, she received the local party's backing, but the dispute had undermined her confidence in her ability to do everything. Her 'addiction to motherhood' had effectively scuppered her political career. Henceforth the couple's political ambitions were to sit on Frank's shoulders.

EIGHT

The Lord-in-Waiting

The 1945 general election took place on 5 July, two months after the German surrender. The conflict in the Far East continued until August, when the dropping of atom bombs on Hiroshima and Nagasaki hastened the Japanese capitulation. By that time Clement Attlee had been Prime Minister of Great Britain and Northern Ireland for over a month, in command of the first-ever Labour majority in the House of Commons.

After his successful conduct of the war, Winston Churchill, and indeed many in the Labour Party, had expected a Conservative 'khaki victory', but, as polling day drew closer, Attlee and his colleagues grew more optimistic. The Conservatives' failure to offer any sort of vision of a postwar Britain to an electorate anxious to make a fresh start contrasted sharply with Labour's commitment to wide-scale nationalization and its promise, a crucial factor in the landslide victory, to introduce a Beveridge-style welfare state. One of the Conservatives frustrated by his party's reliance on Churchill's past record was Quintin Hogg, defending the Oxford City seat he had won at the 1938 by-election against Antony Norman for the Liberals and Frank Pakenham for Labour. A member of the progressively minded Tory Reform Committee, Hogg's credentials were not so different from Frank's. Both were somewhat donnish in appearance and academic in background, unafraid to speak of Christian values and morality at the hustings. (Though a friend of

141

Father D'Arcy, Hogg was a convinced Anglican.) While Frank could score points by rightly pointing to his key role alongside Beveridge, any kudos he gained in the eyes of the electorate from his wartime service was undermined by a combination of Hogg's (and Norman's) distinguished military exploits and Beveridge's open endorsement of Norman. When Hogg shrugged off his war wound, Frank could only reflect on his own inglorious failure to make it to the front line.

Hogg's friendship with the Pakenham family further complicated the campaign. An old admirer of Elizabeth's, when he called at Chadlington Road on the eve of the hustings, everyone managed to be very civil about the election battle ahead except for young Paddy, who refused out of loyalty to his father to get an extra tea cup for Mr Hogg. In the middle of the campaign, Elizabeth's father died, so party politics were put to one side for a moment when Hogg called again to offer his condolences.

Frank fought a mediocre campaign. His instinct for publicity, seen to effect with the pre-war 'Private Pack' newspaper pictures and later in organizing the press coverage for Beveridge, had started to backfire. Riding through the city in a pony and trap with Elizabeth, Judith, Rachel and Michael allowed him to counter any Churchillian rhetoric about totalitarianism and present himself instead as both a family man and a likeable eccentric – in case the Oxford electors had not already realized. However, his attempts to suggest that Hogg was less than dedicated to his constituency misfired badly. The Conservative candidate was on the selection committee of the St George's division of Westminster and a letter to the *Oxford Mail* during the campaign, signed by a little-known trade unionist, indicated that Hogg had unsuccessfully sought the nomination there instead of in Oxford. When Hogg threatened to sue the editor for libel, Frank telephoned and admitted that he was behind the letter. Hogg made great play of this on the platform and the gloves were off.

As ever, Evelyn Waugh was on hand to mock Frank's efforts and rub salt into his wounds in the name of friendship. Returning with him by train from a memorial service in London for Basil Dufferin, who had been killed in action in Burma, Waugh suggested that Frank should stand 'as an eccentric foreign nobleman who had beaten the record for demobilisation'. Later the same month, on the eve of the Oxford poll, Waugh ended a letter to John Betjeman, 'Vote for Pakenham, the old booby!'[1] In pinpointing the reasons for his victory in 1945, Hogg wrote in his autobiography: 'Frank crudely overreached himself and early on in the campaign practised some sharp tactics which rebounded badly on his own head.'[2] He might have added that Frank, a wonderful after-dinner speaker and polished wit in any social gathering, was not a particularly effective speaker from the hustings, especially since his new-found Catholicism inhibited his previous penchant for personal invective. In the pre-television era such a failing was a handicap for any budding politician, especially in a marginal seat.

Hogg naturally omitted to mention the key factor in the election result: the exclusion of the working-class districts of Cowley and Headington. Frank managed to reduce Hogg's 1938 majority to just under 3,000, an achievement given that seven years earlier he had been facing a single opponent. Until the last minute Frank continued to hope for victory. The announcement of the election result was delayed until 25 July to allow the servicemen's votes, cast in the overseas theatres of war, to be counted. When news began to leak out that these had been overwhelmingly in favour of Labour, Hogg seemed vulnerable. Antonia arrived back in Oxford from her boarding school on the day the winner was to be revealed. 'I had my trunk and I got a taxi – a habit not encouraged in the Pakenham household. I made the taxi go round by the Town Hall so I could see my father being elected, but he came second and I burst into floods of tears and got a very unsympathetic welcome at home for having wasted money on a taxi.'[3]

It was a cruel blow to Frank, particularly since Hogg – a contemporary, blue-blooded Old Etonian – symbolized the safe Tory world that he had abandoned by joining the Labour Party. To exacerbate his disappointment, news was flooding in of friends and colleagues elected around the country in the Labour landslide. Evan Durbin, Hugh Gaitskell, Christopher Mayhew,[4] Patrick Gordon

Walker and Richard Crossman would all be playing their part in building the New Jerusalem. Labour easily won West Birmingham (and King's Norton with a thumping majority of 12,000). He alone seemed to have missed the boat.

Once so promising, his political career was in tatters. Whatever reputation he had achieved in the Labour Party would now be eclipsed as a new generation of eager young men, held back by the Second World War, entered Parliament and rose through the ranks. Succour, however, was at hand. When he returned to Chadlington Road from a mournful drink at the Trout for what he had assumed would be a funereal tea, he found Evan and Marjorie Durbin, fresh from the victory platform in Edmonton. Since those early encounters at New College, Durbin had developed a profound admiration and loyal friendship for Frank. Durbin said he was determined to get Frank into Parliament and for the first time they discussed the option for him of the House of Lords.

Edward and Christine Longford were by now clearly not going to produce an heir. In 1932, Christine had written poignantly of the couple's plans. 'We hope to have at least three children. We hope to see Ireland free from the centre to the sea, and we hope to go to China.'[5] They achieved none of them. Edward had grown ever fatter, and when he passed thirty stone, his doctor had told him that he must cut his weight by half if he was to produce an heir. 'Not a crumb', was Edward's response when Christine set out a new diet. She had to make do with mothering him, supporting him as he tried to learn the harp (where his great girth was an obstacle) and applauding his financially draining efforts to support the Gate Theatre in Dublin and, from 1946, to do his bit for Ireland as a senator.

It was not an unreasonable expectation then, Evan Durbin pointed out, that Frank would one day succeed to the title. He was younger, thinner and fitter. As 7th earl, he would be barred from the Commons as a member of the House of Lords. Why not then accelerate the process, Durbin suggested? Labour was perilously short of supporters in the Upper House, especially of those who were young and vigorous enough to see a lengthy and controversial programme of legislation through an overwhelmingly Conservative chamber. Lord Addison, who had led the Labour peers during the war years, estimated that he had a total of sixteen supporters at his disposal in a House of 831 voting members. Only eight of these supporters were up to active and regular service. Attlee would have to create some peers. Could he, Durbin asked, put Frank's name forward in anticipation of the day when he would inherit a title from his brother?

By lunchtime the next day Attlee had been asked by George VI to be Prime Minister. At the heart of his cabinet was a group of five: Foreign Secretary Ernest Bevin; Herbert Morrison[6] as Lord President with overall responsibility for the programme of nationalization; Sir Stafford Cripps, newly restored to the Labour fold at the Board of Trade after his apostasy of 1939; Chancellor Hugh Dalton and Attlee himself. Durbin, with his economic background and track record at the XYZ Club, was appointed as Dalton's Parliamentary Private Secretary and at once set about singing Frank Pakenham's praises.

By the weekend, Durbin had arranged a meeting between the Pakenhams (significantly they were presented as a couple) and Dalton, who was staying with friends at Burford near Oxford. On the surface there was no pressing reason why Dalton should want to help Frank. In the run-up to the Second World War, Dalton had been a hated figure among left-wingers in the Labour Party because of his opposition to talk of a Popular Front. The Oxford party would have had little time for him, nor he for it. At the height of his enthusiasm for left-wing ideas and Stafford Cripps in the late 1930s, Frank had written a scathing article in the *Spectator* rubbishing the personal credo in Dalton's book *Practical Socialism* as 'very tender towards the susceptibilities of capitalists'.

However, Frank, as Durbin pointed out at length, was now a reformed character politically, his Catholicism and his work with Beveridge having banished any previous tendencies to extremism and class rhetoric. As an academic, an economist and a man with intimate knowledge of Beveridge's plans for a postwar welfare state, he would be an asset to the incoming Labour administration.

Dalton enjoyed a reputation for encouraging rising young stars in the party, 'the class of '45', men like Durbin and Gaitskell. George Brown[7] was to note that Dalton had a particular liking for 'university socialites'. Later as Chancellor he had a private list of young politicians who were to be given automatic access to him whenever he was not in a meeting or conference. Thanks to Durbin, Dalton was sufficiently impressed after the encounter at Burford to find time that evening to write notes to several of the leading members of the government commending Frank to their notice. A few days later a call came through to Chadlington Road asking Frank to come to London to meet the Lord Privy Seal, Arthur Greenwood, a stalwart of the 1929 Labour government and the man who commissioned the Beveridge inquiry. Attlee had decided to have several non-departmental ministers in his cabinet to oversee major areas of legislation. Morrison was to be one and Greenwood another, with responsibility for social services and the implementation of Beveridge. Greenwood wanted Frank as his personal assistant. He accepted the post without hesitation.

During the brief period that he spent in Greenwood's office, Frank grew fond of his boss. He spoke for him in his Wakefield constituency and was eager to get down to work, but Greenwood's most influential days in the Labour Party had passed. He had something of a reputation as a drinker, though Frank reported to Elizabeth that he saw no sign of any empty bottles hidden in his desk. However, Greenwood did, he noted, often speak 'through a haze of distant benevolence'. On one occasion, Frank mentioned his friendship with Evan Durbin. 'Oh yes,' said Greenwood, 'I know him well. Such a nice chap. Awful pity that his health is bad. His heart, you know . . .' Frank suggested that perhaps Greenwood was thinking of Hugh Gaitskell. 'Oh, I know him too,' he went on. 'He's another nice chap. His heart's bad also. Funny thing, all the Dalton boys have got bad hearts.'[8]

Before Frank had the chance to get frustrated with Greenwood's ways, he was summoned to 10 Downing Street for an interview with the Prime Minister. The two had met in 1938 when Attlee had visited Oxford in the immediate aftermath of Eden's resignation from Chamberlain's government in frustration at the appeasement policy. Attlee, not usually a particularly effective public speaker, had risen to the occasion and demanded before a packed meeting chaired by Frank that Chamberlain too should go. Such were the passions abroad at that time that Attlee was given a standing ovation and carried shoulder-high down the High Street.

In the wake of his own defeat at Oxford in 1945, Frank had written to Attlee congratulating the new Prime Minister on the scale of Labour's victory. The letter, though it could hardly be described as a deft piece of political intrigue, was clearly more than a courtesy. Frank was blatantly and rather obviously fishing. Wheels were turning behind the scenes. His conversations with Durbin and Dalton had reached the ears of the Prime Minister, who was being assisted by another old New College colleague, Douglas Jay. Attlee replied to Frank's letter, congratulating him on a fight well fought in Oxford. The compliment was misplaced, but the very fact that he had found time to answer was significant. Several weeks later came the call to Downing Street.

Attlee explained Labour's predicament in the House of Lords to Frank and asked him, in view of the likelihood that he would one day inherit his brother's earldom, if he would consider accepting a peerage at once. Frank accepted enthusiastically. Attlee then asked if Frank would agree to become a Lord-in-Waiting, so that he could speak for the government in the House of Lords. It would be the most junior of ministerial ranks. Again Frank accepted. In the space of a couple of weeks he had gone from nowhere to a government post.

While the question of being a Lord-in-Waiting was a new one, the possibility of taking a peerage had been much mulled over following his discussions with Durbin and Dalton. This time he had consulted Elizabeth. He therefore had his reply ready for the Prime Minister. It was one of the defining decisions of his political life. While he was prepared to compromise, accept any way to get into Parliament, Elizabeth initially was implacably opposed. Once he accepted a peerage, she said, there would be no way back to the Commons, no hope of winning a by-election. She had fought the 1935 general election on a pledge to abolish the Lords and regarded it as superfluous. The Commons was where the real action took place. Unless her husband took his place there, he would never wield influence or hold high office. The best he could hope for as a peer, she predicted, was to be Leader of the House of Lords in a Labour cabinet. It would be a poor substitute for heading a major government department. Though the Tories were flexible about giving senior positions to peers, Labour was not.

> It was the House of Commons that to me meant reality and romance [Elizabeth wrote later]. I had lectured endlessly on the grand old men who had operated there and the even grander women who had tried to breach its walls but failed. In a sense I too had failed because I was a woman and I wanted Frank, my alter ego, to succeed. Unprepossessing though I found the central lobby of the House of Commons, decked out as it was with huge marble tailcoats and togas swathing the limbs of Victorian patriarchs, it still gave me a lift of excitement to think that a Gladstone, an O'Connell, a Keir Hardie had trodden these tessellated floors. The House of Lords I had never set eyes on, merely demanding its abolition.[9]

Evan Durbin countered Elizabeth's arguments. Because Edward had not produced an heir, Frank would end up in the House of Lords anyway. Hence any career he might have in the Commons would be blighted. (The possibility of setting peerages aside, as suggested by Waldorf Astor back in the 1910s, was at that time out of the question.) And as a Roman Catholic, Durbin offered, Frank had already saddled himself with a handicap when it came to high office. This was an age when the names of the few Roman Catholic members of the House of Lords were still italicized in Vacher's *Parliamentary Companion*.

The couple came to a decision about the future during a walk around the Dragon School cricket field next to Chadlington Road. Frank admitted he was well aware of the shortcomings of the Lords. One of his standard essays for his politics undergraduates was to discuss the role of second chambers. Yet in the end he and Elizabeth decided that he should accept. It was his only chance to be part of a social revolution about which they had talked, planned and dreamed for years. To sit back as a Christ Church don and see it all happen without having even the small influence that a place in the Lords might offer would be too much. To be in Oxford when the political world revolved around Westminster would be intolerable. To wait five years until the next election, or to pin his hopes on a fortuitous by-election, would be an unendurable ordeal for such a restless figure.

The decision was not made without a tinge of regret. Despite his failure on the hustings, he had been a successful local councillor, and had enjoyed the work of representing a constituency. That avenue would now be forever barred. If he wanted to represent any one group in the Lords in future it would have to be as a self-appointed spokesman. He made sure he would never forget his former constituents by taking as his title Baron Pakenham of Cowley.

In retrospect, Elizabeth believed that they made the right decision. Defeat at Oxford and Durbin's intervention were a happy accident. The Lords was, she suggested, better suited to her husband's increasingly independent line in Christian socialism.[10] There was an element of *post hoc* rationalization in this. Membership of the Lords accelerated his departure from the official party line, already under way when he embraced Catholicism. The less polarized, pragmatic atmosphere of the Lords, where there was a genuine fraternity between members on different sides of the House, allowed him to take up a more singular line. 'I wouldn't have survived in the Commons,' Frank said later. 'To be a top politician you've got to be an egotist, not just to get there but to stay there. Leaders have to show toughness.'[11] Again he sounded like someone making the best of a bad job. His sharp wit would doubtless have made him a formidable opponent in the Commons. While he was not a public platform orator, in the claustrophobic cut-and-thrust environment of the Commons, his sardonic performance would have found a ready and appreciative audience, though he might have faced more ragging than in the polite confines of the Lords, not least for his occasional habit of pronouncing his 'r's as 'v's.

In the short term, membership of the House of Lords greatly accelerated Frank's career. While his rival Hugh Gaitskell had to wait before getting a government job, Frank was up on his feet defending the government's record within minutes of being introduced into the Lords. But before he could take his place on the front bench in 1945, he had to be presented as a Lord-in-Waiting to the King. His title was technically a court appointment, though his role would be a political one.

I had always foolishly assumed that Royalty would begin with something very ordinary and non-committal. Instead, he gazed at me quietly but penetratingly, and after a pause said suddenly, 'Why did you . . . join them?' For a moment I could not for the life of me think what he meant. I was in any case suitably nervous. Could he mean the Catholic Church? No – hardly. It must be the Labour Party – and I realised later it was. It would have been a difficult enough question to answer in any circumstances. I am apt to give the short answer: 'Because I believe that each one of us is of equal and infinite importance in the sight of God.' But that seemed to me, standing there in Buckingham Palace in front of my sovereign, to be liable to smack of impertinence. I stammered out some rather involved account of my political experiences.[12]

At least he didn't make a joke of it, as he might have done on a visit to Cliveden or Hatfield. George VI replied with sympathetic noises, Frank remembered. Evelyn Waugh, however, casts doubts on such a recollection, recording in his diary for February 1946 that Frank had soon afterwards been complaining that 'the King never sees him. He has only seen him once since he has been in office and is not asked to the UNO parties.'[13]

When, on 16 October 1945, Baron Pakenham of Cowley took his place in the Lords, Elizabeth and Antonia watched him from the gallery. At thirty-nine he was the youngest peer to be awarded a title – rather than inherit it – since Beaverbrook in 1916. 'All I can remember is that my father seemed at least forty years younger than anyone else there,' Antonia observed.[14] He enjoyed being the bright young new boy in this elderly environment and quickly made his mark, though not always for his wit but rather with a hefty dose of what might later have been called political correctness. Patrick O'Donovan, a fellow Catholic and an *Observer* journalist, watched him wearing his conscience for all to see at a London restaurant. 'I was with him during rationing at the Gay Hussar. Someone offered him food over and above the ration and he got terribly angry. He thought it immoral.'[15]

Any teething problems in the Lords were soon soothed away under the watchful gaze of the Labour Leader in the Upper Chamber, Lord Addison, a scientist who had been in Lloyd George's 1920 cabinet. During Frank's maiden speech in a debate extending wartime controls over certain basic supplies, he received a kick in the back of the calf from Addison. 'Take your hands out of your pockets,' he rebuked his junior colleague. On another occasion a similarly deft blow was followed by the advice, 'Sit down now. You've got the House with you. You'll lose them if you go on any longer.' His other mentor was the Lord Chancellor, Lord Jowitt. 'He once told me that the secret of advocacy is to find out the worst thing that your opponent can say about your case and then say it yourself in your own way. I may be slightly, but not much, caricaturing when I recall his method of introducing a Bill unwelcome to the Conservatives. "My Lords, I hate this bill. I don't suppose that there is anyone in this House who dislikes it as much as I do. But, My Lords, have we any alternative?"'[16]

Under such tutelage, Frank quickly established a reputation as an effective debater. His early *faux pas* were few and far between. His disregard for detail strengthened his eccentric reputation. 'Ever since I spotted Lord Pakenham, striding out of a Victoria Street shop with a newly-bought collar, unwrapped, in his hand,' John Redfern wrote in the *Daily Express*, 'I have suspected that he was different from the general run of politicians.' Once, when confronted with an unusually full government front bench, Frank took a seat in an adjoining row. Only when he noticed most of the chamber staring at him did he realize that he had sat in the place reserved for the Archbishop of Canterbury.

In his letters to Elizabeth in Oxford he spoke about his excitement at being part of the government, albeit in a minor role. He had been sharing a flat during the week with Nicholas Henderson[17] whom he had met during the war while working for Beveridge. 'We were both ashamed of not being in uniform', Henderson wrote, 'this served as a bond between us.'[18] They rented a studio in Charlotte Street that was once used by Constable.

Back in Oxford, Elizabeth felt underemployed, even with six children to look after. She was appointed to the local Rent Tribunal, an innovation of the Labour government aimed at protecting tenants against their landlords. She would give the occasional lecture on 'Women's place in the New Britain', but such events paled into insignificance next to her husband's accounts of evenings in London spent discussing theology, politics, and the relative merits of the Soviet and capitalist systems with Dick Crossman and Philip Toynbee. Elizabeth would join Frank for ceremonial events; as a Lord-in-Waiting he was expected to attend various court functions – but this was not the political milieu she had desired for the past two decades.

In July 1947, pregnant with their eighth child, she decided after much puzzling – at one stage she put in an offer on a manor house outside Oxford – to uproot and move to the capital. She found a substantial neo-Georgian, Lutyens-style house with an annexe, large garden and tennis court – an invaluable asset in the eyes of her husband – in Linnell Drive in Hampstead Garden Suburb. It had a view of the Heath and was thus part of the Hampstead 'colony', a generic term to describe the cluster of homes of young Labour hopefuls – the Jays, the Gaitskells, the Durbins, the Wilsons and now the Pakenhams – in that area of north-west London.

The house had cost £14,000, a considerable sum by the standards of the day. The couple had lost their other London property – inherited from Uncle Bingo – during the war when structural decay had forced them to sell it at a knock-down price. With Frank's government salary, their small private incomes and an inheritance from Elizabeth's father, they managed to live comfortably, if never lavishly. Much of the awkwardness Frank had felt about his relative prosperity in the early days of his conversion to Labour had now passed.

The loss of her father coincided with Elizabeth's growing interest in religion. Though her husband's conversion had put a great strain on their marriage, prompting in her an angry anti-clericalism, she found herself, almost to her surprise, listening to his views on the subject. Having seen what an important part Catholicism came to play in his life and his politics, she had been forced to reconsider and had slowly mellowed. The loss of her father, with his strict Unitarian views, removed a major psychological obstacle.

It had been the tragically early death of her brother Roger in 1941, caused by a brain tumour, and her despair at his unfulfilled promise that first directed her to thoughts of an after-life. When, soon afterwards, she suffered a miscarriage, possibly of twins, brought on, she believed, by a violent massage for fibrositis, it once again focused her mind on a greater purpose behind this world. That in turn led to sporadic reading of Frank's burgeoning collection of religious books – what she had hitherto described as a 'Chamber of Horrors' and relegated to the bottom shelf of a bookcase in the hallway. Some of the more traditional and dogmatic writers confirmed all her worst prejudices, but others, notably the liberally minded French Catholic scholar Jacques Maritain,[19] came as a pleasant surprise and spurred her on to take up Frank's suggestion that she read the New Testament. John's Gospel in particular appealed to her. When Paddy fell ill with mastoid problems and his fate hung briefly in the balance, Elizabeth found herself turning to prayer.

All the Pakenham children had been christened in the Anglican Church – Judith, Rachel and Michael at a time when their father was Catholic and their mother agnostic. At the start of 1944 Elizabeth took Thomas and Antonia, thus far brought up without any great emphasis on religion, to the High Anglican Church of St Paul's in south Oxford for preparation for their first communion. She accompanied them to church each Sunday and by the autumn of that year was under instruction herself and was received as an Anglican before Christmas.

The Church of England was, however, a halfway house. With others, Frank was a relentless and often foolish evangelist. His conversation about anyone who showed the least interest in his religious beliefs would often include speculation on whether they were 'about to come over' to Rome. In regard of Catholicism, that particular aspect of the zeal of the new convert never faded. With Elizabeth, however, Frank knew not to push her. At her instigation they found themselves talking of prayer and discussed theology. Elizabeth still balked at some cherished Catholic notions – the Virgin Mary remained a problem for her until many years later – but she was bending, partly out of conviction and partly for purely practical reasons. The home-maker could not bear to see her home divided over God.

Each Sunday as the family set off to church, she felt a great emotional wrench as her husband turned one way to go to the Catholic Church and she, Antonia and Thomas the other, to go to St Paul's. Paddy, with a mind of his own and the closest bond to his father, would insist on accompanying Frank. When she discussed her pain at this division in the family with the Anglican Bishop of Oxford, he agreed that it was unnatural. It was Elizabeth, as so often, who had to make the compromise. When she decided to join the Catholic Church, Bishop Kenneth Kirk wrote to her, 'I rejoice that you are both to walk along the same path even though it's not the same as mine.'

After instruction from Father Gervase Mathew, she was received on Easter Sunday, 1946. Frank, predictably, was overjoyed at being a 'household of faith'.[20] The fact that his wife had 'come over' served only to reinforce his own conviction and to increase his eagerness to persuade others to join up. 'My mother could not bear being separated from him in religion,' Antonia said, 'so she had to make the move even if it was on pragmatic grounds. He, on the other hand, had not found that separation difficult.'[21]

Catherine was born in February 1946, and was the first of the Pakenham children to be baptized a Catholic. Her siblings were to follow her, the younger ones as a matter of course. Antonia and Thomas were deemed old enough to make up their own minds.

Antonia did not need, she recalled, to stop to think. She had always wanted to be a Catholic. She transferred to St Mary's, Ascot, a convent boarding school run by the Institute of the Blessed Virgin Mary. Thomas was less wholehearted about conversion and was later to reject Catholicism. He described the events surrounding his mother's conversion as causing a great physical dislocation in his life – he was sent to a Benedictine boarding school – but without altering anything fundamental at home.

It was all very sudden. We moved rapidly from nothing – high agnostic – to Anglicanism. Then we were suddenly told that we were no longer Anglo-Catholics, that we were moving on again. Like Mother Courage our chariot was moving on, and we were becoming Catholics. Antonia asked me if I thought we were ratting. The change meant that we were snatched away from one school and sent to another. As newcomers my parents felt they must be extra conscientious and send us to Catholic schools. But it didn't change the essential character of the family or our relationship with our parents. We didn't suddenly have family prayers. We'd had them before. It didn't change anything.[22]

Change was afoot in Frank's political career. In the autumn of 1946, the Prime Minister reshuffled his government and summoned his Lord-in-Waiting to Downing Street. He offered him the post of Parliamentary Secretary at the Ministry of National Insurance, calculating that, given his Beveridge background, Frank would leap at the chance. The legislation executing the main ideas of the report he had worked on was pending and the job would give him ample opportunity to shine. Confronted with such pressing reasons, Frank said yes, but as he walked back along Whitehall, his doubts grew. It was not so much that he did not want to work on national insurance, rather that there was something else he wanted to do much more. He returned to Downing Street and with what he later saw as extraordinary effrontery and arrogance begged a surprised Attlee to be appointed Under-Secretary of State for War. The memory of his failure as a soldier was still very fresh. When he had been invalided out of the army, Leslie Hore-Belisha,[23] a former Secretary of State for War, had written to him saying, 'if you can't do something in the army, perhaps one day you'll do something for the army'.[24] In the autumn of 1946 Frank saw his chance. Attlee, doubtless slightly taken aback, did not say yes or no at once, but having given the matter some consideration came back and granted his wish.

The Prime Minister cannot have had many junior ministers making such an unusual request, especially at a time when he had a surplus of talented young Labour MPs, held up by the war, eager for ministerial promotion. His indulgence towards Frank can perhaps be explained partly by his own habit, akin to that of Dalton, of encouraging the younger members of his party, but it also seems that he had a particular soft spot for Frank and envisaged a glittering career ahead for him. For his part, Frank later came to rank Attlee alongside de Valera at the top of the list of the men he most admired (though Frank's public defence of de Valera had almost dissuaded Attlee from offering him a peerage in 1945, considering that a man with such opinions must have poor judgement).

Attlee had risen to the leadership of the Labour Party by an accident of history. He was one of the few Labour MPs to survive the 1931 general election. In 1935, following Lansbury's defeat at the party conference, he had been the compromise candidate for the leadership and since then had survived various attempts to unseat him, some of them supported in pre-war years by pro-Cripps figures like Frank. Even after he had delivered victory in the 1945 general election, Attlee had to fight off a challenge by Morrison. Had Morrison succeeded, Frank's career would have been very different. Indeed, he may not have had a political career at all. At a wartime dinner party which he attended with Frank, Morrison gestured at him and said to the hostess: 'Here I am from the lower classes joining the upper classes. He is a member of the upper classes who has joined the lower classes. That always causes trouble.' When pressed on what sort of trouble he meant, Morrison retorted: 'Because he gets keener on the party than the party is on itself.'[25]

Attlee had no time for such class-conscious talk. He came from a well-to-do family, had fought at Gallipoli alongside Frank's father and had shared some of his junior minister's own agonies over reconciling a privileged background with a belief in socialism. Like Frank he had worked among the underprivileged in the East End of London. Furthermore, he was not one of those – like Morrison – who were wary of intellectuals in the party. Attlee was a practical, pragmatic socialist, a position to which Frank had been evolving during the war years. A genuine friendship grew up between the two of them. On one occasion after he had retired, Attlee and his wife Vi took the Pakenhams out to dinner. They went to a restaurant in London's Sloane Square that none of them knew well. 'We had a delightful meal together, but afterwards there was a further moment of embarrassment. He took me aside and asked if I wouldn't mind paying the bill; he would give me his cheque for the amount. "Afraid they wouldn't know me here." He had been Prime Minister . . . but had no more sense of his own importance than if he had been some young Parliamentary candidate.'[26]

Frank, who was one of the few senior Labour figures who continued to visit Attlee right up to his death, liked to point to a Christian side in Attlee that gave him moral authority. 'Clement Attlee was an ethical giant, soaked in Christianity,' he eulogized. 'It was an old-fashioned public school type of Christianity, a tremendous sense of obligation towards the underprivileged.'[27] Yet such a description overlooks Attlee's own denial of Christianity. Questioned by his biographer, Kenneth Harris, he replied, 'I'm one of those people incapable of religious experience. Believe in the ethics of Christianity. Can't believe the mumbo jumbo.'[28]

Newly installed at the War Office, Frank served under Fred Bellenger, the Secretary of State, and the Financial Secretary, John Freeman,[29] a fellow protégé of Dalton. One of the Under-Secretary of State's tasks was liaison with the senior generals. Part of Frank thrilled at the prospect of meeting with those, like his father, who had led their men in battle. Yet another side of him shrank from the encounter because of his own military failure. He decided the best policy was honesty and never made a secret of his own war record. It was almost as if he wanted the generals to absolve him from his sin of omission. Above all, it was Field Marshal Lord Montgomery[30]

157

who performed the act. They would dine together and when the junior minister had to attend an army staff college, 'Monty' was at his side for support.

Among Frank's duties in the Lords was to speak about British policy in occupied Germany. He had long been an admirer of the Jewish publisher and founder of the Left Book Club, Victor Gollancz.[31] During the war years, Gollancz had played a leading role in awakening the British public to the full horror of Nazism and the concentration camps. In the immediate aftermath of the conflict, Gollancz was one of an influential group of voices criticizing British policy in occupied Germany and what he saw as the unnecessary suffering and privations of the German people. Frank stood up on 6 November 1946 to defend the government's policy in the face of such attacks. He had not set foot in the country since the end of hostilities, but postwar Germany was, he conceded, 'a tragic mess', adding, 'a mess of her [Germany's] own making. God forgive me if to say that is to speak unfairly of a people who are suffering as they are suffering now.'[32]

Mentioning God's name did not disguise the fundamental lack of Christianity in a policy designed to wreak revenge on the German people, Gollancz wrote in the *News Chronicle* several days later. The minister's speech had been 'a model of feebleness and futility', Gollancz charged. 'Have these Christian statesmen of ours the slightest idea of what is going on in Germany? Apparently not, for if they had they would not make the idiotic statements that cause such consternation.' In the city of Düsseldorf, in the British occupied zone, Gollancz reported, people were living on between 400 and 1,000 calories per day. 'Four hundred – and I have been in many homes where this has been the daily ration – is half the Belsen rate.' Gollancz's message was not a universally popular one. Many British people felt that the Germans must be punished. At a time of rationing at home, they were not prepared to feel sorry for the vanquished Germans. Forgiveness was out of the question.

However, Frank was stung by Gollancz's criticisms. His own reading had convinced him that forgiveness was one of the cardinal Christian virtues. He felt that as a Christian he was being challenged to forgive the German people. He set to work at once in gathering exact details of what was happening in the British zone of occupied Germany. When he discovered that there was substance in Gollancz's charge that Britain was allowing the Germans to starve, he wrote to Clement Attlee expressing his own difficulty in defending the government position unless steps were taken to improve the situation. The Prime Minister, if he had not already realized, saw that he had a tender conscience on his hands. He summoned his young minister and listened with interest to his plea, but little changed over the severe winter of 1946–7. As well as shortages of food, there was little fuel for heating and an acute lack of housing.

In February Frank was on his feet again in the Lords, defending the government's policy of keeping German prisoners of war in Britain so that they could do reparation work before being sent home. The policy came under fierce attack from Bishop Bell of Chichester,[33] often a lonely voice during the war years in questioning government conduct of the campaign and its insistence on Germany's unconditional surrender. The argument Frank had to put forward was that by doing agricultural labour in this country, German PoWs were contributing to the common task of feeding both Britain and their own country. He was far from convinced by his own words and made his unhappiness known in government circles.

In March he travelled to Austria and saw at first hand people who were desperate, starving and without adequate shelter. His troubled conscience led him, on his return, to bring up the matter repeatedly with more senior colleagues. In April, he was called to Downing Street. Attlee offered him the chance to do something about a policy in which he clearly had little faith. Frank was appointed Chancellor of the Duchy of Lancaster, working directly under the Foreign Secretary to run the British zones of both Germany and Austria. It was to be his finest hour in government.

NINE

The Minister for Germany

Once the Allies had decided upon a policy of forcing the Nazis to surrender unconditionally, it was inevitable that after defeating Hitler's armies the whole of Germany must be occupied. In June 1945 the Allied Control Council in Berlin, made up of Britain, the United States, Russia and France, took on responsibility for running Germany in the absence of a national government. Joint decisions were to be put into effect in each occupying power's zone. The British oversaw the north and west of Germany, the industrial heartland. Berlin, the capital of the Third Reich, was split between the occupying powers despite sitting in the middle of the Russian zone.

From the start, joint action proved impossible. While all four Allies agreed that National Socialism had to be eliminated and the German war machine permanently disabled, little else was decided. There was talk from some – notably the US Secretary to the Treasury Henry Morgenthau[1] – that Germany's industrial base should be smashed, its economic power thereby removed and the country turned over to pasture. Others wanted to see the Third Reich split up into three separate states so as to cripple the German nation for ever. Another viewpoint suggested that the Allies should continue to run Germany for up to fifty years.

After the unhappy experience of 1919, when attempts to get financial compensation out of a defeated Germany had proved counterproductive, the Allies agreed in principle to take reparations in kind, dismantling German industry and shipping plant and machinery back home at the same time as seizing a percentage of remaining manufacturing output. German prisoners-of-war were to be used for ten years to work on reconstruction. The Russians, and to a lesser extent the French, were keener than their Allies on the idea of reparations. Unlike Britain and America, they had suffered Nazi occupation. Their determination to take their revenge on Germany, and not just in their own zone, was one of the causes of the destitution that Victor Gollancz had detailed and which greeted Frank when he arrived in the British zone. The produce of the industrial Ruhr in the British zone was a special target for Moscow and Paris.

Ever the enthusiast for a new challenge, Frank arranged for news of his appointment to be delayed for a couple of weeks to give him time to brush up on what little German he had already grasped in between tennis matches on his pre-war trip to Austria. His chosen method was to study the New Testament for half an hour each morning – a devotion he had taken up on becoming a Catholic – in German. With his usual sharp eye for the value of publicity, when his new job was revealed to the press he let it be known also that he was enrolling his two eldest children, Thomas and Antonia, in German classes. 'It was the most eccentric, horrifying idea at the time,' recalled Antonia. 'People were so anti-German that they talked of killing dachshunds in the street. When I told Mutter Hilda at St Mary's Ascot that I wanted to learn German, she cried and said, "I never thought I would teach that language again".'[2] The press reacted with interest to his appointment. 'Two things only are certain,' said a profile in the *Observer*, edited by David Astor. 'If he fails he will confess to failure. And if he is impeded he will resign.'

Frank's rushed preparations were interrupted by a bout of gastric flu. The family had not yet moved into their Hampstead home, so he received a stream of visitors at his sick bed at the Athenaeum, the patrician setting sitting rather uneasily with the democratic necessity to consult, a suitable image for much of Frank's ministerial life. Never one to bear grudges, he made sure that Victor Gollancz was among those who briefed him. Gollancz's book, *Darkest Germany*, had done much to alert British public opinion to the food, fuel and housing shortages that were afflicting a demoralized German people in the severe winter of 1946–7. 'Victor Gollancz', Frank said later in a tribute, 'did more than any other single man after the last war to awaken the British conscience with regard to the suffering of the German people, especially of the inhabitants of the British zone of occupation. [He] attained an ardour of prophetic fire unequalled among the British public in my lifetime.' Gollancz's biographer, Ruth Dudley Edwards, had a more pragmatic take on those meetings in April 1947: 'Pakenham had a tender conscience and such people were vulnerable to Victor.'[3]

Gollancz and others of like mind had set up the Save Europe Now campaign, aimed at changing Allied policy towards Germany and rescuing its people from starvation. The challenge that Gollancz set Frank was tailor-made to inspire him. Bearing in mind the minister's own views and experience of British rule in Ireland, how could the occupation policy in Germany be carried out without stifling the natural feelings and just demands of its inhabitants? Were the Germans not, like the Irish before the 1921 treaty, prisoners and the British minister, by dint of superior force, the prison governor? Gollancz counselled Frank to aim in this potential battleground for a principle of partnership. To many of his officials' and colleagues' alarm, Frank veered more towards taking the side of the prisoners.

He set off at once for Berlin, where he was to meet the Foreign Secretary, Ernest Bevin, for a briefing about government policy in Germany. Bevin had been to Moscow, trying to persuade the Russians, with little success, to cooperate in reaching joint decisions over Germany on the Control Council. As the Russians extracted their pound of flesh, in the process leaving Germany bankrupt and starving, it fell to the British and Americans to send in emergency supplies to feed the local population. While Bevin had not yet entirely despaired of an agreement being reached – that possibility was finally extinguished at a Foreign Ministers' meeting in London in November – the American delegate, General Marshall,[4] left Moscow convinced that the Russians were stalling in the hope that the ensuing chaos would hasten the spread of Communism across Europe. Back in America, Marshall began drawing up his plan to save Western Europe from the Soviet menace.

With Bevin reflecting on this international impasse on his journey from Moscow to Berlin, Frank had already arrived and caused quite a stir. When his official plane landed at Berlin's Gatow Airport, he was exceedingly fired up for the challenge ahead. 'My sole preoccupation', he recalled, 'was to set foot on German soil and to get on with the job. When the plane came to a standstill, there seemed to my heated fancy to be some delay in pushing forward the steps. Without premeditation or reflection I performed what the *Daily Mail* described as "the Pakenham leap" – quite a number of feet to the ground. At the moment of my leap, however, the steps arrived at a good round pace and collided somewhat violently with my face. My glasses were knocked off, a small cut opened in my forehead, and taken all round it was a somewhat unusual arrival for a British minister in an occupied territory.'[5]

Quite what the assembled dignitaries made of the spectacle is not recorded. A more eccentric, less statesman-like gesture is hard to imagine. The press loved it. Consciously or not at the moment he abandoned protocol, Frank made sure he appeared on the front pages the next day. The bump on his head had almost as dramatic an effect as that sustained at the Mosley meeting. At home his old friends read their papers in amusement. 'Frank's besetting sin as far as my father was concerned', remarked Marina Warner, 'was his love of fanfare and of the ventilation of headlines.'[6]

Having prepared no speech, and without consulting his boss, Ernest Bevin, or indeed any senior British official in Germany, Frank proceeded, with blood trickling down his face, to outline British policy to the assembled crowd. 'I come to Germany in a spirit of goodwill. I am a believer in Christianity, both as regards justice and mercy. In this job I shall attempt to apply Christian principles, not forgetting the past but with my eyes mainly on the future. I am particularly interested in the youth of Germany.'[7]

As a personal credo, it was an accurate picture of his own beliefs and highly individual approach to politics. It was, one observer suggested, the sort of sentiment that could only come from someone who had not faced the Germans on the battlefield. As a statement of government policy, it was ill considered. In a tense international situation, Bevin had no intention of letting Britain be seen as siding with the Germans.

The destitution and hopelessness that greeted Frank when he travelled around the British zone only confirmed his determination to speak up for the Germans. 'The only policy is one of friendliness,' he told his officials as he toured the occupied lands. It was one thing to read the statistics: living standards had dropped by 74 per cent since 1932, the slump year paving Hitler's way to power. It was another to see them at first hand. In his pre-war wrestling with the relative claims of conservatism and socialism, and indeed in his work with Beveridge, Frank the don had operated at an intellectual and cerebral level, weighing up arguments and theories. In Germany as a politician he was greeted by hundreds of individual stories of tragedy. It was as if the people of the British zone became his constituents and he took them to his heart with the same dedication that he had shown to the people of Cowley. Yet he was in a curiously ambiguous position, as both their representative and, as a British minister and representative of the British people, their oppressor.

'It did not make much difference to the general public who was in charge of the Control Commission', recalled Elisa Boness many years later in a letter to Antonia Fraser.[8] Boness was a twenty-year-old German working as an interpreter in Hamburg when Frank was appointed.

I soon realised when I heard Lord Pakenham's rhetoric that changes would be afoot. All German people had up to then been condemned as subhuman by the army of occupation. We had nothing to look forward to and the flame of hope had been truly extinguished. Yet he spoke to us not like a vengeful judge, but implied that things had to change. He almost dispelled the notion that we would be steamrollered into the ground and Germany erased from the map of Europe which had been a serious consideration. He suggested that Europe would be a better place with a cleansed and newly constructed Germany. In short he gave us something to work towards. His words were the beginning of German people pulling themselves up again. Those of us who remember will never forget.

At times his emotional response, working up from personal observations towards general principles, exposed Frank to the charge of lack of political judgement. It certainly reduced his effectiveness in directing the British cabinet. At one meeting with German students at Göttingen, he listened to their tales of woe and promised them immediate action. When he instructed his officials to act upon those promises, they had to explain that it was much more complicated and that with the best will in the world they couldn't hope for much progress. That 'tender conscience' in Germany in 1947 was to make him a thorn in the side of bureaucracy.

One of the first cities that the new minister visited was Düsseldorf. He was met by local German politicians, including the Christian Democrat leader and future Chancellor Konrad Adenauer, and led round the ruins of the bombed-out centre. They stopped off at a school where the children recited poems to their guest. Moved by what he saw, he told them, in what he admits were the first words that came to his lips: 'Never believe that the whole world is against you. Never believe that England is against you. There is much goodwill towards Germany in England. I have seven children of my own. When you grow up I hope that you will come to England and meet my own and other English children.'9 The children then sang his favourite prayer, Psalm 51, the *Miserere*, with its message of forgiveness.

Such heartfelt words were neither an accurate portrait of official policy nor of British public opinion – the latter unconvinced of the need to send food to their recent enemies at a time when basic foodstuffs were rationed at home and therefore certainly not in the mood for forgiveness. Frank recalled that after his impromptu speech to the children, his civil servants grew noticeably irritated. This was not how they expected their minister to behave. They considered he had gone native, but he was not to be put off. He was on a mission. He told his friend Douglas Woodruff,[10] editor of the Catholic journal the *Tablet*, that when he arrived in Germany, he had a feeling of *déjà vu*. It was like the Dublin of his childhood, a people suffering under British rule. He identified the downtrodden Germans with the Irish. Where his involvement had been too late to ensure that the British, in the wake of the First World War, showed a measure of justice to the Irish, he believed that in Germany's case, he had a chance to avoid repeating past errors.

In the ensuing year he was to travel to Germany twenty-six times in all, an average of one trip every two weeks. 'Tearing up and down on foot, in official cars under military convoy, in the omnipresent aeroplane; plunging down mines; exploring the innermost recesses of internment camps; plodding through endless ruins to discover the precise number of calories consumed by pitiable families, I seemed unable to rest and unable to tire.'[11] Perhaps from tiredness, perhaps through his eminently quotable remarks, perhaps from his Christian conviction to speak the truth, Frank was becoming outspoken enough to make Whitehall blush. In a conversation with journalists, which he believed was off the record, he described conditions in the British zone as 'appalling', adding, 'I pray for the Germans night and morning.' It was of course precisely what he would do, but rising politicians with sensitive missions were supposed to be diplomatic with the truth. The next day, he flew back to London to be greeted with banner headlines: 'Conditions in British zone appalling. Pakenham prays for Germans.'

At times his Catholicism caused embarrassment to his officials. When he paid a courtesy call on Cardinal Frings of Cologne, his slavish devotion to Catholic ritual triumphed over any sense of his own importance as the representative of the occupying power. 'When I saw him,' one official said later, 'a Minister of the Crown, going down on his knee and kissing that man's ring, I wished that the earth could have opened and swallowed me.' Behind the flurry of activity and gestures of goodwill and forgiveness, though, did Frank achieve a great deal in Germany? On the ground he was responsible for 26,000 civil servants. Though those in the ranks dealing each day with destitute Germans were sympathetic to Frank's approach, the more senior officials were alarmed at the independent line that their new chief was taking and did their best to frustrate some of his best intentions. While the Military Governor of the British zone, Sholto Douglas, was anxious to relinquish his post and placed few obstacles in Frank's path, his civilian counterpart, Brian Robertson, had little respect for the minister's unorthodox attitudes and was prone to turn to Ernest Bevin for support, especially on financial matters where the junior minister's freedom of manoeuvre was limited. Frank did, however, find an invaluable ally in the American Military Governor, General Lucius Clay, who shared his growing concern about the shortsightedness of the reparations policy. A destitute Germany would be either an eternal burden on the West or a magnet for communist subversion.

The real block to Frank's effectiveness was the Foreign Secretary, Ernest Bevin, who had an instinctive antipathy for the Germans that accurately reflected the contemporary prejudice of many British people. When Frank tried to persuade the Foreign Secretary to echo some of his words of encouragement as a gesture to the German people, Bevin retorted, 'I'm not going to get sentimental over them. I'll leave that to you.'[12] Bevin believed that the Germans only respected strength and that offering them compassion was merely appearing weak and earning their contempt. It was not only personal prejudice that stopped Bevin backing his enthusiastic colleague in his crusade. While Frank had only his German constituents to consider, Bevin was playing a delicate balancing game between Washington and Moscow over the composition of the postwar world political map. Germany was the immediate matter under discussion but Bevin had always to consider a wider picture. While he and Frank shared a conviction that cooperation with the Soviets would ultimately be impossible, Bevin was reluctant to give up on his attempts to play Moscow off against Washington and so keep Britain's independent foreign policy.

Britain controlled four German regions: North-Rhine Westphalia, with a population as large as the Netherlands and encompassing both the industrial complex of the Ruhr and its agricultural hinterland, Lower Saxony, Schleswig-Holstein and Hamburg. The most immediate problem was the shortage of food. The lack of cooperation between the Allies in their zones, plus the handing over of a large chunk of eastern Germany to Poland, meant that whole swathes of the traditional agricultural areas were cut off from the British zone. Compounding the crisis, the western regions saw the influx of an estimated nine million refugees from the east, a combination of those fearful of falling under Soviet rule and ethnic Germans, such as those expelled from the Sudetenland in 1945. The scant food supplies in the British zone were being hoarded by farmers, unwilling to sell their produce in exchange for a German currency that was worthless, thanks to the Russians' inflationary habit of printing marks in the east to pay their soldiers.

When Frank arrived in Germany the people of the US and UK zones were being kept alive on a subsistence diet of 1.5 million tons of food imports grudgingly paid for by British and American taxpayers, as, with German industry in tatters, there was no other money to cover the cost. All the coal the German miners, starving and disheartened, were producing was shipped to France as reparations. In the meantime the Germans had no fuel to heat their homes or run the trains. With an economist's eye Frank soon came to realize that the Germans would never be able to support themselves until they had a stronger currency. That would only happen when reparations stopped bleeding their industry. It was principally over the question of dismantling German factories that he took his stand against his own government, though he did play a supporting role in pressing for and planning currency reform. The British government, pushed by the Russians and French in particular over reparations, had agreed reluctantly to a list of industrial complexes that were to be dismantled. Bevin and the Americans were unwilling as yet to break ranks with the Russians. Germany could be kept down, and peace therefore assured, they calculated, only with Soviet cooperation.

Frank and his officials were for once united in having little stomach for the task, but their complaints cut little ice at the Foreign Office. He did not carry sufficient weight in government circles to get the policy blocked. He could only chip away at the edges, ensuring that dismantling in the British zone was carried out on a smaller scale than elsewhere. Despite his efforts, 1,636 factories disappeared in the British and American zones alone, and Germany's merchant marine was seized as part of reparations. Looking on helplessly, he became more and more convinced that British policy was fundamentally flawed not only in its inhuman treatment of the Germans, but also in its geopolitical ambitions. By concentrating on the recent past and the need to hold down Germany, Bevin was underestimating, in Frank's opinion, the real enemy to freedom and peace, the Soviet Union. Leaving Germany destitute as a punishment for its wartime crimes may have satisfied a widespread desire for revenge, but was simply allowing Russia and its supporters to gain more and more influence.

The Foreign Secretary was not blind to Soviet schemes, and his principal private secretary, Frank Roberts, later wrote that as early as the autumn of 1946 Bevin had grown disillusioned with attempts to work with the Soviets and was leaning more heavily on the Americans.[13] Yet Bevin did not share the suspicion and dislike of the Soviets that Frank had been developing in the war years, fuelled increasingly by the virulent anti-Soviet Communism of the Catholic Church, and which, with his posting to Germany, became a lifelong antipathy.

From the entry of the Soviets into the war on the Allied side in 1941, Frank had been wary of their true motives. He was much influenced by his friend Michael de la Bedoyere,[14] editor of the *Catholic Herald*, who acknowledged the *realpolitik* behind the alliance with the Russians, but held that the Soviets could never be friends of the West. In a leader published in 1941 (which so infuriated Churchill that he considered serving a closure notice on the *Catholic Herald* under wartime regulations) de la Bedoyere wrote: 'We do protest as strongly as we can against any treaty with a power whose avowed policy remains the spread of godless Marxism by inciting world revolution.' Newly converted to Catholicism and switching his allegiances within the Labour movement from the communist-infiltrated left wing to a more centrist Christian Socialist position, Frank endorsed de la Bedoyere's warning and carried his suspicion of the Soviets to his post in Germany. The support the Catholic editor gave to the Save Europe Now movement only increased Frank's respect for his opinion.

In the eastern zone of Germany occupied by the Russians, communists were given special preference in local elections and moderate Social Democrats were browbeaten into an alliance with them. Frank was convinced that the Soviet gaze was spreading across the whole of Germany. He tried to make Bevin and his cabinet colleagues see that the West could not suppress the Russians and the Germans simultaneously. If they wanted a bulwark against the menace of Soviet-style Communism consuming the continent, they needed a strong, united Germany. They may agree in principle, but he tried to warn them that at grassroots level punishing the Germans and keeping them on the poverty line effectively meant pushing them into the arms of the Soviets.

As Frank grew more frustrated at the failure to take this on board, Bevin reacted to each new outburst from his junior colleague – whom he insisted on calling 'Pake-en-ham' – with mounting irritation. Despite the vast gulf between them in terms of up-bringing – Bevin was illegitimate and grew up in great poverty in the West Country – and over policy, Frank maintained a loyalty in public to the Foreign Secretary. Evelyn Waugh even describes him at one of their meetings as 'in a daze of hero-worship of Mr Ernest Bevin'.[15]

Bevin, for his part, viewed Frank with a mixture of respect, irritation and amusement. During the meeting of the Foreign Ministers of the four occupying powers in December 1947, which signalled the progressive breakdown of cooperation in policy towards their respective zones, Frank accompanied Bevin to a dinner at the Russian Embassy. Molotov, the Soviet Foreign Minister, leant over and asked, 'Are you a Marxist, Lord Pakenham?'

'No,' he replied. 'I have studied Karl Marx a good deal, but I am anything but a Marxist.'

'I could hardly expect to find a good Marxist in the House of Lords,' the ambassador retorted.

'That's just where you're wrong,' Bevin interrupted. 'The House of Lords are the only people in England who've got time to read Karl Marx.'[16]

Such friendly banter could not, however, disguise the fact that Frank was failing to convince Bevin of the need to halt reparations at once. Neither was the cabinet moved by his protestations. In her diary Elizabeth recorded a typical exchange of the time. 'Frank had been reported as praying for Germans during the food shortage. Bevin in Cabinet: "We've got Stafford [Cripps] and now Frank praying for the Germans, so we're neglecting no source of supply".'[17]

Frank was faced with an obvious choice, already outlined by the *Observer*: resign over a strategy he found short-sighted or remain and try to ameliorate its worst excesses from within. He decided to consult his confessor, Father D'Arcy, for guidance but found that the Jesuit had a much clearer view than his pupil of the demarcation between matters political and matters spiritual. Spiritual advisers could not give guidance on resignation from the government. Frank learnt not to ask again.

Despite realizing the brief storm of publicity his resignation would cause, and the pressure it would place on the British government, he calculated that he would do more for the Germans in practical terms by fighting from inside Whitehall. It was not an entirely altruistic decision. When he spoke to Evan Durbin of resignation, his old friend pointed out that while the party was tolerant of dissidents and eccentrics within its ranks, resignation from a Labour government was regarded as an unforgivable step. You could battle and criticize from within, but to resign was to injure not just the party but the whole cause, the movement, in a public way. Frank's political career would be at an end. The example of Ramsay MacDonald and Jimmy Thomas,[18] who had abandoned Labour in 1931 and been ostracized by the movement thereafter for their act of betrayal, was still fresh in people's minds. Only those with a substantial following, like Stafford Cripps, could afford to dice with political death and live to tell the tale.

Frank tried to rally support from within the Labour movement to save Germany from death by dismantling. Colleagues like Douglas

Jay described the government as generally upholding the notion that, whatever the vagaries of British public opinion, the Germans had to be fed. 'When Frank started to talk of forgiveness, though,' Jay said, 'it tended to get people's backs up.'[19] Denis Healey, then Secretary of Labour's International Department, saw that Frank was 'quite unpopular with a lot of the party' on account of his pro-German stance. 'I was very pro-German in the sense that I had no anti-German feeling as such. But I think the basic thing with Frank is that he always takes things a bit far. Still if you are a minister your job is to promote what you see as the interests of the policy you represent. And that often makes you unpopular with colleagues. Bevin was a sort of hard-headed, no-nonsense trade unionist and Frank was a committed but unworldly Christian.'[20]

The ultimate avenue of appeal was to Clement Attlee. On numerous occasions Frank sent impassioned pleas to the Prime Minister to save Germany, adding a threat of resignation. Attlee, according to Elizabeth, 'would send one of his terse replies, which totally ignored Frank's threats and generally ran something like this: "My dear Frank, Thank you for writing. I have noted your points. Yours ever. Clem."'[21] On another occasion, Frank attempted to deliver his resignation to Attlee at his room in the House of Commons only to be interrupted by a carefully stage-managed division bell. When the two men returned after voting, Attlee changed the subject and all talk of resignation 'lapsed through mutual inanition'.

Attlee may have lived to regret the day he appointed Frank to Germany, but the Prime Minister was nothing if not a shrewd manager, and he cannot have been surprised at his protégé's independent line on Germany. In fact, his passionate commitment may well have been exactly what Attlee intended. As Chancellor of the Duchy of Lancaster, Frank's freedom for manoeuvre was relatively small. He could only influence everyday affairs. The larger decisions were made by the much more pragmatic Bevin in conjunction with the Russians and the Americans, to whom postwar Britain was deeply in debt. Frank's command of the newspaper headlines gave an exaggerated impression of his powers.

After all, he was a new, relatively untried and distinctly unworldly minister, and a member of the House of Lords. He may have had influential sponsors within the party, including Attlee himself, but it is unlikely that the Prime Minister would have entrusted the task of shaping British policy in Germany to one so inexperienced and unpredictable.

In Germany, too, people began to grow suspicious of the British minister. He arranged a representative gathering in the Opera House in Düsseldorf to try to put as good a gloss as possible on the dismantling policy. Sitting on the platform in front of a Union Jack, flanked by two officials, he tried to explain the case for a measure of reparations and restriction of German industry that might be used in warfare. It was not an argument he endorsed in his heart. His audience showed their disaffection by universal rustling and shuffling of their feet. While such displays made little impact on the cabinet, they did damage his standing in the British zone. 'That afternoon a certain kind of reputation I had acquired in Germany, that of a man about to achieve marvels, disappeared for good,' he wrote in sadness.[22]

Bevin grew ever more exasperated. After a difference of opinion on currency reform, he sighed, 'You do press me a bit hard, Frank, you really do.' In April of 1948 Frank injured his Achilles tendon and was laid up in Hampstead. Attlee came to call. 'I think it is about time you had a department of your own. I've got civil aviation in mind.'[23] Bevin had been applying pressure. Frank did not know whether to rejoice or cry. It was as if a burden was being lifted off his shoulders and promotion would be judged a mark of his success in Germany. In career terms he was being rewarded. Yet he was also being taken off the case, booted upstairs, a blow softened only a little when he was named a Privy Councillor. He felt that he was abandoning the German people and his moral obligations to them.

He managed to assuage his conscience by continuing to visit Germany regularly, attending for example the reopening of Cologne cathedral in the summer of 1948 and by asking awkward questions of his government colleagues about policy there. However, that sense of an uncompleted task stayed with him for many years. As he later remarked, 'I hope to be remembered in Germany not for my achievement but for my endeavour.'[24] He failed to achieve the goals that he set himself: the political one of an end to dismantling and the moral one of getting the British people to forgive the Germans, but they were arguably far too ambitious for one so junior. And there were successes. He oversaw, on behalf of his government, the effective economic and political merger of the British and American zones, a cooperation that was to presage the foundation of the Federal Republic of Germany in the West. The task had already been under way when he took up his responsibilities and continued after he left, but he had played a significant part in it.

Attlee's decision to transfer him came at the outset of the Berlin Airlift. It proved a turning point in history. The Four Power idea of the victors sharing control of Germany was abandoned and replaced by the concept of America and Western Europe aligning in a common front against Soviet aggression. The Soviets' designs on the whole of Berlin and their suspicions of the economic cooperation between the British and Americans led them to block western supply routes into Berlin. Rather than hand over the people of the city to rule by Soviet puppets, British and American planes kept the 2.25 million people in Berlin's western zones supplied for eleven months. Though Frank was about to leave his post, Bevin rated what he had achieved there enough to send him out to Berlin at once to reassure German public opinion. 'I like Berlin,' he told his audience with the full backing of the Foreign Secretary, 'and we have no intention of leaving it.' It did not have quite the impact of '*Ich bin ein Berliner*', but expressed the same sentiment.

On 20 June 1948, a couple of months after Frank had moved on, the currency reform he had worked on came into effect. The western zones became one economic unit and, with German faith in their currency restored, food began to reappear in markets. When he attended the opening of Cologne cathedral in August, he noticed the difference at once. By that stage, too, western German industry, freed of the Russians' insatiable demands for reparations and bolstered by the Marshall Plan, was beginning its rapid climb to European hegemony.

While he played only a supporting role in both the Berlin Airlift and West German economic revival, his involvement in the political reconstruction of first the British zone, then by association the eventual West Germany, was crucial. The Four Powers had agreed at Potsdam in July 1945 that Germany should be helped along the road to democracy. However, there were different biases involved in seeing the process through. The Russians wanted to encourage communists and socialists under Walter Ulbricht to form the Socialist Unity Party, with Soviet patronage in the east. Frank was quick to see the threat this movement might pose if it gained ground in the western zones. He gave his backing to two parties: the anti-Nazi, anti-Communist Christian Democratic Union, which intended to contest elections all over Germany under the twin banners of religion and democracy; and its secular rival, the Social Democratic Union.

With the Americans, Frank handed over local powers to elected representatives in his zone. Thoughts of a fifty-year occupation were soon forgotten. Aneurin Bevan[25] had argued that Frank's appointment to Germany was a mistake because as a Catholic he would favour the Christian Democrats at the expense of Labour's natural allies, the Social Democrats. However, instead Frank developed a good relationship with Schumacher and Arnold, the SDU leaders, as well as Adenauer of the Christian Democrats. In fact the socialists won three of the four local *Länder* in the British zone.

Of the German elected representatives, Kurt Schumacher was the least favourably disposed to the British minister. As a fellow socialist, he was disappointed that Frank worked with the Americans – to Schumacher the epitome of capitalism – instead of joining him in precipitating a proletarian revolution. Frank's fear of the Russians made such a course unthinkable. Schumacher's violent anti-Catholicism – he once called the Vatican 'the fifth occupying power' in Germany – gave them little in common.

Carl Arnold was much better disposed and held a farewell dinner for Frank in Düsseldorf, attended by leaders of German industry, a mark of their respect for a minister whom they had recognized as on their side. Hans Boeckler, the trade union leader, told him, with tears in his eyes, that he would not be forgotten. (One of Frank's lasting achievements in Germany was the encouragement and support he gave to setting up afresh the trade union movement.) Then Arnold stood up to speak, and praised Frank as a friend of Germany. Arnold remained bitterly disappointed, though, at the eventual division of Germany into East and West, and recognized that the British had, by abandoning attempts to placate the Soviets, brought about this partition. Frank was convinced they had had little choice.

Of all the German politicians he dealt with, he was closest to Konrad Adenauer.[26] The future Chancellor and founding father of West Germany had been Lord Mayor of Cologne in the pre-war period and an implacable anti-Nazi. He regained the post in 1945 after the fall of Hitler, but the British dismissed him six months later and banned him from politics. His refusal to fall in with the dismantling of his country made him a character they could do without. Just as he had worked to restore de Valera's reputation from that of dangerous opponent to a statesman with whom the British government could do business, Frank forged a bond with Adenauer after that first meeting in Düsseldorf. He rejected the words of warning from his officials, partly for pragmatic reasons. Adenauer was the elected leader of the CDU and the British therefore had to work with him. Also, the two men shared a belief in the urgent need to rebuild Germany. But the personal sympathy between them should not be underestimated. Both were fervent Catholics, and that immediately created a bond. Both, while regretting the division of Germany, accepted philosophically that there was little they could do about it. Moreover, Frank admired Adenauer's determination in standing up for his country, at the same time as admitting the consequences of the defeat of a regime he had despised. At a conference of European powers in The Hague in the spring of 1948, attended by Frank, Adenauer led the German delegation.

[He] told me afterwards that he and his colleagues had been deeply touched by the fact that Mr Churchill had gone out of his way to receive him personally. 'I wanted', he said, 'to tell Mr

Churchill that I and all of us owed our lives to him – we were Hitler's prisoners, and but for Mr Churchill we would not be alive today. I wanted to tell him that, and to express our deep gratitude.' 'And you did so?' I asked. 'No,' he replied, 'I did not. I knew that the Germans are sometimes said to grovel in defeat. Mr Churchill has described us as always being at your throat or at your feet, and I did not feel that I would be serving my country's interests if I had appeared fawning or fulsome in the moment of national humiliation.'[27]

Besides encouraging the restoration of democracy in western Germany, Frank also placed a heavy emphasis on the need to rebuild its education system. He worked closely with Robert Birley,[28] the head of Charterhouse, who was educational adviser in the British zone. As a don, Frank knew the value of education. His first, emotional visit to the school in Düsseldorf made sure, within his limited control of the budget, that the provision of books and writing materials had a high priority.

If he won plaudits within Germany for his work, there were those in Britain who considered his spell there the zenith of his political career. It was as minister responsible for the British zone that he made his first significant impact on the political scene. The press, from the moment of the 'Pakenham leap' onwards, were behind him. The *Spectator*'s verdict on his spell in Germany was that he had been 'striving with much gallantry and some success to put some heart into Germany'. Among his peers within and without the Labour Party, Frank's crusade did not go unnoticed or unappreciated. Michael Foot,[29] who worked with Victor Gollancz in the Save Europe Now movement, felt that 'both that campaign and Frank's outspoken stance prepared the way in some measure for the Marshall Plan. I'm not saying that without them there would never have been a Marshall Plan, but that we were doing before what Marshall did later. There was a real danger in 1945 that, thanks to people like Frank, wasn't allowed to turn into deep starvation.'

Churchill, too, admired Frank's mettle in standing up for what he believed in. At a Buckingham Palace Garden Party during his period in Germany, Frank was buttonholed by the former Prime Minister. 'I am glad', he said, 'that there is one mind suffering for the miseries of Germany, one English mind suffering for the miseries of Germany.'[30] Lord Carrington,[31] then a young Tory politician, was another impressed by his courage over Germany. 'It was at a moment when the Germans were not the flavour of the month, so to speak, but Frank showed a remarkable farsightedness about Germany and Germany's position in the future. And he was magnanimous. He had a very great magnanimity and understanding.'[32]

His work in Germany led Frank into associations with other groups concerned for the reconstruction of Europe. Among them was Christian Action, founded in Oxford by Canon John Collins.[33] Frank was later to become a loyal patron of the organization, which graduated from preaching reconciliation with the Germans in the 1940s to opposing nuclear weapons and apartheid in the 1950s and 1960s. When Christian Action protested about the treatment of German prisoners-of-war in Britain and the delay in repatriating them, Collins turned to Frank for support in lobbying the government and found the minister sympathetic. Attlee was persuaded to relent and accelerated the process for sending many PoWs home.

'What Frank would dearly have liked to have been', Jon Snow,[34] the political journalist, once remarked, 'is a medieval prelate with enormous temporal powers plus the ability to marry and procreate.' For a year he came close to such a position of supreme political and moral authority. He was responsible for twenty million people in the British zone of Germany and oversaw that duty in the spirit of a Christian crusade to restore the country to economic and political viability. His tenure was one of the most intense, rewarding and simultaneously frustrating periods of his life. Those who worked with him are divided on the extent of his influence on the emerging West Germany. Adenauer certainly made clear his belief that Frank had been one of Germany's principal champions at a time of national degradation and powerlessness.

TEN

The Head of a Nationalized Industry

Two years before taking up his post at the Ministry of Civil Aviation, Frank had been placed in charge of a ministerial committee looking into the deployment of flying boats. He had written to Elizabeth at the time with much amusement and a mass of exclamation marks at such an unlikely appointment for a self-avowed technophobe. Attlee had, however, obviously been sufficiently impressed with his work on this project to suspect that Frank's protestation that he had two left hands in all things mechanical was a pose, playing to the gallery. And so he entrusted him with control of Britain's recently nationalized airlines, its airports and state-funded research and development into civilian aircraft.

The Ministry of Civil Aviation had a reputation for being a political graveyard. The previous incumbent, Harry Nathan, had left to return to the business world. In the six and a half years of Labour rule from 1945 onwards, there were five ministers. When he arrived on 2 June 1948, Frank asked his new private secretary to arrange for some family pictures to be put up on the wall of his office and was told that there was not much point since his predecessors had not tended to stick around for very long. With a tenacity to make his ancestor Wellington proud, Frank stayed put for three years.

His fundamental inspiration for joining the Labour Party had been a desire to right inequalities and injustices in the society around him. To that end, as a politician, he had aspired to a ministerial post in one of the social service ministries. Civil Aviation had no human constituency beyond the ministry's 1,500 staff at head office and the estimated 6,000 at various airports and bases around the country. In essence the minister's role was that of administrator and banker, overseeing operational developments and providing the funding for the state-owned airports and airlines BEA and BOAC.

What others might have considered the perks of the job at Civil Aviation, he disliked. The *bonhomie* of the ex-RAF contingent in the ministry went straight over his head. The growing awareness of technology's potential to transform the world left him admiring but cold. The chance to travel around the British Empire to the opening ceremonies of airports he found tiresome. For an aspiring politician and one with a taste for grabbing the headlines, the Ministry of Civil Aviation offered little that was spectacular or indeed even mildly interesting to the general public. From Clement Attlee's point of view, after Frank's regular appearances on the front pages while in Germany, this lack of glamour was a blessing. For the new minister it was frustrating, boredom-inducing and almost led to his downfall.

However, for all his awkwardness in questioning party policy over Germany, Frank remained a very ambitious man in political terms. He wanted to make it into the Cabinet and believed that his apostasy in Germany had not done him any lasting damage. It was one of the many paradoxes in his personality that at the same time as refusing to play the party-political game, he continued to aspire to high office. Civil Aviation was an interlude where he had to put his head down and tackle an unappealing task in the hope of ultimate salvation in promotion.

Application in matters that did not interest him had laboriously to be summoned up. Elizabeth once wrote in despair in her diary that for every page he said he'd read, he would only have skimmed the first quarter.[1] However, on this occasion he proved to be an excellent administrator, demonstrating that, while details, figures, specifications and careful planning may not have been his natural forte, he was a clever man who could, when necessary, turn his mind to such problems. Top of his list of priorities at the ministry were the tangled finances of the state-owned airlines. The £11 million annual deficit run up by BEA and BOAC was giving nationalization a bad name. Committed to the principle of state ownership, Frank did not believe that this excused poor management, nor that it necessitated endless subsidies from the taxpayer. He wanted the policy to be shown to work efficiently in the best interests of the nation. His economic training enabled him, in the company of his senior officials, swiftly to identify the causes of the operating losses – outdated equipment, overmanning, poor organization and a lack of strategic planning.

He saw the need to invest in modern aircraft for the two corporations and persuaded a reluctant cabinet (by that stage applying an increasingly tight rein on public expenditure as the pressure grew to rearm) to equip BOAC with state-of-the-art, efficient Canadair planes. In his struggle to get approval for the necessary funding, he was enthusiastically supported by the Labour leader in the Upper Chamber, Lord Addison, and by Herbert Morrison, who had overall responsibility for the nationalized industries at Cabinet level. Morrison and Frank had been in opposite camps in 1945, the former scheming to overthrow and replace Attlee, but they moved closer during the late 1940s through a shared belief in moderation as the party became more polarized between Morrison and his supporters on the right, and Aneurin Bevan and his camp on the left. Hugh Gaitskell wrote in 1950 that 'Frank is now more friendly with Morrison than any of the others. He does not like Bevan and was rather horrified when I said that I thought Bevan would almost certainly be leader of the party and therefore Prime Minister sometime.'[2]

At Civil Aviation, Frank worked closely with the trade unions to cut staffing levels – never an easy task for a Labour minister – from 24,000 at BOAC in 1947 to 16,000 in 1951, at the same time as increasing productivity. Many of the jobs went with the closing down of a string of air bases under the ministry's control, scattered around the country. Frank aimed to concentrate resources and was responsible for pushing the development of Heathrow as London's, and indeed Britain's, major airport. With nationalization a relatively new phenomenon, the relationship between the management of the state-owned corporations and their political master was, as yet, ill defined. Frank was unusual in allowing those in charge considerable autonomy in day-to-day and technical details – by dint of necessity given his lack of specialist expertise – but at the same time he kept a close watch as the two airlines moved back towards the black. By 1951, their deficit was only £1 million, and that was mainly accounted for by BEA's domestic routes, where the need to maintain a public service to outposts like the Scottish Islands outweighed commercial considerations.

'Of course,' he wrote later of this period, 'it is all a question of degree and balance; you don't want Parliament, or the Minister for that matter, poking his nose into affairs of day-to-day management. You don't want questions in the House when the train due at 8.56 arrives at 9.06 on a particular Tuesday. But if it does it every day for a year, you most certainly do want intervention on behalf of the public. A question of only day-to-day significance has then passed into a question of general efficiency.'[3]

By showing that he could run an efficient public service without fuss and headlines, Frank managed to put his political star once more in the ascendant in government circles. However, the showman in him could not resist occasionally playing up to his reputation as an eccentric, scatty don. When inspecting new aircraft, for example, he would walk up and down the aisle and congratulate the engineers and designers on how comfortable the seats were. Once, on an official flight, he spied a man sitting alone, away from the main party, seemingly lost in thought. Frank made a special effort by going over to talk to him and offering him a drink. Only later did he learn that the man was one of the senior engineers who was trying to listen to the aircraft engine as part of a safety report. Again when Frank went to greet a visiting Soviet minister at London airport he was accompanied by his son Thomas, by then a teenager and keen on planes. When the younger Pakenham started photographing the Soviet aircraft and various of the surly, affectedly anonymous figures accompanying the minister, he caused a minor diplomatic incident. They suspected the fourteen-year-old of being a cunning British spy, collecting information on Soviet personnel and technical developments.

However, over the crash of a KLM Royal Dutch Airlines plane at Prestwick Airport near Glasgow, Frank's misjudgement severely damaged his political career and effectively destroyed any hopes he harboured of entering the Cabinet within the lifetime of Attlee's government. Just before midnight on 28 October 1948, a KLM Constellation, with thirty passengers and ten crew on board, crashed five miles short of the runway at Prestwick in thick fog. There were no survivors. Frank was on the scene within hours and moved at once to set up a public inquiry under a Scottish QC. When the report arrived the following August during the parliamentary recess, both Frank and his officials felt that its conclusion – that the accident was the fault of the air traffic controllers on the ministry's staff at the airport – was not justified by any of the evidence it detailed. The findings appeared to them to point towards pilot error – a verdict later confirmed by Dutch investigators. His first instinct on reading the report was to defend his own staff against what he considered an unjust accusation. His officials advised him to follow up publication of the report with a statement in the Lords when it reassembled, expressing his own disagreement with its conclusions. Such would have been the pragmatic course for an aspiring politician. A quiet word with more senior colleagues might also have been good tactics, getting them on his side in case the situation became more complicated.

However, Frank did neither. If he was to be confined to a backwater ministry, he felt confident that he could handle the one major incident that was likely to occur during his tenure. To confine his discontent to a statement in the Lords would, he considered, allow the official report too much credence. He intended to make plain his disagreement at the same time as he published it. It was a bad political misjudgement. Those who had written the report were, understandably, horrified and alerted the press. Frank failed to spot any warning signs and after a routine speech in the Lords returned home with Elizabeth from a dinner to be greeted by a reporter from the *News Chronicle* at his front gate. Frank dismissed him, and slept soundly before setting off early the next morning for a two-day visit to a BOAC repair works at Treforest in south Wales and various bases at Filton, Bristol and Bournemouth, where large-scale redundancies had been agreed. As he opened the morning's papers, however, he was greeted with headlines such as 'Storm over Air Inquiry. Minister rejects Findings. It's a Farce' in the *Daily Express*.

Still he failed to see the urgency of the situation. On his arrival in Wales, he drafted a reply to a Commons question on the subject, including a sentence about his duty to defend civil servants who could not defend themselves, without making it sufficiently clear that he was defending them against what he saw as an injustice, rather than simply backing them up right or wrong. Again, he felt that was the end of the matter. He made no attempt to contact any cabinet member and returned to his tour of inspection. That afternoon, the Prime Minister was questioned in the Commons by Anthony Eden from the opposition benches about Frank's actions and the legal precedents for rejecting the findings of a public inquiry. Since he had not been informed by his junior colleague that anything was amiss, Attlee, to his evident discomfiture, could offer no answer. As Frank spent a pleasant evening with his friend Evelyn Waugh at his home at Stinchcombe, discussing everything but civil aviation, a political storm was brewing.

The next morning he was described in the *News Chronicle* as 'a clawing and predatory cat among the legal pigeons'. A message came through from the Prime Minister commanding his presence at the earliest possible opportunity. The cabinet would be discussing the Prestwick affair that morning. By the time Frank got back to London, the evening papers were baying for his blood. 'Sack for Pakenham' shouted the *Star*. Elizabeth, who had seen the headlines, telephoned to pass on messages of support from Hugh Gaitskell, urging his old friend not to resign. 'He says he knows how quixotic you are but on no account must you.' Frank feared that Attlee might not give him any choice.

At Downing Street, the Prime Minister was waiting in the Cabinet Room with the *Star* and its damning verdict spread out in front of him. Frank got a frosty reception. Attlee's immediate concern was the legality of the decision to reject the official report. 'How can you set up a Court and then refuse to accept its decision when it goes against your own men?' he asked. Not satisfied by Frank's assurance that he had been acting within his constitutional rights and determined to investigate further, Attlee instructed him to draft a parliamentary statement. Frank had received a severe rap over the knuckles but at least he had not been sacked.

The following afternoon he returned to Downing Street to hear that government lawyers had exonerated him. Since the official report was advisory, not mandatory, a parliamentary apology for his high-handedness would be sufficient. There was still an unpleasant *mea culpa* to utter in the House of Lords, where he had to cast aside calls for his resignation, but the minister emerged from the ordeal to fight another day.

His reputation, however, had suffered. Whatever other good work he did at Civil Aviation, his mishandling of the Prestwick report dominated Frank's tenure of the ministry. In government circles, he was seen as yet again having caused Labour unnecessary embarrassment. He was not a safe pair of hands. At least over Germany and his public stance against the official policy of dismantling, he had been taking a moral position which some of his colleagues could admire if not endorse. Over Prestwick, his protest that he was defending his civil servants cut little ice. One commentator, Alaistair Forbes in the *Sunday Dispatch*, even went so far as to suggest that, so addicted was he to publicity, Frank had 'stage-managed mock-martyrdom' in order to remind the public of his existence. While Attlee would have seen beyond such a caricature, he did feel let down by someone he had singled out for promotion. 'His professional standards were affronted by the clumsiness with which I appeared to him to have handled the situation,' Frank reflected later.[4]

Attlee called a general election in 1950. The Labour government had not lost a by-election in that parliament. The local elections in 1949 had given grounds for hoping that a Commons majority could be maintained, if not of 1945 proportions. Labour fought on its record – establishing the National Health Service, restoring full employment, creating a balance of trade surplus. The Conservatives, however, pointed to looming economic problems over the cost of rearmament – a result of the deteriorating relationship with the Soviet Union – and to Labour plans for extending nationalization. On a swing of just over 3 per cent to the Tories, Labour's majority was reduced to a wafer-thin five.

Attlee was clearly in the mood for bringing in new blood, and Frank, despite Prestwick, had high hopes of promotion or at least a move. He was disappointed. Hugh Gaitskell was the principal gainer among the younger generation of Labour ministers, promoted to Minister of State for Economic Affairs and, after Cripps's retirement in October, to the Exchequer. The second term in office was not a happy one for Labour. As well as Cripps, Bevin had to step down from the Foreign Office because of ill health, and died in March 1951. Dalton, so much a force in the early years of the Attlee government, had resigned in 1947 over a Budget leak. Although he later returned to the cabinet, he was by then a spent force. Morrison won few admirers as Bevin's successor, especially as the outbreak of the Korean War in June 1950 heightened world tensions. In April 1950 Aneurin Bevan, Harold Wilson and John Freeman resigned from the government over plans to impose a small range of charges in the NHS – a symptom of the deep economic malaise with which Britain was afflicted.

The sense of an era coming to an end only deepened Frank's discontent at Civil Aviation. While he continued to work towards running an efficient public service in the hope of winning back Attlee's favour, he began spending more time on other causes close to his heart. Writing of this period later, he commented:

> the real strain does not arise from what ministers do but from what they feel they ought to be doing. The vigilance of the public operates powerfully on the subconscious. Imagine a devoted GP under constant attack for gross negligence in the local press and you will get a partial analogy. The occupational disease of the good minister is the neurosis, not that he is doing anything wrong but that he is not doing anything like enough.[5]

From childhood Frank had been a restless sort, unable to be satisfied with anything for very long. Three years at Civil Aviation taxed him almost beyond endurance. Beyond his ministerial brief, his interest in Germany had never faded and he continued to press his colleagues on their attitude to rebuilding, latterly as one of the founders of the Anglo-German Society. (He failed to persuade Attlee to be president.) In August 1949, when at Civil Aviation, but still watching with a heavy conscience the British government's activities in Germany, he grew alarmed at what turned out to be one of the final acts of dismantling. He wrote to Attlee threatening once again to resign but this time adding a time-limit for the government to reconsider its attitude. He was called to Downing Street and was convinced that his time as a minister was about to end in a puff of publicity. Attlee began with questions about Elizabeth and the children. When brought to the point, he replied: 'Oh yes. You mean the matter you wrote to me about. Oh that's quite all right: Ernest Bevin's coming back from Strasbourg tonight, and the whole thing's being looked into afresh.' After another volley of questions about the Pakenham family, he said goodbye to his junior minister. 'I shambled out of the room,' Frank recalled, 'uncertain whether I had achieved something quite substantial or been outwitted once again in the kindliest of all possible ways.'[6]

Elizabeth, it seems, was unaware of some of this to-ing and fro-ing. Many years later in her diary she recorded meeting 'Bear, Frank's one-time secretary at Civil Aviation. Bear reminisced how Frank used to keep him late drafting letters of resignation to Attlee over Bevin's German policy and then feel too nervous to go home and tell me, so that Bear would take him out to dinner. Attlee never took them seriously.'[7]

As the Western Allies came increasingly to see Russia and not the Germans as their enemy, Frank's fight for Germany became less of a lonely battle. Within the Labour Party, though, many remained suspicious of both his message of Christian forgiveness and his extreme and unguarded antipathy to communism. His friendship with the emerging West German leader Adenauer and the right-of-centre Christian Democrats – rather than with Labour's natural allies, the Social Democrats – only further divorced him from the mainstream of his own party on the issue of Germany. When he began once again to turn his attention to Ireland, he was out of step not just with his party but with most of the country. In 1948 de Valera and Fianna Fáil had fallen out with the Irish electorate, to be replaced by the supposedly more moderate John Costello[8] and Fine Gael. Though Fine Gael shared with their rivals a dislike of some of the restrictions placed on Ireland as a member of the Commonwealth, there was widespread shock when Costello broke the existing link with Britain without warning or prior consultation. Had de Valera taken Ireland out of the Commonwealth, the British would have been angry but not altogether surprised.

As much as any other British minister, Frank was caught unawares by Costello's action. Yet he and Elizabeth had been dining with the Irish Foreign Minister, Sean MacBride,[9] the night before the Taoiseach made his announcement. A republican whose Clann na Poblachta Party, in coalition with Fine Gael, was opposed to continuing membership of the Commonwealth, MacBride nevertheless discussed with Frank the desirability of Irish attendance at the next Commonwealth summit. During the course of the meal at the Russell Hotel in Dublin, the Foreign Minister had been called away to the telephone. The Pakenhams did not suspect anything, but the next morning headlines in the Dublin papers revealed that Costello had announced Ireland's withdrawal from the Commonwealth while on a visit to Toronto.

The British response was swift and angry. Attlee resisted pressures to rescind any special status allowed to the Irish living in Britain, but he did endorse popular feeling by passing the Government of Ireland Act of 1949, which stipulated that the existing division of Ireland could not be changed without the consent of the people of the north. In practical terms it only underlined what was already a fact, but it was presented as a necessary reassurance for the people of the north. To Frank, the Act was a calculated snub to the Dublin government, asserting Britain's continuing role in Ireland and seemingly delaying further the day when the partition of 1921, thought then to be a temporary measure, would end. He protested to the cabinet in a note but made little impact.

One reason for the amount of freedom to dissent that Attlee gave Frank was the perilous position of Labour in the Lords. He could ill afford to lose him. In 1945 Labour had found itself in much the same position as the Liberals in 1909, with a clear Commons majority but facing overwhelming Tory numbers in the Lords. The peers' attempts to block the Liberals had led to the 1911 Parliament Act, which limited the powers of the Upper Chamber. In 1945, the Conservative leaders in the Lords realized their opposition to the elected government's programme might provoke a further reduction of the Second Chamber's role. To avoid such an eventuality, the Tory peers adopted explicit conventions on self-restraint – the Salisbury Rules, named after the Marquis of Salisbury, Conservative leader in the Upper House. These rules set out that the Lords could not vote down any policies that had appeared in the Labour manifesto – as having been sanctioned by the electorate – though they might suggest constructive amendments. On matters not in the manifesto, the Lords retained a freer hand. The Tories in the Upper House felt that iron and steel nationalization did not pass the manifesto test and therefore blocked its passage.

Labour responded by publishing a new Parliament Bill in 1947 which reduced the period of the Lords' veto from three parliamentary sessions to two. After unsuccessful attempts to reach agreement on this Bill in the Upper Chamber, it was pushed through and, after the Lords' veto had run its course, was passed in 1949. For a while there was talk of a 'constitutional revolution', and, while a crisis was threatening, Attlee and the Labour leadership needed Frank on the front bench, but the menace petered out.

Attlee finally granted Frank the long-awaited promotion in May 1951. It had been suspected for some time that Lord Addison, the septuagenarian Labour leader in the Upper Chamber, wanted to retire. Attlee himself had hinted that Addison could not go on for ever. Frank harboured hopes of taking over from him in a Cabinet-ranking role when the summons to 10 Downing Street came. However, had Attlee entertained such thoughts, the shadow of Prestwick decided him against. Instead, Frank was offered the post of First Lord of the Admiralty, a prestigious and historic office that carried with it a tied cottage in Admiralty House at the other end of the Mall from Buckingham Palace. The First Lord did not sit in the cabinet, though he was expected to play a substantial role in the cabinet's Defence Committee.

This role was one of the more appealing aspects of the job for Frank. At least he would have a voice on British policy in Germany and on the broader question of international alliances, where he had clear views about the threat of the Soviet Union. However, he was undecided about Attlee's offer and asked for forty-eight hours to think about it. 'Please don't think I don't appreciate the honour,' he told the Prime Minister. 'No one who has read a line of British history or got any feeling for it could fail to be stirred. But the Navy deserves the best. Its traditions are everything to it. I don't think I'm the right sort of person. I mean I am too eccentric.' Attlee was clearly wise to Frank's habit of exaggerating his own eccentricity. 'I shouldn't worry about that,' he replied. 'The Navy survived Winston [Churchill] and Brendan [Bracken]. It will probably survive you.'[10]

There were obvious reasons why Frank was unsuitable for the job. He couldn't swim, for example, and straightaway had to take lessons. (His old flatmate 'Nicko' Henderson insisted that the instruction went further – Frank told him, he recalled, 'making undulating movements with his hands', that he had been to see a psychiatrist to overcome his fear of the sea.)[11] What preyed more on his mind was the fact that the day-to-day responsibilities of the First Lord were largely ceremonial. The rearmament programme was well under way and the naval chiefs played the leading role in deciding upon such technical and operational questions. Their political captain was very much an overseer whose interference would be resented. Conscious of tradition and of his own limited knowledge of such matters, not to mention his inglorious war record, Frank knew that he would be in no position to intervene and make his mark.

When he heard that Frank was wavering, Hugh Gaitskell, by now Chancellor of the Exchequer, took his old college friend to lunch. He stressed that, whatever he might think, Frank was not out of favour as a result of Prestwick and his pro-German views. Quite the opposite. He was seen, Gaitskell confirmed, as a future Labour leader in the Lords as long as he did not turn down this opportunity.

At this crossroads in Frank's career, it would normally have been Evan Durbin, not Gaitskell, guiding his choice of path. The three New College men had remained close friends since Oxford days. But in the summer of 1948, while on holiday with his family, Durbin had drowned while rescuing two young children (one of them his daughter) caught in a dangerous current. Durbin's death affected Frank more than emotionally. Durbin had been destined for high office at a major ministry of state and would have been able to use his influence to push for Frank's promotion. Now that prospect had gone. Though he was universally liked, Frank had little by way of a following, as Denis Healey observed.

Frank was odd but then we had many people like that in the Labour Party then and now. After all Stafford Cripps came of an upper-class family and showed it. Beatrice Webb, who was still alive in those days, was the daughter of a peer. Attlee himself was a public schoolboy. It was Frank's manner that was odd. He wasn't a chap who worked with people very much. He never in a sense formed alliances, not because he didn't get on with people particularly but he just was not a political sort of chap.[12]

With Gaitskell's encouragement, Frank accepted Attlee's offer. It was a job that emphasized some of his own ambiguities. Taking the salute and being piped on board His Majesty's vessels both thrilled and appalled him. Never one with an eye for minutiae of dress, as he had shown in the Army, he was not natural or indeed comfortable in the role. But the showman in him enjoyed the public spectacle of it, especially when he was at its epicentre. In August 1951, Gaitskell wrote in his diary: 'Frank and Elizabeth are evidently enormously enjoying his new job, and all the reports I hear about how he conducts himself are excellent.'[13] Another to hear only good words for the new First Lord was his uncle, Arthur Villiers. He sent on to Elizabeth a letter received from one of his 'old boys' at Eton Manor who was now in the Navy. 'I have just returned from the pier where I proudly witnessed the arrival of the First Lord. He did very well. His bearing and manner is excellent, his keenness and attention to both officer and rating. His saluting (best Naval style which is unusual), everything very well carried out.'[14]

Once again Frank had proved that, if he set his mind to it, he could accomplish a task for which he considered himself congenitally unsuited. At Admiralty House, he found himself back in the world of his childhood: the atmosphere of a stately home, servants on hand to attend to his every whim. In the domestic quarters there were reminders of the great and good at every turn. In the blue Axminster of the master bedroom were the marks left by the feet of Lady Diana Cooper's carved and gilded four-poster, designed by Rex Whistler, and installed when her husband Duff was First Lord.[15]

He was not, however, so much at home with some of the trappings of his position. He always insisted on sitting in the front seat of his government car next to the chauffeur – as indeed he had done when a child, distinguishing himself from the other Pakenham children by addressing the staff as Mr and Mrs rather than by their surnames alone. His sister Mary would often express bemusement as to why her brother insisted on sitting next to her driver who had been sent to pick 'His Lordship' up from the local station on his visits out to Herefordshire.[16] Frank could not drive, but refused to abuse the privilege of an official car and driver. One weekend, when he invited Evelyn Waugh to Bernhurst, the author was rather disgruntled to find that the black ministerial car that came to collect him from his London home disgorged him soon afterwards at Charing Cross Station to continue the journey by train rather than conveying him all the way to Sussex.

Frank did, however, take enormous pleasure in the social round that was part of Admiralty House life. His lifelong love of parties took on an institutional significance and he was able to organize gatherings to honour those he admired – notably the Prime Minister. The only blight was that for much of his tenure at Admiralty House Elizabeth was unwell. On the day he took over he received news that she had been rushed to hospital in Hastings from Bernhurst. She had suffered another miscarriage and had lost a lot of blood. 'As I left Bernhurst on a stretcher,' Elizabeth later confided in her diary,

'Mrs Pope [the housekeeper] said to herself as she told me after-wards "I shall never see Lady Pakenham again".'[17] It was a long convalescence during which her eldest daughter Antonia, by now an undergraduate at Oxford, took her mother's place at official functions and enlivened them considerably by inviting her university friends down to join some of the parties. Her contemporary, Kenneth Rose,[18] described one evening painting red lipstick on some of the statues at Admiralty House.

In political terms, Frank did not leave much of a mark on the Navy. His predecessor, Viscount Hall, a veteran of the 1929 Labour government, after five years in office, had left a very tidy, well-run ship. The only matter that detained Frank for any length of time was the need to raise the status of naval aviation within the service and to maintain the pace and flow of finance for rearmament. He was ably assisted in these tasks by James Callaghan[19] as Under-Secretary, though Callaghan recorded in his autobiography that, having carried the can for Hall in the Commons for eighteen months, he felt he had earned a shot at the top job. He had reason to feel doubly aggrieved at Frank. In 1946, he had been promised the post of Under-Secretary of State at the War Office by the Labour Chief Whip. He then went on holiday to Czechoslovakia, only to find that Frank had got it instead, after his impassioned plea to the Prime Minister to allow him to make good in some small measure his war record.[20]

After just five months in post, Frank left the Admiralty when Labour was defeated in the October 1951 general election. The pressures of rearmament and a spiral of bad economic news – rising prices, growing unemployment and a shortage of houses – combined to usher in a Conservative majority of seventeen, though, because of the vagaries of the British first-past-the-post electoral system, Labour actually polled a higher vote than the Tories, 48.8 per cent to their 48 per cent.

There was disappointment but also high hopes in Labour circles that they would regroup and return to office at the next election. Frank felt confident that, judged on his record under Attlee, and with the outgoing Prime Minister's continuing favour, he could count on being a member of any future Labour cabinet. He had proved an asset in the House of Lords, been promoted to the Privy Council, had shown that he could run both a technocratic ministry and a historic institution and had, with occasional lapses, carved out something of a reputation for himself in the public eye as a minister, if not of the first rank, then certainly not of grey self-effacement.

ELEVEN

Look Back in Hunger

In July 1950, Elizabeth sold the house in Hampstead Garden Suburb and moved down to Bernhurst full-time. With eight children, four of them now at boarding school, the habitually tight family finances were more strained than ever, and running two houses seemed to someone of her practical bent absurd. Moreover, her hopes of seeing more of Frank by being with him in London had largely been disappointed. He would be glimpsed briefly in the mornings before hurrying off to his ministry or Germany, and would return late from evening sittings of the Lords. Often he would be away for days on end. The Garden Suburb, Elizabeth had concluded, was neither one thing nor the other. It was too far away from Westminster for her to feel part of political life and not close enough to the countryside for her to feel she had escaped the city.

Her own political ambitions, once so all-consuming, had fizzled out in a damp squib in the 1950 general election, when she had been tempted out of retirement to stand in Oxford against Frank's nemesis in 1945, Quintin Hogg. She was probably the only mother of eight to put herself up for election on a major party ticket in the twentieth century. Hogg's own warm friendship with Elizabeth did something to take the edge off the contest, while the addition of Cowley and Headington, strong Labour areas, gave Labour hope of capturing the seat this time round. However, the national tide was running against Attlee's government. 'I had a new feeling in my bones – that I would be defeated if I stood for Oxford in 1950,' Elizabeth wrote. 'The fight would be a "propaganda" one and none the worse for that. My family would not suffer and I would discharge my political debt.'[1] Quintin Hogg's verdict was that Elizabeth 'was by far the more formidable antagonist'[2] of the two Pakenhams, but her premonition proved well founded. Though nationally Labour scraped in with a much-reduced majority, in Oxford Hogg increased the scale of his own 1945 victory. The woman Nicholas Henderson had heard called 'the Madonna of the barricades' was now definitively out of the front line, although, as Elizabeth wrote later in her diary, there was one unusual attempt to redeploy her.[3] Sydney, the first wife of the Conservative statesman, R.A. Butler, met her and 'offered me a nice Tory seat saying my being Labour was rubbish'.[4]

Harold Wilson and Hugh Gaitskell had come to speak for her at Oxford, as of course did Frank. 'I sat on the platform,' he recalled, 'while our chairman introduced Elizabeth in this way: "Comrades, this is Elizabeth Pakenham. She has had eight children and brought them up herself. And she has done it alone". I muttered audibly: "not quite alone, you know". The chairman repeated with still more emphasis: "and she has done it alone". I felt we both had a point.'[5]

After the election defeat, Bernhurst seemed an appropriate retreat, though it was in a sorry state. The scars of its wartime use by the Canadian military were everywhere to be seen. The ancient oak in the garden had lost many of its lower branches as lorries had brushed against it. Concrete bases of temporary huts remained on the lawns, overrun by weeds. Inside, every surface had been painted standard-issue banana yellow. The basement was riddled with damp where the soldiers had tried to rig up showers. Elizabeth, though, had a vision to turn it into a family home once again and to restore its ravaged gardens. Inside, the banana slowly receded and was replaced by pale William Morris wallpapers and, in the dining room, Pugin Gothic. The drawing room was shaded by a huge tulip tree and, encouraged and advised by Vita Sackville-West,[6] who travelled over to offer guidance from neighbouring Sissinghurst, Elizabeth grew passionate about her garden. It became her creation. 'At heart,' her son Kevin wrote, 'she believed in a good Providence, revealed in all God's creation. Her love of her garden at Bernhurst was an expression of this.'

Frank's outlook was more prone to melancholy, though he struggled gamely to keep up with his wife and see only the positive and the good. Over the relocation to Bernhurst he simply fell into line. 'That move to the country was an extraordinary thing for my father to do since he had no real interest in the countryside,' Rachel reflected. 'Hampstead Garden Suburb had been the country to him, but moving to Bernhurst was not the sort of decision he made.' Having spent most of his unhappy childhood in the country, Frank had little instinctive love for it. The slower pace of life hardly suited his belief that he had always to be active, but, as ever, he adapted. With his knack for camouflaging a lack of interest with an insuperable absence of knowledge, he ostentatiously did not know the name of a single flower or plant in the garden. He would make a show of listening to the land agents who managed the small estate attached to Bernhurst, but he left all matters to them. He often professed in writing his love of the view from the lawn at Bernhurst, stretching over the scene that Elizabeth had so lovingly recreated to the valley beyond, but his interests – politics, academia, meeting people – were best indulged in an urban setting. Even his sporting pursuits were more suburban than rural. He preferred tennis and golf to hunting and shooting, though after 1960, when Bernhurst acquired a swimming pool, he finally conquered his fear of water.

His own contribution to the regeneration of Bernhurst was modest but characteristic. In 1960 he donated some of its land for the building of a Catholic church, a modern, semi-circular chapel dedicated to Our Lady Help of Christians, with a roof like a fan and crescent-shaped pews from Ireland. Until then mass had been in an upper room at the Rose and Crown in Burwash or in the village hall in Hurst Green.

Relocation meant commuting at weekends and lodging once again with Nicholas Henderson while in London. One evening Henderson had invited a colleague, Donald Maclean, back to dinner. Maclean, later to be unmasked as a Soviet spy, soon became drunk, abusive and strongly anti-American in his sentiments. Devoted to the Atlantic Alliance, Frank was drawn into a heated argument with Maclean. From Henderson's point of view, though, Frank's reaction on another occasion to his own bride-to-be was more memorable. 'It is one of the contradictions of Frank's character', he wrote in his memoirs, 'that, in many ways unconventional to the point of being regarded by some as a traitor to his class, and pro-Irish in sentiment, he nevertheless has the traditional English attitude of his generation to foreigners, believing non-whites start at Calais. He had some difficulty in coming to terms with the fact that Mary was Greek, as became embarrassingly apparent when he spoke at our wedding reception and told of his surprise, when he first met her, at the paleness of her complexion.'[7]

Frank's promotion to the Admiralty in 1951 briefly gave him a more imposing billet in the capital, but after Labour's defeat five months later he found himself travelling even further afield – to Oxford to resume teaching at Christ Church. The distance seemed only to emphasize the emotional gap between him and his eight children. In 1946, prior to Kevin's arrival the following year, Paddy had recorded the relative merits of his brothers and sisters:

Antonia is a girl rather clever when laden with responsibility. Mostly she is very nice.

Thomas is a boy keen on photography and bird-watching. On the whole he is very agreeable, a generous boy.

Judith loves her dolls and treasures them. She adores Antonia immensely because Antonia lets her play with her own very exquisite dolls.

Rachel like Judith likes dolls very much, and often makes them dresses of wool and cotton, being skilled in the art of needlework. She is Thomas's pet and Thomas calls her his 'chubby lassie'.

Catherine a very jolly and stout young baby.

Michael is the one I like best and we are both devoted to each other. We both like playing soldiers. I usually let him win a few battles so he is not discouraged. He likes everybody and everybody likes him but he likes ME best.[8]

By the time Frank had relinquished ministerial responsibility and, in the time-honoured politician's phrase, freed up more time to spend with his family, his brood was fast growing up. His return to Oxford coincided with Antonia's arrival at Lady Margaret Hall as an undergraduate. Thomas and Paddy were at Ampleforth, both destined for Magdalen College, Oxford. Judith was sent to a well-known convent boarding school at Mayfield in Sussex. Only the four youngest children moved down to Bernhurst with their mother, where their education followed a less traditional pattern. Catherine and Michael were sent to the local village school. Kevin was too young as yet to join them and Rachel went to an informal day school in Hawkhurst run by Audrey Townsend, Elizabeth's old friend from Oxford.

In a family of eight children, each one inevitably had a distinct viewpoint on their father and their upbringing. Each of course experienced their parents in a different way as age, experience, inclination, exhaustion and material circumstances combined to alter the details, if not usually the main thrust, of the couple's standpoint on parenthood. However, certain general trends can be detected.

With a span of fifteen years between Antonia and Kevin, the eight tended to split into groups. From Antonia's point of view, the cut-off point was the outbreak of war. So she, Thomas and Paddy were one group, while the other five war and postwar children had another childhood altogether. 'We older ones were never part of the corporate upbringing. The other five saw a lot more of my father. First he was invalided out, then they lived with him in London and from 1950 spent at least every weekend with him at Bernhurst. By that time I was a student, then working in London and then getting married and having a family of my own.' Her categorization was largely accepted by the others – though some felt that Antonia and Thomas, with less than a year between them, were very much a unit – 'almost like twins' one remarked – and that Paddy, four years

Thomas's junior and three years older than Judith, floated somewhere in between.

There were parts of Antonia's and Thomas's childhoods that the later children did not share. The first, in those frenzied pre-war days in Oxford, was the almost complete absence of their father. 'It was only when I came up to Oxford and my father was back teaching there that we developed a relationship,' Antonia said. 'It was not an official thing but he taught me privately. In my finals I did by far the best in the papers where he had tutored me. He was a brilliant teacher with a clear brilliance of mind. That set our adult relationship up. He was a politician and I was, for him, a historian of politics. It gave us a lot to talk about.'

Paddy, five years younger, did not see his father as an absent figure.

He was away in London some of the time, but whenever he came home would bring me what he called 'a surprise packet' – a small present of some kind. And he would give me a shilling a week if I learnt to recite a verse of the Bible. I felt he was very close, but I think he perhaps paid me special attention because he was a second son and so was I. Certainly when I was up at Ampleforth and was somewhat undisciplined in my behaviour, he would make the journey, which was a hell of a slog, two or three times a term. If anything I felt closer to my father than my mother, but I don't think I appreciated at the time how loving he was.

Those visits to Ampleforth were, Thomas believed, 'a kind of pilgrimage' for his father. 'We saw him as this kindly figure who came up, we knew, out of duty, but we were grateful because it did mean that we got out to a nice hotel where we could fill ourselves with cream buns and sit on hot pipes without people shouting at us.' Their conversation on such occasions revolved around sport and studies. There would be no display of emotions. The same was true of the weekly letters from Frank to his sons at boarding school. 'There was a difference between his letters and our mother's,' Thomas recalled.

Our mother wrote in a lovely rounded hand about family news. He wrote in his extraordinary handwriting which nobody has ever been able to read. So what the letter actually had was these hieroglyphs in early Linear B or early Minoan script. And you would read the first two pages in early Minoan and then a desperate passage of capitals which, if you looked very, very carefully, you realised it said in large letters 'do please write to me about this before next Tuesday, Your affectionate Dada'. And the trouble was you didn't know what 'this' was.

For Antonia and Thomas, too, there were outings later denied to the others to Pakenham Hall in Ireland. When the first two children were not yet teenagers, they were sent over to stay mainly with the Dunsanys, but with excursions to the family seat and Uncle Edward and Aunt Christine. Though they had much more fun at the Dunsanys – and, when they got off the boat, in the sweet shops of Dublin where rationing was not in force – Pakenham made a strong, albeit often gloomy, impression. They would sit down to lunch with their uncle and witness his tantrums as he complained bitterly that his mound of potatoes was not enough to satisfy his gargantuan appetite. Christine would try – and fail – to persuade him to be satisfied. The childless couple gradually became less and less tolerant of their nephews and nieces, and for the younger Pakenham children their first glimpse of the family seat was as adults at their uncle's funeral.

If Thomas was welcomed, it was because Edward and Christine, who by now had abandoned any hope of having their own children, realized he would one day inherit Pakenham. Unlike his mother, however, Frank himself had a more ambiguous attitude to primogeniture. He would do nothing to spread Thomas's eventual inheritance between all his children – as perhaps a more middle-class parent might have – but years later in the Lords he did vote for a measure which would see titles pass to eldest children, not eldest sons.

Overall, Frank's attitude to his children's education was determined by certain key considerations. First and foremost it had to be an education in the Catholic faith. Beyond that he was at heart a teacher, convinced of the power of education to open new horizons. 'He believed firmly,' Rachel said, 'that knowledge and information were exciting and could give you a better life.' Learning was enhanced by talk and debate. If a topic was ever raised over a family meal, particularly with the younger set who sat down to eat with their father much more often than their older siblings ever had, Frank would engage them in a discussion, which sometimes became heated and was on occasion only solved by recourse, when the food was finished, to a text-book. Yet he never tried to coerce his children into learning. He preferred a different sort of encouragement. When Kevin was still at prep school, he came home at the end of one term with a bad report. 'My father took me to one side and said "your mother is very disappointed. How much did I give you last time?" "Ten shillings." "You must be very disappointed. To cheer you up here's a pound". It was his way of encouraging me and I loved him for it.'

His father's belief 'in the profound power of the human brain to improve by education', Kevin noted, was expressed 'by leading the pupil on to the road of truth, but once there respecting the pupil's right to make his or her own way thereafter'. His father would ask his children searching questions, he recalled, often in advance of their years, and 'was very strong on right and wrong, and more practically, on the obligation to act'. Yet parallel to this broad and enlightened perspective on educating his children, Frank would line up alongside Elizabeth in valuing most highly academic excellence and academic achievement. 'Both my parents were very ambitious for us,' Antonia remembered. 'My mother was particularly interested in girls' education, but we all knew that the way to please both of them was to do well at school.'

Rachel echoed this and felt that the success achieved by Antonia and Thomas had set an impossibly high standard for all those who came after them. 'Both my parents had very high academic ambitions for their children and were tremendously pleased by academic success. There was a competitive atmosphere in that way and I wasn't half as academic as most of my brothers and sisters. Nobody said I was inadequate, but I do remember feeling it when my younger brother Michael used to do his exams at the same time as me and get better results.' Though parental expectations were not unusual in the middle- and upper-middle-class circles in which the Pakenhams moved – and arguably were watered down with the younger children, with Elizabeth yielding to Catherine's demand to go to a finishing school in Switzerland – the extent to which they were emphasized in the household made an impression on outsiders. Marina Warner, a contemporary of Catherine's and one of Frank's godchildren, recalled that 'when I used to visit and was very young, he was vague, but once I was older his attitude (and that of Elizabeth) was very keen – to bring me back to the faith, above all. They were also very interested in achievement.'[9]

His father's view of achievement, though, was shot through with a very basic competitiveness, Thomas pointed out.

He was a very ambitious man himself and he was very keen on success. So by extension he was very keen on all of us succeeding. But that didn't mean in the narrow sense of lessons. It would have been in all forms of everything. So it would appear to us that he would be equally pleased if we were first in the tiddly winks competition or in Greek verse. He wouldn't have had any kind of snobbery. He wouldn't have discriminated. The important thing was to succeed.

Yet despite the premium he placed on education, Frank, as with all other domestic matters, left the detail to Elizabeth. She chose their schools – especially for the girls. Frank's main contribution was to direct her towards the Catholic Eton – the Benedictine boarding school of Ampleforth in North Yorkshire. To later generations of socialists, the idea of choosing private rather than state schools would become anathema, but amongst his colleagues in the Attlee government Frank was not at all unusual in opting to pay. The Longfords scarcely gave it a second thought, save for Elizabeth's worries about how to meet the bills.

Their daughters' education was much more in Elizabeth's hands. At least with the younger set, she was the one who made school visits. Antonia did not receive a single visit when she was at St Mary's Ascot and took it upon herself to leave at fifteen and go to a crammer to prepare for university entrance. Her choice only came to Elizabeth's attention when she noticed that Antonia had brought her school eiderdown and sheets home. 'Won't you need them next term?' she asked. 'No. I've left,' Antonia told her.

Frank's distance from such practicalities when it came to his daughters was again not unusual for men of his age and class, but it made him, Judith felt, more like an uncle than a father.

We knew that he had his work and that it was important. Indeed we regarded it with a certain awe and never questioned his absence. Conversely I honestly don't think that he noticed if I was there or not as a child or a teenager. Nevertheless, at times, when I was really beleaguered, he could be wonderfully tender. He would repeat soothingly: 'we love you, we love you' and even as a shy fourteen year old I would sit on his knee for a precious few minutes. At these times he offered me a sort of life saver, a long remembered source of love.

Mostly, though, his two standard questions to his teenage daughters were 'How's your work?' and 'How's your weight?' Often it was only the latter. For Judith this approach showed his ignorance of 'what hell it is to be a fat teenage girl. He didn't mean to be mean. He felt it was his duty as a father to ask. He was offering sympathy – even solidarity.' Rachel saw it more as reflecting his own fanatical interest in weight and fitness than as evidence of any lack of understanding of teenage angst.

His elder brother was the fattest man in Ireland and I think my father reacted very much against that. He really cared about weight and fitness. He had something called the Alexander Technique which was a way of breathing and I think it involved all sorts of things like the height of lavatory seats. I don't think he ever did anything about it but he was terribly interested in the theory. I remember this awful book with a lot of photographs lying around showing these half-naked men and how they were supposed to sit.

Frank's insensitivity over his daughters' feelings about being questioned – and, they felt, teased – about their weight was symptomatic of the fact that they lacked a common language with which to communicate. With his sons, he could talk about sport, but when he tried to take an interest in his daughters' sporting activities, he struggled. So while he delighted in taking his sons to rugby matches at Twickenham, and occasionally in Cardiff or Dublin, or to play golf at nearby Rye (where he successfully overturned the club's ban on Jewish members), it never occurred to him to include his daughters in such outings. Neither did it occur to them that they might want to go. On the one occasion that he made an effort and took Rachel to pony club, he caused her no end of embarrassment.

I was very self-conscious and was horrified when he announced that he was going to come riding. The whole riding school was thrown into chaos to find a horse big enough for him. He had looked out his old hunting gear – jodhpurs that went down to the knee and then he didn't have boots, so it was socks and shoes. And he'd found a bowler hat. It was absolutely dreadful, a stream of little children and my father leaning back at a ridiculous angle on a horse that was too small for him. Finally I couldn't bear it any longer and I said, 'Dada, can't you see that they're all laughing at you?' He turned to me, completely unmoved, and said, 'Just remember that if people are laughing at you, you're giving them pleasure and that's a good thing.' It was a real lesson for me because it was a policy he carried through himself. He didn't mind if people laughed at him. Well, he did mind, but he didn't let it change his behaviour.

Competition of all descriptions was his keynote contribution when he came to Bernhurst at weekends. This ranged from the simple – sitting round the breakfast table doing a quiz from a newspaper or asking his children (in a fashion akin to his own childhood games) to make lists of the ten best players at a sport or their favourite people or so on – to the involved. 'One of his favourite stories', according to Rachel, 'was about his Uncle Edward Dunsany who decided chess was the only thing he had not mastered and so learnt from the local blacksmith and then beat everyone. So when he visited us, there would be five chess boards set up, and all five of us would sit at one and Uncle Eddie would play us all simultaneously – and, of course, beat us.'

Elizabeth largely took a back seat in such events. On other matters, too, she tried to defer to Frank. Having opposed any form of physical chastisement before she had children, she had changed her view when confronted with the daily reality of keeping her growing family under control. Her sternest sanction was to threaten 'wait until your father gets home'. Frank, though, did not want to play up to the role of supreme court cum hangman. Having begun with a belief in the positive benefits of an occasional smack, he had now, on the basis of his limited exposure to his children, changed his mind and was firmly in the anti-camp. So as a threat he was worse than useless. 'Frank', Elizabeth recalled, 'felt that for a man weighing eleven and a half stone to hit a child weighing five and a half was inhuman.'[10] If there were any smacks then it would be their mother who delivered them, rarely and with no great conviction, the children recalled, though occasionally she was given the light-hearted nickname 'Mummy Ogre'.

On one occasion, however, Paddy, habitually the one who got into most trouble, had taken a hammer to an ornament in the garden at Oxford and smashed it to pieces. Elizabeth was so angry that Frank felt he had to act. 'He came into the room and told me to lie down on the floor, face down. Then slowly and lightly he gave me four taps with his hand. I had to stop myself laughing they hurt so little. "You're controlling the pain very well," he said and then he came out with the old line about it hurting him more than it hurt me. The joke was that on that occasion it was certainly literally true.'

Frank was the softer, more pliable of the two parents as far as the children were concerned. Antonia, as a young child, used to conflate the 'gentle Jesus, meek and kind' of her night-time prayers with her father. And when Elizabeth had worries about the sort of upbringing she was giving their offspring, it was Frank's role to soothe her fears too. In a letter written in 1941, she admitted her concern that she was too strict as a parent. Frank replied at once that his friend, Nicko Henderson, had told him that the young Pakenhams were well brought up and spirited. Elizabeth was reassured.

Aside from his sporting and competitive flourishes, their father, during his weekend visits, could disappear into the background as far as his children were concerned. 'One Christmas at Bernhurst,' Rachel remembered, 'we were all in the drawing room. We had this awful yappy miniature poodle and we were throwing a ball for it to catch, all shouting at the top of our voices. At one stage, the ball ended up on top of the cupboard. During all the commotion, my father had sat reading his paper without noticing us. To get the ball from the top of the cupboard, the dog used him as a ladder and ended up on top of his head, but he just didn't react.'

They wouldn't have dared do such a thing with their mother, for it was Elizabeth who very much was at the helm of the ship. Though her interest in the practicalities of domestic matters was slight – her children used to suggest, half in jest, that she had never changed a nappy – she set the tone of the children's life at Bernhurst. It was largely a spartan one, partly out of inclination – Elizabeth disliked excess or waste and went round turning off lights to save electricity – and partly because money as ever was short. Though they had the trappings, with two houses and a title, the Pakenham family was not wealthy. For all Elizabeth's disinclination to be in the kitchen, they had the minimum of domestic help, a housekeeper at Bernhurst and the occasional au pairs in London who hailed, at Frank's insistence, from Germany. So Elizabeth just had to get on with it. 'Our mother ran the ship,' said Thomas. 'She was really the skipper. He was a kindly presence in the background.'

Neither parent was that interested in food, so the diet was basic. 'A typical high tea,' Rachel described as

consisting of powdered soup and bread and butter. We continued having high tea until we were 16, only joining our parents and older siblings for Sunday lunch. It made us greedy. So we would raid the larder until it was locked and we turned to the vegetable patch or in summer ate the grapes in the greenhouse. There was a sweet jar but it was locked in a cupboard in the drawing room and the key hidden. When it was taken out we were allowed three sweets a day. We all got very excited when my mother had hidden the key in a vase of flowers and, by accident, threw it on a bonfire with the dead flowers. She had to rescue it from the flames. It was charred and never worked properly afterwards so we could get into the cupboard.

Clothes were usually hand-me-downs – again not unusual in large families – but at odds with the worldly image of the family as well connected and successful. If there was a special occasion, something would be made up by Miss Chambers in the village.

Michael used to joke with his brothers and sisters that he would write a book about their childhood called 'Look Back in Hunger'. Antonia, however, regarded her father 'as a Medici of generosity. If you ever asked him, you would get the contents of his pocket which might be nothing or might be a crumpled fiver. We used to think our mother very mean but she was probably struggling to keep the home together.' Judith concurred. 'My mother had to manage the money and that could make her seem penny-pinching. My father was genuinely uninterested in objects or possessions, while she did notice if things were shabby. He left it to her.'

Paddy's experience was that his father could be both generous and understanding. When as a student he ran up debts, Frank would pay them off for him without too much protest. 'I think he regarded the abandoned playboy life I lived at Oxford as not that bad. In a funny sense I think he may have approved of it. He had always worked very hard but there was a part of him that perhaps would have liked to be more relaxed. He was certainly very sympathetic when you were in debt.'

As a man about the house Frank was a walking disaster. Once, when asked to make a cup of coffee, he was found by one of his daughters putting instant granules into a kettle of water and boiling up the lot. On another occasion, told to turn down the heaters in the dining room, he replied that he would if he could but he did not know how they worked. Even using a razor proved troublesome for him, and frequent were the mornings, before Elizabeth presented him with an electric shaver, that he appeared at breakfast with his face a mass of cuts. Judith suspected, however, that her father's eccentricities were sometimes intended to conceal an inherent, if reluctant, adaptability. 'He was a mature personality and he was not going to do things that bored him. And running a home, for example, didn't interest him. Conventionally he earned, my mother kept house and ran the family. However, he had this tremendous affectation of not being able to do things. It wasn't untypical of men then, but he took it to ridiculous lengths. Anyone can work out how to plug in an electric kettle, but he didn't intend to work it out.'

By summer 1952, after two years in the country, the pull of London proved just too great. Several factors were at play – the lengthy separation of Frank from his family, a small improvement in their financial circumstances as Elizabeth began writing, and concern for the younger children's schooling. Bernhurst remained the family home, somewhere to go to for weekends and in the holidays. They rarely went anywhere else in the summer as a family, and on Friday nights would, as Rachel recalled, 'travel down to Sussex in a Dormobile with my mother driving and us all eating white rolls with cheese spread'. Frank would follow on later.

The house they took in London was 14 Cheyne Gardens in Chelsea, close to the Thames Embankment and therefore well placed for the getaway to Sussex. The children described it as tall, dark and cold, its upper reaches with the linoleum floors, gas fires and the bitter bathrooms of a boarding school. The lease was nearing its renewal date and the previous tenants had reputedly lost a child there, so it was available at a good price. Elizabeth employed a decorator to warm up the lounge, dining room and her bedroom, while in the basement was a separate flat, eventually occupied by Antonia and a female cousin. When she came down from Oxford, Antonia had started work for publisher George Weidenfeld.[11] Frank did not play the over-protective father once his daughters became young women, as James Spooner,[12] his former pupil, testified.

> I remember once sleeping in the basement flat at Cheyne Gardens, having driven one of his daughters up from Oxford after a very late party at Folly Bridge. I was slightly embarrassed to be woken by Frank coming into the sitting room and catching me in my smalls on the sofa in his daughter's and niece's apartment. He seemed to take this as perfectly normal and said something like 'Good morning, James, have you been reading so and so? I think you should.'[13]

The proximity of his family brought Frank, who in 1954 started working in London full time, a little more contact, but not enough to disrupt his other concerns. 'We would be sitting around the dining table doing our homework when he would arrive home in the evening in his black homburg,' Judith recalled.

> He would kiss us on the heads, say 'is everything all right?' and then go to his study. The au pair took up a cup of tea. People would call and visit him and be shown straight up to the study or my parents would go out. They were very social. If they ate in, they ate alone together. We would have eaten earlier. Then the next morning we would sit round the dining table for breakfast, he would come in, say 'morning all', plant another kiss on our heads and leave.

Her political ambitions behind her, Elizabeth found other channels. She helped found the Africa Bureau, campaigning on issues concerned with decolonization. She was also increasingly in demand as a commentator on family matters. Having eight children gave her a halo of wisdom. This in turn led to a series of newspaper columns, starting with the *Daily Express* in 1953. Her first article was on Antonia's two imaginary friends. Later she turned to such topics as sibling rivalry. The couple were invited to dinner by Lord Beaverbrook at Cherkley, his home in Surrey, with Frank, for the first time in a long time, playing the consort. In deference to his guests' political sympathies, which differed greatly from his own, Beaverbrook arranged after dinner for a film with a vaguely left-wing moral to be shown in his private cinema. Having heard – or perhaps read in his own newspaper – that the Pakenham children were always hungry, Beaverbrook instructed his butler to fill the boot of Elizabeth's car with provisions for them.

Prompted by her columns on family issues in the *Express*, a publisher invited Elizabeth to produce a book, *Points for Parents*, in 1954. Frank was enthusiastic. For all his avid reading of newspapers, he believed that only a book had any real and lasting substance. The previous year Elizabeth had collected and edited a group of essays entitled *Catholic Approaches*, to which Frank contributed a piece on the Catholic in politics, and Elizabeth a defence – which she later described as unconvincing and half-hearted – of the Catholic ban on artificial birth control. Invitations for her to speak and take part in programmes like BBC Radio's *The Brains' Trust* followed.

Quickly establishing a reputation, Elizabeth, again encouraged by Frank, moved rapidly on to more ambitious projects. After *Points for Parents*, she began to research a full-scale biography of her great-uncle, Joseph Chamberlain. The unavailability of many of the statesman's papers meant that she ended up concentrating on just one episode in which he had been involved as Colonial Secretary, the Jameson Raid of 1896, a buccaneering attempt by Cecil Rhodes to seize Johannesburg and thus the whole of South Africa for the British Empire. The book eventually appeared in 1960 to great acclaim.

One of the reasons behind the move back to London had been concern over the younger children's schooling. Judith had been unhappy from the start at her convent school in Mayfield. One factor in making her dislike the place was highlighted to Elizabeth years later during a casual chat with Lady Hylton and recorded in her diary.

She told me she was at Mayfield with Judith and thought her very clever with a lovely skin like moonlight. She told me a curious story about Judith and the Revd Mother Declan at the time of the 1951 general election. The class were assembled and Mother D told J to go out and brush her hair. After J had left the room she said to the class: 'All your parents will be voting Conservative, but Judith's father will not. So please don't ever mention the election to Judith.'[14]

The other children had also suffered because their father's political allegiances were both well known and out of the ordinary compared with their schoolmates. When Paddy heard at Ampleforth that his father had been appointed First Lord of the Admiralty, he wrote to his parents that 'the gloomy top-table Tories said they hoped you were resigning . . . Dear bovine Miles said he was glad someone was now able to clear up the mess in Civil Aviation, and it was just bad luck on the British Navy.'

Near to the house in Cheyne Gardens, Elizabeth discovered just off the Gloucester Road a good Catholic boys' prep school, St Philip's, which stood Michael and Kevin in good stead for their eventual transfer to Ampleforth and later Cambridge and Oxford respectively. With Judith, Rachel and Catherine, Elizabeth took more of a chance on an untested alternative. More House had recently been founded by the Canonesses of St Augustine in what were, by night, student quarters. The enterprising nuns decided to use them as a day school when the students were out. Judith was the third girl to be enrolled in the new school. Rachel and Catherine followed after a spell at the Holy Child Jesus Convent school behind Oxford Circus. The curriculum at More House was limited. No science was taught, for instance, but all three girls flourished. All studied at Oxford, though Rachel and Catherine's college, St Clare's, awarded external London University degrees.

As schoolchildren living at home with their parents, they were aware of the closeness of the bond between Frank and Elizabeth. 'My parents very much had a separate life of their own,' Judith recalled. 'They made a sanctuary for themselves in the middle of our family life and we were not invited into it. They would eat together in the evenings alone, without us, and talk. They prayed together and they would talk together about politics. I picked up socialism in the air, though I cannot remember being encouraged to explore the issue; the same with Catholicism.' Not all their conversations were on serious topics. In a diary entry for 1979, Frank revealed the 'Randolph Bar (Oxford) Test', something they had jointly devised and enjoyed for many years, though it sounds very much his type of exercise. It was a measure of how attractive a woman was. 'The criterion is how many people would come and speak to you if you stood at the corner of the Randolph Bar', Frank wrote, adding that he had always believed glasses made a woman more attractive. 'Curious how many women I admire who wear horn-rimmed glasses,' he noted. 'Elizabeth', he went on, 'looks marvellous when she puts on her glasses to lecture.'[15]

At the core of Frank's life lay Elizabeth. Although his large family could often create bedlam and distract her attention, she was the still voice of calm, keeping his career on course, warding off moments of melancholy, supporting him when he took unpopular positions. There was still great – and, for those who only knew his public persona, unsuspected – romance in the attention he lavished on her. Though indifferent to his own appearance, he would take great trouble with the clothes he bought her as presents. As the sixties dawned, for example, he walked up to the nearby King's Road to get her a Mary Quant handbag.

With his children, though, as they grew into teenagers, there remained, for all his evident love and pride, an awkwardness and a lack of intimacy. Most would not dream of telling him their problems and he, if he stumbled across them, would look lost. 'A girlfriend of mine was staying with us at Bernhurst,' Rachel remembered. 'We must have been in our early teens. She was in the garden on her own and was upset for some reason or other. My father came across her. "You look rather sad," he said, "here's £5 to buy a hat". He couldn't enter into what was upsetting her but he wanted to help.' Her friends, as a result, thought him wonderfully charming and old-fashioned. His habit of treating teenagers like adults – cross-questioning them on journeys about subjects like the Romantic poets and, most importantly, listening to what they said in reply – endeared him to outsiders, but with his own children he struggled to make that extra step to intimacy that would have marked them out as special. He could not, for instance, even put his arm round them. 'It was as if he thought he didn't deserve it,' Rachel felt, 'which may date back to his own childhood'.

Two of the abiding concerns of his public life did potentially affect them. The first was his Catholicism and the conservative line he took on many contemporary questions of morality. Yet his children had no experience of being pressurized into going to church – that tended to come from their mother – or lectured on morality. 'The most he would say', recalled Paddy, 'was something like "it would be nice if you went to mass".' His one attempt to get the younger children to join him in kneeling down to say the rosary ended up with them collapsing in a heap in fits of laughter and the idea being abandoned. 'It gave him great pleasure if we agreed with him,' said Rachel, 'but there was another side of him where he was consciously trying to please us at his own expense. When I was about 15 he took me and two friends to see *Cat On a Hot Tin Roof* at the Royal Court Theatre. It wasn't his sort of thing at all, but he knew we wanted to see it.'

There were moments when his lack of inhibition about moralizing in public, even when it was becoming increasingly unfashionable in the 1960s, could embarrass his children. Rachel and Judith, both undergraduates, went to hear their father speak in an Oxford Union debate on the motion 'Is chastity an outmoded concept?'

My father was needless to say defending the motion, and he did a perfectly fine speech. Judith and I were in the gallery and he must have looked up halfway through his peroration to see his daughters sitting there. 'And how can you say that chastity is an outmoded concept,' he went on, 'when you look up there and see in the gallery two beautiful examples of perfect chastity?' And he pointed to us. Everyone turned to look at us. I fled and never appeared at the supper afterwards as arranged. The weight of this perfect chastity was too much.

The other pillar in his self-definition was his strong sense of being Irish. With the younger ones, there was little chance of going to Pakenham Hall, given Edward and Christine's antipathy to children. 'When we went to rugby matches,' Kevin remembered, 'it was never in any doubt that we supported Ireland, even if they were playing England. We may not have gone there, but it was the family home rather as a family from the Caribbean settled in England for many years would still regard the West Indies as home.'

His sense of Irishness took on almost mythic proportions. There were, given Frank's habit for telling a good story against himself, other more mundane myths. Rachel's favourite concerned Nancy Hamilton's alleged efforts to gas them all (dismissed by Elizabeth in her diary as 'a fantastic lie').

One of my mother's friends was staying, the story went, and she noticed that this nanny was keeping us quiet by gassing us. She rushed to tell my mother who was so alarmed – and this is where the story falls down in the detail because she would never have done this – that she said 'I must tell Frank'. When she had regaled him with all the details, he reputedly said 'I know what we must do. We will watch and pray. You watch and I will pray'. I don't believe a word of it, but it does, rather neatly, sum up their respective roles in our childhood, one active, one passive but concerned.

TWELVE

The Criminologist

While his colleagues on the Labour front bench in the Commons buckled down to the task of opposing a Conservative government with an elderly leader in Churchill and a fragile majority, Frank was left in the Lords facing the resident Tory majority. For the first time he experienced the practical disadvantages of being in the Lords rather than the Commons. While the party had high hopes of causing the government difficulties in a finely balanced elected chamber, there was little prospect of fruitful opposition in the Lords.

Loss of ministerial office, moreover, meant he had to relinquish his London base at Admiralty House and his ministerial salary. As a member of the Lords, unlike his colleagues in the Commons, he could claim no salary. A system of reimbursing peers' expenses plus an attendance allowance was not introduced until 1957. He needed to find paid work. As a member of the aristocracy, Frank was always considered by his friends in the Commons to have no financial worries. 'Hugh always seemed to think of me as better off than I was, or to underestimate my financial responsibilities,' he wrote of Gaitskell.[1] As a second son, he had inherited only a fraction of the family's wealth which his elder brother, Edward, was now pouring into the bottomless pit of the Gate Theatre in Dublin. Both he and Elizabeth had small private incomes from their parents, but these had quickly been spent on the day-to-day costs of bringing up and housing eight children.

The logical thing was to return to the only profession other than politics that he had enjoyed – academia – and the city that had been as close to a home town as he had ever found – Oxford. Through his old friend Robert Blake,[2] he found a part-time post back at Christ Church teaching politics. Among his pupils were his daughter, Antonia, and James Spooner. Much of what he taught was recent political history and Spooner recalled that Frank took an iconoclastic line. 'He insisted I read Beaverbrook's trilogy on the Lloyd George government. It was, he said, "not by any means all true but living history nonetheless at the time". I remember being slightly shocked when he said it could be necessary for a Minister to lie in public.'[3] Reflections on his own recent spell in government notwithstanding, what remained with Spooner was Frank's commitment as a teacher, even if it took unconventional routes. 'It was his real interest in his pupils and his involving them in all sorts of things he was doing that enchanted one. I was the only son of a war widow with no connections at Oxford and it was fascinating and exciting to be asked to lunch [by Frank] with many well-known people including Hugh Gaitskell and Agnes Headlam Morley. He really opened up Oxford and the world to me and I was eternally grateful to him.'[4]

So much had changed since the frenzied late 1930s and the fight against appeasement. Frank was now a peer and an ex-minister in a government whose politics were inimical to many of the privileges upon which Christ Church rested. He spent from Thursday to Saturday at Oxford and as a part-timer never quite slotted back into college life. Some traditions, though, he was soon to discover, had remained unchanged since his own Bullingdon days. He was reading in bed one evening when he heard the shouts and approaching footsteps of the Loders Club, part of the smart social set. 'He was just falling asleep,' Elizabeth recorded in her diary, 'when he was roused by a lot of whispering and giggling outside his bedroom. He lay quite still. Suddenly the door was pushed open. One man came in. Frank lay stiller. There was dead silence. As the door opened inwards, the intruder could not see Frank, only the end of his bed. His nerve broke. He bolted out again and they all rushed away, instead of breaking F's rooms as they had intended.'[5]

Those of his students who were not involved in such high jinks were undergraduates fresh out of the forces and anxious to complete their degrees as soon as possible and start their careers. A few caught his eye, and none more so than a young Australian Rhodes Scholar, Roger Opie, who was reading Modern Greats, by now rechristened Politics, Philosophy and Economics. Opie, who went on to teach economics with great distinction for many years at Frank's Alma Mater, New College, was sent to Lord Pakenham for political history. 'He took me under his wing. I got the impression that if anyone was prepared to work, he saw it as rather novel.' Opie found that as a tutor Frank was habitually more interested in people and personalities than with issues and concepts. 'If something interested him, he then felt he could enthuse you. And he had known so many of the people we were studying. And even when he talked about Gladstone – whom he obviously hadn't known – you felt that he knew that atmosphere. He'd say things like "I don't think you can trust Gladstone an inch" or "Oh, Disraeli was a real charmer".'[6]

While other members of the college, to judge by the Loders incident, felt that Frank was importing his own political prejudices into the tutorial room, Opie found him free from any pronounced bias, though the experience of serving a socialist prime minister was an integral part of his political outlook. 'He would make it clear that he had been a member of a Labour government. It was always there, but he didn't use it to say "if only Gladstone had been more left-wing . . ." or anything like that.'[7]

In the aftermath of Labour's defeat Frank was approached by the publishers Chapman and Hall, who wanted him to write an account of the past 100 years of British foreign policy. With his recent experience under Bevin at the Foreign Office and his knowledge of the 1921 treaty with Ireland, he could claim some expertise in the field. However, Germany had been an exceptional case. International relations had never greatly interested him. Domestic policy remained his principal concern. His interests were parochial – he would have counted Ireland as part of his own parish – rather than global. It was not, therefore, a terrible wrench to turn down the Chapman and Hall offer when Jonathan Cape came up with a lucrative alternative of £2,000 to write his memoirs.

Born to Believe, published by Cape in 1953, covered Frank's early years, his conversion to socialism and Catholicism, and included an insider's view of the Attlee government. The style was personal, with plenty of his by-now trademark self-satire, but not particularly reflective. It was not in his nature to look back over events as anything other than a source of stories and anecdotes and this gave the book a here-today-gone-tomorrow quality. Some reviewers also found him guilty of rushing to publication and overestimating his own importance and interest to the public. Political memoirs are usually the remit of senior figures in government who have retired from top public office. Frank, by contrast, had not made it into the cabinet and was still full of ambition to serve in a future Labour administration. Any claim he might have to a higher literary purpose than that of recording events and conveying his personal philosophy was received sceptically by the critics. 'Lord Pakenham, on his own showing, was born to believe a number of things,' said *The Times* review, 'and among them was the fact that it is wise for a public figure to write an autobiography before the age of 50. This, also on his own showing, is a doubtful proposition.' While noting his 'acute ear' for good anecdotes, *The Times* found him prone to praise everyone he came into contact with and lacking sufficient intellectual rigour and political judgement to make his own story interesting. After the unqualified success and continuing reputation of *Peace by Ordeal*, *Born to Believe* had a decidedly mixed reception.

Evelyn Waugh had tried hard to persuade him to rewrite the book on the justifiable grounds of the damage its loose and anecdotal style would do to his intellectual reputation. Writing in his diary on 28 September 1952 with cruel clear-sightedness but an evident affection for his victim, Waugh outlined an argument with Frank over the manuscript of *Born to Believe*.

I overstated the badness of the writing. I said I wasn't shocked at a politician writing like that but at a don's. It might be worthy of a second year undergraduate at Brasenose. I had in the preceding days taken a physical revulsion to the manuscript and couldn't bring myself to touch it. When challenged to find clichés, I failed. Left on bad terms and with the feeling that all Frank's protestations of friendship are blarney and his sense of Catholicism, uplift.[8]

Waugh invited his old friend to come and spend two weeks with him at his home in Italy where they could rewrite the manuscript together. He was in effect offering a masterclass. Frank declined. There was his dislike of travel, his antipathy to being shown how to do something by the overbearing Waugh, but most of all he did not think improving his literary style was worth two weeks of his time. When he had tried harder with *Peace by Ordeal*, he had written well, but now his interests were less in achieving plaudits from other writers and more in getting a political message over. His prose may not have been perfect, but he was content that it was adequate to its primary purpose.

Born to Believe, with its heavy emphasis on Catholicism, strengthened a growing association in the public's mind between Frank and his religion, as indeed it was meant to. He was in great demand as a high-profile lay champion of the Christian cause. He was invited, for example, to a Cambridge Union debate with A.L. Rowse[9] on the motion 'God made man in his own image and likeness'. Rowse defeated him by four votes.

The intertwining of the Catholic and socialist influences in his life continued also to affect his reaction to developments within the Labour Party and his party profile. His Catholicism was as important a feature as his ministerial achievements, and consequently his essay in Elizabeth's collection *Catholic Approaches* on the Catholic/Christian in politics became a standard theme in his countless talks to audiences up and down the country. He never felt entirely easy with the topic since it seemed he was, immodestly in his own eyes, claiming the moral high ground. Yet, inevitably, such was the case. 'After all,' he admitted, 'when one lectures on "The Christian in Politics", one is not far from saying: (i) A Christian in politics is a better man than other politicians. (ii) I am a Christian in politics, therefore I am better than, at any rate, most other politicians. (iii) And it may interest you to know in what my special virtue consists.'[10]

In expanding on that virtue, Frank would draw a distinction between Christian policies and programmes on the one hand and the conduct of the individual Christian in politics on the other. In the latter case, it was a question of a minister or parliamentarian applying his faith and conscience to his work. He had followed this principle in his approach in Attlee's government, notably over Germany. In so far as specifically Christian policies can exist, Frank saw them in operation mainly in the social field, and it was towards this wider, though ill-defined, area that his thoughts were turning in the early 1950s.

I remain unrepentantly convinced that even though the conclusions of the natural law are open to anyone with a brain to think with, the average Christian, with and without supernatural aid, is much more likely than the average non-Christian to try to give effect to them. So although in theory I agree that any enlightened social policy could be hatched by non-Christians, in practice it is much more likely to emerge from a Christian source, whether or not it can be ascribed to it beyond all possibility of argument.[11]

He was searching for a new mission, areas and issues where he could make a distinct contribution, where politics and faith had common ground in their upholding of the equality of all individuals. Freed of the constraints of running a department of state, he now had the luxury – from his vantage point in the becalmed House of Lords – of choosing the issues with which to make his mark as a Christian socialist. While his ambition to return to high office remained strong, he began to focus on areas which were not the staples of British political life.

The crusades that had hitherto supplemented Frank's daily parliamentary and ministerial diet were by now waning. Over

Ireland, his attempts to get his senior colleagues and newspaper editors like David Astor to take seriously the question of reuniting north and south had failed to arouse interest. His continued protestations of nationalism were scorned by some of his friends. In July 1952, Evelyn Waugh recounted to Nancy Mitford his meeting with the 'poor Frankenstein Monster' in London. Frank, Waugh said, 'believes that he is under private instructions from the late King [George VI] to solve the Ulster problem by having Princess Margaret declared Queen of an independent and united Ireland'.[12] It was a story that Frank subsequently denied – 'Evelyn put down what amused him or what he thought would amuse his correspondents' – but it has the echo of something he might have raised as a speculation over lunch.

On Germany, Frank found himself increasingly subsumed in the mainstream of his own party's thinking. The Labour front bench in the Commons took a pro-German line, backing government plans to rearm West Germany and allow it to join the Atlantic Alliance. Although Frank's own theme of Christian forgiveness of the Germans was not widely taken up, the need to build up a bulwark against the expansion of Communism and the significance of Konrad Adenauer as an ally of the West were both recognized. Frank had taken an early lead in questioning the prevailing pro-Soviet, pro-SPD sympathies in his own party. It was over Labour's attitude to German rearmament and the Atlantic Alliance that Hugh Gaitskell and Aneurin Bevan were to clash repeatedly in the early 1950s, with Frank's old room-mate leading the front bench's opposition to Bevan's anti-American stance.

A larger struggle was taking place in the Labour Party in the early 1950s between those who responded to the reverse of 1951 by advocating a period of consolidation on the achievements of 1945–51 and those who wanted to press on with further nationalization and socialist policies. With Shadow Chancellor Gaitskell and Herbert Morrison leading the consolidators, and Bevan and Harold Wilson at the head of the progressive group, the two camps fought their corners over a number of issues, of which German rearmament was just one. They were also battling for the future direction and leadership of the Labour Party, with the question of Attlee's successor never far from the surface. Frank had little time for Bevan and sided wholeheartedly with the consolidators, who won out after the 1955 general election defeat. When Attlee subsequently resigned, Gaitskell defeated both Bevan and an out-of-touch Morrison on the first ballot for the Labour leadership. Yet it was a contest over which Frank could exert little influence.

Compared with the heady days of running the British zone in Germany and battling with the Foreign Secretary, he found academia and life at Christ Church rather pale and unchallenging. Looking for a new challenge, at the end of the summer term in 1953 Frank asked his student, Roger Opie, bound for further academic work in the autumn at the London School of Economics, to come and work for him over the long vacation on a study of the causes of crime which he had set up with funding from the Nuffield Foundation. Here was the new mission he had been seeking since he left the government, an area where his Catholicism and socialism could operate hand in hand.

Prisons had been part of his life since the late 1930s when he visited Oxford Jail on behalf of his constituents in Cowley. When he returned to Oxford after his military service and work with Beveridge, he briefly took up prison visiting again but during his period in Attlee's government he had had little time to spare. Occasionally, however, an old face from the past had turned up to ask for his help. During one particularly heated discussion at the Foreign Office when he was Minister for Germany, Frank was interrupted by his secretary to say that he had a visitor. The man in question, a lay preacher with a long record of custodial sentences for homosexual activity whom he had befriended when he was in Oxford Jail, had come to seek his blessing for his forthcoming wedding. When the groom revealed that he had not told his future bride of his past, Frank, 'after some humming and hawing', advised him not to come clean but, if the truth ever came out, to refer his wife to him.[13] With that he said goodbye and returned to Bevin's office to continue their debate. Six months later, the lay preacher's wife contacted Frank to say she had discovered the truth about her husband. He entertained the two to lunch at Simpson's and managed to smooth the waters. The episode taught him an important lesson. Spontaneity and warmth are indispensable for winning the regard and confidence of those who turn to you for help, but it requires forethought and follow-through to be effective. The after-care of prisoners should not be left to well-intentioned individuals but to dedicated bodies. The thought echoed in his mind as he began looking into the causes of crime.

The idea for the investigation had come to Frank in a flash one morning as he read *The Times* on 1 December 1952. The article detailed how crime was on the increase. This rise had come at a time of growing prosperity and expanding social services under the Attlee government. Frank had worked with Beveridge in the belief that eliminating want would create a more equal and therefore a better world. Instead, higher living standards for those on the lower rungs of society seemed to have accelerated crime. Faced with this conundrum, which gnawed at his most cherished socialist beliefs, Frank decided that a new Beveridge was needed to examine why crime had increased as poverty had decreased.

He began by approaching Beveridge himself but his former boss, now in his seventies, declined to take up the gauntlet. Through David Astor at the *Observer*, Frank was put in touch with Leslie Farrer-Brown of the Nuffield Foundation, who agreed to fund a two-year investigation into the causes of crime. Frank would work from Nuffield's headquarters in Regent's Park when he was not at Christ Church and would be assisted by a team of secretaries and researchers, in effect his own ministry team in exile. The aim, announced with some ceremony to the press, was to publish a report that would both produce an accurate picture of the extent and nature of crime in Britain and reveal the motivations of those involved in criminal activity.

Within that framework, author and commissioner had differing priorities. Frank's mind was typically racing on to the conclusions and the practical action that would follow. Nuffield was keen on a thorough-going assessment and compilation of existing knowledge and data on the subject. They wanted Frank to don the mantle of social scientist – rather than politician – to study crime just as a meteorologist would study climate. 'They were much less ready than I', he admitted later, 'to grasp at limited evidence with a view to immediate action.'[14]

This divergence of purpose was to dog the entire inquiry and accounts for the uneven way it collected evidence. Psychiatrists, sociologists and various bodies involved in the treatment of offenders would come to Nuffield Lodge to present their views and undergo cross-examination by Frank and Dr Grunhut, a reader in criminology at Oxford, Frank Milton, a north London magistrate, Dr Stafford-Clark of Guy's Hospital and Dr Trevor Gibbens of the Maudsley Hospital. In addition to this formal and academic approach, Frank spent a great deal of time visiting prisons – fifteen are listed in his final report – borstals, remand homes and approved schools. On such missions he was usually accompanied by Honor Jones, who had previously been Secretary to the Howard League for Penal Reform. As a result of these visits, and through personal contacts, he also talked at great length to offenders and ex-offenders. As he commented in the foreword to his final report, 'Those who have worked among ex-prisoners will sympathise with my admission that my scientific interest in individuals yields easily to a sense of human kinship.'[15]

While Nuffield was looking for facts and figures backed up by painstaking research, Frank, moved by the individuals he met, wanted to act to change a system which he felt was hopelessly inadequate, notably in the after-care of offenders once they had left prison. He quickly became convinced that the search for statistical evidence was fruitless and instead drew his conclusions from individual cases.

The disparity between the two approaches left his inquiry with a confused sense of purpose. From the start some of the Nuffield staff found his attitude informal and unbusinesslike. Roger Opie remembered that he was just told to turn up to start work one Monday morning at Nuffield Lodge. He never had a written contract or terms of reference. But it was neither in Frank's nature, nor was it his intention, to engage in a long, detailed inquiry. His instincts, fine-tuned at the Ministry of Civil Aviation, were those of the initiator and delegator who spots an issue and then sets his team to work. He regarded it as an advantage as head of the inquiry not to know anything at the outset about the causes of crime. To be successful, he felt, you needed to think yourself into the role of someone who is ignorant but who wants to learn, a representative of the public.

Roger Opie recalled his own reaction to this way of working.

He seemed to think that as a PPE man I could do anything. He thought that clever people when asked the right questions in the right way at the right time would come up with the answers. A subject would occur to him and at once he'd be on the phone to three or four people whom he just happened to know who were experts in the field. There was a somewhat arrogant, upper-class element in thinking that no problem couldn't be solved. But it was also the academic in him. What he had that many academics lack though was energy, interest and concern.[16]

While his team were dealing with the central issues in the inquiry and an ever-lengthening list of submissions, Frank got more and more sidetracked by the cases of individual prisoners and in the failings of the prison system as he observed it. Consequently, the original scientific purpose of the causes of crime inquiry fell by the wayside. Thanks to Frank's social connections and his public standing, doors were opened wherever he cast his gaze. The Home Office cooperated, though Roger Opie said that their attitude was distant, cool and not altogether helpful. Yet for all the seriousness that surrounded the investigation, it was still seen in penal reform circles – and in the Home Office on Dr Opie's evidence – as essentially a dilettante effort, an amateur dipping his toe in waters best left to expert navigators.

One year into the two years that had been allotted for the inquiry, Frank was offered, out of the blue, a full-time job at the National Bank and immediately leapt at a new challenge. He told his backers at Nuffield that, with their leave, he planned to accept. He felt that his work with them had reached its limit and was sceptical of the chance of reaching any proven conclusions about the scale and nature of crime. The foundation agreed to him cutting short the research, but they were not happy about his suggestion that his 'findings' should be published under Nuffield's logo. Frank was the first to admit that measured in strictly scientific terms, the total product of the inquiry did not amount to much. 'If scientific categories were going to be insisted on in dealing with the questions "What are the causes of crime?" and "Why has crime increased so much in Britain?", the total answer after a year was in one sense a lemon. And it was not likely to look much different a year later.'[17]

Frank abandoned the Nuffield inquiry in 1954 and it was not until four years later that his personal account of proceedings appeared as *Causes of Crime* under George Weidenfeld's imprint, with Roger Opie receiving a hefty co-writing credit. Sonia Orwell,[18] who had read the manuscript, persuaded Weidenfeld that, whatever Nuffield's reservations, the book should be published. It began by laying great emphasis on the fact that no accurate assessment of the extent of crime was possible because the Home Office did not provide the necessary statistics. Indeed, the first chapter concluded that it was impossible to say unequivocally that there had even been an increase in crime since the war. (Frank was to take up this matter in various public addresses in the mid-1950s, including a speech to the Magistrates' Association in 1955 where he appealed for a new statistical department to be set up at the Home Office and for a unified set of figures on crime covering all the country's police districts.)

Causes of Crime then considered the 'reasons' quoted for the alleged upturn in crime. In addition to events that were specific to the period – the wartime dislocation of social mores, the economic shortages that came with peace and the introduction of the welfare state and its supposed encouragement of a 'something for nothing' mentality – the book mentioned broken homes, the media, police failings, a general decline in morals, the collapse of the family and the weakening of religious belief. Each of these 'reasons' was investigated with detailed summaries of some of the expert witnesses' evidence. The conclusion was in effect that there were as many causes as there were crimes. No effort was made to evaluate and grade the list.

Frank's opinions shone through the book, which became, after Nuffield's withdrawal, a personal statement. The Christian outlook on crime was discussed at length, reflecting what Roger Opie saw at the time of the inquiry as Frank's personal concern with questions of sin, evil, the devil and redemption. Having noted the lack of accurate statistics that would allow a scientific evaluation of the supposed decline of religion, Frank concluded with his own conviction – without a shred of supporting evidence – that 'there is little crime to be found among active members of the Christian churches'.[19]

In a section advocating 'A New Approach to Crime', based largely on his observations when visiting prisons, he touched fleetingly on excessively long sentences that were out of proportion to the crime committed; the need for prison to act not just as punishment but also as a place for rehabilitation; and the relationship between sin and crime.

The book reached few definite conclusions. The answers it sought to the questions addressed by the inquiry could not be backed up by the sort of statistical data that Nuffield had hoped would be forthcoming. In that regard the whole exercise can be said to have lacked any authority and therefore to have failed. Yet it certainly did contribute to growing pressure on the Home Office to put substantially more resources into collecting accurate data, a task which R.A. Butler as Home Secretary was to initiate at about the time *Causes of Crime* was published.

More pertinently, though, the book signposted a new avenue of activity for Frank. In allowing him to visit prisons, the inquiry drew his attention to a field that hitherto had interested few rising and ambitious politicians, the rehabilitation and after-care of offenders. As in Germany and Ireland, Frank would initially take up the cause of unpopular individuals, then his concern would spread to the wider issues in which they were embroiled. The inmates he met on his visits to Britain's prisons became a new 'constituency' and, like those over whom he had responsibility as Minister for Germany, this group was neglected and hated by British society. The Establishment's hostility only served to deepen Frank's resolve to help them. He determined to use his own privileged position to their advantage.

Here was a new crusade, an unpopular cause he could champion. To those who had already watched his many changes of course, it was another public volte-face to amuse and irritate them, but lying behind it was almost two decades of private and little-publicized prison visiting.

Frank felt uniquely qualified to take on such a role because he was both inside and outside that Establishment. To focus his efforts on unpopular causes was both a way of making a mark in the normally neglected chamber of the Lords and, more importantly, a means of turning his military failures to good effect. He would be, as he liked to put it, 'the outcasts' outcast', someone who could sympathize with the plight of those on the margins because of his own marginalization during his wartime breakdown.

Fear of damaging his political career never once entered Frank's mind as a reason to avoid the prisons' issue. First, he did not see any conflict in his convictions about prison reform as they dovetailed with his political beliefs. Second, while he retained his ambitions for high office, his view of party politics was becoming more ambivalent and he was less involved in the daily struggles that were convulsing Labour as it came to terms with electoral defeat. Third, he was attaching an increasing importance to his search for a distinct and personal expression of his Christian socialism.

Frank saw at once that he would have the field of crime, in particular the treatment of offenders and ex-offenders, largely to himself. Penal reform was seen as an issue for individual campaigners rather than as a vote-winner for politicians. However, as a member of an unelected chamber, unconcerned with how electors would respond to his involvement with criminals, as a politician with a record for taking an independent line, and as a man who had already experienced the disapproval of those around him, Frank could afford to follow his instincts.

The concern with sin and redemption that Roger Opie had noted during the causes of crime inquiry was also part of Frank's interest in prisoners. At the most basic level, he was responding to the line in Matthew's Gospel: 'I was in prison and you came to see me.' He came not to judge or urge prisoners to repent, but simply to express his solidarity with them over the period of their ordeal. 'I can't help judging them, disapproving of the crimes they have committed,' he wrote, 'but I constantly remind myself and tell them that we are all sinners. I don't get on a pedestal. They have failed and I am conscious of having failed during the War. My spirit was willing but my flesh was weak. That could equally apply to them.'[20]

Catholicism preaches forgiveness. This, to Frank, was the distinguishing Christian virtue and one which he now set out to act out in his life. While they may have offended against the laws of the state, he questioned whether prisoners have offended against God's law any more than any other member of society. 'As I see it,' he wrote, 'we can never be sure that someone who commits a wicked crime is in the sight of God any more wicked than we are.'[21]

One of the first cases in which Frank became involved was that of Christopher Craig. In 1952 Craig had shot and killed a policeman who had caught him committing an armed robbery. His accomplice, Derek Bentley, already in custody, had shouted to Craig, 'Let him have it, Chris!' At their trial it was accepted that Bentley had been telling Craig to shoot the policeman (though forty-five years later the verdict was overturned). As a minor, Craig could not receive the death penalty but Bentley, who was mentally retarded, could and did. Bentley's death was to become a *cause célèbre* of the campaign to abolish capital punishment which Frank joined in the mid-1950s. Initially, though, it was the fate of Christopher Craig that attracted him.

Craig was in Wakefield Prison, one of the establishments Frank visited as part of the Nuffield inquiry. The two met and Frank was impressed by the efforts Craig was making at rehabilitation, training as a fitter, improving his education and in general behaving as a model prisoner. After several meetings with Craig's family, he began to lobby the Home Office for the young man's release. He pointed to

Craig's unhappy family background, the influence of his older brother Niven, who was involved in crime from an early age, Christopher's inability to read and write and to his subsequent dramatic change and reform when in prison. To keep Craig locked up for decades would serve no good purpose, Frank was convinced. He had been punished and now there was every chance that he would make a good and honest citizen. Frank was just one of a number of prominent people who took up Craig's case and in 1962, after serving ten years of his sentence, he was released.

Another notorious case to attract Frank's interest was that of Michael Davies, convicted in 1953 of a brutal murder on Clapham Common in south-west London and sentenced to death. The psychiatrist who had examined Davies was one of the experts Frank consulted during his Nuffield inquiry. The connection brought Frank on to the case and he quickly came to share the psychiatrist's conviction of the young man's innocence.

Frank decided to commission a private detective to compile a dossier of evidence. He turned to a retired army officer and one-time policeman, Major Matthew Oliver, whom he had first met in Germany, where Oliver was serving as a military attaché. For three months Oliver – who was unpaid but worked on the case, as he later put it, 'out of friendship for Frank' – re-examined the case. His report, which exonerated Davies, was then passed by Frank to the Home Secretary who, having considered it among other submissions, was persuaded first to spare Davies the gallows and later to release him after seven years in prison. Major Oliver saw it as 'a negation of natural justice that he was never granted a Queen's Pardon', but Frank was at the gates of Wormwood Scrubs with Elizabeth when Davies was released and took him off to breakfast in Richmond.[22]

While Frank's lobbying on behalf of Craig had excited few headlines, his connection with Michael Davies was taken up with gusto by the press. In August 1956, the *News of the World* reported that Frank had received a death threat as a result of his campaign on behalf of Davies. He was warned to drop the case or risk being 'done in' with a razor. Relatives of the victim of the Clapham

Common stabbing criticized him for his interference. Already known to be interested in prisons through his work with Nuffield, he was fast establishing a reputation in the press as the prisoners' friend. With his early successes on behalf of Craig and Davies, he became a focus for those complaining of the rough justice handed out to them.

Frank, zealous about his new project, wanted to investigate each and every case, to visit anyone who wrote to him. One of the privileges of being a member of the House of Lords was that he could make visits at any of HM prisons without prisoners having to use up one of their precious family visiting slots. After 1957, when peers were allowed to claim their expenses, he was able to get a little financial assistance in his travels.

Though the showman in him undoubtedly enjoyed the coverage gained by his involvement with high-profile individuals, the bulk of the cases he adopted concerned prisoners who were not well known, where his work went unreported. The charge laid against him that he sought out only infamous criminals was unjust. On the whole, he responded to cases brought to him. Inevitably sometimes he was duped. His friend David Astor believed that he was often taken in by prisoners because 'he was one of nature's innocents. He was a very clever, very talented, very experienced child. There was nothing worldly about him though he could move in the world.'[23] There is much truth in this, though the agnostic Astor missed a crucial point about Frank's Christian crusade over prisoners. He was not overly concerned with guilt or innocence. He wanted to awaken society's conscience to the way it was treating all those in jail, regardless of whether they deserved to be there.

THIRTEEN

The City's Best-known Socialist

It had been the offer of a job at the National Bank, one of eleven clearing banks in the City of London, that brought Frank's work for the Nuffield Foundation to a premature end. In the autumn of 1954 he became Deputy Chairman and took over as Chairman at the start of 1955 at the Bank's headquarters on Old Broad Street in the Square Mile. While there had been a long tradition of Conservative politicians taking up posts in the City once their careers at Westminster came to an end, the appointment of a socialist ex-minister was highly unusual. Moreover, Frank had not held any post at the Treasury. That the new chairman retained hopes of holding high office again, and continued to speak from the opposition front bench in the House of Lords, was unprecedented.

The City was not sure what to make of Frank. As a descendant of the Jerseys who had owned Child's, an Old Etonian with a first from Oxford in Modern Greats, where he had specialized in economic theory, banking and currency, he could not be dismissed as a lightweight. Yet his politics, his reputation for eccentricity and his continuing, albeit minor, role in the leadership of a party that had a long history of antagonism towards the City made him suspect. Even the intervention of his widely respected uncle, Arthur Villiers, nearing the end of his career as a director of Barings, could not prevent Frank from being blackballed by the City Club, one of the Square Mile's more exclusive institutions.

The National Bank – taken over in the 1970s by Williams and Glyns Bank and they in turn by the Royal Bank of Scotland – was a unique institution. Its Anglo-Irish roots called for a chairman who had standing on both sides of the Irish Sea. Founded in 1835 by Daniel O'Connell, the 'Great Liberator' and the man who led the campaign that resulted in the Catholic Emancipation Act of 1829,[1] the National Bank had, like the Pakenham family, grown in wealth and influence in an era when the Irish and British economies were as one. In 1859 it had joined the London clearing banks system. There was nothing paradoxical then about a bank whose funds were largely provided in Ireland but whose head office was in London. Branches had been opened all around the British Isles.

By the time that Frank took over as Chairman, though, the treaty of 1921 had effectively separated three-quarters of Ireland from Britain and the relationship between the National Bank's investors, two-thirds of whom were in Ireland, and its investments – mainly in British government securities through the London market – was a delicate one. The National Bank was the only financial institution that attempted to bridge the gap between London and Dublin, with boards of directors in both capitals but London taking precedence. Of the other banks functioning in the Irish Republic at the time, the majority had their headquarters in Dublin and two were based in Belfast. None had a branch network like the National's in Britain.

In London there was a clear view that the National was an anachronism. The first time Frank attended a meeting of the clearing-bank chairmen, one remarked, lightheartedly but pointedly, 'I always say you oughtn't to be here.'[2] The Bank of England had had to be carefully nurtured by Frank's long-serving predecessor, Michael Cooke, to ensure that the National's dual position was maintained. Cooke was seventy-three in 1954 and, after twenty-one years as Chairman, had been anxious to retire for some years. However, he had failed to find a suitable successor whose credentials would pass muster in London and Dublin, who would be able to lunch with other chairmen in the City and move easily around the branches in Ireland. The obvious candidate, Antony Acton, a member of the board with ample banking experience, had no Irish links and was not a Catholic. Though religion was kept out of business, the National counted many Irish religious orders among its clients and had to take their preferences and prejudices into account. Cooke was not looking for a figurehead but for someone who would be prepared to exercise close, day-to-day control. He was a shrewd man who had worked his way to the top from the most junior post. He was able to see through Frank's distracted air and self-satire to the qualities that brought him success as a manager and financial controller of nationalized industries when he was at Civil Aviation.

The approach came through John Dulanty, retired Irish High Commissioner in London and one of those who had dissuaded Frank from resigning in 1949 at the time of the Government of Ireland Act. He met Cooke at the Reform Club and listened to the terms and conditions. The job would not be a short-term appointment. While he would be able to continue his work in the Lords, the Bank had to come first. Frank was initially in two minds. Cooke was immensely respected and reputedly able to take over every job in the bank at a moment's notice. Frank would not be able match that sort of expertise, and while he had proved himself as a manager, his own approach was more that of an initiator and delegator. There was also the question of becoming less involved in the inner counsels of the Labour Party. Though the Lords was not a significant area for Labour under a Conservative government, Frank still retained an influence on the leadership, especially through his close personal ties with Hugh Gaitskell.

The two lunched at the House of Lords to discuss Cooke's offer. Gaitskell was against Frank accepting. He doubted the contention that an inside view of the City would be valuable to the party. Gaitskell was much more optimistic than his old friend that Labour would win the 1955 general election. In such an event, Frank would be in line for leadership of the House of Lords and a post in Cabinet, Gaitskell pointed out. If he went to the Bank and committed himself to a lengthy stay, he would have to decline such an offer from the Prime Minister. Attlee himself was much more flexible when approached by Frank. 'The Tories do it: why shouldn't you?' he told his young colleague.[3]

From a practical point of view, there was a strong financial motivation to accepting the post. As Chairman, Frank would be able to abandon Christ Church, support his family and pay their school fees. He decided, against Gaitskell's advice, to put the party to one side for the time being at least. It was a choice that shows how far he had travelled since he first joined Labour less than twenty years previously. Then a distraction from politics would have been unthinkable. By 1954, the glitter had tarnished. The same realization was leading him to branch out into the field of prison reform. He had experienced ministerial office, still nurtured ambitions, but was looking for a new challenge. The Labour Party was no longer his all. Accepting the post was another indication of his ability to compartmentalize areas of his life – his politics in one box, his prison work in another and now his 'day job' in a third. He would be the first to point out the interconnections, but the reality was that for much of the time they were separate and often pulled him in opposite directions.

To those on the left of the party, for example, Frank's decision to go and work in the City only emphasized their suspicions of his background and Establishment ties. He was a Tory toff returning to his roots. At best he was exposing himself to the charge of being a good-time socialist, around and keen when the party was in government and ministerial office was on offer, but looking elsewhere when times were harder.

Such accusations, which significantly reduced Frank's standing in the Labour movement, failed to take into account the isolation and financial constraint he suffered in the Lords, and underestimated the lure of the National's offer to him. To be a socialist in the City, the head of a clearing bank yet still an active politician, was a unique opportunity. To a maverick like Frank, habitually so fascinated by anomalies, by people who could not be pigeon-holed, it was irresistible.

Working for the National Bank also appealed to his sense of his own Irishness, though his brother Edward greeted the news of his appointment with a snort of laughter. 'The best news for years,' he laughed, 'I'll break him with my overdraft.' (Edward's subsidies of the Gate Theatre in Dublin had all but exhausted the family coffers.)[4] Since his first meetings with de Valera and *Peace by Ordeal*, Frank had taken the cause of Ireland to heart and regarded himself, despite his Ascendancy roots, as an Irishman and a nationalist. Though he had chosen to make his career in England and had, in terms of where he lived and his children's education, turned his back on Ireland, the chance of heading the National Bank, with the largest branch network in the country, gave him an opportunity to play a significant role in Irish life for the first time. Indeed, the ambiguities of the National's position, straddling the Irish Sea, reflected Frank's own dual allegiances. The fact that so many in the City of London thought such a dual role was anachronistic shows just how marginalized the Anglo-Irish had become by the new political arrangements between the two countries. Thomas Pakenham, who like his father tried to uphold that twin allegiance, described the concept of being British as the key to his father's seemingly anomalous position. 'It was not a question of him being English or Irish. He came from an Anglo-Irish family and was, in that sense, both British and Irish. The two were not incompatible. It was not unlike the position of Scottish and Welsh aristocratic families. They would send their children to English public schools just as my father's parents did. And he retained that dual allegiance, carrying an Irish passport while going on British government business, for example.'[5]

As Chairman of the National Bank, Frank had the role of passionate amateur. He and his board of mainly distinguished and respected citizens were insulated from the day-to-day business that was handled by the professionals. Technical knowledge and business acumen were the preserve of the general managers, while public contact and overall decision-making remained the responsibility of the board and its chairman. Where Michael Cooke had cast his gaze over the whole organization, with an eye for even the smallest of matters, Frank quickly moved to delegate lesser details to his general managers. He had neither the expertise nor the interest to keep such a tight rein of control.

Over major issues he would consult his directors much more than his predecessor had done and worked to achieve a consensus. In his time at the bank he appointed the entire Irish board and four out of the six English directors. John Leydon, the Irish Chairman, played a significant part in the building of Ireland's economy in the inner counsels of Prime Minister Sean Lemass.[6] Frank subsequently took pride in having promoted David Montagu to the English board. At thirty-three he was one of the youngest men ever to make it on to the board of a major clearing bank, but Frank's concern, besides Montagu's business expertise, was that the commercial banks in Britain in the 1950s were biased against Jews in high positions. At the time of Montagu's appointment, Frank estimated that the only other Jew on the board of any joint-stock bank in the City was the deputy chairman of Lloyd's. 'During my time in the City,' he wrote, 'I would not describe this as deliberate anti-Semitism. In charity one might call it an evil legacy, but the result was the same. The highest positions in the City were virtually closed to Jews.'[7]

While at one level being a chairman was akin to running a ministry, at another Frank found that the collective responsibility of two boards of directors was a change of direction, working with a team rather than as a leader. 'The members of the board of a bank share the responsibility for policy and for results. The Board of the Admiralty', he mused, 'presents a superficial analogy, but that is recognised fiction. The only ultimate responsibility within the department is that of the Minister, i.e. the First Lord. In this sense a bank chairman could never feel the strain of personal responsibility in any way so acutely.'[8]

However, as a minister, his ultimate responsibility had been to a cabinet of which he was not a member, and beyond that to the electorate. At the bank there was a greater freedom of manoeuvre. Commercial considerations were the only valid criteria in most decisions. There was little opportunity for publicity or pandering to the electorate. 'In banking,' he wrote of his period as Chairman in the 1950s, 'there is an absence of public knowledge and public discussion of the performance of particular institutions. This, while relieving the strain of public scrutiny, restricts, though it does not destroy, the field of public trust.'[9] Results rather than intentions and fine words were the mark of a successful bank chairman. A politician, by contrast, could escape liability for his failings as long as he could talk his way round them.

There were areas where Frank left his imprint. He was very keen that the National should expand its branch network and he persuaded his fellow directors to concur. No new English branches had been opened since 1921 and he was determined to build up the British side of operations, especially in the south-east. He also took a greater interest in meeting his staff and their welfare than had hitherto been expected of the chairman. He was a passionate advocate of unionization and was the first bank chairman to address a meeting of the National Union of Bank Employees. To his own staff he pledged that no one at the National should receive less in pay than his or her equivalent colleagues at other clearing banks. In a more relaxed vein he played host once a year at Bernhurst to a cricket match between a bank team and an eleven from Hurst Green. In his dishevelled whites and slightly too short trousers, he joined in with the National's employees before standing them lunch at a local hotel.

Co-ordination of the Irish and British sides of operations involved many journeys across the Irish Sea. Frank made around eighty visits to Ireland in his eight years as Chairman, though he made a point of never using his position to interfere in Irish politics. However much he felt himself an Irishman, he knew that his sphere of political operations had to be restricted to Britain.

At the outset of his reign, the Irish staff of the National were engaged in a go-slow over conditions. By the end of his period, he had won their affection. They presented Frank with a scroll that paid tribute to him as 'an honoured chairman' but more significantly as 'a great friend'. 'There was a man called Arthur Quirk [recalled Christine Longford] who used to drive him [Frank] all around Ireland to see these sub-offices of the Bank, in quite out of the way places. He was an enormous success. Bank clerks are encouraged to play games and Frank has always been very good on athletics. He would always know the form of practically any footballer in any small town in Ireland. He always talked to bank clerks about that. They'd never had a visiting chairman who could talk to them like that.'[10]

There was overlap with his prison reform concerns. He intervened in the case of a young employee who stole £300 from his branch in Ireland and was dismissed. Planning to leave for Canada to avoid the disgrace, the miscreant was contacted by Frank, who arranged to see him. The Chairman gave the young man a rosary and promised to keep in touch. Within four months he had paid back the money out of his wages in Canada and in later years was to return to Ireland where he and Frank became friends.

The balance sheet on Frank's tenure at the National Bank was in the black, according to several eminent observers. Business in England and Wales increased three times faster than the average of its competitors. The *Daily Telegraph* paid tribute to his business flair and shrewdness. The *Economist* described him as a successful amateur banker. The use of the second adjective is significant. For despite the energy and enthusiasm with which he threw himself into the job, and his wholehearted decision to make the bank his first priority, the world of politics still laid claim to some of his attention. Banking never quite overtook politics in his affections.

As a socialist in the City, he tried to prove Gaitskell wrong and operate as an effective double agent for his party. He embarked on a long campaign to bring about a cessation of hostility between Labour and the City. He arranged a series of lunches with influential figures in the Square Mile for Hugh Gaitskell, Harold Wilson, Aneurin Bevan, Frank Cousins,[11] the union leader, and James Callaghan, his former number two at the Admiralty and, after Gaitskell's election in late 1955 as Labour leader, a hot tip to be a future Chancellor of the Exchequer.

Little was achieved, though some very pleasant lunches were had. The conflict of Frank's two careers was highlighted in 1957 when, in the midst of a financial crisis, the Conservative Chancellor of the Exchequer, Peter Thorneycroft,[12] called in the clearing-bank chairmen for a full and open discussion. Great emphasis was placed on secrecy. Frank had already noted how his presence among the clearing banks' delegation as an ex-Labour minister and opposition spokesman in the Lords had embarrassed Thorneycroft's predecessor, Harold Macmillan, and he was scrupulous about leaving politics out of such gatherings. One item that was not raised at the meeting was that a substantial increase in the bank rate was intended. However, news of the rise leaked out somehow and speculators were able to take advantage. There was an outcry, followed by angry scenes in the House of Commons, with Harold Wilson leading the opposition's demands for an inquiry and hinting at collusion between the Conservative Party and the City. Frank found himself with a foot in both camps. He sympathized with Labour's anger and could see the political capital to be made out of Wilson's accusations, but was sure from his inside knowledge of how the City worked that news of the bank-rate increase had not come the way his colleague was suggesting. He likened his position at the time to that of Winston Churchill who, when asked which side he was on in the Spanish Civil War, replied 'both'.

The Parker Inquiry was set up to investigate the leak and exonerated all concerned. As it was published, Frank, with his dual vantage point, was tempted into print by the *Daily Telegraph*. On 31 January 1958, he defended the standards of professionalism in the City, adding: 'I am not coming forward to say that those I have met in the City are morally better than politicians, but I will certainly swear they are no worse.' He continued with words that were to rebound upon him: 'Some of the most eminent of the leaders in the City have recently vindicated their integrity, never doubted by anyone but a fool or a knave.' Tory MPs seized upon this remark as an indictment of Harold Wilson, who had led the Labour assault over the leak. Frank had to write hurriedly to Wilson, pointing out that he had not meant to suggest he was a fool or a knave. Wilson accepted his apology, but to those who were suspicious of the self-proclaimed socialist in the City, the incident was further evidence that the two interests were incompatible. To others it simply confirmed their impression of Frank's naïveté and capacity for misjudgement.

However, in the City the article was greeted with great enthusiasm and Frank suddenly received a flood of luncheon invitations. He decided to exploit these – and try to undo the damage his article had caused in his party – by reviving his attempt to build bridges and so invited along prominent Labour colleagues. In the run-up to the 1959 general election, with the prospect of a Labour victory, both sides expressed an interest in such a *rapprochement*. Frank even managed to persuade other chairmen to consider the appointment of ex-Labour ministers to their boards. However, the sweeping Conservative victory at the polls destroyed any momentum.

Most of his surplus energy was channelled into work for prisoners. His observations of prison life for the Nuffield report and his friendship with individual prisoners had opened his eyes to the shortcomings of existing provision for the after-care and resettlement of offenders. The various Discharged Prisoners' Aid Societies, set up in Victorian times, were run by good-hearted individuals but were failing to help ex-convicts rehabilitate, often leaving them jobless, homeless and prone to return to crime. Furthermore, the societies were regarded by their 'clients' as part of the prison Establishment, a service offered out of duty rather than out of genuine concern. In keeping with his benevolence towards individual prisoners, Frank recognized the need for an organization that would be sympathetic with those newly released. The New Bridge put that radical idea into practice.

Two ex-prisoners in particular were associated with Frank in the establishment in 1955 of the New Bridge: Lord Edward Montagu[13] and Peter Wildeblood. They had been two of the three men convicted of homosexual offences amid sensational headlines in the early 1950s. Montagu knew Frank's daughter Antonia slightly and the two peers met at Wakefield Prison during the causes of crime inquiry. Though he had no connection with Wildeblood, a *Daily Mail* journalist, Frank sought him out in Wormwood Scrubs. In his account of his prison ordeal, Wildeblood was later to write:

Two things kept me going. One was the visit every three weeks of Lord Pakenham who was preparing a report for the Nuffield Foundation on the causes of crime. He must have exhausted my views on the subject during the first few visits, but he kept on coming for as long as he was able. Sitting with him there in a room without a warden in the dingy grey suit which I had worn for six months, with my hands scarred by the mail bag needle and my fingernails black with ingrained dirt, I could feel I was still a person. I can never repay him for what he did for me during those months.[14]

Wildeblood was being treated as a social leper, and with his own breakdown of 1940 in mind, Frank found that irresistible. His willingness to be associated with both men seems strange in the light of his own often outspoken homophobic views. His conviction that homosexuality was sinful pre-dated his conversion to Catholicism and was bound up with the puritanism of his childhood and early experiences at Eton. It was not an unusual attitude for men of his generation, but Catholicism exacerbated it. Gay relationships, according to the Church, offended against nature and sex's divine purpose – namely procreation. Yet in all his dealings with those in trouble of any sort, Frank made a distinction between the sin and the sinner. It was an old Catholic adage coined by Saint Augustine that 'you hate the sin but love the sinner' and it became his by-word. He refused to judge individuals – the sinners – but instead judged their crimes – the sin.

For many the problem with this approach was that it required the sinner to acknowledge his or her sin – in Wildeblood's case that being homosexual was sinful. In less open times, he was prepared to make that concession, but for others subsequently it sounded like a mark of intolerance. Yet in these days, when homosexuality was a criminal offence, it was Frank who opened the first debate in Parliament in favour of the Wolfenden report published in 1956. It recommended that homosexual acts in private between consenting adults over twenty-one should be decriminalized. Frank was in the vanguard of the libertarians. When the Commons avoided discussing the report, he used his platform in the Lords to take a forward stand for implementation. During the debate, on 4 December 1957, Lord Boothby[15] referred to him as 'the non-playing captain of the homosexual team'.[16]

After Montagu's release, Frank had dinner with him at the White Tower Restaurant in London. He expressed his eagerness that

Montagu should take his seat again in the House of Lords and not feel forever stigmatized. The subject naturally led them to discuss facilities for rehabilitation of ex-offenders and Montagu revealed that, since his release, he had been besieged by requests from former inmates who hoped that he, a wealthy man, would understand their plight and lend them a helping hand. He told Frank that he was considering starting the equivalent of Alcoholics Anonymous for ex-offenders. The two decided to pool their efforts and set up a new body which would make good the deficiency. Its aim would be to befriend prisoners and help them find a useful role within society once more.

There followed a dinner at which supporters from various areas of Frank's life gathered with Montagu and Wildeblood to endorse the new venture – among them David Astor, Sonia Orwell and Victor Gollancz. The original intention was to call it the Bridge, but there was already a left-wing body of the same name. So the word 'New' was added – both Victor Gollancz and Edward Montagu were later to claim the credit for this combination. The first official meeting of the New Bridge took place in January 1956 at Rubens Hotel in central London. Bill Hewitt, the writer, was elected the first chairman with Norma Opie (wife of Roger) the secretary and Canon Collins of Christian Action, Frank and his daughter Antonia, who had commissioned Wildeblood to write about his prison experiences for Weidenfeld, as members of the executive.[17] Many were soon to withdraw from an active involvement because of other work. Hewitt stood down as chairman, but Frank, who replaced him, seldom missed a meeting for the next eight years despite his commitments in the Lords and in the City.

The first obstacle New Bridge encountered was antipathy from the Home Office and the press, who dismissed it as a society organized by homosexuals for homosexuals. The involvement of Montagu and Wildeblood, still remembered after the sensationalism of their trial, and the appointment of a homosexual as secretary to succeed Norma Opie, was much commented on. Whether Frank showed good judgement in allowing Montagu and Wildeblood to be so publicly associated with the New Bridge was questioned even by supporters. Yet the whole purpose of the organization was to provide a bridge between prison and society for ex-offenders. Hence to have discriminated against two founding members would have been to go against the spirit of the organization and would have pandered to precisely the sort of ill-informed hostility that New Bridge was aiming to make a thing of the past. Yet Frank might also have reflected that in any attempt to change opinions it helps to begin with the public on one's side. To alienate them at the outset, to allow New Bridge to be dismissed, however unjustly, as something it was not, was to weaken its impact and its campaign. Given public hostility to prisoners in general, he was merely making an already uphill struggle harder.

The second problem facing New Bridge was that, in their enthusiasm to launch the new organization, its founders did not clarify their purpose nor how they were going to achieve it. Talk of befriending prisoners simply resulted in a constant stream of visitors queuing up at New Bridge's first offices, situated in a church crypt, hoping for a hand-out. When they were offered advice and counselling instead, some were disappointed.

Again, in setting up New Bridge, Frank was the initiator who drew up broad parameters and left the day-to-day running of the charity to its staff. He envisaged an organization unashamedly siding with the prisoner, working to help individuals rather than lobbying Parliament or ministers over more general issues. He would undertake the latter himself. In effect New Bridge was broadening the scope of his own prison visiting. In its early days, before probation officers routinely went into prisons, New Bridge worked to set up after-care arrangements for those about to be released. In addition, it trained and recruited prison visitors and later ran a specialist employment service.

What was needed was the acceptance by the community for the first time [Frank later wrote] of a specific responsibility for providing a minimum standard of welfare for the ex-prisoner. That was the social principle. What was needed in administrative practice was a national network of after-care officers, supplemented by voluntary efforts. Some of the voluntary effort should be state-aided, some of it, like New Bridge, quite independent. It was not sufficient to assume the Welfare State could look after ex-prisoners through the same services – the Ministry of Labour, the Assistance Board etc – as were adequate for other citizens. Prisoners need special help because they are specially handicapped.[18]

One of the reasons New Bridge was reluctant to provide direct financial help to prisoners was its shortage of funds. Frank threw himself zealously into persuading his wealthy friends and, through them, institutions to provide financial backing. The minutes of the early meetings abound with reports of fund-raising functions and balls, often organized by Frank.[19] Several of his contacts in the City proved generous, one senior official of another bank making a particular impression on Frank by revealing that he too was a socialist in the sense that he wanted to follow Christ's instruction to the rich man to give up his worldly goods.

Occasionally, in their enthusiasm to help out, Frank's friends could prove an embarrassment. Lord Boothby, a colleague of Elizabeth's on various *Any Questions* panels and a member of the House of Lords, attended a New Bridge ball and was asked to say a few words. 'With great geniality,' Elizabeth reported, 'he began "There is no audience I like so much as a captive audience. That is why prisoners are the best audience in the world." No laughter. The ex-prisoners present looked as black as thunder.'[20] In spite of such *faux pas*, the charity's bank balances managed to stay in the black while its work and its staff numbers increased.

The largest obstacle to New Bridge, however, were the existing after-care organizations. In the House of Lords in 1961, Frank was to describe the system that greeted him when he undertook his Nuffield inquiry as 'a nonsense, a shambles and a mess'. The Discharged Prisoners' Associations, for their part, regarded New Bridge as interlopers whose very existence amounted to a condemnation of past efforts. This mutual hostility is evident in the minutes taken by New Bridge of a meeting in October 1957 between

14 Hugh and Dora Gaitskell in 1950. The Labour leader and Longford shared digs in Oxford, when Gaitskell had also proposed to Elizabeth. The two couples went on to become firm friends. Both men were rising stars in the Attlee government. Longford's political ambitions were dashed by the tragic death of Gaitskell in 1963.

15 The Longford children in the garden of their Hampstead home, *c.* 1950. From left: Judith, Antonia, Catherine, Rachel, Kevin, Paddy, Michael and Thomas.

16 *Opposite*: Longford at Bernhurst on Christmas Day, 1959. His daughter Antonia remarks, 'A typically ambivalent expression to family festivities.' *(Hulton Deutsch Collection)*

17 The leader of the House of Lords and his Prime Minister: Longford and Harold Wilson at the wedding of Rachel to Kevin Billington in 1967.

18 'Lord Porn': the Marc cartoon inspired by Longford's celebrated trip to Copenhagen's red-light district, part of his private commission of inquiry into pornography in 1971. *(The Mark Boxer Estate)*

19 Friend of the friendless: Longford played host in London to the disgraced former American President Richard Nixon in 1978.

20 The Longford family in the 1980s: (*standing from the left*) Paddy, who qualified as a barrister; Michael, British Ambassador to Luxembourg; Kevin, who works in the City; Antonia, award-winning historian; and Thomas, another award-winning historian; (*seated from the left*) Judith, poet and campaigner; Elizabeth, Frank and Rachel, novelist and children's writer.

21 Supporter of good causes: Longford with Fr Mark Elvins at a centre for the homeless in Brighton.

22 Elizabeth, with a view of Bernhurst.

23 Frank with one of his great-grandchildren. Philip Howard once wrote in *The Times*, 'Longford needs an *apologia pro vita sua* less than most . . . His monuments stand and sit all around him.'

Frank and his team and the Royal London Discharged Prisoners' Aid Society. This body had been blocking New Bridge's attempts to get a representative on the discharge board for London's prisons. The only sop they were prepared to offer was a promise to refer ex-prisoners, when appropriate, to New Bridge. Despite Frank's best attempts at reconciliation, the two bodies left the meeting as discordant as they had started, and the carefully written minutes cannot disguise a frosty and suspicious atmosphere.[21]

Despite all these obstacles, though, prisoners and well-disposed characters within the system soon realized that New Bridge was the place to go if you were genuinely seeking to make a fresh start. Frank subsequently liked to recall that one day, a couple of years after the charity had started, he received a visitor at the National Bank's headquarters. The man announced himself as the father of one of the prisoners Frank had been visiting. He had spoken to the prison governor about the support his son would be given after five years inside. 'If you're asking what the state is going to do,' the governor had answered, 'the answer is nothing. You'd better go and see the chairman of the New Bridge.'[22]

Though New Bridge took up much of Frank's 'spare' time outside the bank, it furthered and deepened his knowledge of the penal system and – in the Lords, in Whitehall and on public platforms – intensified his appeals for reform of some of its worst aspects. The brutality of the prison regime, the routine insensitivity with which prisoners were treated, and the appalling conditions in many of Britain's jails shocked him. In overcrowded prisons, there was a lack of facilities and of a will to undertake any sort of rehabilitation aimed at sending inmates back into society as reformed characters.

From the initial debate he opened in the House of Lords on prisons in 1955 (the first-ever debate about prisons in the Chamber), Frank laid great stress on what he called 'the three evil ones' – overcrowding, understaffing and shortage of work for prisoners. Such efforts at bringing the prison service forward in the fight for resources and attention in Whitehall bore fruit in the late 1950s when a reforming Home Secretary, R.A. Butler, decided to make a priority of the Prisons Department, hitherto a neglected domain. In a speech in March 1957, Butler stressed the necessity of more research into the causes of crime, better after-care facilities and a prison-building programme through which offenders could be treated according to their needs rather than their deserts. Frank could not help but be delighted that many of the points he had been pressing for were part of the Conservative Home Secretary's programme. In February 1959 a White Paper, 'Penal Policy in a Changing Society', appeared.

Butler's good intentions were not translated into quite the revolution for which some had hoped. Prison overcrowding increased rather than diminished over this period. The launch of a £4 million prison-building programme coincided with an upturn in the crime rate and hence a growing prison population. From 2,000 sleeping on average three to a cell when Butler became Home Secretary in 1957, the number had risen to over 7,000 when he left office in 1962. Frank soon became disappointed with Butler's pledge for reform. His dissatisfaction was not due to political rivalry but to the dismay of an ardent prison reformer at the limitations and pragmatism of a Home Secretary with other concerns to occupy him. His attitude to Butler demonstrates how deeply he had taken the cause of prison reform to heart, to the point of blinding him to political realities such as the public reluctance to spend money on jails. Consideration of public opinion on spending, especially at a time of economic belt-tightening, was an unavoidable part of Butler's job, and played a part in his retreat from the cause of prison reform. 'If he had been entirely engrossed in penal work [Frank later wrote of Butler] he would hardly have acquiesced so tamely in the frustrating of his high and genuine ambitions. He would have tackled the staff situation, and the work situation in detail, and called the attention of the nation to both.'[23]

Such is the verdict of a campaigner, not a politician. Others judged Butler the most conscientious Home Secretary on the prison issue since Churchill. Butler's wider responsibilities at the Home Office and his designs on the leadership of his party, already once frustrated by Macmillan, did not allow him to push the unpopular prisons issue too far lest it compromise his political career. For

Frank, to judge by his verdict on Butler, there would have been no choice. He had never had much taste for party in-fighting and tactical manoeuvring when principles were at stake. His prisons crusade was carrying him ever further away from the Labour mainstream and political preferment.

Frank made several other determined bids to promote greater reflection on the state of Britain's prisons. In 1959, building on his experiences at New Bridge and hoping that Butler's interest in after-care might signal a window of opportunity with Whitehall, he worked with Peter Thompson to produce a report on existing provision for prisoners once they were released. Thompson, a devout Christian, had made a name for himself in 1958 when he arranged and paid for the defence of a man who had stolen his briefcase. He followed this up by trying in various ways to provide facilities to help ex-offenders, but without much success. He decided to establish a private inquiry into prisoner after-care and had persuaded Lord Gardiner, chairman of the Bar,[24] to chair it but there would be a delay of three months until he retired and so could take up the post. Thompson decided not to wait and so at the suggestion of another Labour peer, Lord Merthyr, turned to Frank. Other members included two Catholic MPs, the Conservative Peter Rawlinson[25] and Labour's Bob Mellish.[26] A public relations man, Thompson managed to attract a good amount of press publicity for the launch of their investigation.

However, it was not an entirely harmonious collaboration. Despite their shared belief, Frank and Thompson did not combine well together from the outset. Much of the legwork for the eventual report – and the drafting of its recommendations – ended up being carried out by the honorary secretary Jack Donaldson,[27] who hitherto had not been much involved in the prison reform field. In terms of impact, though, the report was one of Frank's more successful attempts at detailed examination of a public issue. Unlike the causes of crime inquiry, it produced specific recommendations about training and work facilities in prisons and how to manage the transition from jail to independent life in the community afterwards. The recommendations were taken up first in a government report and later in legislation that carved out an extended role for a professional probation service. 'I cannot shake off the illusion, if it is one,' Frank later wrote, 'that our Pakenham–Thompson committee had much to do with the establishment of the government's own enquiry into after-care of prisoners.'[28]

Christianity was becoming an increasingly significant factor in his writing and thinking on prisons as he moved beyond practical concerns to examine the philosophy that lay behind Britain's penal system. Building on his personal links with prisoners, he tackled some of the conflicts that his work had raised in his mind. In 1961 he produced an extended and very personal essay, *The Idea of Punishment*, for the Christian publisher, Geoffrey Chapman. Written in academic and occasionally convoluted style, the essay addresses principally the question of whether, as a Christian, Frank believed that prisoners should be punished. Having unashamedly taken their side in the work of New Bridge and in his visiting, he was often accused of advocating that no one should be sent to prison at all. *The Idea of Punishment* attempted to set the record straight.

Essentially it expanded on the idea of loving the sinner and hating the sin, accepting that crime has to be punished but that criminals are sent to prison as a punishment, not in order to receive more punishment when they are there. A prerequisite of the essay was therefore to balance God's law against man's laws, to establish a relationship between crime and sin. Frank quoted St Thomas Aquinas – 'the commands of human law cover only those deeds which concern the public interest, not every deed of every virtue' – to support his own view that the vast majority of our sins must pass unnoticed by the state. All crimes were sins, but not all sins crimes. How then should the state punish those sins which contravene its laws? Punishment, Frank suggested, had four aims – retribution, prevention, reform and deterrence. On familiar ground for those aware of his work with New Bridge, he attacked the state's failure to match its commitments over reform of prisoners with actions.

Reform has established itself in practice as the life's objective of the leaders of the prison service, of all their dedicated members, of the whole probation service, and of many magistrates, doctors, clergy and others concerned with the lives of prisoners . . . Few of us who have had much to do with prisons would deny that a prison sentence is capable on occasion of benefiting a man. We have probably all met with one or two men who were better for a period in gaol. Hardly anyone, however, will seriously argue that in general our prison system as we know it is likely to have this effect. One would need to be far removed from reality to claim that at present we ordinarily send a man to prison to promote his welfare. We ordinarily send him to prison to keep him out of circulation (prevention) and to discourage him and other members of the community from committing a like offence (deterrence).[29]

However, his extended essay was not a political pamphlet and won little favour among his colleagues in the Labour Party. Responding to Frank's plea for greater understanding of ex-offenders, for example, Aneurin Bevan commented: 'I must remind Frank Pakenham that Christ drove the money-changers from the Temple. He did not open the doors wide for them to enter. He drove them away. If we go on to apply the principles of Christianity to contemporary British society, they must have been done elsewhere rather better than they have been done here.'[30]

Away from Westminster, *The Idea of Punishment* could be seen in a truer light as a philosophical and theological examination of punishment in general and the notion of retribution in particular. While Frank and other Christian campaigners for penal reform were united with their secular counterparts in condemning the lack of any notion of reform in Britain's prisons, they parted ways significantly over retribution. Many of the latter group held that criminals were medically unwell, that it was circumstances that led them to break the law, that they therefore carried no moral responsibility for their crime and should not suffer society's retribution but rather its concern and understanding. Those who claimed that criminals are simply sick were, Frank wrote, 'abandoning all belief in the freedom of will whether in a Christian or secular sense. In particular one is abandoning the view that we shall one day be judged by God according to the moral or immoral use we make of our freedom of choice in this world.' If crime is dismissed as sickness, there would be no attempt, he continued, to distinguish between good and evil. 'Clearly therefore a Christian can have nothing to do with this doctrine that crime is disease.'[31]

In *The Idea of Punishment*, Frank wanted to distance himself from such a doctrine. Concern and understanding did not preclude retribution, which indeed he saw as an integral part of reform. As a Christian who believed in free will, he wrote that those who commit crimes carry a moral responsibility for their actions. It was the acknowledgement of their moral responsibility that started prisoners on the road to reform. In linking reform to retribution, he was anxious to stress that the latter should not be regarded negatively as society extracting its pound of flesh from the criminal. He preferred to use the term 'debt to society' rather than the word 'retribution'. In associating reform with retribution, he was placing the responsibility with society as well as with the individual prisoner. Locking people away in prison and imagining the problem was solved was insufficient. Prison was the first stage of their rehabilitation as full members of society and the success of that process depended not just on the criminals, but on those charged with their welfare.

'The Christian judge,' he suggested, 'in the full knowledge that he also is a sinner like the man in the dock, judges with love and then does all he can to help the prisoner repay. And in that duty, the prisoner is seen to be no lonely or isolated figure – no second-class human being. For repayment is the task of all.'[32]

FOURTEEN

The Reluctant Earl

The period between the Labour Party's electoral defeat in 1959 and Hugh Gaitskell's early death in 1963 was one of the most bitter and stormy in its history. Over unilateral disarmament, membership of the Common Market and the relationship between public and private ownership, it was deeply divided. Hugh Gaitskell was defeated at the annual conference in 1960 over nuclear weapons and soon afterwards faced a leadership challenge from Harold Wilson, seen by those on the left as the successor to Aneurin Bevan, who had died in July of that year.

Conflict brought out the best in Gaitskell as he battled to save his party from collapsing into factions after three successive defeats at the polls. Hitherto he had failed to convince the electorate and many of his colleagues that he was at all remarkable. His public oratory had never matched the private eloquence that had brought tears to the eyes of Marjorie Durbin when Gaitskell, as a young don, described the sufferings of the working class during the Industrial Revolution. Aneurin Bevan's famous jibe about 'the desiccated calculating machine' had stuck. Yet in these tumultuous years from 1959 to 1963 Gaitskell's passion and determination, well known to close friends like Frank and Elizabeth, to fight for his beliefs and his party moved even his staunchest opponents. He successfully reversed the 1960 set-back at the annual conference the following year and put a renewed and united Labour Party, committed to social democracy and a more equal and just society, on course for an eventual victory at the polls in 1964. 'We had both looked upon Hugh as our ideal leader,' Elizabeth later wrote, 'an orator since his "Fight, fight and fight again" speech, every inch a Labour democrat and known to us through an intimate friendship of over thirty years.'[1]

Gaitskell was struggling to adapt the Labour Party to the changing economic and social conditions which had transformed postwar Britain, many of them set in motion by the reforms instigated by Attlee's governments. Improvements in the standard of living of the working class had in particular eroded Labour's solid electoral base. People who had moved out of the urban ghettos were no longer so ready to identify themselves as working class. The old rallying cries of nationalization and full employment had been annexed by the Conservatives during their long spell in office. Tony Crosland,[2] another of Gaitskell's closest supporters, argued for a complete overhaul of the party ideology in his book, *The Future of Socialism*. 'The much-thumbed guide-books of the past must now be thrown away.' Douglas Jay, another prominent Gaitskellite, took matters a stage further in an article in the magazine *Forward* in 1959 where he advocated that Labour should change its name to represent a new image.

Frank lined up alongside Gaitskell in the many battles he fought during this period. After the leader's defeat on the nuclear issue at the 1960 conference Frank was one of the prominent supporters of the Campaign for Democratic Socialism. Set up by Gaitskell's backers, the campaign aimed to rally the party behind his reform programme, especially the urgent task of overturning the unilateral resolution. Frank shared his leader's belief that for Britain to abandon all nuclear capacity, however linked with the Americans, would be to abdicate any role in the postwar settlement, of which Bevin had been one of the principal architects. His attachment to the Atlantic Alliance, first forcefully stated during his time in Germany and reinforced by his anti-communism, was no less passionate than Gaitskell's. Yet, as a Christian, Frank was also deeply troubled by the destructive capacity of nuclear weapons. Long-standing colleagues like Canon Collins of Christian Action were in the forefront of CND protests at Aldermaston. He attempted to square the circle by advocating, somewhat idealistically during the cold war, a world government equipped with an international peace force that would eliminate the need for weapons of mass destruction. His argument was that the nuclear deterrent was a temporary expedient which could be negotiated away. He was immensely impressed by bodies like the United Nations, though he failed to address its inability to break out of the limbo imposed by the Soviet–American rivalry on the Security Council. Habitually the initiator, the academic looking beyond what was politically possible, he was constantly scattering the seeds of reform, some of which were inspired, fired others and became crusades, and some of which were unrealizable pipe dreams.

Over nationalization and the commitment to public ownership enshrined in Clause Four of the party's constitution, Frank was an equally firm Gaitskellite, endorsing his old friend's conviction that, after three successive defeats, Labour had to modernize and adapt itself to a mixed economy. The promise of widespread further nationalization had, many Labour supporters believed, frightened off the electorate as early as 1951. Equally the state control of a range of basic industries between 1945 and 1951 had not subsequently provided the cure for capitalism's cycle of boom and bust that Labour had believed it would when first advocating public ownership. While continuing to acknowledge that there was a role for nationalization and for its expansion, Gaitskell, aware of the need to convince a sceptical electorate, was attempting to redefine its status in the Labour programme. It would continue to be an important part of Labour's ideology, but not the only, nor indeed the crucial, part. He stressed instead Labour's commitment to certain moral values to which equality and fraternity were central and public ownership subordinate, an instrument not a goal. Frank, whose socialism sprang from a belief in the fundamental equality of all men, and whose Catholicism had only served to strengthen his belief in the moral mission of politicians, heartily subscribed to Gaitskell's reforming zeal in this area. It had, after all, been his doubts as to the economic efficacy of Labour's programme that had delayed his joining the party back in the 1930s.

Of the major issues in this period it was only over the Common Market that Frank differed from Gaitskell. Their disagreement came in 1962 after the Labour leader had earned a standing ovation at the annual conference at Brighton by revealing for the first time on a public platform his rejection in principle, if not in practice, of membership of a European Community. Unable to catch the chairman's eye during the conference debate, Frank took issue with the Gaitskell line in a newspaper article the following weekend. 'Never had Hugh Gaitskell risen to such oratorical heights. But for many of us who listened it was a heart-breaking experience,' he wrote in the *Sunday Pictorial*. He was later to record his own preference for George Brown's ardently pro-Europe speech which immediately followed Gaitskell's rousing address.

Frank was enthusiastic about the European vision, inspired by his own experience of the rebuilding of Germany and his friendship with Konrad Adenauer, one of the most fervent backers of closer economic cooperation between the European nations. A united Europe would be the first step on the path to his dream of a world government. The framework of a European Community would provide an excellent structure, Frank felt, within which to resolve the Anglo-Irish impasse over Northern Ireland, an abiding concern. Another element in his pro-Common Market views was his Catholicism. His old Oxford friend Douglas Jay, an ardent opponent of the European Community wrote: 'I felt no disillusion towards Frank as a pro-Marketeer. He was a devout Catholic and I noticed that to many such the Common Market tended to be equated with Christendom and Eastern Europe with the anti-Christ.'[3]

Isolated in the Lords and with only one foot in the political world because of his work at the National Bank, there was little in practical terms that Frank could do for Gaitskell. The reality was that their friendship was intensely personal, dating back to the days when they had shared digs at Oxford and both fallen for Elizabeth Harman. Gaitskell often referred to Frank as 'my oldest friend'. Other senior Labour figures – Jay or Crosland, for example – may have been his closest friends in political terms, but with Frank there was a special bond.

There were, however, areas where Gaitskell sought out his input. It was to Frank that he turned in 1958 for advice in drafting party policy on Northern Ireland. Frank's dual allegiance, only emphasized by his post at the National Bank, had over the years in opposition led to various missions. One, predating Gaitskell's approach, concerned Sir Hugh Lane,[4] an Irishman who had made his reputation in England and who had been a prolific picture dealer before he was drowned when the *Lusitania* sank in 1915. In a late addition to his will he bequeathed his collection of French Impressionist paintings to Ireland but the codicil was not witnessed. His paintings – including Renoir's *Les Parapluies* – therefore ended up in the National Gallery in London to the intense disappointment of the Irish. The dispute over ownership rumbled on for over forty years and involved such Anglo-Irish figures as W.B. Yeats[5] and Lady Gregory.[6] Frank was drafted in as a mediator acceptable to both sides in 1956 at the request of the Irish Prime Minister, Sean Lemass. Under a compromise suggested by the Duke of Wellington, it had been proposed that the collection should be shared between Dublin and London, and spend half the year in each city. In furtherance of this plan, Frank visited Prime Minister Macmillan at Downing Street in August 1957. The two had met occasionally, when Macmillan spoke for Lindsay in the 1938 Oxford by-election and later at an Anglo-German Association dinner. Macmillan gave his backing to the Duke of Wellington's compromise – as had the Irish government – and eventually the trustees of the National Gallery in London were persuaded to yield. For his part in ending this forty-year battle Frank was awarded an honorary degree by the National University of Ireland.

To some in Ireland in the 1950s, through his high-profile role with the National, Frank had become a familiar if eccentric figure. The Irish rugby union international and later business magnate, Tony O'Reilly,[7] recalled first meeting Frank in 1956 after the bank chairman had been enthusiastically cheering Ireland in a match with France. 'I was naked and singing lustily with the rest of the team when a large figure in a black overcoat and Homburg hat joined me in the shower. He talked excitedly about the game. I watched with fascination as the brim of his hat filled up with water and the water finally cascaded over the edge of his hat like a gigantic fountain. This, I said to myself, is a true Irish rugby supporter.'[8]

Labour's policy had changed little since Attlee's Government of Ireland Act of 1949, which guaranteed the people of the North a veto over any change in their status as part of the United Kingdom. While realizing that it would be impossible to get Gaitskell to reverse such a position, Frank attempted in notes and conversations to steer him with a more conciliatory line towards Dublin.[9] If he succeeded, it was more by dint of what Gaitskell didn't say rather than what he did. Frank was asked to look over drafts of both the manifesto produced for 1959 by the Northern Ireland Labour Party and the text of Gaitskell's own rallying cry to Labour candidates. Both ended up as bland documents which made almost no mention of the constitutional position, and concentrated instead on the economic problems of the province. There were hints at a realization of the routine discrimination in housing, education and employment that Catholics suffered under the Northern Ireland Parliament at Stormont, but again the tone was that of trying to stand above any impression of sectarianism.

Frustrated by the experience of working with the leader's inner circle on this issue, Frank subsequently became much more outspoken on the problem of the partition in the North. In a debate in the Lords in December 1960 on the future of Ireland, he departed substantially from the party line and reiterated his views in a lengthy piece for the *Observer* advocating what became known as the Cardinal d'Alton[10] solution. The Catholic churchman had given an interview in which he suggested that the two parts of Ireland might unite as one republic but return to the Commonwealth, thereby offering the Loyalists of the North a continuing link with the British Crown and evidence that the Dublin government, in their willingness to rejoin the association of ex-colonies which they had left in 1948, was prepared to make concessions. It was a novel solution which earned some applause on both sides of the Irish Sea, but it had few backers and little hope of success. Yet again Frank was standing outside the mainstream.

By the late 1950s Frank knew that any hopes he had of holding office in a future Labour government rested mainly on Gaitskell's esteem. This realization did not, however, make him sycophantic, and occasionally he would rebuke his old friend. During the battle over Labour's defence policy, he wrote to Gaitskell in June 1960 warning him of the danger of becoming isolated. 'I am convinced that you are . . . infinitely the best leader available . . . But . . . your leadership is in real jeopardy . . . I find a widespread conviction that you expect loyalty without providing the opportunity of consultation which your leading followers might reasonably expect . . . particularly some who are younger rather than older than you and me and who are somewhere near the middle of the road.' It was a mark of Gaitskell's esteem for Frank's friendship that, on receiving the letter, he rang him at once and arranged a meeting that very afternoon.[11]

Frank believed, however, that for all the show of warmth, his acceptance of a peerage in 1945 had created a certain distance with Gaitskell. The leader had no time at all for the House of Lords, and while he talked of Frank holding the leadership of the Upper Chamber in a future Labour cabinet, he was adamant that a peer could not run a major ministry in a socialist government. Indeed, in 1958, when he agreed to Conservative plans to introduce life peerages in the face of vocal opposition from those like Jennie Lee[12] who wanted the Lords abolished at once, he emphasized that election to the Commons was a prerequisite for entry into a Labour cabinet except in the cases of the Lord Chancellor and Leader of the Upper Chamber.

Gaitskell's summary dismissal of the Lords occasionally irritated his old friend. In his diary Richard Crossman recorded a dinner conversation with Frank and Elizabeth after a World Government rally in Brighton in February 1961. 'As we talked, it became clear that Frank's experience was the same as the rest of us. He just couldn't take Hugh's inability ever to thank him or to show any appreciation for what he has been doing. "I know that the House of

Lords doesn't matter, but it would have been nice if Hugh could, once even, be aware that I have been opening debates there for him for three years."[13]

While he was part of Gaitskell's inner circle of friends, a place where politics was the only topic of conversation, Frank remained outside the heart of the Labour Party organization throughout the 1950s and early 1960s. He was regarded by most colleagues in the Commons as amiable, even colourful, but his past record and his current position in the City left them unimpressed. Besides occasional contributions to the press on the direction of party policy and speeches in favour of candidates around election time, he languished in the Lords. The speeches he made were never heard by his fellow party members in the Commons. In 1956, for example, he wound up the opposition's attack on the Conservative government's handling of the Suez crisis and its disregard of the United Nations, countering Alec Douglas-Home's[14] sterling defence. Frank concluded his speech with great aplomb: 'Everyone on these benches feels as strongly as I do.' When he turned, he realized that there was no one on them.

Though Labour's tenuous numerical position in the Lords began to improve in 1958 with the introduction of life peerages, Frank reflected ruefully on his decision in 1945 to accept Attlee's offer of a peerage. There was no way back, or so it seemed, until Anthony Wedgwood-Benn,[15] the son and heir of one of his fellow Labour peers, Viscount Stansgate,[16] began a determined and high-profile campaign to allow members of the Upper Chamber to disclaim their titles and thereby (in his case) hold a seat in the House of Commons. A door opened that Frank had thought closed for ever. Benn won his battle in 1963 when the Peerage Act, shaped by a joint committee of both Houses, was passed.

Benn's campaign offered Frank the chance to contemplate once more a career in the Commons, and his dream was to be Home Secretary so as to overhaul the Prisons Department. It was an ambition that he made the mistake of confiding to Evelyn Waugh, who in turn wrote to Ann Fleming that if Frank ever got the Home Office, 'we should all be murdered in our beds by sexual maniacs'.[17]

260

Elizabeth, who had always had doubts about the wisdom of their joint decision in 1945, was enthusiastic about her husband's suggestion of renouncing his peerage. There were difficulties, though. There was the question of finding a seat. More immediately the National Bank, and the comfort of a chairman's salary, would have to be renounced to permit a return to full-time politics. After seven years, though, Frank had exhausted his interest in the City. No one could claim he had not lived up to his promise to Cooke to leave his mark and he had already identified a worthy successor with the right credentials for the National and its Anglo-Irish ward.

The major obstacle to such a scheme, however, was that the proposals being drawn up as a result of Tony Benn's campaign did not include peers of first creation, only inherited titles. They did not, in short, allow those like Frank, who had accepted a peerage, then to renounce it within their lifetime. His situation was complicated by the fact that in 1961 he had inherited a title as well. His elder brother Edward, the 6th Earl of Longford, had died suddenly on 4 February at the age of fifty-eight. The cause was a massive stroke brought on by overweight – he was said to weigh thirty-four stones. Though it was an Irish earldom and therefore carried no entitlement to a seat in the Lords, Edward was a member – though he had never attended – by dint of being Baron Silchester, the English title given to the Pakenhams in 1821. So the planned legislation would allow Frank to disclaim the Silchester title but not that of Baron Pakenham of Cowley, created for him by Attlee in 1945. If he was to get into the Commons, it would mean fighting for an amendment to the bill and that, Frank calculated, would require the support of Gaitskell. (The Labour leader had written to him at the time of Edward's death expressing his sympathy.)

Edward's death had made news in London, thanks to glowing obituaries from the likes of John Betjeman. Frank, though privately estranged from his brother, was anxious to pay him tribute in public for all he had done for Dublin theatreland, but in response to journalists' questions about moving to Ireland and taking up residence as the lord of the manor, Frank pointed out truthfully, 'I haven't got sixpence to my name'. In 1959 he had signed over Pakenham Hall as it was then, and any money left after Edward's profligacy – principally two Messien lions and a Russian diamond necklace held in a Bank of Ireland vault – went to his 26-year-old son Thomas as a way of avoiding two lots of death duties. (The lions were later sold to the Metropolitan Museum in New York.)

He did, however, inherit the title. His staff at the National Bank report that he found it very hard at first to adjust to being Lord Longford. When people would call asking for him by his new name, he would look puzzled for an instant before realizing that they meant him. Elizabeth decided to publish under the name of Longford rather than Pakenham. 'I had by no means made the name so famous that I must cling on to it; besides Longford had fewer letters and was easier to pronounce correctly.'[18] As Frank was now an earl, his daughters received the courtesy title Lady.

When he approached Gaitskell about his idea of renouncing his peerage, Frank was amused at the Labour leader's reaction. 'But do you mean that you wouldn't mind giving up your title?' Gaitskell asked. 'I told him', Frank recalled, 'that I wouldn't mind at all. I honestly think that that surprised and pleased him. He seemed to have thought that it would have seemed a real sacrifice; that that kind of honour mattered to me, perhaps for family reasons.'[19] Next to the prospect of claiming a major department of state in a reforming socialist government, there was no sacrifice in renouncing a title that he had inherited by default.

In the face of Frank's determination to amend the Benn bill, Gaitskell was evasive. When Frank then broached the subject of his being in the Commons, Gaitskell avoided making any commitment. (It may have been that he was aware of Frank's ambitions to be Home Secretary. Gaitskell was the lover of Ann Fleming, to whom Waugh had written.) The Labour leader needed time to think. He had not been at all enthusiastic about Benn's campaign from the start, seeing it as irrelevant to the electorate. Even when persuaded to join cross-party talks on the issue, he remained suspicious that the Conservatives were trying to use the issue to bolster the powers of the Lords, where they had an in-built majority.

Frank and Gaitskell parted amicably. There were various references to the matter when the two met in the ensuing months, but nothing was promised. By December 1962, however, when the Longfords had dinner with the Gaitskells, the Labour leader spoke in enthusiastic terms to his old friend about the chance of adding an amendment to the Peerage Bill then going through Parliament.

Gaitskell had used the intervening period to put Frank to the test on a delicate task. His vote of confidence at the December dinner indicated that he felt the assignment had been successfully carried out. At his leader's request Frank had taken on the chairmanship of an all-party committee looking into London's government. It was set up, under Gaitskell's patronage, at a time when the Conservative administration had announced unpopular plans to reorganize the old Inner London Council. Though Gaitskell had told Frank that the members of the committee had specifically asked for him as chairman (Frank, with his background in local politics in Oxford and in social services via the New Bridge, accepted his words at face value), he was being foisted on the group, which operated out of a small office, paid for by a donation of £2,000 from a Labour parliamentary candidate, Robert Maxwell.[20] The inquiry itself failed to deflect the Tories, but the members were won over by their chairman and finally paid handsome tribute to him.

The London government inquiry was in fact just one part of Frank's growing burden of extra-curricular activities after making the decision to prepare the ground for a return to full-time politics. After seven years of trying – though not always succeeding – to avoid the limelight as a bank chairman, he took on a wide range of high-profile appointments. Since July of the previous year he had led, with Douglas Jay, a unit trust which aimed to attract trade union money into industry. Drawing on the knowledge Frank had gained in the City, and designed to promote greater partnership between workers and management, the unit trust invited 180 trade unions to take stakes in industry. In a similar vein, in June 1962 he became deputy chairman of a Wider Share Ownership Council, again trying to break down the barriers between different sectors in industry – though this later venture was a cross-party initiative with Maurice Macmillan, the Prime Minister's son, in the chair. In March 1963 Frank joined his fellow Catholic Leonard Cheshire[21] and the actor Peter Ustinov[22] in sponsoring a call to 5,000 young Britons to volunteer to join a world police force, part of a continuing interest in the notion of world government.

Without knowing Gaitskell's final verdict on his hopes of re-entering the Commons, Frank boldly announced his resignation as chairman of the National Bank in July 1962. He would be serving several months' notice and would not be free until the start of 1963. In the *Evening News* Frank described his return to full-time political life as 'making my small but uninhibited contribution' to the Labour Party. He refused to be drawn on his hopes for high office in a future Labour cabinet.

He had needed to break his link with the bank before he could start campaigning for the necessary amendment to the Peerage Bill and selling himself to constituency parties as a potential Labour candidate for the House of Commons. While his work at the National had left him space for regular forays into the Lords, to aim for the Commons while still chairman would be to compromise his position, Frank readily recognized. With his political pulse now beating fast, Frank viewed his release from the bank chairmanship with a mixture of regret and relief. Eight years was the longest continuous period he had held one job. Given his tendency towards restlessness, the duration was quite an achievement, as he acknowledged in his remark: 'I had a feeling that if I stayed much longer at the bank I should have shot my bolt.'[23]

He regretted leaving behind employees for whom he felt a genuine affection. They had become like an extended family. As well as the scroll from the Irish staff, he also received as a parting gift a shiny red Mini and a course of driving lessons. His lack of coordination and general mechanical ineptitude were to triumph over any will to learn. After two sessions and an unhappy experience around Sloane Square in central London he handed over the rest of his lessons to his daughter Judith and promised to try again later. After another unfortunate attempt on the drive at Bernhurst with his son Kevin, where the Mini ended up embedded in an apple tree, he gave up entirely.

Gaitskell's positive words about disclaiming his peerage at the dinner party of 7 December 1962 gave Frank good reason to look forward to 1963. In the course of the evening, Gaitskell had mentioned feeling unwell because of an illness that he had picked up on a trip to Paris. He had been showing signs of strain for some months and in June had blacked out during a television recording, but none of his close circle were unduly alarmed. Indeed, Frank's impression was that the Labour leader was on good form that evening. On 14 December, Gaitskell was admitted to Manor House, the trade union hospital at Golders Green, with flu. Tests proved inconclusive and he had discharged himself by Christmas and was talking enthusiastically about his planned trip to Russia in the New Year. However, he was back in hospital in January and died several days later at the age of fifty-six, victim of a rare immunological disease. 'To those who had worked closely with Gaitskell the loss went deep [writes his biographer Philip Williams], like the unexpected and premature death of a parent. For a generation of politically-minded progressive people – teachers, journalists, trade unionists, civil servants – an inspiration went out of public life.'24 Even among his opponents there was obvious grief. Harold Macmillan moved the adjournment of the House of Commons on hearing the news – the first and so far only time such a mark of respect has been made for an opposition leader who had never been prime minister.

Both the Longfords were deeply saddened by the loss of one of their oldest, dearest and most loyal friends. Later Frank reflected that he missed Gaitskell more, not less, as time went by. A remark by Denis Healey over dinner, recorded by Elizabeth, pointed up what for her was a shared approach to politics between Frank and Gaitskell that transcended all the other differences. 'Denis said Hugh's mistake had been, even in Cabinet, to try to educate people as well as persuading them. He could not bear to feel that they agreed with him for any reason but full understanding . . . . The education pitfall is what academics fall into . . . it's an indulgence, Denis said, they must do without once they are in government.'25

Both educators, both men who picked over issues with logic, both with a tendency to get impatient, the two had shared much in common and Gaitskell's death affected Frank much more than

Edward's had done. Despite having a very large circle of friends, only a handful of people had an enduring significance in Frank's life. Elizabeth was at its centre, unrivalled. Then there were his children and a small group of intimate friends, like Gaitskell and David Astor, most of whom he had known since his youth, and with whom he could relax, talk openly and give free rein to his wit. Beyond that there was a vast array of social contacts, people for whom the warm-hearted Frank felt a great affection but from whom, as a man who struggled with intimacy, he withheld a part of himself. He would play the eccentric and entertain them with amusing and self-deprecating stories that revealed little of himself.

The future for most Gaitskellites without their leader obviously depended very much on who took his place. For Frank, however, the personal loss of Gaitskell was matched by the blow that his death dealt in career terms. Of all his closest friends and confidants in the party from the time of his conversion, Gaitskell had been the most important. If he had aimed at holding high office in the Labour Party since joining in 1936, Gaitskell had increasingly become the key to achieving that goal. Now he had gone. Frank was without an influential supporter in Labour circles, though he had many friends. Just as he had been re-entering the political battle alongside Gaitskell, his general had been carried off. In political terms, it was a loss from which he never recovered. Gaitskell took with him to the grave whatever plans he had for Frank in a future Labour cabinet. Those close to the Labour leader are divided as to what may have been in his mind. 'I think Hugh was very loyal to Frank [said Denis Healey] and had he lived I think Frank would have had a larger role than he eventually did. Hugh was not only loyal to his friends, but he listened to them.'[26] Douglas Jay was less sure. 'Hugh would have admired Frank's qualities but he lacked Hugh's political judgement, his knowledge of personalities. He had been a part-timer out of office and would have been debarred by membership of the House of Lords from the highest offices.'[27] Though Jay was one of Gaitskell's inner circle, he did not recall discussing with his leader the subject of Frank disclaiming his peerage, which raises the question of how committed Gaitskell was to the plan in the first place.

As a peer Frank did not have a vote in the ballot to choose Gaitskell's successor. There was no natural heir among his supporters. Tony Crosland and Denis Healey were too young. Douglas Jay and Patrick Gordon Walker had no strong following. George Brown, Gaitskell's deputy, was the obvious candidate. Yet he had never been a Gaitskellite either in spirit (he had, on many occasions, expressed his disdain for socialist intellectuals) or on various policy issues, most notably over Europe. To Crosland, Brown was a 'neurotic drunk' and he was one of those who persuaded James Callaghan to stand as an alternative candidate on the right. Of the two Frank preferred George Brown, if only for his ardent Europeanism, but was, according to Crossman, 'lukewarm' and would have been happy to see either in charge.

The centre and left – including Elizabeth, habitually more radical than her husband – rallied behind Harold Wilson who, since his 1960 quarrel with Gaitskell, had moderated his own stance while still maintaining a radical veneer. Frank and the Gaitskellites saw Wilson as an opportunist seeking to seize the legacy of a man of principle. Crosland described a Brown–Wilson contest as choosing between a drunk and a crook. Christopher Mayhew, Frank's old student, summed up the distaste of many on the right of the Labour Party for Wilson.

> Politicians tend to be either 'be-ers' or 'do-ers'. That is to say, some of them want to be something – a Minister or a peer, or a Whip, or a social success; and some want to do something – to abolish nuclear weapons, or unify Europe, or reform the electoral system . . . Gaitskell was a single-minded 'doer' and Wilson a single-minded 'be-er'. Gaitskell was committed to social democracy and the Atlantic Alliance. Wilson – witness the famous photograph of the short-trousered schoolboy in Downing Street – was committed to taking up residence at No 10 and staying there as long as possible.[28]

Frank had particular reason to fear Wilson's accession. Though they had been acquaintances for years and neighbours in

267

Hampstead, where their children used to play together, the two had not moved in the same circle. Wilson was somewhat looked down on by the Gaitskell circle of Hampstead families. Kenneth Younger,[29] a Wykehamist like Gaitskell, would delight their gatherings by performing a satirical song about Wilson. Frank candidly admitted to Wilson's biographer in old age that 'the Gaitskellites were not very nice about Wilson. He was felt to be an upstart. Socially he was from a different class.'[30] Such exclusion merely confirmed what had been Wilson's experience at Frank's hands at Oxford in the late 1930s. He had been on the fringes of Labour while Frank held centre stage. Frank had not paid the younger man any great attention. At the core of his disdain was a feeling that Wilson, though cunning, determined and sharp, was not very bright. Reporting on Wilson's speech on science and the future of socialism at the Scarborough conference, Frank emphasized the academic gap between them. 'The faithful son of an industrial chemist from Huddersfield, he would feel that kind of future in his bones, while some of us Old Etonians and Old Wykehamists from the South of England could think it out best with our minds.'[31]

In political, as well as social, terms Wilson and Frank were poles apart, with Wilson's earlier role as Aneurin Bevan's protégé – Dalton once called him 'Nye's little dog' – enough to make him suspect. Frank's principal political reservation over Wilson concerned his vacillation over the Atlantic Alliance. (This particular worry was, however, quickly laid to rest after Wilson's election when he retained Patrick Gordon Walker, a committed Atlanticist, as Shadow Foreign Secretary.)

In the ballot of Labour MPs, the division in the right allowed Wilson to pose as a unity candidate and see off Callaghan in the first round and Brown in the second. Having already publicly announced that he was leaving the bank and re-entering politics full time, Frank had no choice but to attempt to work with the new leader. The influence he had previously enjoyed, though, was lost. If Wilson was suspicious of the social snobbery of the Gaitskellites, he was hardly likely to go out of his way to help a hereditary peer in their midst. He agreed to back Frank's attempts to amend the Peerage Bill, but with little enthusiasm. Any role he envisaged for him would centre on the Lords. Dingle Foot[32] moved the amendment but, with no signal from the Labour leadership, it was soundly defeated. Frank Pakenham was never to reappear.

Stoically accepting his life sentence in the Lords, Frank was swept up in a flurry of activity in the spring and summer of 1963. From the opposition front bench he was leading economic and education debates, and tackling issues such as racial discrimination, women in industry and the press. Yet all the shortcomings in terms of influence of being a member of the Upper Chamber remained, and with Wilson rather than Gaitskell at the head of the party Frank was even more out on a limb. His mind, restless as ever, turned to other interests to fill the available time and absorb his energy now his great political project seemed doomed to failure.

He wrote a second volume of autobiography, published in April 1964 by Hutchinson. Originally Harold Harris of Hutchinson had wanted Frank to write on the narrower subject of being a socialist in the City but that would have been too constraining for him. He ended up expanding the original proposal to take up the story from *Born to Believe* and the fall of the Attlee government in 1951. Its title, *Five Lives*, reflected the many facets of Frank's work. Accounts of his work at the bank, with prisoners, in the Lords, and latterly alongside Hugh Gaitskell, were interspersed with two 'interludes' on Ireland and in praise of Elizabeth's talent, and capped by an epilogue by his daughter Judith on Frank as a father, his fifth life. The book was hastily assembled, a collection of thoughts without a strong narrative line. His secretary at the time, Angela Lambert,[33] recalled: 'He wrote in his usual terribly undisciplined and random fashion, whereby he'd think about it over the weekend and occasionally jot down a few notes and then dictate quite fast something which really should have been just a working basis but which always went straight in verbatim.'[34]

Roy Jenkins[35] was later to reflect on Frank's literary style. While praising the energy, gusto and eclecticism of his writing, he felt his colleague could be criticized both for a lack of meticulous scholarship and for his prose. 'Subjects are often unceremoniously hauled in by the scruff of their necks and the simple device of beginning the sentence "Incidentally" . . .' This tendency to inconsequentiality and lack of stringency in structure was, Jenkins added, offset by a fulsome generosity in Frank's comments about individuals. 'Compliments come naturally to Lord Longford. Almost every book cited is "impressive", "invaluable", "brilliant" or "penetrating" and almost every noble family justifies its nobility. There is, however, sometimes a hint of steel beneath the velvet. He can clothe a rebuke in a compliment with unique skill.'[36]

Five Lives appeared to mixed reviews in April 1964. Some of the accusations against *Born to Believe* were echoed: that it was somewhat arrogant of Frank to think that a minister who had not been in the cabinet, was in mid-career and had been out of office for thirteen years, was interesting enough to justify not one but two excursions into autobiography. Six months later Elizabeth's painstakingly researched *Victoria RI* became an overnight bestseller, was heaped with praise by the critics and went on to win the James Tait Black prize for biography.

It was Judith's epilogue to *Five Lives* that caught the attention of the popular press rather more than her father's account of his career to date. Near the day of publication the *Sunday Mirror* ran a full-page article entitled 'My Father – writhing in a belly dance while my mother placidly combed her hair'. It was a précis of Judith's account of her father's early morning efforts to keep fit and slim. Frank's public reputation as an eccentric showed no signs of diminishing.

His large number of friends from all areas of life and every shade of political opinion often brought Frank to the fringes of the great public controversies of the day. The summer of 1963 saw Britain obsessed by the Profumo affair. The involvement of the Conservative Secretary of State for War[37] with a call-girl, Christine Keeler, who was also associated with a naval attaché at the Soviet embassy, blew up in the face of a Conservative government, led by an unpopular and ageing prime minister unable to lift Britain's economy out of a slump. Frank knew several of the key players in the drama that unfolded first in court and then in the pages of every newspaper. Profumo had been introduced to Keeler by Stephen Ward, an osteopath fashionable in London society who rented a country cottage on the Cliveden estate of Bill Astor. Astor's name was linked with that of Mandy Rice-Davies, an associate of Keeler's.

Frank had known Bill Astor since student days and the Bullingdon point-to-point. Though his friendship with Astor's younger brother, David, was closer, Frank had continued to visit Cliveden and had been there just before the Profumo scandal broke, demonstrating to Astor's wife, Bronwen, his newly acquired ability to swim. Bronwen Astor[38] recalled that as soon as her husband became embroiled in the controversy, Frank was one of the first to offer help and support to the couple at a time when they were shunned by friends in society and virtual prisoners in their home.[39] He continued to stand by them until Astor's death in 1966 and beyond, supporting his widow in the late 1980s when *Scandal*, a film account of the whole affair, reopened old wounds. As with the prisoners he visited, it was not a matter of guilt or innocence that prompted Frank but rather loyalty to friends in trouble. At the time of the release of *Scandal* he took Bronwen Astor to lunch at the House of Lords but seemed not to understand her continuing need to clear her late husband's name from any suggestion that he was improperly involved with Mandy Rice-Davies.

Frank had known John Profumo slightly before he became a household name, but was to become a good friend afterwards, exposing himself again to the charge that he deliberately sought out the notorious, finding a certain glamour in their activities. While the Labour front bench in the House of Commons attacked Profumo over a potential breach of national security, Frank's concern was a moral one. Here was a man brought to his knees by the press and public opinion. While he could not condone Profumo's actions, he could sympathize with him as a sinner in his current predicament. There was the element of public failure which Frank could recognize. He saw someone whom society and his colleagues could not wait to judge, but whom he was not prepared to condemn or shun.

In the debate on public and private morality his innate puritanism and his Catholicism made him take a hard line. In principle he was intolerant. In his view, those who broke their marriage vows showed a weakness in character that made them unfit to hold high office. Yet his intolerance of breaches of the moral code did not preclude tolerance and forgiveness of the individual perpetrator. Profumo had acknowledged his sin, taken his punishment and should, Frank advocated, be left alone. A few months after Profumo resigned in June 1963, he invited him to lunch – without any publicity. Finding his guest conscience-stricken, blaming only himself and determined to rebuild his life with his wife Valerie, Frank recorded that the meeting left him with 'an irresistible conviction – whatever the past and future may hold for him and me, at this moment he is nearer to the Kingdom of God than I am'.[40]

A third figure at the centre of the affair, Stephen Ward, had met Frank briefly during one of his visits to Cliveden. He had even offered to use his professional skills to relieve Frank's fibrositis. Frank, knowing about Ward's voyeuristic interest in prostitutes, could not bring himself even to contemplate accepting the offer. Ward's evident pleasure in his lifestyle left little room for talk of sins and sinners. The problem with basing one's approach on this idea was that the sinner has to admit that he has committed a sin in the first place. While Profumo's public penance was complete, Ward was unrepentant.

The osteopath was subsequently crucified in court and abandoned by his friends. Frank tried to contact him but his approach came too late. Ward committed suicide. No one else among the osteopath's erstwhile friends and clients would speak openly of him, but Frank agreed to an ITN interview request. He began by stating his own belief that what Ward had done was wrong and could not be tolerated by society. 'But with him lying dead at our feet how can one fail to ask, "Which of us is qualified to cast the first stone?"'

His conduct during the Profumo scandal served once again to emphasize the gap between him and the party leadership. While Wilson worked successfully to make political capital by exploiting the affair to discredit Macmillan and his government, Frank was worrying about the moral well-being of the central players. It was not only over

Profumo that Frank's Christianity put him out of step with his party in this period. The early 1960s saw the start of the Second Vatican Council in Rome, summoned by a reforming Pope, John XXIII, who wanted the Catholic Church to get to grips with the modern age. In April 1963, the Pope published *Pacem in Terris* (*Peace on Earth*). For Frank it signalled a change of heart in the Vatican and in his Church towards socialism, hitherto regarded by clerics throughout Europe with suspicion bordering on positive hostility. The Pope even appeared to be taking a softer line on communism.

However, the time-honoured Catholic attitudes to divorce, contraception, homosexuality and assisted fertilization changed little in this reforming period – at least on an official level. When these matters came up in Labour Party debates and in the House of Lords, Frank felt obliged as a Christian to state his Church's beliefs, no matter how discordant they were with those of his colleagues. Other outspoken Catholics in the Lords at the time, like Lord Iddesleigh, made their contribution from the cross-benches, but Frank tried to combine the roles of a Catholic – and one clearly identified as such in the public eye – and a Labour politician. When inevitable clashes occurred, it was his party, not his Church, that saw itself compromised. His daughter Antonia recalled an argument they had in the early 1960s over Conservative plans, backed wholeheartedly by Labour, to make contraceptive pills freely available on the NHS. 'He stuck at nothing in his condemnation of that. When I tried to talk about the real world, he wouldn't have any of it. I think anytime in politics where the doctrine of the Catholic Church pointed one way and the doctrine of the Labour Party another, he stuck with the Church.'[41]

She attributed her father's inflexibility over questions like contraception to more than a blind adherence to the papal line. 'My father, because he had no sexual experience before marriage, and I would go to the stake saying had none other than a very happy married life, found it impossible to understand anything extra-marital or premarital, the guilts, the hopes, the fears, the way the world carried on. It wasn't that he was uncharitable about it. He just couldn't understand.'[42]

On another occasion, he spoke out in a House of Lords debate against artificial insemination by donor.

There are some of us whose main interest in public questions derives from a desire to help the weak, the afflicted, the poor, the old and the lonely. This sentiment would seem to place us naturally and easily on the side of the childless couples, but whatever we like to call our ethics, Aristotelian, Kantian, Utilitarian, Humanitarian or simply Christian, we must all be aware that immediate happiness, while a laudable objective to be promoted by all scientific means, is not the highest value here. Grapes cannot be grown from thorns or figs from thistles. It is literally impossible to help anyone, a childless couple or anybody else, however humane our purpose, by evil means.

Such uncompromising talk of evil from a front-bench Labour spokesman did not pass unnoticed in his party. As Douglas Jay put it: 'I always felt that Frank answered to a higher set of principles than those of party. There was an element of the Edwardian politician about him, above party concerns, speaking on principle. But on social issues, he was right behind the Labour line. It was on moral matters that his Christian principles came into conflict with party politics and his principles always won out.'[43]

One area where Frank's principles were in line with those of his party and where his public reputation might be used to enhance Labour's image was that of penal reform. In the middle of 1963, Wilson invited him to chair a committee on the prevention and treatment of crime. As a peer, an academic and a man beyond reproach who wore his Christianity on his sleeve, Frank was the natural choice to chair such a high-minded initiative. The original idea for Labour's report on crime did not come from Harold Wilson. The suggestion was made by Joan Bourne, a member of the party's research department whose brief was minority issues and who had come to know Frank through her interest in penal reform. She approached her head of department, Peter Shore,[44] who in turn took the proposal to Wilson with Frank's name as chairman included in it.

It was Wilson, however, who seized on the scheme both as a way of occupying Frank and also, more importantly, as demonstrating to the electorate, in the run-up to an election, that Labour took the question of crime prevention and penal reform seriously. Other members of the working party included Gerald Gardiner, later Lord Chancellor, Alice Bacon[45] and Baroness Serota[46] among eight future ministers. Tom Driberg, a left-wing MP and member of the National Executive, was a late recruit. Although Driberg was an Oxford contemporary and interested in penal reform, Frank was initially opposed to his membership. Driberg was gay and made no secret of the fact, delighting in shocking his colleagues in the House of Commons tea-room with news of his latest conquests. Like Stephen Ward before his downfall, Driberg offended Frank's principles by his unashamed behaviour which was not, Frank believed, compatible with being a politician. However, other members of the working party persuaded him to compromise his personal principles for the good of the cause. Driberg was an influential figure in party circles and would be a useful ally in advocating that the final report should be adopted as official policy.

The impending election gave the exercise a great sense of urgency. If the report was to shape party policy, it had to be completed in record time. With Joan Bourne as secretary giving direction to the group's deliberations, Frank curbed his natural inclinations to be a lone crusader on the issues involved and instead worked hard to achieve a consensus between his colleagues. Other members of the working party, such as Baroness Serota, were later to pay tribute to him for managing both to enthuse them about radical solutions while at the same time keeping the group on common ground and to schedule. The resulting report, *Crime: A Challenge to Us All*, was published on 18 June 1964 and in terms of legislation was the most influential in which Frank was ever involved. It had a profound effect between 1964 and 1970 on the Labour government's policy on law and prison reform in general and in particular on the Criminal Justice Act of 1967 which introduced the parole system. Hitherto there had been discretionary release for some 'model' prisoners before they had completed their sentence. Following the recommendations of the Longford Committee, the 1967 Act allowed those who satisfied local and national parole boards to be released with as much as two-thirds of their sentence still to run. Frank and his working party felt that the prospect of earning remission would encourage prisoners to change their behaviour and smooth their readmission into society. It was the high point of Frank's attempts to bring a more humane approach to punishment and rehabilitation.

Some of the report's proposals concerning young offenders (for example the idea of Family Courts) were not implemented, but remained the aim of campaigning organizations for years to come before finally being achieved. Others quickly passed into law. Its recommendations on the setting up of a Family Service to coordinate and centralize all other efforts in that area were to inspire the Labour cabinet to set up the Seebohm Committee, of which Baroness Serota was also a member. As a result it was legislated in the Children and Young Persons' Act of 1969 that all government work concerning family matters should be carried out in a single department within each local authority.

The report also made the abolition of capital punishment a priority. It was generally accepted on the Labour benches that abolition was a good idea. The fact that the future Labour government in 1964 included so many ministers who had been working on the report accelerated the issue through the Commons voting system.

Some time before the 1964 general election, Harold Wilson had visited the retired party leader, Clement Attlee, now an earl and a member of the Lords, to seek his advice on various appointments if, as looked likely from the polls, Labour should win. Their conversation turned to Frank and the leadership of the House of Lords. There were those who felt that Frank had disqualified himself by taking too Catholic a line over various moral matters in the previous months. Two other candidates – Lords Silkin and Alexander – were also being talked about.

From Wilson's point of view, the advantages of appointing Frank outweighed any problems with disgruntled colleagues. For a start any cabinet he constructed would be exceptionally short on experience of government after thirteen years in opposition. Frank, at the Admiralty, had been 'of cabinet rank' and possessed in the circumstances a relatively lengthy ministerial track record. Equally, Wilson would need to appear generous to the Gaitskellites. Giving Frank a place at the top table would satisfy that need without ceding him any real power.

When their discussion came to the leadership of the House of Lords, Attlee told Wilson he was in no doubt. 'It must be Frank,' he said. And so it was decided, though Frank knew nothing about it until after the narrow election victory of 1964. Waiting for the call to come from 10 Downing Street in his Chelsea flat with Antonia, who was expecting a baby, Frank was nervous. 'It was an agonising time for him. The telephone did obviously ring finally – though only by tea-time. He talked a lot while we waited. At first he was very confident and talked about wanting to be in the government. But there were doubts, things he didn't agree with Wilson over.'[47]

At Downing Street, Wilson told Frank of his conversation with Attlee, then offered him the leadership of the Lords. The mention of Attlee was almost as if Wilson was disowning any responsibility for the appointment himself. Attlee's patronage, so important in starting off Frank's ministerial career and in sustaining it when he made himself unpopular with other colleagues, proved decisive in securing him a place in the cabinet.

FIFTEEN

The Leader of the House of Lords

Being in the cabinet had been Frank's goal since he joined the Labour Party in 1936. In pursuit of such a position he had been deemed by some a class traitor, endured ridicule, and lost friends. Yet the lustre of success in achieving a political lifetime's ambition could not disguise the fact, from the moment when Wilson told him that he was being appointed on Attlee's recommendation, that it was an empty triumph. The new Prime Minister had no plans to use Frank as anything more than a way of keeping the House of Lords quiet. The 1964 manifesto had made plain Labour's view of the Upper Chamber. 'Certainly we shall not permit effective action to be frustrated by the hereditary and non-elected Conservative majority in the House of Lords.'

However hard Frank tried to convince himself that simply being in the cabinet would ensure him a substantial role in shaping legislation, he knew in his heart that he was on the margins, at best an irrelevance to many of his colleagues, and occasionally the butt of their jokes. He had left office in 1951 as a rising star, at the heart of an influential, soon to become dominant, grouping in the Labour Party. In 1964, at fifty-nine, he was regarded by many in the party as already too old to hold high office. Without Gaitskell, he had no private access to power.

Part of the problem, he freely admitted, was that the Lords was of no interest to the rest of the cabinet. 'It made me ineffective,' he admitted subsequently. 'The other twenty-two members saw each other every day in the Commons. There was a fraternity. I saw them only at full meetings of the Cabinet.'[1] So his speeches there went unnoticed. He liked to recall that at one crucial juncture of the dispute with Ian Smith over the future of the colony of Rhodesia, soon after the Unilateral Declaration of Independence in November 1965, it fell to him to make a statement for the government in the Lords before it was announced in the Commons. It was vital that the Upper Chamber gave its consent that evening. Wilson was in the gallery and was evidently impressed by Frank's deft and efficient handling of a matter about which several of the peers on the opposition benches harboured strong feelings. Next day Wilson congratulated Frank in front of the cabinet on his performance. 'I think it came as a real surprise to him,' Frank realized.[2]

In this regard he was a victim of his own success in handling the Lords. There was enormous potential for a conflict between a small Labour majority in the Commons, brimming with ideas and schemes to put into effect after years out of office, and a Conservative majority in the Lords, able to block that legislation. Frank had no explicit guidance from the Prime Minister as to whether he would have welcomed a clash with the Lords or whether he wanted no trouble from them. So he took his silence as indicating the second and thereby forewent his opportunity to attract the attention of his colleagues.

A survey of the House of Lords completed in 1968 showed that 116 Labour peers faced 351 Conservatives, with 41 Liberals and 554 peers who sat as independents on the cross-benches. The Labour front-bench team in the Upper Chamber was beleaguered. 'As Leader of the Opposition I had an army behind me,' Frank's opposite number, Lord Carrington, remarked. 'As Leader of the House Frank only had a platoon.'[3] The non-attendance of many of the hereditary element among the Conservative and cross-bench peers evened matters out. In theory, if Frank and his chief whip received the support of most of their colleagues and of an above-average number of cross-benchers, they could carry the day. Harold Wilson made it a point of policy as prime minister to refrain from creating sizeable numbers of Conservative life peers – except when it was unavoidable. At the same time, he bolstered the ranks of his own party in the Lords with life peers who were prepared to put in a day's work for their title.

However, even such a determined approach could not alter the fact that, as Leader of the Lords, Frank faced defeat on every bill that he tried to put through the House. With Labour's formidable legislative programme he opted to employ skill, diplomacy, and often good humour, not to mention winning the cooperation of the Leader of the Opposition, to ensure that the Lords did not become a major constitutional stumbling block. He was, Peter Carrington reckoned, personally popular on all sides of the House. 'Frank was extremely adroit. He was an extremely good debater. And he could be extremely sharp. But it was always saved by a wonderful sense of fun and humour. Except on very rare occasions when we got under his skin and prompted him to bite back, he always responded in great good humour with a joke, a laugh or a quip that was never personally wounding.'⁴ Many fellow Lords would already have noted Frank's detachment from routine party politics and therefore respected him.

His eccentricity lay in his manner and appearance. It did not affect his abilities as an organizer. By seeking a consensus and by keeping the House in good spirits, he managed to get the business done. As ever, he was the delegator. His deputies – Lord Champion before 1966 and Lord Shackleton, son of the explorer, afterwards – took care of much of the day-to-day timetabling, while Frank was involved in cabinet committees and other such duties.

While Frank strove to avoid a clash between the Conservative majority in the Lords and the Labour government, he was not blind to the need to reform the Second Chamber. Having sat on the front bench continuously since 1945, he had dwelt – often as a result of bitter personal experience – on the shortcomings of a largely hereditary institution and its place in the British political system. Labour had fought the 1935 general election on a pledge to abolish the Lords. The fracas of 1948 over iron and steel nationalization had led Attlee's government to curtail its powers further. Despite modifications with the arrival of life peers in 1958 and Tony Benn's disclaimer in 1963, the Lords in 1964 retained the power to delay government business by two parliamentary sessions. Restrictions on the sort of bills where it would exercise its veto were largely informal. The Salisbury Rules, drawn up when Labour came to power in 1945 to forbid Tory majorities in the Lords from blocking issues that formed part of the government's election manifesto, had no basis in statute.

Frank was convinced that the hereditary principle of the House of Lords needed weakening in order to rationalize its position as watchdog of the Commons. Its attempts to influence parliamentary decisions would then no longer be greeted angrily by an electorate unwilling to accept the interference of unelected noblemen. Deprived of any other focus in government for his reforming ardour, Frank turned his attention to the subject of the House of Lords. It was the aspect of his work in the Second Chamber that impinged most directly on cabinet meetings.

Reform of the Lords had an obvious personal appeal. Since his decision to accept a peerage in 1945 had, more or less, consigned his political career to the Upper Chamber, it followed that he would want to make the Lords work as effectively as possible. If its irregular constitutional position could be sorted out, then its politically active members could demand an end to their marginalization when it came to government jobs. Since the 1950s, when the family had first started going down to Bernhurst, Frank had played a round of golf at the weekend in Rye with Commander Henry Burrows, clerk assistant in the Lords. As they strode along the fairway, the two would discuss how the composition of the Lords could be modified to secure its position in the constitution. Burrows's favoured solution – the two-writ scheme – won Frank's backing. All members of the Lords would continue to have the right to come and speak, but only those who were created peers, either before or after the introduction of the scheme, would be allowed to vote. Hereditary peers would lose the right to vote, though some of their number, like Frank himself, would be given voting peerages to enable them to maintain their active participation in events. The in-

---

built Conservative majority, derived from the hereditary element, would be removed and the main anachronism, from a democratic point of view, would be consigned to history.

It was a pragmatic proposal. The two-writ scheme would not completely disenfranchise the hereditary peers. It would in particular reduce the antagonism that a less gentlemanly solution would have aroused on the Tory benches in the Lords. Evolution rather than revolution was the approach. As Leader of the Lords Frank worked with his cabinet colleague, Lord Gardiner, the Lord Chancellor, to prepare a plan based on the two-writ scheme. He introduced the idea to the cabinet in June 1966 with high hopes that he would be given at least cautious encouragement to pursue the matter further.

The previous item on the agenda had generated much disagreement, and Frank's proposal, to his profound dismay, was treated as light relief by his colleagues. Even those who bothered to listen mistook his emphasis. Barbara Castle recorded in her diary that the plan was 'excellent in tone about the need to reduce their [the Lords'] powers'.[5] Frank's protests that the question was not of a reduction of powers but of a change of composition failed to move her and most of the rest of the cabinet. Wilson responded: 'Whatever may be said about the last topic, I can imagine nothing quite so divisive as an attempt to reform the House of Lords.'[6]

Frank then further undermined his position by angry talk of resignation, a threat he had no intention of carrying out. The cabinet was not in the mood to be bullied. He backed down but resolved to carry on the fight. The appointment of his old Oxford confrère, Richard Crossman, as Leader of the House of Commons in the autumn of 1966 provided the required opportunity. At the June cabinet meeting Crossman had provoked much of the laughter that had greeted Frank's proposal with his remark, 'I'm all for a Second Chamber which is indefensible when any alternative must be a check on progress.' Barbara Castle noted that Frank displayed 'shocked pain at such "cynicism"' but that this in turn 'had us almost rolling in the aisles'.[7]

However, only a matter of months later Crossman had revised his opinion and determined on reform of some of the procedures of the

House of Commons and of the Lords at the same time. He lived up to his reputation as 'Double Crossman' by effectively annexing Frank's scheme and then trying to exclude the Leader of the Lords from an active role in its implementation, preferring to work with his close friend and protégé Lord Shackleton,[8] as well as Lord Gardiner and Roy Jenkins as Home Secretary. After much discussion and debate with his circle of advisers, Crossman came to the Prime Minister and his senior cabinet colleagues in the autumn of 1967 for advice over how to proceed with Lords reform. George Brown, First Secretary, still felt that it was an unnecessary distraction from the pressing question of unemployment and would be judged as such by the electorate. James Callaghan, Chancellor of the Exchequer, was more in favour but torn between Crossman's two proposals of either a one-tier approach – which eradicated the hereditary element and made working members with inherited titles into life peers – and the two-tier approach, in essence Frank's two-writ scheme. Crossman favoured the second.

In spite of such prevarications Crossman managed to get top-level backing to proceed on the basis of including a general pledge to reform the Lords in the forthcoming Queen's Speech and then negotiating with the Conservatives and Liberals as to the exact details. It was only at this point that Crossman took Frank into his confidence, a remarkable delay and a huge snub given Frank's responsibility at cabinet level for the Upper Chamber. Frank had clearly heard the rumours of what Crossman planned, and had grown frustrated at being excluded from the consultations, as revealed by Professor Bernard Crick,[9] then working with Crossman. 'He sent for me as academic secretary of the Study of Parliament Group. "What does Dick intend for Lords' reform?" When I said I didn't know, he muttered out loud "Won't tell" and dismissed me peremptorily. "Why the hell does he ask me," I screamed to Private Office in the corridor, "he's in the bloody Cabinet". "They are a rough lot, professor; they don't tell him much".'[10]

A working group was established over dinner in Chelsea in October 1967, consisting of Frank, Gardiner, Shackleton, Crossman and Jenkins. 'When all this had been agreed Frank said he thought that I should lead the delegation [Crossman wrote in his diary]. I must say this was very good of him because as Leader of the House, he would naturally like to lead it himself. Considering how passionate he is about this and how much he knows and how little I know, he has shown an astonishing power to put his personal feelings behind him and a real care for the cause we all have at heart.'[11] Frank had decided that the cause was more important than any hurt feelings at his continued relegation to a subordinate role. Crossman was more likely to make it happen.

Though Crossman led the negotiations and steered them through cabinet, and Shackleton did much of the detailed drawing up of the reform package with the Tories, Frank remained actively involved. Understanding the ways of the Lords and its gentlemanly approach rather better than Crossman, he brought the two sides together over dinner at the Café Royal to dispel any antagonism. He also made it his business to keep Carrington and his team fully briefed on Labour's attitudes, a courtesy which could annoy Crossman. In his diary for 24 October 1967, just before the announcement of the reform scheme in the Queen's Speech, Crossman complains that the Tory leaders in the Commons knew via Carrington the precise wording of the proposal 'because Frank Longford can't resist talking to them out of office hours'.[12]

Though Conservative approval was obtained for a reform package very similar to Frank's preferred two-writ scheme, it was never made into law. Crossman moved in November 1968 to be Secretary of State for Health and Social Security and the measure thereby lost its most eloquent spokesman in the Lower Chamber. The bill was delayed in the Commons by an unlikely combination of resistance from Frank's son-in-law Hugh Fraser[13] and Enoch Powell[14] on the Tory right, and Michael Foot on the Labour left. Foot rallied those of like mind to rebel against the Labour whip with his argument that the Lords should not be reformed but abolished. To tinker with its composition would be to give an unelected chamber an unwarranted place in the system, Foot said. Powell and Fraser, a former Tory minister, were opposed on the basis that any change would alter the constitutional balance. Their long-running battle held up the bill to such an extent that Wilson in 1969 lost patience with a scheme that had never been a top priority anyway and quietly abandoned it. If Frank had ever doubted the indifference of the Labour Party to the Lords, here was proof.

The majority of his speeches in the Chamber were on routine business; some of them were simply reading out other ministers' statements. Occasionally though, a subject would arise about which he felt passionate. The most notable example was the arrival in the Lords of a private member's bill legalizing abortion, introduced into the Commons by David Steel[15] and passed by the Lower Chamber. Opposition to abortion is the keystone of orthodoxy in the Catholic Church and Frank was implacably against the measure.

Though Steel had received backing from Roy Jenkins as Home Secretary and the cabinet was generally in favour of the measure, the issue was left, in theory at least, to the conscience of individual members. However, the government had granted parliamentary time to Steel in the Commons and its tacit approval was no secret. To oppose the measure, Frank would be seen to be going against the spirit of the government and the cabinet of which he was a member. He would be justifying the criticism in party circles that their Leader in the Upper House was more Catholic than socialist.

If the bill had been a straight government measure, Frank would have had to resign over it. Given its quasi-official status, he decided instead on the eccentric course of taking temporary leave of absence from his post to speak from the back benches against the measure. As a manoeuvre, it was without precedent constitutionally. As a gesture, this went down very badly with his cabinet colleagues. As a ploy to sway the House of Lords, it failed miserably. One observer recalled that when Frank spoke, it was the nearest the Lords ever came to booing anyone. He stated clearly that life, in his opinion, began at the moment of conception and that abortion was therefore murder. He developed the 'thin end of the wedge' argument and asked how long it would be before the law allowed elderly members of the House to be bumped off on the grounds of their advanced years. Some responded with cries of 'Shame!'

It was arguably a tribute to Frank's usually sure-handed mastery of the Lords that, within months of taking office in 1964, Wilson named him to a second post, that of Lord Privy Seal, but it was again an empty gesture. Under Attlee such non-departmental posts had been filled by men with overall coordinating responsibility for various areas of government policy. Wilson continued this policy with, for example, Douglas Houghton,[16] the Chancellor of the Duchy of Lancaster, covering the separate ministries of health and social security in cabinet, but as Lord Privy Seal, Frank was given no additional brief. In an interview in 1977, Wilson attributed his failure to employ Frank in any broader role than the Lords to the fact that 'senior ministers didn't take him seriously enough'.[17] He was excluded from the chairmanship of any of the cabinet committees for the same reason. He did sit on the important economy and defence and foreign affairs committees. He was kept busy, but it was more a case of perpetual motion than getting anywhere. Movement should not be mistaken for action. According to Wilson, 'On the financial thing and his [Frank's] expertise in the bank, he always had his chance in committee to make his points, but I don't think the Treasury or the Chancellor would have regarded him as a financial expert just because of the Irish bank. I mean he knew his way round but he wouldn't have been au fait with the really hard, tough Treasury and Bank of England decisions.'[18]

Frank did not easily accept his fate as an irrelevance in cabinet. He lobbied Wilson intensively for greater responsibilities and was successful in winning concessions on two occasions. Yet, both times, he failed to exploit the opening to leave any mark on the government. In December 1965, Wilson reshuffled his cabinet, moving his close ally Barbara Castle to Transport, replacing her at Overseas Development with Tony Greenwood, until then Colonial Secretary, and awarding Frank Greenwood's old job. According to Wilson, Frank had been 'pressing for an administrative job to combine with his part-time Leadership of the Lords'. (The Prime Minister's description of leading the Upper Chamber as 'part-time' employment was telling.)[19]

Such was the number of talented ministers at Wilson's disposal in 1964 that he was forced, initially at least, to leave such rising stars as Roy Jenkins outside the cabinet. Seen in that light, his offer to Frank of the Colonial Office was not quite as insubstantial as it may seem now. After all, it had been a key ministry when run by Elizabeth's ancestor, Joseph Chamberlain, in the early years of the twentieth century, and the appointment did mean that Frank at last had behind him a department, rather than a small private office in the Lords.

The major 'colonial' dispute of the day was over Rhodesia and UDI, but Wilson had already made it clear that he was taking personal charge of this area and excluded Frank completely. Furthermore, with the new Commonwealth emerging to replace the old Empire, he undisguisedly intended to subsume the Colonial Office into the Foreign Office as soon as possible, and asked Frank to accelerate the winding-down process. Indeed, some critics argued that his very appointment was part of that scaling down. Essentially he was being handed another administrative task, rather than the opportunity to make policy.

Frank's secretary at the time, Angela Lambert, recalled that, despite such drawbacks, he was delighted with the appointment. For the first time in fifteen years he was back in a ministry with all the paraphernalia of civil servants and support that such a post entailed. Yet he was stripped of the colonial secretaryship just three months later after Labour's victory at the March 1966 general election. Lambert attributed this failure to several factors. 'First of all he was in his sixties then and there were a lot of young people around. Secondly he didn't change. He didn't become any more organised or hard-working. He didn't master his briefs. He never got over the conviction that if you carried papers around with you for long enough, they would be absorbed by a process of osmosis. He didn't read and study them and his PPSs used to have to make summaries of them for him.'[20]

While leadership of the Lords came naturally to Frank, involving thought and diplomacy, not endless hours of reading documents which he found tedious, the colonial secretaryship exposed his lack of application. As a young ambitious politician in Attlee's government, he had been prepared to buckle down to unpleasant tasks like his post at Civil Aviation, in the hope of future preferment. However, by the time Wilson awarded him a department of his own, he knew that he commanded little respect and therefore had little incentive to apply himself. There was no hope of further promotion. As became increasingly obvious to those around him, Frank's mind was turning more and more to matters outside the political mainstream, like prison reform.

'In Cabinet [said Denis Healey, Defence Secretary in this period] any minister can play as big a role as he wants to and being a peer doesn't prevent him at all. Frank was just not very political in an odd way. He was not an organisation man. Essentially he was one of these chaps who was 150 per cent committed on any issue which he felt strongly – like penal reform – but on many issues didn't have strong feelings. He was marginal because of his nature. He didn't aspire. He liked to do well and he liked to be well regarded but he didn't want to work hard to do well.'[21] In other words, through Labour's thirteen years in opposition Frank's tendency to become engaged in other issues, to take up a crusading stance, had lowered his tolerance of the everyday issues of government. He was only interested in matters that touched on one of his own personal areas of concern.

In 1964, when first a minister, his diary[22] showed that he continued on a regular basis to attend debates and give talks at various university Catholic chaplaincies, some as far afield as Nottingham, to participate in events for the Anglo-German Association, Eton Manor Boys' Club and New Bridge, to visit individual prisoners, and to keep up a busy social life, with receptions at the Irish embassy to greet the national rugby team before their match against England at Twickenham, lunches at the Lords with old friends like Hugh Gaitskell's widow and new acquaintances like Laurens van der Post,[23] and then dinners with the Women's Advertising Club of London at the Savoy or the Building Societies' Association at Quaglino's (he had been on the board of the Brighton-based Alliance Building Society).

If he was disappointed with Frank as Colonial Secretary, Wilson did give him one further chance with a more creative brief in addition to leadership of the Lords. Mindful that he had considerable knowledge of social services and that this was the area where he could potentially make the biggest contribution, Wilson agreed to allow him to undertake an investigation into youth services nationwide. In some respects it was a continuation of the committee on crime that Frank had headed in 1963–4. He had felt then that there was not sufficient attention paid to the needs of young people. His new brief was to include not only advice and counselling, under the auspices of the Ministry of Education, but also the treatment of young offenders, part of the Home Office's field of responsibility.

Both relevant ministers – Tony Crosland and Roy Jenkins – were less than pleased at the Prime Minister's concession to Frank and felt that he was interfering in their domain. An argument ensued, with Jenkins and Crosland successfully combining in cabinet to limit the scope of the Longford inquiry. 'When it was over [Jenkins recalled], he upbraided us in the middle of the road outside 10 Downing Street. I think he was quivering with (probably well-justified) rage, but what he actually said was, "I will still write very favourably about you both in my autobiography but not quite so favourably as I would have done until this morning."'[24]

The abortive youth inquiry was not Frank's only attempt to bring his expertise as a prison reformer to bear on the policies of the government. As a cabinet minister, he felt the Home Office should treat him with a little more respect than they had done hitherto when he lobbied them over individual prisoners. Roy Jenkins, appointed Home Secretary in 1965, was not impressed.

Frank was always on the side of the prisoners. He was considered by the Home Office officials to be very wrong on a lot of things. He was a man of immense charm but there was this flibberti-gibbet aspect to Frank. I don't think he would have been a good Home Secretary. I'm afraid that we made jokes about Frank as a prison reformer within the Cabinet and the Home Office. His willingness to pursue something he believed in and his absolute indifference to ridicule or to criticism were absolutely admirable, but they were not balanced, I'm afraid, by a discriminating judgement. Therefore he was just as likely to get involved in a bad case as in a good case.[25]

There were occasions, despite Frank's best intentions, when his involvement with individual prisoners or miscreants clashed with his ministerial responsibilities and landed him in trouble with his colleagues. In May 1965, the papers picked up the case of a cleaner at the Longfords' Chelsea home who appeared in court charged with stealing a pearl and diamond ring worth £105. She was found guilty at Marlborough Street Magistrates' Court and sentenced to two months in prison. Frank paid for a solicitor to defend her. It was seen as an eccentric gesture, but the point was clear for Frank. He was not interested in guilt or innocence, only that the accused should be treated fairly.

In December 1967 (when, admittedly, Labour was in a stronger position, with its Commons majority increased from four to ninety-six at the 1966 election, and therefore less sensitive to what the cabinet saw as Frank's excesses), the *People* did a full-page spread on 'The Moving Story of the Peer and the Prostitute'. It was based on an article Frank had written in the magazine *Christian Action* and reported how the Leader of the House of Lords had befriended an Irish prostitute called Annabel, found her a home in a convent and given her a new life. To Frank, Annabel's story was one of redemption, and he told it in that spirit. To his critics and some of his colleagues, though, it portrayed Frank in a curious light, the politician who cared not only for people's material well-being but also for their souls.

His continuing friendship with Christopher Craig and his brother Niven was to cause Wilson most blushes. Soon after Frank joined the cabinet, Niven Craig was allowed to work out of prison on a hostel scheme. His fellow inmates, jealous of the privileges he had won and ascribing them to his friendship with Frank, wrote to two Conservative MPs to complain. They accused Frank of having a homosexual relationship with Niven Craig. Even though there was no evidence to back the claim, one of the MPs raised the issue of Frank's undue influence in an adjournment debate in the House of Commons.

In the ensuing row, Wilson imposed a rule that ministers would not be allowed to visit prisoners without the Home Secretary or himself being informed. Frank therefore had to curtail his visits, though he did get round the bar by sending his secretary. No sooner had the Niven Craig accusations been forgotten than his younger brother Christopher, released from jail in the early 1960s through the efforts of Frank and others, announced that he was getting married. He invited Frank to the wedding. Given the recent publicity, Frank reluctantly felt he must seek the Prime Minister's advice. Wilson asked him not to attend the ceremony lest it place any more strain on the government's – at that stage wafer-thin – majority. 'Until 1966,' Frank remembered, 'when the majority in the Commons increased, there was a siege mentality, a feeling that you should avoid stepping out of line at all costs.'[26] After considerable hesitation, Frank fell in with the Prime Minister's wishes, but invited Craig and his fiancée to dinner at the White Tower on the eve of the wedding. The curtailment of his liberty to follow up his long-standing mission to prisoners and ex-prisoners was the price of holding high office. Yet in view of the limited influence he was gaining as a result, Frank began to wonder whether it was a price worth paying.

Other than establishing a reputation with his cabinet colleagues as being something of a loose cannon, it is hard to see how Frank affected the course of the Wilson government. No other cabinet has been so picked over posthumously through the publication of diaries written by some of its principal players. Yet, in the accounts of Richard Crossman, Barbara Castle, Patrick Gordon Walker and Tony Benn, Frank hardly figures. There are occasional cruel asides about his ineffectiveness, but on the major issues that divided this turbulent group of ministers, he rarely played a leading role. He himself was later to describe his usual attitude to the regular Thursday morning cabinet meetings as one of 'I ought to get my word in, in order to show that I was not sulkily aloof.' It was such a dispiriting performance that 'thoughts of lunch alone sustained me'.[27]

On the crucial matter of the government's commitment to maintaining the value of sterling in the face of a balance-of-payments deficit, for example, Frank, despite being a member of the cabinet's finance committee, was neither consulted before the decision was taken to defend the pound at all costs, nor was he informed when the policy began to run into serious trouble.

In July 1966, Frank travelled up to London from Bernhurst by train with an old friend from the National Bank. His companion's warning about the impending need to devalue sterling – despite the government's repeated denials that it would happen – prompted him to take the unusual step of telephoning the Chancellor when he arrived at his office. When the two met, Frank outlined a package of measures that he felt would ease the run on sterling – including a prices and wages freeze. Callaghan told him that it was too late for such action. The cabinet was going to have to decide the next day whether or not to devalue. Callaghan was opposed but George Brown, at the Ministry of Economic Affairs, was strongly in favour.

Because the sides in cabinet were evenly balanced, Callaghan needed Frank's vote and so arranged for him to talk to one of his economic advisers at the Treasury. 'As leader of the House of Lords,' Elizabeth recorded in her diary, 'he [Frank] had no economic information, though a Cabinet Minister. So he went first to Robert Nield, who gave him a Wilson line (anti-devaluation) without once indicating that he, Nield, did not agree with it. Then Frank saw McDougall (also top civil servant) who gave same view, but from personal conviction. Finally Frank saw Douglas Jay who, as President of the Board of Trade, gave apparently convincing anti figures. Afterwards Frank made some arrangements to get economic figures from people like Burke Trend,[28] but he says that none of them ever gave their own opinion.'[29]

Frank went with the last person he'd heard from – Douglas Jay – and voted on this occasion not to devalue, though the cabinet was later to change its mind. The fact that it took an old colleague from the National Bank to alert Frank to the true seriousness of the matter demonstrates his detachment from the inner workings of the government. The episode shows also how Frank was seen as simply a voting counter to be won over in cabinet disputes. Yet real power in these years lay elsewhere. The Prime Minister preferred to by-pass the cabinet and work either with small groups of ministers or with his own team of advisers, the so-called 'kitchen cabinet', which included Wilson's political secretary, Marcia Williams,[30] Gerald Kaufman[31] and Joe Haines,[32] his press officer. Wilson tried, whenever possible, to make the cabinet a rubber stamp. It meant that Frank was doubly marginalized.

Roy Jenkins, who in 1967 replaced Callaghan as Chancellor after the devaluation crisis, recalled Frank in cabinet mainly for his good-humoured contributions. 'I remember him making some very good jokes but to say that he was a weighty member would be an exaggeration.'[33] On one occasion, Frank's dual allegiance embarrassed his colleagues when in 1966 he attended the fiftieth anniversary celebrations in Dublin of the Easter Rising. He sat next to President de Valera on a platform at an event commemorating a revolt against British authority in Ireland.

> Wilson attempted in response [Jenkins said] to lay down a rule about travelling. It was really a matter of rebuking Frank but he tried to couch it in a general rule. He always tried to be emollient. 'It would hardly be appropriate,' he said, 'if members of the Cabinet went off for holidays in Vietnam.' And Frank said: 'But I think, Prime Minister, very few members of the Cabinet have family homes in Vietnam.' It convulsed the Cabinet. It was a good example of the way Frank dealt with something by being extremely funny but self-deprecating at the same time.[34]

In August 1967, when he was hard at work on the truncated youth report and taking second lead in Crossman's grand design to reform the Lords, Frank was summoned by Wilson and asked to stay on for another year to see the latter project through. Wilson had decreed a retirement age of sixty for all cabinet ministers, but Frank had already passed this. There had been hints about his future in the press and much speculation, but here Wilson was both paying him a compliment and telling him that his days were numbered. He made it plain that he wanted a younger man in charge in the Upper House and had Lord Shackleton in mind for the job.

Frank assented to the arrangement without much of a fight. It would give him time to complete the youth report and he was realistic enough to understand that if he saw the report through and aided the passage of the House of Lords reform, he would have reached the limit of his achievements as a cabinet minister. However, events overtook him. By the autumn of 1967 the Wilson government was in the midst of a deepening financial crisis. Sterling had been devalued by 14.3 per cent on 16 November and government expenditure was being cut everywhere. Wilson's phrase 'no sacred cows' set the tone for the exercise. Many suggestions hit at some of the central commitments in Labour's programme. Prescription charges, the issue over which Wilson had resigned from Attlee's government in 1951, were reintroduced in spite of fierce opposition from Jennie Lee, then Arts Minister. National insurance went up. Council house and road building was cut. Free school milk for secondary school pupils was stopped. The F 111A bomber order was cancelled – Frank had sided with its backers. British commitments east of Suez were slashed – again against Frank's wishes. In total, £716 million was saved.

The raising of the school-leaving age to sixteen was also deferred for two more years. It had long been a central tenet of Labour's manifesto and the postponement caused justified anger, especially among those cabinet members like James Callaghan, George Brown and Ray Gunter who had enjoyed only the bare minimum of education. They made a fuss but did not resign. It was Frank who had benefited from the most privileged of educations, and who had unhesitatingly sent all his children to private schools, who chose to go over an impediment to the improvement of the state education system. His vehemence surprised those colleagues like Douglas Jay who recalled that he had shown little interest over education policy in general, aside from occasional forays to defend Catholic schools within Whitehall.[35]

Yet the education issue was not as tangential to Frank's main areas of work as it might at first have appeared. His inquiry into youth services and his personal contacts with young prisoners had raised his awareness of the role education plays in forming adult

294

characters. He was an instinctive teacher who could see that dedicating resources to a good foundation of learning would avert trouble in the future. He had loudly opposed the proposal on these grounds from the moment it was mooted in cabinet, but while other dissidents like George Brown finally acquiesced, he stuck to his guns. He must have known that, as a marginal member of cabinet, he stood little chance of forcing the government to change tack. Furthermore, since Wilson had already indicated that Frank would be dismissed in the autumn, the Prime Minister was hardly going to kowtow to his wishes in order to retain him for a mere eight months longer.

In his letter to the Prime Minister, Frank spoke of the breaking of a promise. 'The step proposed [he wrote on 15 January after his final cabinet meeting] is apparently condemned by those whose opinions I value most in the educational world. It is sharply opposed, as I see it, to the long-term policy and fundamental ideals of our party and to the pledge that we gave as recently as last September. It is inconceivable that I should commend such a step to the House of Lords.'

The breaking of a pledge was the main contention for Frank and, more particularly, reneging on a neglected and marginalized group of the community, the fifteen-year-old sons and daughters of poor families who could not afford to continue their education. He wrote later:

I was leaving a Cabinet where the sanctity of promises seemed to be on the point of losing its significance. This question of whether a government is ever entitled to abandon a commitment is full of difficulties . . . I should not like to go to the stake, therefore, for too rigid an interpretation of the rule that a government's undertakings must be kept in all circumstances to the letter. Nevertheless, in the case of raising the school-leaving age, the economic advantages of the postponement seemed so trivial, the moral commitment so recent and so glaring, the educational issue so obvious, that I have never had any doubts that it was a resigning matter as soon as I realised that postponement was on the way.[36]

295

Frank bailed out before he was pushed. As Denis Healey put it, 'For Frank it wasn't much of a sacrifice but it was a genuinely felt issue.'[37] Resignation was the only course left to him to mark his distaste for the Wilson government's policy-making. He chose to play his hand over an issue where the duplicity and pragmatism of the government was most glaring and at a moment when it would attract most attention. He could not afford to fudge as he had done with Attlee over Germany. While he had known that Attlee was reluctant to lose him, he harboured no illusions as to Wilson's attitude. Frank had to issue his ultimatum and then act upon it.

Harold Wilson was polite, if not devastated, in his response.

My Dear Frank, Thank you for your letter of January 15 confirming your decision to resign from the Government because of the reasons stated. I know how strongly you feel about this, though naturally it is a matter of regret to me and my colleagues that you should now be leaving us. As you know from our discussion last August, I was most anxious for you to remain in your position to launch and see through the discussions about the future of the House of Lords, a subject in which you have played such a distinguished part for many months. I am sorry that in these circumstances you will not be able to see the discussion right through to the end, but I should like to thank you for all you have done in that capacity, and more widely as a member of the government. Yours, Harold.[38]

Though it was more an appreciation of Frank's usefulness in the Lords than a testament to his enduring contribution to the government, Wilson's letter did at least acknowledge what had been a significant step for a senior colleague. No other member of the cabinet managed to put pen to paper. Only Lord Gardiner made any attempt – at the last minute – to dissuade Frank. On the eve of the crucial cabinet meeting, Gardiner called on the Longfords at their Chelsea flat and employed all the skills he had learnt as a barrister to try to persuade his colleague to stay on, but to no avail.

Some of the other cabinet members were scornful. Tony Benn wrote in his diary that Frank's loss 'will not be a serious one'.[39] Crossman noted that 'Cabinet is greatly strengthened by having Frank Pakenham out and Eddie [Shackleton] in'.[40] Patrick Gordon Walker reported that Wilson 'did not seem to mind at all'.[41] The rest were simply so caught up in their other responsibilities that they scarcely noticed his departure. They had grown accustomed to taking little notice of him. Years later, facing Roy Jenkins in the House of Lords, Frank extracted a small measure of good-humoured revenge. He recalled his own resignation in 1968. 'There was the compensation', he told the House, 'of many people having been kind and sympathetic.' After a pause for effect, he continued: 'The noble lord, Lord Jenkins of Hillhead, for instance, told me afterwards that he had very nearly written to me.' The Upper Chamber collapsed in laughter.

Central to Frank's failure as a cabinet minister was his inability to thrive in the poisonous atmosphere of the Wilson government. As he had risen to leave the cabinet room of 10 Downing Street after being appointed Leader of the House of Lords in 1964, Wilson had promised, 'We'll have a lot of fun together.' The impression given by various accounts of the Labour cabinets between 1964 and 1970 is that they were anything but fun. The diaries of Richard Crossman, Tony Benn and Barbara Castle, whatever their respective merits as accurate accounts of events, all suggest that the spirit in which proceedings were undertaken was not comradely or kind.

The Prime Minister himself was largely responsible for the malaise. While other Gaitskellites were slow to come round to Wilson, Frank was willing to work with him. On a personal level, their relationship was cordial. Both perceived themselves as outsiders, but each was in a different kind of exile. Wilson was looked down on by the upper-class Gaitskellites of the Hampstead set. Frank would always be part of the social elite from which Wilson felt excluded. Yet where Wilson rose to lead his party, Frank was on its margins.

Politically, Wilson's greatest failing in Frank's eyes was a lack of integrity in his public conduct. From the outset he had severe reservations about Wilson's leadership style and the beliefs – or absence of them – that underpinned his government. The Labour historian David Marquand has written of 'the atmosphere of shabby expediency which hung over the government like a pall'.[42] Wilson's pragmatism was incompatible with Frank's view of politics as a moral crusade, but it went deeper than pragmatism. 'Frank says', Elizabeth wrote in her diary, 'this is really the flaw in Harold. Though in many ways a nice, kind man, he is not basically honest.' On another occasion, she recorded Frank's dislike of Wilson's 'extreme self-centredness'.[43]

Given such high standards, Frank would probably have felt uncomfortable in most cabinets, but the infighting in Wilson's 1964 team was particularly pronounced and was fuelled by the Prime Minister's paranoia. In a 1984 essay on Harold Wilson, amid a great deal of praise for his former leader's qualities, Frank made two specific criticisms: first, that he was too open with the press, and second, that he talked too freely to everyone, partly out of friendliness, partly out of a desire to impress. There was more than a touch of personal hurt in these comments. Virtually from the instant he joined the cabinet, Frank was hearing rumours that the Prime Minister wanted to replace him with a younger man. He talked openly in 1965 of wanting to replace Frank in the Upper Chamber with an ennobled Frank Cousins, the trade union leader brought in as Minister for Technology in 1964. Patrick Gordon Walker had lunch with Wilson in April of 1966, just a month after the Prime Minister had confirmed Frank in office. But Gordon Walker notes that Wilson 'thought poorly of Frank Pakenham'.[44] At a press conference later that year, Wilson was asked about rumours of a cabinet reshuffle. He replied that there had been much speculation about the leadership of the House of Lords and that he didn't want to comment on the matter at that moment. The implication was clearly understood by his audience. While the Prime Minister protested to Frank that he had been quoted out of context, one of the Lobby later showed Frank his notes to confirm Wilson's remarks.

In July 1965, less than ten months after forming his government, Wilson told Cecil King[45] that Frank was 'quite useless – mental age of twelve'.[46] Wilson was later to qualify these remarks, saying that he was referring not to Frank's intellect but to his innocence.[47] 'When I was told the remark,' Frank later joked, 'I misheard and thought he had said 112. In that context a mental age of twelve doesn't sound so bad.'[48] As ever, he turned hurt and rejection into a joke. He even sent out copies of the Cecil King *Diaries*, where the remark appeared, as Christmas presents.

'I expect', Frank later reflected, 'I was something of a nuisance in Cabinet. I was always going on about morality. It was like a gay party of people drinking wine and brandy and I was the only teetotaller. Very tedious.'[49] On one occasion, he was challenged by Tony Crosland, the Minister for Education, over a speech he planned to make in the Lords that afternoon which claimed to be speaking for a 'Christian cabinet'. Frank did a quick head count and replied: 'I make it eleven Christians and beginning with the top three – Harold Wilson, George Brown and Jim Callaghan – six non- or anti-Christians, and four don't knows. I don't know what they think about religion and I surmise they don't.' Crosland's only response was to ask where he fitted into the picture. Frank had him down as a 'don't know'.[50]

Whatever the religious beliefs of those who sat round the cabinet table, Frank was one of the few who saw a direct link with his work. Barbara Castle recalled another cabinet meeting in January 1965 when the issue of pensions came up again. George Brown complained that there was 'too much morality and not enough politics' going on around the table. 'Lord Longford nearly swooned at this. He said limply that he hoped he had misheard the First Secretary, but George waved him airily aside.'[51]

His Christianity sometimes publicly conflicted with the Wilson cabinet's commitment to humanistic concerns of scientific and technological advances. In March 1965, for example, he castigated the BBC for a sketch about birth control in the satirical *Not So Much a Programme, More a Way of Life*. The government did not appreciate his Catholic objections to artificial contraception. Moreover, his proselytizing interest in the fate of his colleagues' eternal souls exposed him to ridicule. In a diary entry recording a visit from Frank, Evelyn Waugh captured this eccentric, evangelizing tendency: 'Frank made a splendid entrance to Sunday breakfast, his face, neck and shirt covered with blood, brandishing the Vulgate, crying "Who will explain to me Second Corinthians five, six?" or some text. Of every name mentioned Frank asked: "What chance of their coming in?" [to the Church].'[52]

Given such a context, the most surprising aspect is that Wilson kept Frank in the cabinet for over three years and that Frank wanted to stay. When he resigned he abandoned party politics altogether. The latter decision was not sudden. It was the result of a change of perspective and priorities in his work. He had always regarded politics as a means to an end and not an end in itself. As it became obvious that the desired end could not thus be achieved, he began to withdraw from the battles of Wilson's cabinet, where he was feeling increasingly superfluous. His interest in politics, in political personalities and in the activities and tea-room gossip of Parliament continued, but close scrutiny of the workings of the cabinet had been a great disappointment.

After so many years on the Labour front bench, Frank found the unfamiliar state of no longer having any authority on his side of the House rather unsettling and potentially embarrassing. The Labour peers, however, attempted to reassure him of their goodwill by giving him a bust of himself by Judith Bluck (a neighbour from Hurst Green) which won a bronze medal at an international exhibition in Paris. At the presentation, Frank replied to Lord Shackleton's affectionate tribute with one of his favourite quotations from the Scottish novelist Archibald Cronin's *The Stars Look Down*: 'Though he had failed to lead the van in battle, at least he was marching with the men.' It had not been a glorious resignation, he acknowledged, but had been tendered for the right reasons.

On the same occasion Frank pledged his full support to the government and vowed to avoid embarrassing them in any way. Within a couple of weeks, the man who had resigned over a broken promise himself went back on his word. In a debate over the government's plans to limit the number of Kenyan Asians, expelled from their own country but holding British passports, who could enter the United Kingdom, Frank voted against Labour's proposal. It did not deflect the scheme, but was, if confirmation were needed, further evidence of Frank's view that there was a crucial lack of principle at the heart of the Wilson cabinet. Seeing that he was voting against the government of which he had so recently been a member, Lady Violet Bonham-Carter[53] challenged him. 'Surely you are going to resign over this?' 'Resignation', Frank replied, 'is one thing you can't do twice running.'[54]

SIXTEEN

The Leader of the Opposition to the Permissive Society

For three decades since he had joined the Labour Party, Frank had worked towards holding high political office. The experience, when it came, was a disappointment to say the least. There had been little chance to make the world a better place, as he had fervently hoped, but only the sour taste of in-fighting, double-dealing and cynicism left from sitting round Harold Wilson's cabinet table. And now what? He had jumped before he was pushed, and retirement stretched out before him with plenty of sidelines but without the unifying focus of his life in politics. The scrap-heap loomed. Without constant activity, melancholy introspection once more threatened.

He could harbour no hopes of a Lazarus-like resurrection from the grave, as the response of his cabinet colleagues to his loss made abundantly plain. While they continued with their internecine struggles and jockeyed for position under their paranoid leader, Frank retreated to the back benches in the Lords. They scarcely gave him a second thought. His political obituaries had been mostly kind, albeit brief. *Punch* struck a harsher note with this epitaph:

> Lord Longford steeled his mighty mind,
> Gritted his molars, and resigned.
> How sad for his heroic pose
> The headlines 'Only Longford Goes'.

Behind the cruel wit lay a fair summary of what the general public had assimilated about Frank. He was clever, he was principled, but he was largely irrelevant. It was a verdict that might have crushed him, but instead, with his talent for turning adversity into virtue, he set about converting what had been extra-curricular activities into his life. The needs that had prompted his social crusades, after all, remained as urgent as ever for all his efforts from within the political establishment. Maybe from the outside he might make more progress, especially since he would no longer be circumscribed in any way by party-political considerations.

One avenue he explored as a means of finding renewed purpose was writing. In 1969 he published what he always referred to as a 'small book' on humility. Malcolm Muggeridge,[1] a close friend and neighbour, once a celebrated humanist, later a prominent convert to Catholicism, used to claim that this was Frank's most self-revealing book. 'Those autobiographies of his weren't worth writing,' he told an interviewer. 'They don't tell you anything about the man. But there's more of him in that little book on humility than anywhere else.'[2] The central dilemma it tackled was one that had been omnipresent throughout his political life: how to act as a Christian in public life, whether to take obvious pride in your position and achievements, or whether to recoil from any publicity or recognition.

His abiding flaw, as many had already observed on the basis of incidents like the Pakenham Leap, was his fondness for publicity and the limelight. His brother-in-law, Anthony Powell, no great admirer of Frank's, as his published diaries made plain, once described him as 'the antithesis of those individuals who lack "image"'.[3] John Betjeman's biographer, Bevis Hillier, had Frank down as 'ink-hungry' – 'Longford not only clamours for attention; he remains in some degree the child clamouring for attention.'[4] And, in one of the classic own goals of his career, Frank, seeking as ever to make people laugh at him lest he be taken too seriously, began telling how he had gone into a bookshop and asked why they did not have his new book on humility in the window. It was a fanciful and untrue adaptation of a story he told in the introduction to the book about Bishop Ullathorne,[5] one of the Catholic hierarchy, who, when lecturing on humility, was asked by a student which was the best book on the subject. Ullathorne replied: 'There is only one and I wrote it myself.' Yet it was such a good story that it soon spread and grew to eclipse the content of the whole book. It was perhaps the most often repeated anecdote about him. 'All my life,' he admitted in old age, 'I have suffered from a fatal desire to amuse which I have never been able to resist.'[6] Yet he knew the dangers. He once remarked to his former student and friend Philip Toynbee: 'It's dangerous to tell stories against oneself because people always remember the stories but forget who told them in the first place.'[7]

The temptations for a senior politician to discard humility were great, Frank candidly admitted in the book. 'When people say or think that politics is a dirty business, they have usually in mind the temptations against honesty. But I soon realised from my own direct experience that the temptations against humility were much more insidious. The politician is encouraged to think of himself as a very fine fellow. His power for good or ill depends upon his popularity. It is easy for him to see the achievement and maintenance of this same popularity as a primary obligation.'[8] How far this was confessional, as Muggeridge suggested, and how far a condemnation of his former cabinet colleagues, is impossible to establish, but it certainly has the ring of acknowledging a besetting sin. Frank's conclusion, however, was clear. The aspiration towards humility, as well as forgiveness, was for him a key Christian virtue, something to be sought after and aspired to, the ideal. Auberon Waugh, his godson, described this fervent desire to be truly Christian in the eyes of the world as Frank's 'crucifixion complex'.[9] Part of that complex was to go on record as aspiring to be humble, thereby risking the ridicule of those who subsequently charted his every shortcoming. It was rather like, he later remarked, writing a book about the secret of a successful marriage after being divorced three times.

His choice of such an unusual subject was a sign, for those who had not yet realized it, that Lord Longford was no average politician but one for whom moral choices and obligations superseded worldly success. While it may be argued that his thesis had come rather late in the day – since his political career was over and it was easy to preach what he no longer had to practise – Frank's decision to tackle such an elusive subject as humility was indicative both of his indifference to former party colleagues' opinion and of his intention not to disappear from public view altogether. Far from being a backward-looking book in the style of the memoirs and diaries favoured by most politicians, *Humility* set an agenda for future endeavours.

Frank had slowly managed to pick up some of the threads of his pre-cabinet minister work when he left office. He was reappointed as a director of the Alliance Building Society, a lucrative post which he had held while at the National Bank but which he had relinquished on joining the cabinet. He also was named a director of the Martin Luther King Fund and – by Harold Wilson – Chairman of the Attlee Memorial Fund. The latter had been set up in 1965, when the former Labour leader was still alive, and continued after his death, under Frank's leadership, to raise funds to build Attlee House as part of the facilities at Toynbee Hall in the East End, where the ex-Prime Minister had once been Secretary.

These posts, though, were more the traditional retirement sinecures of the mainstream politician than the sort of substantial work Frank was seeking. That appeared out of the blue at the end of 1968 when the Catholic hotelier, Charles Forte,[10] asked him to join the board of the publishing house he had bought, Sidgwick and Jackson, with a view to taking on the chairmanship in May 1970. It would be a part-time post, but very much an active one. Frank was not simply to be a figurehead to create confidence among authors and bankers, but an involved publisher. While as a youngster he had little time for books, he had become increasingly embroiled in the literary world – through his own efforts in print, through those of his family, and by virtue of his daily and incessant reading of spiritual and theological tomes.

It was an imaginative appointment by Forte. Frank was, after all, nearing retirement age, and some questioned whether he would be able to make any sort of impact. A shrewd businessman, Forte was – like Michael Cooke before him – able to see beyond Frank's air of eccentricity and distraction to perceive that he had a sound grasp of the world of books and moreover was the sort of well-connected figure to attract big names to his publishing house. Moreover, because of his own ability to attract headlines, he would ensure that everyone would have heard of Sidgwick and Jackson. In a field that in 1970 was still dominated by maverick gentleman publishers, often of eccentric disposition, the post would fit Frank like a glove.

Frank's approach was similar to his attitude at the National Bank. He was happy to delegate most day-to-day decisions to his managing director, William Armstrong, but he insisted on being consulted over which books would be published and over the treatment of staff. He had found himself another mini-constituency. Various employees at Sidgwick and Jackson from his time as chairman until 1980 and later as a director until 1987, remembered him welcoming anyone with a problem into his office at the firm's headquarters in Bloomsbury for a glass of sherry and a friendly chat.

His efforts to improve Sidgwick's list soon bore fruit. Among his greatest triumphs was to persuade the Conservative Prime Minister, Edward Heath,[11] first to write a book about sailing – which leapt to the top of the bestsellers' chart and stayed there – and then a follow-up, written after his election defeat, on music, which was also a runaway success. Heath was not without his frustrations for a publisher. In her diary, Elizabeth wrote of Heath: 'Frank has found enormous difficulty in getting him to answer a single question on the book he is supposed to be doing for Sidgwick on Sailing'.[12] In general, Frank tried not to let his own concerns influence commercial decisions. He made no attempt, for example, to turn Sidgwick into a religious publisher. Occasionally they would produce a book in which he had a personal interest. John Grigg[13] was commissioned to write a life of Frank's old friend Nancy Astor. Claud Cockburn – originator of the idea (which Frank rejected outright) of a late 1930s 'Cliveden Set' – was signed up to record his impression of this period in *The Devil's Decade*. John Phillips, whom Frank had visited in Maidstone Prison, produced a memoir of his starring role, as John Vassall, in a spying drama in the early 1960s. Concerning Ireland, Margery Forrester's bestselling biography of Michael Collins was published by the firm. It was on Elizabeth's recommendation that Sidgwick took Molly Gillen's *The Prince and His Lady*, which had failed to excite other publishers but which received critical acclaim. And when the company decided to move into the field of children's books, Frank published two – *Robin Hood* and *King Arthur* – written by his daughter Antonia several years before, with illustrations by her teenage daughter Rebecca.

Some of his other ideas for authors proved more controversial. His commissioning of Diana Mosley[14] to write about the Duchess of Windsor caused a heated family argument, with some of his children holding that her fascist past made her an unsuitable person to do business with. Frank applied to her the same 'sin and sinner' formula to argue that whatever her past 'crimes', she was a long-standing friend and one he would not abandon. The problem which he failed to address was that she, at least in public, had made it clear that she did not regard anything in her past as a 'sin'.

During Frank's time at the helm of Sidgwick and Jackson, they won the Publishers' Publicity Circle silver trophy three years running, and in 1977 the Allen Lane award for best publisher of the year. While the achievement was one shared by everyone in the firm, as Frank was the first to point out, the transformation in Sidgwick and Jackson's fortunes was marked under his chairmanship. He had set himself the goal of moving the company up a notch or two on the publishing ladder – from small to medium sized. The number of books was increased and, within four years, he was able to report to his board that turnover had quadrupled thanks to bestsellers like the Heath volumes and Shirley Conran's[15] *Superwoman*. In 1978 he was chosen as one of six 'great English publishers' by the *Sunday Times*. With typical self-deprecation, Frank attributed his inclusion to the fact that one fellow publisher had withdrawn from the list when he heard who else was on it.

He combined his work at Sidgwick's with other excursions into print. In 1970 Hutchinson published his authorized biography of his old friend Eamon de Valera. Since the early 1930s when they had first met, the two had been firm friends and the years did not diminish Frank's admiration for de Valera. The book had been five years in preparation with Frank's co-author, Tom O'Neill of the National Library of Ireland, doing most of the research work sifting through de Valera's papers. Frank's contribution was his special knowledge of the events leading up to and following the 1921 treaty – recorded in *Peace by Ordeal*. His long-standing but intermittent role as unofficial emissary between the British government and the Irish leader permeated the text and there was an intimacy in some of the accounts of de Valera as a family man that Frank was able to provide as a result of the many occasions on which he had stayed at the president's residence in Dublin's Phoenix Park. Also evidence of Frank's involvement was the attempt to define de Valera as a man of religion. In de Valera's work Frank found that political achievement and Christian duty were interwoven.

The biography was well received on both sides of the Irish Sea and sold well in America, though the criticisms directed at Frank's partisan approach in *Peace by Ordeal* to de Valera's role in the 1921 negotiations were reiterated by some reviewers. However, the weight of new material in the biography was acknowledged and its enduring status as a standard work on a man who dominated Irish politics for fifty years was assured. Publication in November 1970 was marred by only one small slip on Frank's part. He travelled to Dublin to give the Irish president a special presentation volume of the book as part of the launch celebrations. Much to his embarrassment, and to the delight of the headline writers, he misplaced the gift on the eve of handing it over to the eighty-eight-year-old president.

In 1969, just before British troops arrived in Northern Ireland as sectarian tensions grew to fever pitch, Frank had been approached by Hodder and Stoughton, as a man with Anglo-Irish connections and a long-standing interest in the subject, to write a book about Ulster. He accepted the idea in principle and set about his research, making repeated trips to Belfast to talk to senior politicians and Church leaders on both sides of the conflict. He found that he had grossly underestimated the extent of popular anger in the North. With the situation on the ground changing from day to day, he decided that trying to write a book on Ulster on the basis of research trips from London was a hopeless task and he abandoned the project.

During the 1970s his work with prisoners inevitably brought him into contact with growing numbers of IRA convicts in British jails. His role in visiting some of them, linked to his outspoken Irish nationalism, caused speculation that he was 'soft' on the terrorists, but it was an impression that he was at pains to dispel. He repeatedly and unequivocally denounced the IRA campaign of violence from the floor of the House of Lords. One of the bombers' targets was, he pointed out, his own son-in-law, the ex-Tory minister Hugh Fraser. In October 1975, an explosive device attached to the front wheel of Fraser's green Jaguar, parked outside the family home, killed his next-door neighbour, Dr Hamilton Fairley.

It was through his prison work too that he became interested in the problems of homeless young people in London. His involvement with disadvantaged youngsters dated back to his childhood links with the Eton Manor Boys Club. He had been engaged on an inquiry into youth services when he left the Wilson cabinet in 1968 and later that year spent a brief spell in charge of the National Youth Employment Council. As early as 1960, though, he had spoken to the executive committee of the New Bridge about the need for what he called a 'junior New Bridge', geared specifically to young offenders.

With the ending of his government career, he was finally able to realize this dream. The New Horizon Youth Centre was launched in November of 1968 from the crypt of St Botolph's Church in Aldgate in the City of London, offering help and advice to youngsters. It was a pioneering venture, stressed Jon Snow, one of its first employees. 'New Horizon was the first of its kind. Before then there had been no provision for young people in need in the capital. Frank had no idea what he was doing, but he could see youngsters on the streets and he knew he had to help them.'[16]

New Horizon was not, however, an instant success. *The Times* criticized its brief as 'unclear' and the involvement of John Profumo – a typically generous but unguarded gesture by Frank – attracted some adverse comment. Young people did not flock to its doors at

309

first. Frank sat waiting with one assistant in St Botolph's for callers, and there was scarcely a knock at the door. He attributed this failure to location and, through a contact at New Bridge, was able to find new headquarters in St Anne's Church in Soho. He also recruited some young blood in the shape of Martin Walker, who had caught Frank's eye during student protests at the Hornsey College of Art the previous year. Frank had been called in as a mediator and had befriended Walker.

As the client base began to grow, Frank took more of a back seat. It was Walker whom the youngsters wanted to talk to, not an elderly peer. Instead Frank raided his address book to take care of fund-raising. There were fundamental differences between the two men which were to take New Horizon away from the original course that Frank had envisaged. Walker had no time at all for Christianity and rejected the notion of, as he later described it, 'handing out soup and sacraments'. He felt uncomfortable with New Horizon's location within a church building, and, despite a rapid increase in the numbers of those using the centre, felt that the link with organized religion – however tenuous – might put off potential visitors.

Yet for Frank the Christian element was the key to his vision of New Horizon. The very name has biblical overtones. His aim was not to force his own personal beliefs on those who came to ask for help, but, just as he did in prisons, to offer support unconditionally. He was never an evangelist in the narrow sense, but neither was he afraid to talk of his Christian convictions when challenged.

Walker left after a year and a half, and was replaced by Jon Snow, the son of an Anglican bishop. Snow recalled that the most difficult task for Frank at New Horizon was bridging the age gap with the young visitors. 'He was extremely uncomfortable in conversation. Part of his Catholicism was, I suspect, about being uncomfortable with sinners. And gauche. And yet he stuck at it. The youngsters started on the basis of laughing at him and on occasions even abusing him. Then, because he sat and took it and even asked sensitive questions, they had to think again. That was how he broke through in prisons too. Of course, it could work both ways. Because he was open, he could end up by being duped.'[17]

While Walker found the Christian ethos to be a barrier between him and Frank, Snow praised the founder's tolerance. Writing of the initial period when he was around in the office, Frank noted: 'It was, however, of immense value to have the place run actively day by day . . . for a short time, and to have to answer telephone enquiries of all kinds, including requests for abortion to which I was chilly.'[18] Yet a year and a half later, Snow found that front-line experience had made Frank more tolerant. 'He gave us complete freedom to do whatever we felt was right. For example, he felt very strongly about abortion, but if he'd walked in and heard us advising somebody on how to get to the Brook Advisory Clinic, there's no way he would have interfered. For one who was so often portrayed as intolerant, he was immensely tolerant.'[19]

New Horizon continued to grow, moving to new premises in Drury Lane and, in 1972, by a vote of the staff, changing its role to that of a seven-days-a-week walk-in centre, open until late at night and offering hostel accommodation. Frank regularly dropped in to see how things were going, but his role became increasingly restricted to fund-raiser.

Though he may have been judged a marginal figure in political life by many of his colleagues, most notably in the Wilson cabinets, he received a sign in April 1972 that he was held in high personal esteem by the monarch. The Queen appointed him a Knight of the Garter. The Most Noble Order of the Garter had been founded in 1348 and membership was in the personal gift of the sovereign. It was an exclusive – some say the most exclusive – club, with just twenty-four members at any one stage.

The announcement of his appointment caused much comment and was generally taken a sign of royal approval for his various crusades over Ireland, prisoners and Germany rather more than as a mark of his seniority as a politician. The Duke of Edinburgh, in an effort to inform himself of social problems in Britain, had, for instance, invited Frank to dinner at Buckingham Palace to discuss prison reform. Harold Wilson, however, in a 1977 interview, dismissed such an explanation for the awarding of the honour. 'I would have thought the answer was rather simple,' he said, denying any personal role in the matter, 'that she was wanting one or two people on the Labour side and he was a minister of Cabinet rank going back to her father's reign.'[20]

With the award came the duty to design a banner to hang in St George's Chapel – he chose the crest of the Irish Knights of St Patrick, stressing once again his dual allegiance – and to attend the annual Garter ceremony at Windsor Castle plus various royal receptions. Among the latter, Frank derived greatest pleasure from meeting unlikely figures at Buckingham Palace. As Elizabeth wrote in her diary after one such event: 'the person Frank was most excited to meet is Irish rugby player, Willy John McBride, captain of Lions'.[21] The strict dress code of the Garter Knights was, however, beyond him. On one occasion, he turned up wearing a pair of Union Jack cufflinks out of a Christmas cracker – and told people about them. He never bothered with purchasing his own robes – unlike Harold Wilson who, as Elizabeth pointed out, 'had bought all the gear' – but borrowed a spare set each year from the RAF and would travel to the ceremony on the Underground. Sometimes the odd juxtapositions in his life were only emphasized by his royal diary dates. After attending in 1986 the Queen's 60th birthday thanksgiving in St George's Chapel with the other knights, he had to hurry off for a debate in a west London pub on morality organized by the Campaign for Homosexual Equality.

Frank's appointment to the Knights of the Garter was doubly controversial because days before the announcement was made he had unveiled plans which were to make him the butt of every satirist for the rest of the decade. He was to head an independent public inquiry into the subject of pornography. 'Lord Porn' was born.

On questions of sexual morality, he had rarely budged in principle from a black-and-white Catholic viewpoint, though in individual cases he had been much more tolerant. Sex outside marriage was, he believed, wrong and any exploitation of sexuality degrades a precious gift from God. It was a fairly standard position for many of his generation, at least in public, but the 1960s and the development of a more permissive society had made such a stance sound fundamentalist. Not that Frank expounded it very often in that decade. Given *carte blanche*, he would always return to subjects like crime, prisons, young people or Ireland before he would hold forth on sex. Certainly pornography had not figured at all in his public pronouncements – or indeed in his private thoughts. When Jon Snow was working with Frank at the New Horizon Youth Centre, they would occasionally go into Soho for lunch. 'We would pass enormous lurid breasts hanging out of doorways and he wouldn't even notice. I felt we could probably have run into a naked woman in the street and he wouldn't have noticed.'[22]

Until he began preparing for a debate on pornography which he initiated in the House of Lords on 21 April 1971, Frank had scarcely given the subject more than fleeting attention. With the abolition of the Lord Chamberlain's role as theatre censor in 1968, various plays and revues had begun to attract popular interest and prompt political debate. Frank, though no avid theatre-goer, was intrigued and made it his business to see what all the fuss was about. He had walked out of a play called *America, Hurrah!*, mounted at the Royal Court in London soon after censorship was lifted, when a huge four-letter word was displayed on stage, but the real starting-point for his anti-pornography crusade came in the summer of 1970 when he left *Oh! Calcutta!* at the interval in disgust.

He had been prompted to go to see *Oh! Calcutta!* by an article in *The Times* on 26 August 1970 by Sir Alan Herbert, president of the Society of Authors, and one of the prime movers in the relaxation of the law on obscenity in 1959. Herbert argued that the production showed that the new liberalism in the theatre had gone too far. 'My colleagues and I, in 1954, began a worthy struggle for reasonable liberty for honest writers,' he wrote. 'I am sorry to think that our efforts seem to have ended in a right to represent copulation, veraciously, on the public stage.' Frank wondered out loud, reading the piece, if some form of censorship was now needed.

Oh! Calcutta!, which its producer Kenneth Tynan[23] described as 'elegant erotica', set out to offend from the start – the safety curtain was decorated with a large pair of buttocks, with the word 'bum' added in case anyone should miss the point. It followed this up with scenes of attempted rape, flagellation and a liberal sprinkling of obscenities. Frank went to the revue with his son-in-law, Hugh Fraser. When Elizabeth and Antonia had expressed an interest in accompanying their spouses, they had been told that 'it isn't the sort of thing one goes to with ladies'. This was evidently man's business, but not to be put off by such Edwardian stereotyping, they secretly got two tickets and sat in a separate part of the theatre. 'We bounced out at the interval,' Antonia recalled, 'saying "Lord Longford, have you any comments on this disgusting show?" as though members of the press. Then we all four went and had dinner together.'[24]

Finding himself in agreement with Herbert, Frank decided to raise the question of pornography in the House of Lords. Yet he felt no real sense of mission until, in the course of taking soundings, he was handed explicit magazines and booklets which, he was informed, were circulating among schoolchildren. These so shocked him that he felt impelled to act. The crusading spirit within him had been awakened. One of his abiding concerns during the subsequent pornography inquiry was the potential damage that pornography could do to the young. Through New Horizon and in a variety of other ways, he had tried, sometimes falteringly, to keep the needs of young people in the forefront of his public activities. 'I don't think that he was ever interested in the use of pornography as pornography, old men in raincoats hanging round Soho and that kind of thing,' said Marigold Johnson, a college friend of Antonia's who worked as his assistant in the later stages of the report. 'It was principally his teaching thing, an old-fashioned idea that society must protect the young. It was the effect pornography might have on children and young people that worried him.'[25]

Elizabeth was adamant that from the outset her husband tackled the subject out of a sense of public duty. 'Far from being a cover for his own smutty-mindedness, as some critics suggested – just as our eight children were once said to be a cover for his own homosexuality – porn was distasteful, utterly boring to him. Neither of us had read a word of it until the campaign opened, and Frank was profoundly thankful not to have to read another line after it closed. Though an exceptionally amusing after-dinner speaker, his wit depended not at all on dirty stories.'[26]

With assistance from the Home Office he began by looking into the prevailing legal position on obscenity. He soon became convinced that the law was not strong enough to counter the menace posed by pornography. 'I think he had made up his mind long before the committee ever met,' remembered Marigold Johnson. 'They were the umbrella under which he was able to put together something which he had already decided needed to be written.'[27] Frank also prepared for the Lords debate by reading the handful of other reports undertaken on the subject. There was an American Presidential Commission inquiry which had tentatively established links between sexual violence and pornography. By contrast, in Britain, the Arts Council – of which his daughter Antonia was then a member – had commissioned a working party under the chairmanship of John Montgomerie which reported in 1969. This had come down in favour of a laissez-faire approach, concluding that there was no evidence to suggest that obscene publications did any harm and that restrictions should therefore be lifted because they interfered with freedom of expression.

The government itself had no official position on the subject. In March 1970, the Labour Home Secretary, James Callaghan, had backed the police in their attempts to clamp down on pornography. In November of the same year, his Conservative successor declined a request in Parliament for an inquiry into the workings of the obscenity laws.

Frank was quickly made aware that there were some, especially in church circles, just as concerned as he was about what they perceived as the growth in pornography. In the autumn of 1970 a group of Christians protested outside another London play, *Council of Love*, and one of their number, Lady Birdwood, attempted unsuccessfully to mount a private prosecution against it. In east London Christians demonstrated outside cinemas showing what they considered to be pornographic films. In November of the same year, the Church of England's Board of Social Responsibility produced a report, *Obscene Publications: Law and Practice*, which contained a strongly worded attack on the growth of pornography. Two months earlier, the Archbishop of Canterbury had called on

Christians everywhere to protest at blasphemy and obscenity. And in March 1971, the Bishop of Blackburn led a protest march to demand higher moral standards in society.

Christianity provided a vital common ingredient for the majority of campaigners. Because of his own faith, Frank was naturally sympathetic to these groups and was soon working closely with them. As part of his research in preparation for his House of Lords speech, he came into contact with the devout Christian and rising Conservative star, John Gummer MP,[28] who in 1971 published a book entitled *The Permissive Society*. It argued that the new emancipation had brought negative rather than positive benefits, and highlighted what the author saw as the failure of experiments with permissiveness in Denmark. Most significantly, he teamed up with Mary Whitehouse,[29] a teacher from Shropshire who in 1964 had founded the Clean Up TV campaign, becoming in 1965 Honorary General Secretary of the National Viewers' and Listeners' Association. Ridiculed in the press, Whitehouse had displayed great courage in refusing to be silenced by such a wave of criticism.

By the time Frank stood up in the House of Lords in April 1971, he had already attracted enough media attention to make him feel that he could not leave the matter to rest after addressing the Upper Chamber. There had been newspaper articles, radio debates and the first flood of correspondence from the public. He had clearly touched a nerve. Therefore in advance of his speech he had discussed with prominent Christians in the anti-permissiveness movement the idea of establishing a committee to investigate pornography. Though he subsequently maintained that he had no idea that his remarks in the Lords that day would release the tide of national interest that was to follow over the next eighteen months, he had already started to lay plans for another Beveridge-style report.

In the Upper Chamber, Frank quoted various examples of materials he had seen – including, just a few days before the debate, a school sex education film, *Growing Up*, which included graphic sections on masturbation – to demonstrate his contention that the young and impressionable were at risk. There was, he said, a free trade in what he described as obscene and evil materials. While nobody liked censorship, he acknowledged, least of all himself, what was being produced in the name of freedom was depraving and damaging its audience.

He floated the idea that the government should as a matter of urgency set up a commission to look into agreeing a form of control that would answer public concern, but this was a ruse. He was close enough to ministers to know that they would not. Failing such an official inquiry, he continued, he and a group of individuals would prepare a privately funded report. From the government benches, Lord Eccles, as Frank had expected, declined to make this an official matter but wished the proposed private initiative well. Lord Beswick, speaking for Labour, responded in similarly general terms. Other old friends of Frank's on the Labour benches were, however, vehement in their opposition to his suggestion of limitations on freedom of expression. Dora Gaitskell, ennobled by Harold Wilson as a mark of respect to her late husband, joined with Jennie Lee and Lord Willis to denounce the proposal. Even Elizabeth was initially opposed to her husband's crusade on anti-censorship grounds, 'until I read some of the hard porn that was circulating in comprehensive schools among girls of twelve. If one is against racism, sadism and sexist exploitation, one must be in favour of banning these cesspits that degrade the name of "book".'[30]

Frank's outspoken attack in the Upper Chamber was widely reported the next day in the press. Few other speeches in the comparative backwater of the House of Lords can have made such an impact. Letters poured in by the sack-load, the vast majority echoing his concerns. Among the many offers of support was one from the Dulverton Trust, a grant-giving body set up in 1949 out of the proceeds of a tobacco fortune. It included an interest in religion and education among its remits. It was a godsend, for Frank had announced his plans to set up an inquiry before having any financial backing. He gratefully accepted, apparently unconcerned that his inquiry into the damage being done to the young by pornography was being paid for with money from the tobacco industry.

From the start, some of those around him believed that he was being guided, by zealots, into disaster. 'I felt that the porn thing was an interesting example of how Frank can be manipulated,' recalled Jon Snow. 'There were other people in that campaign who clearly did have a very organised axe to grind and they used Frank. Some fairly unattractive forces managed to muscle in on his innocence.'[31] His status as a former cabinet minister made him quite a catch for what had hitherto been fringe groups. Marigold Johnson, however, disagreed. 'I don't think it is fair to say that Mary Whitehouse hijacked him. He was very much on the same wavelength as her. What did go wrong with the pornography report was to do with the number of people who were on his commission for the wrong reasons. It was absurdly large to start with. For some it was a social thing. Many of them just put their names to it and never turned up.'[32]

Despite Frank's previous experience with similar private reports, the pornography inquiry was different in several respects. Most significantly, there was no restraining factor. Nuffield had struggled, unsuccessfully on the whole, to make him begin by proving his hypothesis in 1954 that crime was on the increase, before going on to theorize as to the cause. With his crime working party for the Labour Party and his group on London government, there was some higher authority to answer to, someone to monitor progress and give a gentle nudge on the tiller. Even with the Pakenham–Thompson report, he had been restrained by the presence of a co-chairman. Over pornography, the whole inquiry was very much his show, a self-constituted watchdog serving a public that certainly existed but which was ill defined. The Dulverton Trust gave him a free hand.

The only restraining factor was the other members of the committee. When he announced the composition of his inquiry team on 21 May, Frank was attacked in the press for packing the committee with friends, fellow Christians and those who shared his opinions. The *New Statesman* denounced the whole venture as 'full frontal hypocrisy' and the *Guardian* accused his colleagues of being 'stooges'. Some had already been advising him in the run-up to his House of Lords speech. Through Mary Whitehouse he met Professor Norman Anderson, chairman of the House of Laity in the Church of

England and vice-chairman of the pornography committee. Yet given his own beliefs and the prominence of the Churches in highlighting the menace of pornography, it seemed natural to Frank to include their representatives. Other clerics who took part were the Archbishop of York, Dr Donald Coggan, Bishop Christopher Butler, one of the auxiliaries to the Catholic Cardinal Heenan, Dr Ronald Williams, Anglican Bishop of Leicester, Bishop Trevor Huddleston,[33] the anti-apartheid campaigner, then Bishop of Stepney, Lord Soper, the Methodist leader, the Jesuit Father Thomas Corbishley, who had written the foreword to Frank's book *Humility*, Canon Sydney Hall, dean of King's College, London, the Revd Joseph McCulloch, rector of St Mary-le-Bow in the City of London, and the Revd Keith Steven of the Church of Scotland committee on moral welfare. Among prominent Christian laity who were members of the commission were the broadcaster Jimmy Savile, Lady Masham,[34] and the journalist Peregrine Worsthorne.[35]

Frank also recruited several of his old friends, including Dr Agnes Headlam-Morley, an academic who had advised him when he was working in Germany and who had become a family friend, Lord Shawcross,[36] Attorney-General in Attlee's government and later chairman of the Royal Commission on the Press, and Malcolm Muggeridge who, after publishing *Something Beautiful for God*, his tribute to Mother Teresa of Calcutta, was on his way to joining the Catholic Church. All had some form of expertise to offer, but Frank had not been careful enough to avoid giving the impression, unjustified by subsequent disagreements over the drafting of the final report, that he was packing the committee.

In his introduction to the final report, Frank claimed to have attempted to construct a committee made up of representatives of the Church, the law, medicine, the teaching profession, the arts, industry, and social services. True to his word, there were members from most of these areas, some of them distinguished in their fields. Over half the eventual members were not known to him before the committee began its work. However, the over-representation of the Church and the corresponding shortage of figures from the world of the arts gave the inquiry more the semblance of a crusade than an investigation. Frank was particularly disappointed that the novelists Kingsley Amis[37] and Elizabeth Jane Howard,[38] then husband and wife, refused to sign the final report. They would have given the committee's findings more standing in literary circles. Amis and Howard did contribute an essay on freedom of expression in literature, which was included in the final document.

In its brief, the committee pledged 'to see what means of tackling the problem of pornography would commend general support'. The fact that pornography was regarded as a 'problem' again gave the impression that the inquiry was from the start bound to come down heavily on one side of the debate. Frank himself acknowledged in his introduction to the final report: 'It would not be true to assume that all those who took part in our inquiry agreed with my House of Lords proposition that pornography was a manifest evil, though anyone who thought that I was completely on the wrong tack would hardly have agreed to serve under my chairmanship.'[39]

Whatever the disputes over composition, Frank embarked on the inquiry with a new spring in his step, putting his responsibilities at Sidgwick and Jackson on the back burner. 'What he loved about doing it was that he was the centre of attention. He was no longer a back number. Wherever he would go, people would be saying to each other, "Isn't that Lord Porn?"' recalled Marigold Johnson.[40] Having slipped into relative obscurity after his resignation from the cabinet in 1968, Frank found in the pornography inquiry a public role once more.

In his organization of the inquiry, he adopted much the same pattern as he had with previous ventures. He employed a small office team to take care of administrative and secretarial matters, and he invited interested groups and individuals to present oral and written evidence for inclusion in the final report. Because of the scope of the subject under review, and Frank's innate impatience – no speech should last more than eight minutes, he once said, and no report take more than a year – different areas were dealt out to sub-committees. Professor Anderson chaired the group looking at the effect and control of pornography, Malcolm Muggeridge those who investigated broadcasting, Father Corbishley sex education, James

Sharkey cinema and theatre, Ronald Kirkwood advertising and so on. Frank kept for himself the detailed questioning of individuals involved in the pornography trade and it was to him that all the correspondence from concerned members of the public was directed. In practice, he held the reins of control tightly. It was he, for example, who set up meetings with newspaper editors and proprietors.

Marigold Johnson, who accompanied him, witnessed his technique of investigation. 'He didn't behave in the way an official commission of inquiry would. He, in effect, tried to persuade newspaper editors to be caricatures of themselves. We went round and had endless cups of coffee with the likes of Larry Lamb[41] and David Astor. And Frank would ask whatever question he thought would get the right answer. "But surely you would draw the line at naked women on page three?" to David Astor. And David would say "Of course I would, Frank" because that wasn't what the *Observer* wanted.'[42]

Frank also spent much time trying to find sociological and statistical information on the damaging effects of pornography. Though he worked with several academics who believed there was a link, the final report could not prove cause and effect conclusively. To Frank this was not a drawback. He had never hoped for absolute proof and believed that, however extensive the inquiry, it would have been impossible to reach a completely unequivocal conclusion. 'A fair-minded person reading our report must concede that pornography sometimes does harm. How often it does harm and how much harm it does, and what kind of harm is done by particular kinds of pornography remain questions which are never likely to be finally disposed of [he wrote later]. From the angle of practical policy they have, I believe, been much clarified by our exertions.'[43]

There were moments, however, when he found the lack of scientific back-up frustrating and disheartening. He commissioned Maurice Yaffe, a research psychologist at the Institute of Psychiatry in London, to conduct a survey into the harmful effects of pornography, hopeful that it would prove that there was at least a strong case to answer. To his deep disappointment, the resulting paper came back with no conclusions. It was the one moment during the inquiry, his close colleagues say, when Frank spoke privately of giving up. In the end, Dr Yaffe's survey was tucked away as an appendix to the report, with a note added by a child psychiatrist and an educationalist who were members of the main committee describing it as 'not helpful'.

There were also times when he was tempted to readjust the focus of the inquiry and direct it more towards the damaging effects of the portrayal of violence in the media. Several of the academics he consulted – and a large number of his correspondents – identified the graphic depiction of violence as a more easily quantifiable danger to impressionable minds. Frank began to follow up this avenue – going to watch Stanley Kubrick's film, *A Clockwork Orange* – but such efforts were not sustained.

Though there were some who felt uneasy about the pornography committee from the start, there were few who mocked it mercilessly in the late spring of 1971. The satirical magazine *Private Eye*, which managed to get one of the committee to leak reports of proceedings, did its best to turn the whole venture into a joke, but nationwide notoriety did not descend upon Frank until he decided to visit Denmark at the end of August 1971. The Arts Council working party had concluded in 1969 that the free availability of hardcore pornography in Denmark had reduced sexual crime by as much as a quarter. John Gummer, in his book *The Permissive Society*, rejected this proposition. In view of the disparity of opinions, Frank decided that his own inquiry would not be complete without a firsthand investigation of the 'Danish experiment'. He ignored all advice to the contrary, as Malcolm Muggeridge recalled: 'When the Danish expedition was on, he wanted me to go. I said, "Absolutely out of the question because you'll be made a monkey of by the press." I knew because I'd been a journalist and I know what I would have felt if someone had said "Go and cover Lord Longford in Denmark." I'd have jumped at it. I told him I didn't think it was wise either from his point of view or from the point of view of the credibility of the report we were supposed to be producing. But he couldn't see it. He had a strange feeling that to be in the public eye was per se good.'[44]

Not only did Frank ignore Muggeridge's advice and go to Denmark, he also agreed to being accompanied by a group of journalists, or rather he stated beforehand that it was not for him to stop anybody coming. 'This was treated as a warm invitation. If I had known how much excitement our trip would arouse, I might have been less cordial,' he later wrote.[45] It is no excuse. Muggeridge had already made the situation clear to him. Much of the two-day visit was spent meeting Danish officials and Church leaders, seeking their opinions about the effects of Denmark's liberal laws. The claims of those who argued that sex crimes had gone down in Denmark since reform of the obscenity laws were debunked. No such evidence existed, Frank and his team heard from Danish officials.

From the moment they had seen Frank reading the Bible on the plane over – 'I am preparing myself for the ordeal we are going to have to face', he told them – the press corps sensed that there would be more column inches in the unofficial aspects of the Copenhagen trip. First there was a full day of meetings. Despite the prevailing view of him as some kind of nineteenth-century puritan, Frank did show glimpses of his witty side. When a British embassy official briefed him on which clubs to visit, Frank replied with a smile 'You seem remarkably well informed.' Later he and his five companions (Mary Whitehouse had gone to Rome instead to present the Pope with a book she believed was corrupting schoolchildren) split into three teams, each with £10 to spend, and set out to experience something of Copenhagen's notorious night life. Accompanied by Dr Christine Saville, a prison psychiatrist with much experience of drug addiction whom he had met through New Horizon, Frank paid £7 a head to witness a live sex show. A fat middle-aged man with his trousers round his ankles was on stage being attended to by a naked dancer with a battery-operated vibrator. It did not take Frank long to see enough to know he had to leave. 'In a sense the audience were almost more horrifying than the performers [he recalled]. To join in "the fun" even by remaining there at all seemed to be sharing the humiliation to which the girl was subjected. The fact that she appeared not to realise her own degradation increased rather than diminished one's sense of revulsion from those who had brought her to this.'[46]

Yet, despite his horror at what he had seen, and the baying of the press, Frank and his companion proceeded to another club. 'Peer defies the Whip' cried the *Guardian* headline the next morning. 'A beautiful young woman pressed a whip into Lord Longford's hand and invited him to beat her. His Lordship declined,' ran the report. Confronted by the model – who turned out to be a man in drag – Frank had walked out of the club. 'Don't think me faint-hearted,' he told Gyles Brandreth, one of his team in Copenhagen. 'I had seen enough for science and more than enough for enjoyment.'[47]

In one evening, he had destroyed the credibility of the pornography inquiry. To the journalists who accompanied him, it was a dream of a story – the serious-minded, if eccentric, inquirer who was so shocked by his subject that he had to run from the room, Lord Longford, with his noble cranium and mad scientist's tonsure, rejecting the charms of Denmark's very own Miss Whiplash. Though he had earlier told the *Guardian*'s correspondent that he would not be corrupted by seeing Copenhagen's seedy clubs, Frank had underestimated how alienating he would find the whole experience. Had he listened to the advice of his friends and colleagues, a little more worldly wise, he would never have found himself in such a situation, in the glare of media attention.

However, his blind faith in publicity, his previous enjoyment of research and his obstinate refusal to heed wiser counsels combined, in a few short minutes, to turn his inquiry into a laughing stock. Even the *Observer* in a generally favourable profile – written, many assumed at the time, by Frank's old student Philip Toynbee with help from his editor, David Astor – asked: 'How can one deny that to walk indignantly out of such a performance, which he was supposed to be watching in a data-collecting mood of appraisal, showed some confusion in his approach?' Far from coming to investigate, Frank appeared, on the evidence of his swift exit, to have made up his mind already.

He had placed himself in a no-win situation. To have stayed at the first show would have been to confirm all the suspicions, thinly veiled by some journalists, that he was nothing but a dirty old man disguising his own lascivious lusts with a high-minded inquiry. To walk out and then to go to a second show to repeat the experience simply made him look foolish. As he himself described the experience: 'I was sitting there like a stage professor in a house of ill-fame.' Yet throughout the visit, he continued to court the press pack. 'Frank pretends to be wary of the press,' Gyles Brandreth wrote in his diary, 'but in truth he can't get enough of them. This trip to Denmark has turned us all into ludicrous figures of fun, but he doesn't seem to mind.'[48]

On his return from Copenhagen, Frank made a great show of handing over to a blue-coated official at the airport all the pornographic material he had collected while in Copenhagen. He believed the man to be a customs officer, but he was in fact a courier from American Express. Eventually the Chief Customs Officer was summoned. The next morning Frank could at least take comfort in the fact that his inquiry was international headline news. 'To every Englishman,' America's *Time* magazine began its report on the affair, 'Francis Aungier Pakenham, the Seventh Earl of Longford KG PC, is better known as "Lord Porn".' He was also being ridiculed in every quarter. Some writers were dismissive in an affectionate way. *Daily Express* columnist Jean Rook labelled him 'a strayed and silly old goat'. Others were more cruel. A *Daily Mirror* leader described the whole Danish episode as 'sensationally foolish'. Robert Robinson dismissed the inquiry as 'the lost cause of 1971'. Mark Boxer produced a cartoon exploiting Frank's height and bald pate to turn him into a walking phallus.

Stories began to proliferate in the tabloids about 'Lord Porn'. One told of how he was stopped at an airport customs desk and asked to explain why he had a suitcase full of pornographic magazines. Another located the same event in a Soho Street. In another he had been invited to become a playmate at the Playboy Club. In a *Guardian* profile he was portrayed as a self-righteous and zealous Christian attempting to pull society back from the precipice of hell. It was an image that echoed through the work of other journalists who covered the inquiry. Where previously Frank's vocal

Christianity had been regarded as on the whole admirable or at least harmless and a feature to distinguish him from other politicians, in the context of a pornography campaign that was aiming at censorship it became another stone to throw at him.

The sort of personal mockery that Frank endured cannot only be explained by his subject, his approach or the offence it caused in the liberal arts and media establishments. Among the tabloids in particular, there was a palpable sense of vying to make him look more ridiculous. His every move prompted a 'Lord Porn' headline. If he was seen lunching in Soho, it would make a story. When Rachel published a novel with a bedroom scene, the papers cried out 'Lord Porn's daughter shocks father'. He became one of the first in a long line of tabloid anti-heroes, public figures who, because they have caused offence to the prevailing attitude of the papers, have therefore to be destroyed by ridicule, often with their own unwitting assistance – witness Copenhagen. In the early 1970s, the *Sun* was just getting into its stride of personality assassination and page-three pin-ups. By his anti-pornography crusade, Frank was seen to be attempting to stop the great British public getting its daily diet of busty beauties. And because of his attitude to publicity he just walked into every trap, as Jon Snow remembered. 'It was the height of the controversy and I had arranged a charity football match to benefit New Horizon at West Ham. Frank insisted on playing and turned up in some rather grey knee-length shorts. As we walked out on the pitch, there were a group of Bunny girls entertaining the crowd and beckoning to him. "You better avoid going anywhere near them," I said to him. "Imagine the photographs". The next minute he'd walked over there and was posing with them. He couldn't help himself.'[49]

He managed to give the appearance of laughing off most of the hostile publicity. He had long been indifferent to what people said if he thought he was doing the right thing, but he was also a man given to introspection and self-doubt. During the pornography inquiry, the barrage of criticism did begin to get to him. 'He really did care what people said,' according to his daughter Antonia. 'He got quite angry sometimes. And good for him. He minded being a figure of fun.'[50]

In his introduction to the committee's final report, however, Frank appeared philosophical. The work he had undertaken, he wrote,

> has brought me an extraordinary amount of personal notoriety. There will be those who feel that this personal publicity could have been handled more prudently. They may be right. I would not be the one to judge. From the beginning it was obvious that all of us, and I particularly, were bound to encounter vehement opposition – some of it frankly based on vested interest but some of it deriving from libertarian convictions. One would expect that we would be either ignored or denounced or ridiculed. In the event we have certainly not been ignored. For a time we certainly were denounced but rather halfheartedly. In a country as proud, on the whole rightly, as Britain of its rational discussions, it is hard to go on denouncing an inquiry as such. So ridicule it had to be.[51]

His close friends, few of whom agreed with his stance on pornography, nevertheless admired his resilience in the face of attack. 'Frank really is a person of great moral strength,' said David Astor. 'His capacity to follow his own line, regardless of what any and everyone may say, is, I think, a very great achievement.'[52] Others, though, felt that he was so wrapped up with his new crusade that he was riding rough-shod over their feelings. In 1971, soon after the wedding of their daughter, Marina, to the writer William Shawcross, Frank's old Eton friend Esmond Warner and his wife Emilia were invited to spend the weekend in Sussex with Hartley Shawcross, an old ministerial colleague of Frank's and his wife, so that the in-laws could get to know each other better. Frank and Elizabeth were invited to join the party for the dinner. As soon as the ladies had retired, Frank immediately asked what the men round the table thought about pornography. 'The discussion quickly became very extreme,' Marina Warner was later told by her husband. 'People were talking about masturbation and my father found it such an inappropriate subject that he got up and threatened to leave and break up the whole party. Meanwhile a Czech refugee friend of William's who was at the dinner made Frank positively boggle when he told him "I agree that there is a problem with pornography. It is too expensive".'[53]

Ridiculed he may have been, but on the day the pornography report appeared, 21 September 1972, he starred on nine radio and television programmes. Those who expected him to be a push-over were surprised by his vigorous and feisty defence of his report. Only on BBC Radio's *Midweek* did he lose his rag and accuse the presenter of being partisan – an error for which Elizabeth, listening down at Bernhurst, was later gently to rebuke him. By contrast, when Diana Dors,[54] an actress celebrated in her youth for parading round Venice in a mink bikini, took the chair in a debate on Southern Television on the pornography report, she made plain her agreement with its author and the two became friends.

There were many others who did not subscribe to the view of Frank as a joke. A couple of weeks before publication he had been one of two speakers at a Savoy luncheon to honour 'Men of the Year' on the grounds of courage and achievement. At the time of publication, he was the subject of a BBC Television *Panorama* programme and numerous newspaper profiles. He came fifth in a BBC Radio poll of 'Men of the Year' for 1972, behind Enoch Powell and Edward Heath but ahead of Harold Wilson. The public were not as hostile as the press.

On the establishment of institutions, the report came down in favour of a body to uphold public decency in various areas – broadcasting, cinema, the theatre. On the question of sex education, it advocated a shift in responsibility from teachers to parents. The report also included a draft bill to amend the Obscene Publications Acts of 1959 and 1964 and the liberalizing Theatres Act of 1968 'to make further provision for prohibiting the public exploitation of indecent matter; to penalise the exploitation of actors and models for purposes of obscene or indecent shows and pictures'. The bill would make it illegal both to display in a street or other public place any written, pictorial or other material which was held to be indecent and to produce or sell any article which 'outraged contemporary standards of decency or humanity which were accepted by the public at large'.

Though the report was completed and signed in July, it did not appear until September, when it was published in paperback by Hodder and Stoughton under its Coronet imprint and went on to be a bestseller. On the eve of publication, the *Daily Mail* offered Frank £10,000 for serialization rights. He was inclined to accept. 'I tried to explain to him that if he did that [Malcolm Muggeridge recalled later] he would get absolutely no serious press attention at all. It meant cutting himself off from any possibility of being taken seriously. And it was only with some difficulty that I persuaded him to see that. In other words, on this question of publicity and the media, he is in a way a tremendous innocent.'[55]

A few siren voices did note that the report made a case to be answered against pornography. 'It may well prove [the *Daily Telegraph* wrote in a leading article the morning after publication] that the research by the Longford committee investigating pornography is of more value than the actual recommendations which it makes. Few people will have any doubts, after reading the report, about accepting two things as established fact – one is that the commercial exploitation of pornography has extended and is expanding vastly. The other is that in many cases pornography does lead to sexual attitudes which cause unhappiness and social malaise.'

The overall verdict was damning, however, and most of all damning of Frank. His political career may have already been over when he embarked on the pornography inquiry, but his work with prisoners and over penal reform was still continuing. He was a leading and respected spokesman for that cause in April 1971. By damaging his public reputation in Copenhagen, by allowing the press to make him a laughing stock, he diminished his own ability to further the campaign that had long been the closest to his heart. Among those who felt most aggrieved at his conduct of the inquiry and the fall-out that came in its wake were his friends in the penal reform movement. His dabbling in other areas lessened his effect as their spokesman. His judgement would now be suspect forever.

On an official level, the report had little effect on government policy. Robert Carr, the Home Secretary,[56] spoke of the menace of pornography at the Conservative Party conference shortly afterwards, but he rejected changing the obscenity laws. Attempts by back-benchers to raise the subject in Parliament quickly subsided. In November, eighteen months after Frank had first mentioned pornography in the Upper Chamber, the Bishop of Leicester opened a debate in the Lords on the report he had put his name to. It was a gentlemanly affair. Publication did not seem to have swayed many of the members from the position they had taken in April of the previous year. To that extent, the report must be judged a failure. It neither prompted legislation nor fuelled a continuing campaign.

The contents of the pornography report were quickly forgotten. No commission was set up to pursue the subject. Some of the members of the committee – notably Mary Whitehouse – pressed on. Frank remained friendly with many of them, but after publication he left the subject alone. He rarely mentioned it again in public. He vehemently denied, if challenged, that he changed his mind. He probably simply lost interest. 'He is like quite a lot of men of action,' said Marigold Johnson. 'They move on to the next thing. They don't waste time wondering if they did the right thing. They don't brood.'[57]

What did persist was his national celebrity. Throughout the autumn and winter of 1972 the press ran story after story about 'Lord Porn' – from tales about him being offended by the saucy calendar in his local café (unlikely, given his lack of interest in his surroundings) to reports that he and his wife occasionally swam naked in their pool at Bernhurst. In March 1973 his visit to the cinema to see *Last Tango in Paris* made headline news: 'It's Lord Tango'. Whatever the other failures of the pornography report, it succeeded in making Frank a name to conjure with.

Later developments did, however, show that he was not quite so wrong or out of touch as was suggested at the time. The first direct result of the inquiry came quite soon after publication. Part of the investigation had focused on the organization of the trade in pornography which was carried out, Frank began to suspect, with the connivance of senior figures in the police. At about the same time as he was going to Copenhagen, Frank employed the same private investigator, Major Matt Oliver, who had helped him with gathering information to clear Michael Davies of the Clapham Common murder back in the 1950s. Oliver compiled a dossier revealing malpractice by the police. Frank was unsure about how to proceed. When he consulted his committee they made it plain that it was not within the remit of the inquiry to tackle police corruption. Frank could not let the matter rest and he decided, in a private capacity, to hand over the information to Sir John Waldron, Metropolitan Police Commissioner, who promised to investigate.

Frank also encouraged Oliver to take his dossier to the *Sunday People*, which put a team of undercover reporters on the case. In February of the following year the paper ran an exposé on police corruption and the pornography trade which in the summer of 1973 resulted in eighteen senior officers being tried and sentenced to a total of 116 years in jail. Although the history of the pornography inquiry is largely one of journalists working against Frank, in this instance a successful partnership was forged.

A year after publication the *Daily Telegraph* reported from Copenhagen: 'Danes curb sex clubs after Longford's visit'. While the British press had laughed at Frank's antics, the Danish media had presented the very fact that their capital was inspected as the centre of Europe's porn industry as a national disgrace. Moves were made to tighten up the prevailing libertarian laws and clubs were closed. Amsterdam took over Copenhagen's role as the mecca for pornographers. Later in the 1980s, Margaret Thatcher's Conservative government introduced a series of measures that were very much in the spirit of revoking the unfettered freedoms of the 1960s and 1970s. The Broadcasting Standards Authority was just the sort of watchdog that the Longford committee suggested, though its brief is broader than obscenity. Legislation was also enacted giving parents a greater say over matters like sex education in schools – another recommendation of the report. An Indecent Displays Act in 1981 tackled the type of pornography that could be put on open shelves. Frank broke his silence on the subject to speak in favour of this measure in the Lords.

In 2001, when Gyles Brandreth, subsequently a broadcaster and Conservative MP, published his diaries which covered the

Copenhagen caper, he added a postscript. 'At the time, both in my diary and in the press, I mocked the commission's activities. Nearly 30 years later, it is self-evident that most of what Lord Longford was predicting has come about. I wonder, was he right all along?'[58]

SEVENTEEN

The Literary Longfords

Though hitherto regarded, thanks to the efforts of Frank and Elizabeth, as a political family, the Longfords found themselves in 1969 suddenly awarded a new label – the literary Longfords. Books had always been around the house, and reading had been encouraged by parents who valued education and learning highly, but for the children, raised with the latest political debate and the latest political stars at their dining table, it came as a surprise. 'I think people suddenly had this notion that when we all got together, all we would talk about was books,' said Rachel. 'The reality was that it was still politics that dominated family gatherings. At breakfast and from their bedroom at night we could hear my parents discussing the issues of the moment, testing their own viewpoints and working out how they would be involved.'

Though Frank had been the first to venture into print back in the early 1930s, his achievements were surpassed in the late 1960s by first his wife and then various of his children. His chief contribution to the collective image of a bookish clan was his role in charge of the publishers Sidgwick and Jackson, though his own books started to appear with ever greater regularity in retirement from government. If they were not greeted with the universal critical acclaim and prizes lavished on the efforts of Elizabeth, Antonia, Thomas, Judith and Rachel, then at least his flair for getting himself noticed meant that they were always reviewed.

333

Frank never showed any disappointment that none of his children followed him into front-line politics. Paddy had a theory that he had been christened Patrick Maurice Pakenham so he could either be PM Pakenham or Paddy MP, but was, he said, 'put off politics by the sight of my parents trudging out in the evening to endless, dull town hall meetings and soirées'. Michael's career as a British diplomat was perhaps the closest to Frank's calling, especially when in January 1991 he was sounded out about being Ambassador to Ireland, a post Frank advised him against, fearing his son would feel equally English and Irish and hence torn. Frank, though, was never that interested in foreign affairs, save for his time in Germany.

Of his other children, though some were involved in political campaigning on various issues, none stood for election. Thomas and Kevin were closely involved in the British–Irish Association, Rachel took up prison reform, becoming a trustee of New Bridge and co-editor of *Inside Time*, the only national newspaper for prisoners, Judith chaired an organization fighting for justice for migrant workers, Paddy joined forces with his father and set up the Help Charitable Trust in 1988, directed mainly at prisoners, and Antonia was involved from an early age in various international literary causes, setting up the Writers in Prison committee of English PEN. Antonia and Rachel both served as presidents of English PEN.

Thomas had various theories on the family's shared tendency towards writing. 'That cheerful, optimistic temperament we have inherited from you', he wrote to his father in 1969, 'must have its darker side: at any rate, a taste for melancholy. It is this – a streak of melancholy – that must be common to most authors. How else to explain the self-exile; the "long, tranquil, lonely days" as Evelyn Waugh called them, facing an endless supply of blank paper; the writing and the non-writing; the wrestling with the devil for the soul of one's narrative.' However, Thomas continued, after spending an evening with his brothers and sisters, he had thought of another cause of the family's mania for writing: 'We are not writers at all. We are talkers disguised as writers. Ten talkers in one family, and no listener: it was inevitable that half at least – the weaker half perhaps – should be driven to take refuge in authorship in order to try to find an audience.'[1] If it was Elizabeth's international success, from the 1960s onwards, as a biographer that was the most obvious source of inspiration for her children, their father's own bookish background as a teacher and an academic should not be overlooked in their choice of career.

In 1969 Foyle's Bookshop organized a lunch to celebrate the achievements of 'the literary Longfords'. 'One family, seven writers, twenty books' ran the publicity for the event at the Dorchester. Elizabeth's star was blazing bright. After the huge success of *Victoria RI* in 1964 on both sides of the Atlantic, she had embarked on a biography of the Duke of Wellington, her ancestor by marriage, Frank's great-great-uncle. As well as being given full access to Wellington's archives at Apsley House in Piccadilly and Stratfield Saye in Hampshire, she travelled to Waterloo and the Iberian Peninsula to research her subject and his famous battles at first hand. Occasionally she twisted Frank's arm to accompany her but his antipathy to travel remained strong. His sister Mary proved more willing and, with the keen eye of a soldier's daughter and a soldier's widow, more useful.

The first volume of Wellington appeared in 1969, collecting that year's *Yorkshire Post* literary prize. (The second volume came out in 1972.) Appearing at the same time was Antonia's *Mary Queen of Scots*. It too garnered transatlantic acclaim and, like *Victoria RI* before it, was the recipient of the James Tait Black prize. Thomas had begun writing soon after Oxford and his scholarly *Year of Liberty* – on the Irish rebellion of 1798 – was another family book published in 1969. Joining it on the bookshelves was Rachel's first novel, *All Things Nice*. Judith had already completed textbooks on *The Gordon Riots* and *Women in Revolt* before being published as a poet and later a novelist. Catherine may not have yet made it into the British Library's catalogue, but was a writer on the newly founded *Sunday Telegraph* magazine. 'It is in fact becoming rather ridiculous', Michael wrote to his mother in 1969, 'that every time I open a paper I see a member of the family smiling out of it. Are you all seeing the same press agent or is there an entire firm under contract?'[2]

Frank was quizzed by reporters at the Foyle's lunch as to what it felt like to be the spouse of a famous author. Lightheartedly, he recommended three possible reactions. 'Feigned indifference: Reply, "I did notice she was scribbling a lot lately". Therapeutic analysis: Say that writing is a first-rate thing for keeping a woman out of mischief. Self-satisfied: Assume that you did it yourself and say "We had a bit of trouble with the last chapter but we ironed it out".' His true feeling, in regard of his wife's and all his children's achievements, was a tremendous and undisguised pride. Any fleeting sense of being sidelined was immediately soothed by the naturally modest Elizabeth. 'She was an extraordinary woman,' Rachel wrote, 'but the most extraordinary thing about her was that she behaved as if she were quite ordinary. Perhaps this was partly because she so admired my father and thought of him as far more distinguished than herself.'

In addition to the literary efforts of his wife and children, there was also Frank's connection with his three sisters (Julia had died in her fifties of cancer), all of them published authors, and Violet's husband, the novelist, Anthony Powell. Violet, Mary and Pansy all lived long lives, but there were few bonds beyond blood that linked them to their brother. Mary and Violet were country women and Conservatives. Though Violet and her husband enjoyed the company of Elizabeth and her children, they were not close to Frank himself. Powell and Frank had been contemporaries at Eton but had had little to do with each other.

It was occasionally suggested that one of Powell's best-known fictional creations, Widmerpool, in the *Dance to the Music of Time* sequence of novels, was based on Frank. It was not a compliment. Widmerpool was described as 'so wet you could shoot snipe off him'. As ever, when faced with an insult, Frank repeated it against himself, even to journalists. This left Powell, who denied any link, amused, especially since he knew Frank had not read the books. 'In point of fact,' he wrote in his diaries, 'I cannot imagine ever even considering Frank as a model, least of all when I began the sequence. Frank uses up all his own "image" in publicity, leaving nothing in suspension, something essential in creating a novel-character based in real-life.' He did concede, however, that in his books Frank 'has developed certain Widmerpoolian overtones' in terms of 'phraseology and verbiage'.[3]

Amid all the acclaim in 1969 for his family, there was a terrible tragedy. In August, soon after the Foyle's lunch, the Longfords had to shoulder the hardest blow that can befall a parent. Elizabeth was away in Warsaw with Rachel, visiting her old friend Nicholas Henderson, then the British Ambassador in Poland where Michael served as his Second Secretary. Catherine would normally have spent the weekend at Bernhurst with her parents, but with Elizabeth abroad decided to go to East Anglia with a girlfriend. Early on the morning of 11 August, as they were returning to work with a photographer friend, a lorry collided with their car. All three were killed instantly.

Cruelly Frank first heard the news from a journalist on the London *Evening Standard* who telephoned him to get his reaction. Antonia, who hurried over to be with her father, remembered, even in this moment of desolation, his extraordinary faith. 'He had to go and identify Catherine's body. I was enormously struck by how strong and noble he was. He really did believe she had gone to a better world. His faith was propping him up in a world that otherwise would have been unendurable.' At a moment when darkness might have engulfed even the most convinced believer, Frank's faith survived its most extreme test. He was sustained most of all by his belief that Catherine was with her maker. That did not take away the profound sense of loss he felt, though when he explained his conviction it could disguise the huge sense of loss that lay behind it and make him seem cold and removed. At Catherine's funeral, her old friend Marina Warner spoke to him and said some words about the terrible loss. 'He replied "The good die young, and they go to heaven".'[4]

Though Catherine had been a natural rebel and the most willing of Frank's children to challenge him on any range of subjects in often heated disagreements, they had developed a closer bond in the years immediately before her death. Their relationship may have been more extreme, but followed a pattern largely true of all his children. As they grew into adults, he became more approachable, more interested in them and their opinions, and in awe of their achievements. In particular, while he did not expect them to follow his own line on matters of the day, he was delighted when they did. He expected very little but correspondingly could be thrilled by the least gesture. He had been particularly proud of Catherine's appearance with Malcolm Muggeridge in a television debate where she defended the 1968 papal encyclical *Humanae vitae*, which outlawed artificial contraception. As he wrote later: 'Her mind was still fresh and eager. In a sense her loss was all the greater because her powers were only just beginning to blossom, but . . . she had already in the deepest sense found herself, and she had nothing to fear in this life or the next one.'[5]

The loss of his child was to concentrate his thoughts on a question that had been in the background of his work with prisoners for years – the feelings of the victims. 'I had never been a victim of a serious crime and therefore it had been hard for me to say how I would feel towards the perpetrator', he wrote. 'The closest I came was with my daughter's death. The lorry driver who caused it also died in the crash. But had he lived, I was not sure how I would have felt towards him. I thought I would have gone to visit him in hospital. I hoped I would have gone to see him in hospital. I would have seen it as a duty.'[6]

The internal struggle between his instinctive response and the suitably Christian one was more evident in this passage than perhaps it had been at the graveside. For Elizabeth, coping with Catherine's death was more visibly an ordeal. It was the severest test of her basic optimism. Frank's melancholy streak arguably made him more accepting of the downside of God's mysterious ways but Elizabeth's Catholicism was not as deep-rooted as her husband's. She had assumed it dutifully to keep the domestic peace and so her children felt that Catherine's death was a make-or-break time for her faith. In 1986 she was able to write:

I think I have got over it. I am sometimes asked whether my faith helped: belief in immortality and a personal resurrection. My answer is that nothing lessens the pain at the time. I remember Frank being sent for by Mrs de Valera, a devout Catholic and wife of the Irish president, soon after Catherine died. 'Tell Elizabeth', she said to him, 'that I cried every day for a year when our youngest son was killed in a riding accident. She will do the same. But now I would not have him back.' Faith saved me from asking the terrible questions, 'Why? Why her? Why me?' I also had a growing conviction that Catherine was all right. It was a comfort to be able to do something for her . . . if only to say a Hail Mary.[7]

Christ's mother, a feature of Catholicism that had given Elizabeth great difficulty when she converted, became a comfort to her in her moment of grief.

A memorial to Catherine was later unveiled in the Hurst Green church, and the family established the Catherine Pakenham Prize in memory of their sister. Since 1971 – in conjunction with a series of national newspapers including the *Sunday Telegraph* – it was awarded to young women journalists, like Catherine, at the outset of their career. Rachel was one of the stalwarts of the judging panels, taking over in the 1980s as chairman from her mother.

In subsequent years, the Longfords faced the challenge of living through the failure of the marriages of four of their surviving children. While their marriage was held up as a national monument to the institution, their children were not so fortunate. In 1975, Antonia and Hugh Fraser parted after almost twenty years of marriage and six children. In 1980, Patrick and his wife, Mary, divorced after having two children. Two years later it was Judith and her lawyer husband, Alec Kazantzis, and in 1984, Kevin and his wife Ruth. The circumstances in each case were different, but no parent would want their child to go through the trauma of a marriage break-up. For Frank this was complicated by Catholic teaching that marriage was for life and remarriage impossible without first going through the Church's intrusive annulment process. Here, painfully close to home, his ideals were being tested by the realities of life. Augustinian formulas about loving the sinner and hating the sin were, he discovered from his children's reactions, no answer when the 'sinner' refused to regard themselves as such.

His pain was further exacerbated by the contrast between his public pronouncements – opposing in 1969, for instance, the relaxation of divorce laws – and the experience of his children which, inevitably, given his high profile after the pornography inquiry, was remarked upon in the press. 'I acknowledge that in a few cases these provisions for getting rid of an unwanted wife after a few years may, on balance, increase rather than diminish the total happiness [he had told his fellow peers in 1969]. But I would say, with absolute conviction, that in the vast majority of cases these provisions will have a very cruel impact and for that reason I am totally against this Bill.'

His use in that debate of phrases like 'the guilty partner' and 'the innocent partner' demonstrated a somewhat black-and-white understanding at that time of the issue under discussion. His initial lack of compassion when faced with Antonia's well-publicized break with Hugh Fraser – which prompted a period of estrangement between father and daughter – sat uneasily with the compassion he showed to the prisoners he visited. It was compounded by his heavy-handed paternalism when he had always been a remote father. With Antonia, he belatedly recognized that he couldn't bend a grown woman (she was forty-two at the time of the break-up), whom he had taught to be independently minded, to his will and so he accepted her second husband, Harold Pinter.[8] The prolonged period of alienation was therefore ended. Though he delighted in Pinter's success, and latterly was grateful for his practical assistance in continuing his prison visiting, they were never close.

Elizabeth was more immediately accommodating, even if she shared Frank's basic disapproval. It was she who built the bridges after the rows that ensued and helped heal wounds and end estrangements. Her keen interest in the arts and theatre made it easy for her to establish a warm relationship with Harold Pinter, and for fifteen years she enjoyed sharing family holidays with Antonia and Harold until she felt too frail to continue.

If, at the beginning of my married life [she wrote in her memoir], when my children were being born, some prophet had told me that we would be a Catholic family and yet we would have these divorces and second marriages, I would have felt amazement, disbelief and great unhappiness. But for most people life doesn't strike with one great hammer blow – it gradually happens, and you get used to it, you accept. You know the people involved, you admire them and love them whatever has gone wrong, and so you're buoyed up. You know it isn't the end.[9]

With the subsequent marriage break-ups, Frank was less condemnatory, less concerned with what he once described as his children's 'good name' and instead more intent on showing his understanding and on building relationships with a second generation of in-laws. Judith recalled how 'both my parents, my father just as much, said many times to me spontaneously how much they loved and admired Irving [Weinman], my second husband, and later how grateful they were for his conversation and visits'. When Judith and Irving, an American novelist, married quietly on a boat in Key West, Florida, Frank organized a celebration lunch at the House of Lords on their return.

Despite the impression given of him in the press as a hard-line puritan, in practice he was more flexible. 'He has always been very consoling,' Judith said. 'I was very ill when my first marriage ended and my father really put himself out to visit me. He was always wonderful when you were in real trouble. You could count on him.' Kevin used the same word – consoling – in relation to his father's attitude to him at the time of his divorce and remarriage. And Rachel placed this approach in a wider context.

If you asked his guidance or help, he would show a real interest that was not just theoretical. While we, his children, would never have dreamt of asking his advice on something like contraception, a good friend of mine who had known him since childhood was struggling with the question and turned to my father for help. He wasn't in the least condemnatory and took her to see a Jesuit

341

priest he knew well. He sat outside when she went in to talk to the priest who counselled that she could ignore the official ban on artificial contraception. It went against his own beliefs but that wasn't the point. He wanted to help her.

Such episodes, though, did not weaken Frank's attachment to Catholicism and its principles. He simply tried to adapt when his children didn't do what he would have wanted them to do. Even later, when he became active in the Catholic Women's Ordination movement, taking part in its protests outside Westminster Cathedral, he dismissed any suggestion that he was putting himself outside the Church. 'He remained', Judith remarked, 'a devoted son of the church. It was his home. He had the House of Lords but that was more a political club. I think he felt he had lost the Labour world after Gaitskell's death while the prison world was where he did his battles.'

The marital breakdown of Paddy came a year before the premature end of his career as a criminal barrister. His adult life was beset by a series of traumas. In September 1963, when he was out sailing with two friends, their boat capsized in the English Channel. Paddy alone survived. He spent eighteen hours at sea and swam ashore at Hastings, not far from Bernhurst. Subsequently his behaviour was periodically eccentric and self-destructive, causing anguish to his parents and preventing him from fulfilling his potential. Elizabeth's response tended to be tougher, though in practical ways she went out of her way to support Paddy and his children after he had been forced to give up work. Frank was more indulgent, prone to make excuses for Paddy. 'I think that he saw something of himself in me and so perhaps put me in a special category to be treated differently,' Paddy said. 'We were certainly unusually close and that may have been something to do with the experiences we shared – not the least of which was our enthusiasm for sport.'

In general, however, Frank's relationship with his adult children was warmer and closer than it had been when they were younger. 'Once he got free of having to earn his living and the ambition of trying to get to the top,' according to Judith, 'he relaxed a good deal. He had a very vivid old age.' There were, of course, heated debates about politics. Not all of them supported all of his campaigns, but he enjoyed fielding their views. Bernhurst remained the hub of family life, with increasing numbers of grandchildren dropping by at weekends.

Frank's lack of interest in babies and small children had remained unaltered with the arrival of most of the next generation.

In May 1967 [Antonia recalled], my sixth child Orlando was born. I think there had been some complaints in the family that my father never took an interest in his grandchildren and my mother had a word with him. When anybody is in hospital Dad was determined to visit them. For him it was a corporal work of mercy. I was in Guy's and in bed – you had to be in bed when Dada visited otherwise it wasn't a visit. Anyway he'd been very busy with various Cabinet matters but he walked in and went straight over to the cot and said: 'Hello, hello, what a sweet fellow' and then gave a very satisfied smile. When he turned to me I couldn't help laughing. The cot was empty. Orlando was in the nursery but my father hadn't noticed.

However, by the 1990s, when Kevin's youngest children were toddlers, a change was almost forced on him. 'Hermione, Ben and Dominic grew up, like others of their generation, accustomed to being cuddled by adults,' said their father, 'and with their grandfather they saw no reason why he should not behave with them like everyone else. So they didn't really leave him with any choice. Before perhaps he had not trusted his emotions to do it, but he seemed to enjoy it.'

EIGHTEEN

The Only Friend of Myra Hindley

In September 1972 the hysteria surrounding the pornography inquiry was at its height. The final report was due out any day. Frank was headlines in every national newspaper. Since Copenhagen his work had been generating smiles and mockery, but the mood turned to anger when it was revealed publicly that he had been privately visiting Myra Hindley in prison since May 1969. To those who knew little about Frank's long record as a friend of prisoners and who thought of him only as 'Lord Porn', it was a horrifying revelation which at once altered his status from misguided eccentric to potential danger to society and hypocrite. While he was prepared to castigate those who sought relief in pornographic magazines, he wanted society to rehabilitate a woman whose crimes were regarded as among the most heinous ever committed. A Jak cartoon of the time pointed out the paradox. It showed Frank addressing his anti-pornography committee: 'Then as soon as we've got all the pornographers in prison, I'll start a campaign to get them out.' Even to those who knew of and admired Frank's commitment to marginalized causes, the news of his connection with Hindley came as a shock.

Few murders have so shaken and repelled the public as the crimes committed by Hindley and her lover, Ian Brady. They were arrested on 7 October 1965 after the brutal bludgeoning to death of seventeen-year-old Edward Evans by Brady with Hindley's assistance

344

the previous evening. When detectives began investigating that crime, the trail led them to Saddleworth Moor above Manchester and ultimately to the graves of ten-year-old Lesley Anne Downey, who had disappeared on Boxing Day 1964 and John Kilbride, twelve, who had vanished on the night after John F. Kennedy was assassinated. In the neat, unremarkable council house Brady shared with Hindley and her grandmother in the Manchester suburb of Hattersley, police found a tape recording of Lesley Anne Downey's tormented last hours and photographs which Brady had taken of her.

The trial at Chester Crown Court of the Moors murderers, as they became known, dominated the news in April and May 1966 and left an indelible mark on the public consciousness. In court, as Brady's admiration of Adolf Hitler and the Marquis de Sade was detailed, the gruesome tape recording played and the crimes against defenceless children recounted, Hindley sat impassive, betraying no emotion and showing no remorse. They were both convicted and sentenced to life imprisonment. So high was the level of public anger and disgust that a petition of 30,000 names was collected demanding the return of capital punishment for the couple. In his bestselling book about the case, *Beyond Belief*, Emlyn Williams summed up the popular wish for revenge at the time of the trial. 'Their continued existence is indeed hard to tolerate. Public feeling being what it is – and about these two the public will have a long memory – it is unlikely they will ever be released, and it is natural for taxpayers to be incensed at the thought of their being maintained, for life, by the State.'[1]

Much of the horror at the crimes focused on Hindley, though from the start it was clear to police that she had been Brady's accomplice, a willing helper in his evil schemes but not the instigator. The idea that a woman, whose body is designed to bring children into the world and whose traditional role has been as a nurturer and protector of the young, could take part in such atrocities engulfed Hindley in a storm of national hatred. The photograph of her used at the trial, and ever after, as a Medusa-like blonde with a stern, unyielding expression and a blank stare, became an icon of crime and evil doing in the twentieth century.

At the trial Hindley never once tried to distance herself from Brady or anything he had done. At one stage she described him as her 'god' and she remained fanatically loyal to him. She made plain that what he had done, she had done. It was her overwhelming desire to see Brady again, once she had begun her sentence, that prompted her to write to Frank. She maintained subsequently that she knew nothing of his reputation as a campaigner for penal reform. She did not approach him as a soft touch but rather through the good offices of Lady Anne Tree, who was visiting her in prison and who knew of Hindley's fervent desire to have face-to-face meetings with Brady rather than just a correspondence. It was Lady Anne Tree, knowing of Frank's interest in prisoners, who suggested putting Hindley in touch with him.

Frank's approach to prisoners had long been based on a refusal to sit in judgement and an unconditional offer of forgiveness and friendship whatever their crime. It was his unshakeable belief that no prisoner was beyond redemption. While the public put Hindley in a special category, beyond the pale, he refused to do so. To him she was neither a monster nor evil. Yet he was initially cautious about leaping to Hindley's rescue. The enormity of her crime – like that of the former concentration camp guards he had met when he was a minister in Germany – made even him pause to draw breath for a moment. Before agreeing to get involved in lobbying the Home Office, he arranged to visit her at Holloway Prison. After talking to Hindley, he still was not convinced that greater contact with Brady would be of any benefit to her. However, after listening to others who had been visiting Hindley, he was brought round to the view that the prospect of seeing Brady again was important to Hindley's emotional equilibrium and he agreed to make representations on her behalf. Though he failed to make much headway with the Home Office, Frank gradually became more involved in her case. He began visiting Hindley every three months.

Elizabeth, who had always supported her husband in his mission to prisoners in the past, was opposed at the outset. 'I didn't want Frank to have anything to do with these people. I wanted him to keep his hands clean of these monsters.'[2] It was significant that over both pornography and Myra Hindley, the two crusades that did so much to damage Frank's public image and eclipsed his record as a politician and reformer, Elizabeth began by advising him against taking them up.

Frank was determined, however, to press on but accepted at first the wisdom of doing so without attracting any publicity. Through his contact with Hindley, he began corresponding with Brady. His relationship with Brady, which continued for many years, was principally conducted at an intellectual level. Frank would send him books to read (including his own volume *Humility*, Elizabeth's life of Wellington and Antonia's *Mary Queen of Scots*) and then discuss them with him by letter and on regular visits. After a fourteen-year struggle he persuaded the Home Office to send Brady to a special hospital for the treatment hitherto denied him by officials.

It was his friendship with Hindley, though – a very different relationship from that with Brady – that has won him notoriety and dwarfed in the public mind his wider campaign for prisoners. In the early 1970s he saw the Moors murderers gradually drift apart, Brady in no fit mental state to contemplate release, but Hindley hoping that one day, in the distant future, she might be set free. Hindley subsequently said that Frank played an important part in her decision to return to the Catholic faith of her teenage years. Other prison officers who befriended her were just as important, but Frank gave her the courage to start taking the sacraments again in spite of the adverse reaction she feared from both fellow worshippers and clergy. Her renewed faith completed her break from Brady, who despised religion. At the same time it cemented her bond with Frank. Though many, including not a few senior Church figures, doubted the sincerity of her conversion, seeing it as a ploy to present herself in a better light with the parole authorities, his belief in her genuine return to religion was echoed by the chaplains and Christians who visited or wrote to Hindley.

Their shared Catholicism was a central topic of conversation during Frank's visits – first at Holloway, then in a series of prisons around the country. Both had no inhibition in talking openly about God and faith and how it affected their lives. Both shared a devotion to St Francis. Frank had joined the Catholic Church in a Franciscan parish, while Hindley's most loyal friends among the clergy were Franciscan priests and brothers. Both read extensively on religious topics – Frank with his daily diet of spiritual books and Hindley the *Divine Office* and a wide range of other texts by Christian figures. Yet the friendship that developed between them was not just to do with religion. Hindley put Frank's devotion to the cause of her release down to a kind of Sir Galahad complex, wanting to ride in on his charger and save her. Through that devotion, she became an honorary member of his family. They discussed his children and grandchildren, exchanged birthday cards and gifts.

Once converted to Hindley's cause, Elizabeth Longford occasionally joined her husband on visits. The first time was at Holloway in December 1976. In her diary she wrote:

Myra, very slim, was dressed in a long skirt and white blouse, her long dark brown hair loosely combed – very pale complexion and dark blue eyes – black lashes and regular eyebrows. Never in a hundred years could anyone have guessed she was the blond hussy of the media ten years ago, with hair in a bird's nest and brazen expression. The impression she now gives is of deep sadness. Her voice is low and rather husky . . . She showed us her bandaged and swollen leg and knee and the marks of her two black eyes were still visible . . . She then told us the story of the assault by a young prisoner who had a record of violence but had been going 'straight' until she saw the *News of the World* article recalling the Moors murders and sloganing 'These monsters must never come out'. She rushed at Myra, dragged her head down by her hair shouting 'You bastard – You child murderer' and kicked her in the face and elsewhere with her heavy shoes. Myra lost consciousness but was saved in the first place by the lesbian singer Janie Jones. Her case needs airing in the press if she is ever to get parole, so I persuaded her at last to agree to publicity. Frank said this was valuable and got a letter into the *Guardian* just before Xmas. Hitherto Myra had shrunk from using the press. She kissed me goodbye, putting one hand at the back of my fur hat. I responded, feeling deeply moved and unhappy at the whole ghastly tragedy.[3]

By the time of that visit, Frank's interest in the Hindley case had been 'outed' in the press and was now well known, but it was only slowly that Hindley allowed him to press more forcibly the case for her release. If anyone was inhibiting his zeal to go out and convince the world she was a reformed character who deserved parole, it was Hindley herself. Following the *Guardian* letter, Frank managed to get her permission to allow Harold Evans,[4] editor of the *Sunday Times*, to publish some of her letters which set out her profound remorse at her crimes. The public remained unconvinced and Frank's efforts over the years were damaged when in 1987 she broke her silence about Brady's role in the deaths of Pauline Reade and Keith Bennett, always thought by police to be victims of the Moors murderers but never proved to be such, and agreed to assist in a new search on the Moors for the children's bodies. Publicly Frank presented it as an act of compassion towards their parents made at the cost of damaging her own chances of parole. Yet to the press, it served only to reinforce their image of a calculating woman who had hidden the evidence of the killings for years.

He also tried to persuade Hindley to express her remorse in a letter to Ann West, the mother of Lesley Anne Downey and a vocal campaigner against parole. In his diary entry for 15 January 1981, considering the apology sent by another of 'his prisoners', Shane O'Doherty, to the victims of his IRA parcel bomb, he wrote: 'It would indeed be helpful if Myra could send a similar apology to Mrs West. But Myra clings to her own sincerity which makes it harder.'[5]

Yet he never wavered from his belief that Hindley should be judged by the authorities on the basis of her efforts at reform rather than the popular prejudice against her. The extent to which her cause became a personal crusade for him throughout the 1970s and 1980s, overshadowing his concern for other prisoners similarly afflicted, many of whom he visited, can only be explained by a certain allure she held for him – not unlike the fascination she held for the general public. It was certainly not the love that some critics hinted at. Rather, with his long record as a prison campaigner, he wanted to put himself to the test, to practise what he preached – unconditional forgiveness even for a woman whose crimes he saw as horrific. For most people it would be one thing to offer unconditional forgiveness to a prisoner who had defrauded the tax authorities, but quite another to forgive a woman who participated in the sadistic killing of children. Frank's Christian conviction, passed through his own almost coldly logical mind, demanded that no sin be any more or less forgivable than another. He then took that one step further. Not content with accepting the challenge for himself in regard to Hindley, he tried to evangelize society and persuade others to forgive. It was, as Jon Snow described it, an attempt 'to stake out a moral and spiritual position that no politician ever even begins to think about'.[6]

As a public figure and one with an abiding belief in the efficacy of publicity, he did not limit himself to lobbying Whitehall over Hindley. He attempted, in a principled, brave but naïve fashion, to win over public opinion, calculating quite correctly that without it behind her Hindley would never be released. Yet he placed too much faith both in the public's capacity to follow his example of forgiveness, and in the media's willingness to promote such a message. Hindley's name on the front page of newspapers sold extra copies. The press had no interest in presenting her as a reformed character. Their stake was in maintaining the spectre of an evil monster who could one day be let loose on society. Frank simply became part of their strategy, paraded by the press as the 'loony' peer, 'Lord Wrongford' as the *Sun* dubbed him, who had been tricked by a scheming murderess. However hard he fought against such casting, he found it impossible to change minds.

The first of his many skirmishes with the press over Myra Hindley occurred just a week before the pornography report was due to be published. The *Daily Express* had learnt that the governor of Holloway, Mrs D.M. Wing, had taken Hindley for a brief walk outside the prison walls. It was not an unusual privilege to grant model prisoners, but the *Express* was intent on exploiting the anger that the public would feel at such a special concession to a hated prisoner. Frank, when telephoned by a reporter, said that he knew nothing of Mrs Wing's initiative but that it sounded to him like an excellent idea. The Home Secretary, Robert Carr, thought otherwise and rebuked Mrs Wing.

The Home Secretary had a surer grasp of what his electorate wanted to hear. Frank's response, typically, was not shaped by a politician's pragmatism, but by his knowledge of the prisoner and his conviction that she was a reformed character. The public had not witnessed that transformation. Nor did they want to. There was a hint of arrogance in Frank when he miscalculated such revulsion. As over pornography, he was sure he was right and was convinced that if he stated his views often and clearly enough, he would win others round.

When he was proved wrong and his statements about Hindley began to attract a negative response, Frank's natural impatience came to the surface. He would speak testily and provocatively to those who challenged him, for example, when he appeared on the BBC TV discussion programme *Kilroy* and said that anyone who did not believe Hindley should be released was stupid. 'He had a brilliant mind and complete commitment to the cause,' said Hindley's solicitor Andrew McCooey, who appeared on the same programme, 'but there was not a standing back to consider the views of the man in the street, to ask, "Am I being perceived as being obsessed, as having an axe to grind?" Objectivity and understanding of others' feelings was very important in dealing with this case.'[7]

Faced by a sympathetic journalist, or in private conversation, he could make a strong argument for releasing Hindley that rested not on her personal attributes but on the workings of the parole system. In an interview with the *Catholic Herald* in June 1985, after the National Parole Board had just rejected Hindley's application, he made such a telling case that the paper backed his campaign in a leading article. The local review board, he said, had recommended Hindley's release on licence. They had based such a conclusion on the Home Secretary's instructions that prisoners should be judged primarily on the basis of whether they were still a danger to society. Hindley posed no danger at all, had been punished enough and should be freed, they concluded. In the vast majority of parole cases the judgment of the local experts is endorsed by the National Parole Board and sent forward to the Home Secretary for approval. In Hindley's case, however, the local board's ruling was summarily dismissed at a higher level. Frank believed that this move was due to the weight of public opinion and the then Home Secretary Leon Brittan's[8] unwillingness to handle such a political hot potato. Yet, according to Frank, the Parole Board had no mandate to consider such factors. Parole was judged not on what was acceptable to public opinion – and particularly a public opinion manipulated by tabloid journals which carry labels on files about Hindley instructing that her name always be prefixed by the adjective 'evil'. Parole should be determined by the standards the Home Secretary himself had set out – was the prisoner still a danger to society? – and by the regulations laid out in the law that Frank himself had played a substantial part in introducing after his 1963 report on crime was taken up by the Labour government.

Such an argument steered clear of the emotional minefield that surrounded any suggestion that Hindley was reformed, but its effectiveness still rested on a Home Secretary having the political courage to release her. As a politician of many years' standing, Frank should have known that, with public opinion rightly or wrongly vigorously opposed, no ambitious minister would take that risk. 'Myra Hindley would always be one of the symbols of crime and to be seen to go soft on her was to be seen to go soft on crime,' said her solicitor Andrew McCooey. 'No Home Secretary was going to take the decision.'[9]

If public opinion prevented Hindley being released, rather than any belief in the Home Office that she was a danger to society, then Frank played a part in stirring rather than soothing popular fears. By linking himself with her, in effect mortgaging his own good name and reputation in pursuit of her cause, he undoubtedly made a great sacrifice, but equally the interest of 'Lord Porn' in Hindley's case meant that many more stories were written about her than would have been otherwise. He contributed to keeping her name in the news.

Hindley was aware almost from the outset that Frank's campaign could backfire on her. Unable to speak out for herself, she was a silent and increasingly disturbed onlooker as he tried to put her case. Time after time, he would conclude his visit to her by promising that he would answer any journalist's question about her with a simple 'no comment'. Then days later she would read his comments with what she described as a mixture of anger and frustration. When he engaged in a war of words over her case with Robert Maxwell in the *Daily Mirror* in the mid-1980s, she pleaded with him to keep quiet, but he was unable to, and when challenged on subsequent visits, he would respond that he could not face St Peter at the end of his life with a clear conscience if he thought he had turned down an opportunity to do her good. His sense of mission was so strong that he stubbornly continued on a course that even the woman he was supposed to be helping considered damaging. The crusade once again had almost grown more important than the person. Hindley's conviction that his public campaign was doing her harm made no impression on him.

Hindley was not the only one who grew increasingly alarmed at the negative effects of the campaign. David Astor felt moved to raise the question of its efficacy with Frank in the late 1970s.

He was absolutely right to defend her as a human being when no one else would [said Astor], but accidentally he did her harm by exciting the press, encouraging them to treat him as a 'loony lord' and therefore make her position worse. Frank was very reluctant to see this when we talked about it. He thought that to go quiet about Myra's case would be seen as abandoning her. He was horrified at the idea that he might have been counter-productive to her and to himself. It was to help both of them that I got involved. I agreed that if Frank would lay off, the quid pro quo would be that I would visit Myra along with Peter Timms, a former prison governor. Frank bought this compromise only with a great deal of difficulty.[10]

Frank and Astor could not have been more different in their approach to publicity and in particular over how to handle Hindley's case. While Frank believed that minds could be changed through the media, Astor shunned any personal attention and, as a former newspaper editor, was aware that courting the press could have adverse effects. Though he was convinced on meeting Hindley that she should be paroled, Astor believed a low profile was in her best interests. Frank was increasingly marginalized from the mid-1980s onwards from Hindley's campaign to obtain parole. He continued to lobby privately – out of the media's eye – for her eventual release and to recruit prominent figures to her cause, but she even began to limit his visits to her for fear of the publicity they generated.

Though Elizabeth backed Frank in his public campaign to have Hindley paroled, she was more aware of questions of how to present the issues. In Hindley's case, in particular, he could neglect the grief and anger of the parents of her victims. 'When my mother showed me a first draft of her memoir, *The Pebbled Shore*,' Antonia recalled, 'there was a section about Myra and their friendship which followed directly on from another about the joy my mother derived from her many grandchildren. When I told her how insensitive this might appear – that she had enjoyed her grandchildren while the parents of Myra Hindley's victims would never know that joy – she immediately saw my point and deleted the section, but my father simply didn't understand why she had done it and told her to leave it in.'[11]

In general, Frank did not take much notice of hostile reporting and reactions to his views on Myra Hindley. 'If rude letters came in, he would simply throw them in the bin,' said one of his long-time secretaries, Barbara Winch. 'Occasionally the writer would say something that would make him reply, but he could take as much as he could give.'[12] On one occasion, though, he did allow himself for once to show in public his anger at constantly being laughed at and teased because of his support for Hindley. Elizabeth recorded in her diary Frank's visit to the Garrick Club, 'where he met Judge Melford Stephenson who gave him a sherry and his usual genial greeting (which F greatly disapproved of) "How's Myra?" F: "I am giving lunch to a West Indian; I hope you will be kind to him." "Why do you ask?" "I thought you might be anti-black." Big man standing near: "We're all anti-black, aren't we? But we know how to behave in a club".'[13]

Yet in his calmer moments, Frank wasn't without self-knowledge. In 1995 he appeared on a televised debate with Winnie Johnson, mother of Keith Bennett, and gave his usual robust plea for Hindley to be paroled, but the next morning in his diary he wrote: 'I asked myself whether, if I had to do it again, I would do it any better. I concluded that I should have expressed at the beginning (what I took for granted) my profound sympathy for victims and their relatives.'[14] The problem was that viewers did not take it for granted.

He could also be humorous about the press's fascination with his relationship with Hindley. In 1985, Elizabeth recorded in her diary arriving back a day early from a holiday in Portugal with Antonia. 'Frank jokes about Myra being found in bed with him.'[15] Hindley for her part sometimes responded in kind. On Frank's ninetieth birthday she wrote to him comparing him to Robbie Ross, who had raised his hat to Oscar Wilde as he was taken away, with bowed head and manacled legs, after conviction.

Though it attracted more publicity and took a disproportionate share of his effort and time, Frank's campaign for Hindley was only a part of his broader work with prisoners. He continued to be involved with New Bridge, witnessing its growth into a respected organization in the penal reform world, offering a specialized employment service to ex-prisoners and *Inside Time*, the only national newspaper for those in jail. He took considerable pleasure in the growing involvement in New Bridge of his daughter Rachel and her interest in visiting prisoners.

When Frank became involved in prison reform in the 1950s, there were no ex-prisoners' organizations like New Bridge. By the 1980s, largely inspired by his efforts, that gap had been filled. It was his legacy. Equally, when he first initiated debates in the Lords on conditions in Britain's jails, he was a lone voice, calling attention to an issue that had not previously been discussed. Again in the 1980s he was a member of a large parliamentary all-party penal reform group. It was time to hand over the mantle.

Some, indeed, took the view that, because of his association with Myra Hindley and his notoriety in the press, Frank was less than an asset to groups set up to lobby on prison policy. When the Prison Reform Trust was established in September 1981 by David Astor among others with the aim of informing public opinion on the topic, Frank was treated with deference but – much to his chagrin – excluded from any active participation. He was judged to be a barrier to communicating a new message on prisons. 'The idea [he wrote rather crossly after attending the launch] is that fresh faces and fresh voices should be introduced into the penal scene. The trouble about that is that these novices, however distinguished elsewhere, may take years to learn about prisons and the Trust initially intends to operate for only three years.'[16]

Even if he was now on the margins of any organized lobby, the letters from prisoners continued to come in and, with his platform in the House of Lords and his ready access, as a former cabinet minister, to Home Office officials, he turned his attention increasingly to a one-man crusade, visiting prisoners and taking up individual concerns. He would travel several times a week until well into his nineties to see someone behind bars. Some of those he sought out were infamous, though it was a description he disliked. He preferred to see such people as those that no one else would contemplate visiting, men such as Dennis Nilsen, jailed for murdering gay men and then dismembering their bodies, whose developing interest in art and music he encouraged, and Peter Sutcliffe, the 'Yorkshire Ripper', in Broadmoor. Another was a violent offender who had changed his name by deed poll to Charles Bronson after the American film star. 'The first time I met him,' Frank wrote, 'I was told that he was the most violent man in the prison. Was I ready to go into his cell alone? I had no option except to chance it. I asked him what he had been doing that day. He said "Two thousand press-ups". I said "I used to do a dozen a day. I'll see if I can do one now". [He was in his eighties at the time.] I went down on the floor and with some difficulty did one.

We have been friends ever since. He is full of fun and, in a strange way, talent.'[17]

Without attracting any attention at all, he also visited prisoners whose cases never hit the headlines, but who were lonely and desperate. The charge often levelled against him that he visited only those with well-known names was nonsense. He would respond to anyone who appealed to him, regardless of how far he had to travel and with no interest at all in their guilt or innocence. Andrew McCooey remembered a good example of this little-seen side of Frank's work.

> I was representing a young man who had brought drugs into the country. He was arrested, charged, sentenced and sent to Albany. He was from a wealthy family in Holland but his parents disowned him. He was HIV positive. Frank was prepared to travel to the Isle of Wight just to say he cared. That's the sort of thing the *Sun* doesn't publish. And the young man was very pleased that someone of such high standing would go all that way to, if nothing else, hold his hand, notwithstanding that he was a criminal, that he had AIDS. In those situations Frank was someone you could always turn to. It was a noble thing to do.[18]

Frank had a routine before setting off on a prison visit. 'I pray beforehand that I might be of some use and I pray for the person,' he said. 'I sometimes suppose that he's paying me and then I try to make sure that our half hour talk isn't dull.' With someone like Nilsen, he explained, 'my approach is just to listen. If he wants to talk about his crime, I let him. If he doesn't, I don't press him. He said to me, "If I knew why I did it, I wouldn't be here now."'[19] Part of Frank's introspection was a gift for listening, for forgetting himself and concentrating on others, and it proved an invaluable asset in his prison visiting.

Seen from the other side of the visiting room, he could be a life-saver in the dreary routine of prison. Rosie Johnston, convicted in December 1986 of drug-related offences after the death of her friend Olivia Channon, was the daughter of a family friend of the Longfords.

When I was first in prison he rang my mother and said he could come and visit me as a peer without depriving me of other family visits and asked if I would like to see him. The week that he was due to visit the snows fell. The prison was completely cut off. We couldn't get letters, food, anything, but he got there. He got a train and then a taxi and bullied them to battle through the snow and there he was, I couldn't believe it. Nothing else had got in through the prison gates for weeks. He was wearing a big grey coat but he didn't have any hat. There were snowflakes in his hair and his pate was practically blue. I had no preconceptions. I knew that he visited Myra Hindley but that didn't bother me. In fact I was fascinated. When you're in that situation, you've been in prison for two months, any visit is completely welcome. We completely and totally hit it off. He's the biggest flirt. That was what I couldn't believe. He just flirted – he'd say, my dear you are charming, you've got such a charming face. When you look like shit and you've been eating white bread for months, it was wonderful. He gave me a copy of the *Spectator* and we sat down and talked a lot about lesbians. It was so funny. He said, 'Well, tell me are there lots of lesbians here?' And I said, 'Yes, of course.' And then we had a good giggle about that. We just giggled really.[20]

She recalled that his connection with Hindley meant that many of the women she was imprisoned with treated him with suspicion, bordering on disdain. 'They couldn't understand why I wanted to see him. "What do you want to go and be visited by that loony who visits Myra Hindley for – daft bugger." I'd say, "I don't think he's daft." They were very suspicious of him. Because he was championing Myra Hindley they thought he must be either under her influence or mad.'[21]

Although it was his Christian beliefs that inspired his prison visiting, Frank did not try to push his faith on those he met, according to Johnston.

He did talk about Christianity – in a didactic way, that what he felt with Myra Hindley was that Christians should forgive each other, and I can't disagree with that. But I made it clear that I was never ripe for conversion. But I don't think he did it with a view to convert. He just talked about it because it was his thing like I talk about my work. I think he had a terribly strong sense of suffering and people who were in a position where they cannot get help. He did have a crusade. The penal system is not a vote winner, an electoral issue. It appealed to his sense of injustice. He wanted to make it better. He took on his own shoulders the injustice of a group of people who have no rights and cannot speak for themselves and who have no one to represent them.[22]

After her release, Frank invited Johnston to lunch in the House of Lords. It was a gesture he made to most of the prisoners he visited when they were set free, an attempt to ease their integration back into society by bringing them to the seat of the Establishment. Occasionally it could land him in trouble – as when he invited ex-IRA bomber Shane O'Doherty – but most of the time the gesture of friendship passed unnoticed, save by those to whom it was extended.

His efforts on behalf of prisoners also stretched to standing up for them when they were in court. However, his interest in prisoners damaged the credibility a retired cabinet minister would normally carry as a character witness. Judges came to doubt his judgement. In August 1982 Judge Cooke, sitting in the Inner London Crown Court, listened respectfully as Frank spoke up for thirty-nine-year-old John Masterson, a habitual offender whom he had met while on a prison visit. Frank asked the judge to favour a suspended sentence on Masterson, who was convicted of an assault charge, but a prison term was awarded. Another judge, hearing the case of Eddie Richardson at Winchester Crown Court in October 1990, was predicted to hand out a sentence of fifteen years, Frank liked to recall. After Frank had said a few words as character witness, the judge made it twenty-five. Richardson obviously did not bear a grudge and, as he developed his talent as an artist, was later to paint a portrait of Frank.

While the judge had paid little attention to Frank's appeal, it caught the attention of Bernard Levin,[23] writing in *The Times*. Levin had been one of the fiercest critics of the pornography report, but was apparently converted by Frank's long campaign for prisoners. 'Everybody asks the wrong question about Lord Longford, viz., is he barmy? The question is not worth asking: of course he is barmy. What we should be discussing is something quite different: is he right?' Levin wrote that he was quite prepared to take Frank's word that there was 'another side' to Richardson and that Myra Hindley was a reformed character. He expressed his admiration for Frank's indifference to those who ridiculed him and asked why the Churches had not joined him in his crusade. 'If there is one dominant theme in Christian scripture, it is surely that no one, no one at all, is past hope of redemption and forgiveness.' In speaking of the possibility of redemption – however idealistically – Frank was, Levin said, acting as Christ would and pointing to a central dilemma that society and the Home Office preferred to ignore. Whatever prisoners have done, are they beyond salvation? In refusing to accept that they are, Frank had Levin's support.

Prompted by Elizabeth, Frank invited Levin to lunch at the House of Lords to thank him, but when a few weeks later, on the occasion of his eighty-fifth birthday, his children presented him with a framed copy of the article, Frank revealed his ambiguous feelings about it. 'It was Rachel's idea,' Elizabeth wrote in her diary. 'She had had it beautifully (and expensively?) framed. But it turned out that Frank hated it!!! The children arranged for it to arrive dramatically in the dining room. Frank took one look at it and then frankly turned away his face. When called upon for a speech of thanks he muttered the quotation [from the article] about "economy of expense and economy of effect". Whereupon Kevin called out "I haven't paid my contribution yet, so I shall not pay it". Afterwards Frank realised his various mistakes and apologised all round. I have hung it in the hall at Bernhurst.'[24] Criticism, even when couched in the midst of a rare piece praising him, could still wound Frank, for all his protestations that he was indifferent.

Levin's raising the much-neglected question about what Christ would have done is important in evaluating this area of Frank's prisons' crusade. His work with individual prisoners was directly inspired by his Christianity, by his daily reading of the Bible. It made him an unlikely campaigner in the secular atmosphere of the late twentieth century. He would have fitted more easily in the era of William Wilberforce and Lord Shaftesbury as they tackled – from much the same social background and religious convictions as Frank – slavery and working conditions in factories.

In the Gospels, Frank read that Christ did not judge. He did not take the moral high ground but offered unconditional forgiveness. When He was among the sinners and the prostitutes like Mary Magdalene, they recognized in Him, unlike the scribes and Pharisees, that lack of judgement and they were drawn to Him. He did not want to put them in their place. 'In his own very small way, Frank tried to imitate Christ [said Andrew McCooey]. A lot of Christians can make you feel uncomfortable because they are righteous and judgemental. But Frank was not like that. And prisoners sensed that in him, his concern and forgiveness. It endeared him to them. He touched the values that in your heart of hearts you know are right. He cared for people, for the underdog and he always had time for you. It's the closest you can come to what a Christian can be.'[25]

Roy Jenkins, like Bernard Levin, was moved to change his mind by Frank's long campaign for a changed attitude to prisoners. 'I think Frank showed dedication to the issue and even though he was a nuisance to successive Home Secretaries, he did a lot of good. I deeply respected him for his dedication on the issue and his absolute indifference to being put down or made to appear ridiculous by the press. Running through my slight impatience with what I regarded as his occasional misjudgements, there was an underlying streak of admiration and a feeling that on balance, though an irritant, he did good.'[26]

NINETEEN

The Man with the Stick

In 1997, the *Oldie* magazine, edited by one of Frank's fiercest critics, Richard Ingrams,[1] and aimed at fifty-year-old-plus readers, bestowed on the Longfords the title 'Lovers of the Year'. By that stage they had been married for sixty-six years and were going strong at the start of their tenth decade, dividing their time between Bernhurst and their London flat, where Paddy lived across the courtyard in the same block. Both his parents were busy working on books. Frank attended the House of Lords every day and visited prisoners several times each week. There were regular parties as they jointly and individually reached another landmark, the Garter ceremony, and even for Frank a new newspaper column – in the *Catholic Herald*. 'No London party felt quite complete without the presence of Lord and Lady Longford,' wrote A.N. Wilson,[2] 'she always immaculately turned out and radiantly beautiful into her nineties, he resembling, at first glance, a professor who had for some reason been sleeping rough for months in the same tattered pin stripe suit, his bald pate often adorned with a piece of greyish Elastoplast.'

Elizabeth's hearing had been failing for some time and poor eyesight eventually forced her to stop driving at eighty-nine, but she remained as vigorous as ever, writing and commentating on royal matters. In 1989 there had been a scare when she was discovered to have a spinal tumour, but when it was removed it proved to be benign. Frank celebrated their enduring love in verse when she recovered and came home.

> And if at times I've seemed to fail in love
> There's never been a failure of desire
> I've yearned with every waking moment and above
> All earthly things to melt into your life.[3]

Over his own health problems he took a wittier line. Poor eyesight – a congenital affliction, suffered also by Mary and Pansy – eventually stopped him reading. He would ask those around him to read sections of newspapers – including the Irish rugby score – out loud to him. He refused to allow losing his sight to curtail his remorseless journeying around the country. Until he was eighty-seven he would go jogging every weekend at Bernhurst. He gave up, he used to say, when people walking started to overtake him. His refusal ever to be still saw him in later years turning visiting into an art form. There were his trips over to Robertsbridge to see the Muggeridges – before Malcolm's death in 1990 – and journeys down to the coast at Hastings by bus every Sunday morning to call in on his old colleague, Major Matt Oliver, and a more recent acquaintance, Anthony Marlow whom, characteristically, he was hoping to convert to Catholicism. When he tripped over a kerb and was forced to use a stick, he enjoyed, as ever, laughing at himself.

> There once was a man with a stick
> whose moves were remarkably slick.
> He said 'after my wife
> the stick is my life,
> is the thing that makes me tick.'[4]

In February 1992, aged eighty-six, he had a more serious accident. Elizabeth described in her diary how he fell on the stairs at Bernhurst while paying a night-time call of nature. There was no light and he bashed into a grandfather clock and broke two ribs and ruptured his spleen. 'Then he groped up to the backstairs bathroom and finally reached his dressing-room where I found him white and shocked at 7.30am. He didn't want to disturb me. I felt absolutely stricken.' He was rushed to East Sussex Hospital, where doctors decided his spleen had to be removed. 'Rachel and I were waiting for him in men's surgical when he came back from the operating theatre and he came rolling in on a trolley, clasping both hands above his head like a victorious boxer.'[5] Within two weeks he was back in the Lords. Within two months he threw away the medicine that he was supposed to be on for the rest of his life.

The eccentricities in his dress became more pronounced. At one Garter ceremony, the loose-fitting trousers he was wearing began to slip down. Clutching on to his stick for balance and therefore without a free hand, he had to summon assistance to stop them ending up round his ankles. On a visit to Tullynally to see Thomas and his wife Valerie, he was put in the Tower Room because his habit of waking up early tended to disturb Elizabeth. When he got to his room, she wrote in her diary, he was disorientated briefly. 'Then not realising it was all laid out for the Sunday tourists who visit Tullynally, he called for Thomas. When Thomas said "where are your pyjamas, Dada?" Frank picked up his father's uniform jacket of the Life Guards and said "this will do".'[6] On another occasion when he arrived by taxi after Elizabeth at his son Kevin's west London home, he forgot what number he lived at. 'He wandered up and down the street for 15 minutes,' Elizabeth recorded, 'until I noticed his absence and Kevin rescued him.'[7]

Though he could occasionally exasperate Elizabeth – as when in a restaurant he mistook her hearing aid for a piece of pasta and ate it – the couple did not like to be parted. The one exception they made was when it came to holidays. With Antonia and Harold, Elizabeth enjoyed a series of Mediterranean trips. Frank, with his lack of interest in travel, would always start off by saying he was coming but would then make an excuse. Everyone knew what he was up to, but it was never publicly acknowledged. Even in her diary, Elizabeth kept up the pretence. In August 1983, she went with the Pinters to the south of France. On the third she wrote: 'Frank arrives on Saturday for two days, though the betting among his children and

grandchildren is that he will find an excuse. I know he will come.'
Two days later, she was proved wrong. 'A dreadful blow and
disappointment. Frank rang up to say he had had a gastric attack
last night and could not travel (naturally and rightly) tomorrow . . .
I offered to come home but of course he would not let me.'[8]

The one compensation was that when she returned, he would
have been pining and there would often be a love poem or gift
waiting for her. In 1990 when she got back from Greece, he had
written:

> Last night I lay in bed bereft of you
> A victim of anxieties and dreams
> The new day comes and maketh all things new
> Tonight I lie securely in your arms.[9]

This was a great love affair. The couple's togetherness was
celebrated many times over. In 1993, the National Portrait Gallery
unveiled a double portrait by Lucy Willis, who won over the normal
restless Frank during sittings by talking of the lessons she had given
prisoners at Taunton Jail. Elizabeth liked the result. 'She avoided
getting his mouth turned down – which is often natural to him when
not talking – and with the most perfect speaking eyes.'[10] On their
golden wedding anniversary, Patrick Lichfield[11] photographed them
with their grandchildren. 'I feel touched and proud,' Elizabeth
wrote, 'perhaps as the successful proprietor of a Garden Centre feels
as he looks along the rows of healthy plants, shrubs and young
trees.'[12]

Frank's interests and talents adjusted little to accommodate old
age. He took immense pride in his children and grandchildren and in
particular their achievements. 'He was always the first person to see
and call me if my book was in the best-sellers' chart,' recalled
Antonia. Less mobile, he resorted more and more to using the
telephone and once a week would dutifully call his three surviving
sisters, Mary, Violet and Pansy (who became a Catholic in Rome in
1981). In public life, he remained a fine speaker and used old age to
his advantage. Prince Charles described him as one of the best he

had ever heard in the Lords.[13] In 1991 he chaired a Foyle's Literary Lunch for the comedian Ernie Wise.[14] Elizabeth, though biased, considered Frank the wittier of the two. 'Frank was very funny indeed and got more laughs than anyone, except for some strings of "funny stories" told mechanically by the professional comedian who proposed the vote of thanks. Frank's was entirely personality humour. He did not tell a single funny story.'[15]

His interest in signing people up for the Catholic Church continued unabashed. On meeting Jack Dromey, the union official who had married his politician niece, Harriet Harman,[16] he confided later to Elizabeth that he believed Dromey was about to return to the Church. On another occasion, the Longfords had dinner with Frank's old secretary, now a successful novelist, Angela Lambert, and her daughter Caroline who was studying comparative religion at Strawberry Hill. 'Frank of course,' Elizabeth wrote indulgently in her diary, 'thinks she is "on the way".'[17] To some – like the former Tory minister and diarist, Alan Clark[18] – he even offered informal instruction.

Some of his views, once the standard position of his age and class, could sound outdated and on some matters his prejudices hardened as he looked on at the effects of a more permissive society. His homophobia, for instance, became more pronounced despite his earlier noble efforts to promote the Wolfenden report. After one of Elizabeth's birthday parties, there was a family debate as to why one of the guests had been condescendingly dismissive of Antonia's success as a writer. 'After they had all gone,' Elizabeth recorded, 'we discussed what could have prompted him to be so aggressive. Frank said it was because he was a homosexual. Harold said he was drunk. Antonia said he was just jealous. I said he had known A since she was a girl and thought he was being paternally constructive.'[19]

Though he remained committed to the Labour Party and turned up at local branch meetings in Battle in Sussex and Chelsea near the London flat, he viewed it in later years with a good deal of detachment. 'I feel more ambiguous now about socialism [he said]. If I'm asked, "Are you in favour of socialism?", I would always say, yes. It's rather like being asked if you're against sin. There is only one answer. Equality remains the most important thing. As a moral ideal, as the goal of socialism, it has not changed. But the superficial things have changed. Socialism used, for example, to mean nationalisation, but now all that has changed.'[20]

If there was a moment when he might decisively have turned his back on Labour it was in 1981, with the founding of the SDP by, among others, his old cabinet colleague, Roy Jenkins. Labour's drift to the left under Michael Foot (for whom Frank was once mistaken in a hospital waiting room on account of their shared lack of interest in dress) had seen it embrace unilateralism and question the Atlantic Alliance, to Frank the keystone of any British foreign policy. Those on the right of the party departed in substantial numbers, among them Frank's son Kevin, but the Longfords remained dedicated to fighting from within to save the party they had joined almost fifty years previously. 'At my age,' he told his friends, 'the question of leaving the Labour Party does not arise.' In an article in *The Times* on the day of the special Labour conference at Wembley in January 1981 to agree on how the leader should be chosen, Frank gave a fuller account of his reasons for not following Jenkins. Under the banner 'Why I must stay', he noted that there was nothing new in the charges of extremist infiltration of local Labour groups. It was a question of having the courage to stand up and fight. 'When I was elected to the Oxford City Council for the Cowley and Iffley ward in the late 1930s, my colleague on the ticket was a communist organiser who was narrowly defeated. "Crypto-coms" were not unknown in our party, but complacency, or alternatively impotent rage, are no substitute for dealing firmly with anti-democratic forces. I must hope and pray that democratic socialists will bestir themselves more actively than in the past.'

Moving on to the argument about the future direction of the party, Frank defended his continuing allegiance in personal terms:

The Labour Party with all its faults stands, as it has always stood, for an idea, for a belief that all men and women are of equal significance in the sight of God and should be treated accordingly in human arrangements. Or to make use of a Christian text: 'When thou givest a feast, thou shalt call the poor, the maimed, the lame and the blind and thou shalt be blessed.' Black, white, yellow and brown, all are included. No one questions the motives or for that matter the Christianity of those who adhere to other parties. But no other party proclaims as lofty an aspiration as does the Labour Party. As long as I can continue to work within the party, for the causes and ideals I believe in, I cannot see myself leaving it.

Elizabeth had supplied the last line, and it was, in effect, a statement from both of them. When they took their seats at the Wembley conference, Roy Hattersley[21] was among those who came to congratulate Frank. Despite Michael Foot's defeat at the end of the gathering, Elizabeth told her husband on the journey home that 'they' – the left – 'have over-reached themselves'. Her political instinct was characteristically acute. With the 1990s and the advent of Tony Blair, Frank was reassured to see a more moderate line, and the presence of so many Christian socialists – Blair included – in the 1997 cabinet. Also at top table was Elizabeth's niece, Harriet Harman, though she was not close to them, something they occasionally found puzzling and disappointing. Frank's reputation for eccentricity may have put her on her guard. Certainly in 1987, when Roy Jenkins was contesting the election for the Chancellorship of Oxford University, his agent was keen to solicit Elizabeth's endorsement, but almost relieved when informed that Frank would be backing a rival, Robert Blake. '"Roy doesn't want any pressure over Robert", she told me,' Elizabeth wrote in her diary indignantly, 'as if actually glad that Frank was opposing her candidate!'[22]

Frank did have his concerns about 'New Labour' and in 1999, when the Prime Minister addressed the Labour peers, was quick to raise them.

As the senior Labour peer [he wrote in his diary], I had been invited to ask the first question. 'Is some redistribution of wealth from rich to poor still part of the New Labour ideal?' He rattled off a long answer touching on many points, mentioning redistribution as he swept along, but leaving the audience no wiser about the government's reply on my question. He left on me, and no doubt on others, the impression of being a really good man. New Labour seems to most of us old-timers a different party from the one we joined . . . . I am happy, for the moment at least, with my assessment of New Labour. It is not the same as Old Labour, but a little child of Old Labour. That is to say, one of its parents is Old Labour. The other is Tony Blair himself.[23]

Blair himself evidently reciprocated this admiration. In October 1999, with the passage of legislation that would exile all but a small number of hereditary peers from the Lords, he wrote to Frank offering him a life peerage – as Baron Pakenham of Cowley – to enable him to continue to sit in the reformed Lords.

Only a couple of weeks before the Wembley conference in 1981, Frank had made his final appearance as a party spokesman in Parliament. After a thirteen-year gap since his resignation from the cabinet, he was drafted in by the Chief Whip, Lady Llewelyn-Davies, to wind up for the opposition a debate on the disabled. It was a subject that he had held dear since 1970 when he piloted Labour MP Alf Morris's Chronically Sick and Disabled Persons Bill through the Lords. He sat on the front bench again, albeit briefly, doomed at the end of the debate like Cinderella to return to the shadows from whence he came. His swan song left him feeling exhilarated.

As the years passed, he attended more and more memorial services for old friends, often called upon to give the address, and found he knew fewer and fewer of the contemporary major political players. The Longfords had a personal link with Margaret Thatcher. They had lived in adjoining streets in Chelsea and, in the late 1970s, the Thatchers, who had a house at Lamberhurst, came to dinner with the Longfords at Bernhurst. Frank liked Denis Thatcher well enough, the two sharing a love of rugby and the same experience of being the butt of cartoonists and satirists. Though he admired Mrs Thatcher as 'a sincere but unintellectual Christian', he found her policies and, in particular, the social inequality that they promoted, antithetical to what he regarded as the essence of Christianity.[24] Elizabeth was more cutting in her diary after the dinner. 'Cold, cold. Funny how clever Tories are nearly always cold, whereas warm ones like Willie Whitelaw[25] are dull.'[26]

One of the privileges of the House of Lords at that time was that you never had to retire. Frank had retired twice from politics – compulsorily in 1951 and voluntarily in 1968. He had also retired from the National Bank in 1963 and from the chairmanship of Sidgwick and Jackson in 1980, but in the Upper Chamber the concept had no meaning. As a long-serving member of the Upper House, Frank watched as his former cabinet and government colleagues came to the end of their Commons careers and filled the benches around him. He acted as sponsor to Harold Wilson when he joined the Lords – and, it should be noted, lest the puritan tag attach itself too firmly, to Baronness Wootton, a confirmed atheist.

His other great activity of old age – besides prison visiting – was to write. He produced another volume of autobiography in 1974. *The Grain of Wheat* was published by Collins and covered his activities in the decade since he had joined Wilson's cabinet. *The Sunday Times* thought it an important enough book to run a large extract at the time of publication, featuring Frank's own account of his visit to Copenhagen. Some reviewers, however, were not convinced of its merits. Richard Ingrams, who as editor of *Private Eye* had been responsible for some of the most damning satire about the pornography inquiry, dismissed *The Grain of Wheat* in *Books and Bookmen*. He wrote of Frank: 'His political achievements are minimal, his writings are piffle and his pronouncements on religion and pornography are entirely worthless.'

Undeterred, Frank filled his time as his political activities wound down with profiling some of the people he most admired. In 1974, the same year that *The Grain of Wheat* appeared, he also produced a biography of Abraham Lincoln and a very personal portrait of Jesus Christ. 'Not another autobiography, surely,' Osbert Lancaster[27] quipped. While the subject-matter was hardly original, the attractions of Lincoln are obvious to someone like Frank, who attempted to take a moral rather than a pragmatic line in politics. In 1976, he published a brief life of John F. Kennedy which was overtaken by events. Anxious as ever to believe the best of people, he ignored persistent rumours of Kennedy's womanizing to present his subject as a Catholic statesman answering to a higher moral code. He even managed to secure an interview with Kennedy's widow, Jacqueline. 'Frank back from giving a lecture on Lincoln and Kennedy in States,' Elizabeth wrote in her diary. 'He had tea with Jackie Onassis on Fifth Avenue. He was terrifically hypnotised by her huge black eyes and thought she wore dark glasses out of consideration for others, knowing their power.'[28] In spite of its shortcomings, his book on Kennedy was a bestseller in Ireland.

After a life of St Francis of Assisi, who – like Frank – had befriended the marginalized, he reverted in 1980 to contemporary biography with Richard Nixon. His fall from grace in the Watergate scandal had been a public humiliation which had left Nixon an outcast. As such, Frank found him irresistible. It remained a character trait in his later years. If people were in trouble he would rally to their cause. On one occasion, he attended a drinks party for Harold Wilson and got talking to Marcia Williams, doyenne of the Wilson kitchen cabinet and someone who in the past had had little time or respect for Frank. 'Frank had his first long friendly talk with Marcia after dinner,' Elizabeth noted, 'when she told him she was on the brink of a nervous break-down, everyone was so horrid to her. F suggested giving her lunch in the House and taking her to a Thursday Labour Party meeting under his wing. I can't quite believe in her total desolation (sympathetic as I often feel) as she was so dressed up.'[29]

After finally completing his long-promised book on Ulster in 1981, he was drafted in at the eleventh hour to produce an official portrait of Pope John Paul II to coincide with the Polish pontiff's visit to Britain. Elizabeth had been the first choice of the publishers, but she was tied up with her research for *The Queen as Monarch*, and suggested her husband. He took to the task with alacrity and managed to secure a private interview with the Pope in the Vatican. In 1975 he had been accorded the rare honour of the Grand Cross of the Papal Knights of St Gregory. He joined a club almost as exclusive – in Catholic terms – as that of the Garter Knights. There were only two other recipients of the medal in Britain.

In 1982 he produced *Diary of a Year*, detailing his activities throughout 1981. It was a more successful book than many of those that had gone before, carrying the reader along with witty asides and a procession of well-known names and revealing in the process something about its author. Auberon Waugh, Frank's godson and a critic with a reputation for being just as cutting as Richard Ingrams, wrote a mostly kind review in the *Sunday Telegraph*. 'For the first time in his life, he has written a vastly entertaining book which reflects that goodness, that intelligence and that genuine, usually lovable, eccentricity.'

Heartened by such praise, Frank's literary output increased as his other work dwindled. *Eleven at No 10* in 1984 told of the prime ministers he had known, while *One Man's Faith*, published the same year, was another exercise in autobiography. *The Search for Peace*, which appeared in 1985, pondered again the Irish problem among others, while *The Bishops* in 1986 and *Saints* in 1987 were both collections of essays about some of the Christian figures Frank revered.

A History of the House of Lords appeared in 1988, with an introduction by Elizabeth, once a fervent opponent of the Upper Chamber. *Forgiveness*, published by a small independent printing press in 1989, was intended as a companion volume to *Humility* and depicted another of the central Christian virtues and a recurrent theme in his own life. In 1991, he began a trilogy of books on prisons policy with *Punishment and the Punished*, followed in 1992 by *Prisoner or Patient*, about the subject of the mentally ill, especially close to his heart, and in 1993 by *Young Offenders*. In 1995 he published a final volume of autobiography – *Avowed Intent* (a title chosen by Elizabeth) – bringing together all the versions that had gone before.

Some of the books in this extensive bibliography betrayed the signs of having been hastily written. The trilogy, for example, was a collection of transcripts of interviews carried out by Frank and typed up by his devoted secretary of three decades, Gwen Keeble. Having identified an interesting area and carried out his research, Frank let himself down at the last hurdle and assembled rather than wrote the book. There was also a good deal of overlap in many of the volumes. Marigold Johnson, who continued to work part-time with Frank once the pornography report was over, recalled that his approach to meeting a publisher's deadline was unusual.

He would sit in his office with all the various talks, notes and bits of books that he had already written on any related subject, and he would then say, 'I'm going to work now' and we would all disappear. And then he would come out and get his secretary, Gwen, to retype it. Occasionally I caught a glimpse of these manuscripts. He would just recycle paragraphs, chapters, pages quite ruthlessly. And he would cross things out and say, 'That will do.' That's how he has managed to turn out so many books in such a short period.[30]

Often the final assembly of a manuscript would be completed on a Sunday afternoon at Bernhurst in his study with Barbara Winch, who worked as his part-time secretary there for thirty-three years.

He would dictate bits and pieces and then reach into a big bag of papers that he carried with him and pull something out. He'd then tell me to stick it altogether with glue and staples. 'But it will look such a mess' I'd say, but he told me 'it wouldn't matter to the publishers'. Even in all the muddle though, he knew exactly where everything was and had to go. He read a book as a mechanic knows an engine. So if he wanted to find a paragraph, he knew exactly which page it was on. He had a photographic memory for those things – and telephone numbers.[31]

Frank himself never laid claim to any great literary talent. Years before he had turned down Evelyn Waugh's invitation to spend time together fine-tuning *Born to Believe*. Prose style was not a priority. He wanted by his books to prompt coverage for some of the subjects that interested him. His name was usually enough, if not to draw a large publisher's advance, then to attract a healthy crop of generally respectful reviews. It was Elizabeth's carefully crafted, thoroughly researched biographies and investigations into the state of the monarchy that keep the family finances afloat.

His final book came out in 2000, an edited version of the prison diaries he had been keeping for years. It repeated many previous themes – as well as new ones, including his violent antipathy for the policy of the Conservative Home Secretary in the mid-1990s, Michael Howard,[32] whom he likened to the Devil. It showed yet again the range of prisoners that he journeyed to see beyond the few well-known names. There were references to his small victories on behalf of individuals – having people with mental illnesses transferred to the hospital wing, getting books and educational materials into prisons for those who aspired to learn and so on. The launch – at one of his favourite haunts, the Irish Club in London's Eaton Square – was surrounded by much coverage in the press, as well as serialization in *The Times* and *Daily Mail*, but soon afterwards one of the prisoners he had mentioned in the text sued him for breach of confidence. A judge ruled that the book had to be withdrawn. While Frank was not devastated – the book had, in his terms, served its purpose by raising the profile of prison visiting – he did have reason to feel aggrieved at the action taken by someone he had put himself out to help while he was behind bars. Soon after the court hearing, the same man approached Frank and asked if he would appear as a character witness at his forthcoming trial on fraud charges. Even though it involved a long train and taxi journey to Suffolk, Frank, by now almost blind and walking with a stick, agreed to do it.

His favourite form of entertaining remained until the very end of his life a large lunch at the House of Lords. Elizabeth sometimes joined her husband but increasingly preferred to stay down at Bernhurst. In her absence Antonia or Rachel, with or without their husbands, would make up the party. Occasionally Frank invited fellow peers to join the group. His friends in the House ranged across all ages, from those like James Callaghan whose ministerial careers stretched back almost as far as his, to relative newcomers like the Domenica-born barrister, Patricia Scotland.[33] Marigold Johnson and her husband, the newspaper columnist Paul Johnson,[34] often attended such events. 'They were always very funny, very lively lunches. You talked about everything under the sun. Frank had always done his homework to such an extent that not a single moment passes when he wasn't introducing a topic that was of interest to one of us. No politician, active or not, could have handled the groups of disparate people he gathered better. It was like a star performance and he kept all the information in his head.'[35]

At the start of 2001 Elizabeth suffered the first of an ongoing series of mini-strokes that left her mentally unimpaired but unable to cope with domestic arrangements. She decided to go into a nursing home in Notting Hill, close to where her children lived, though she made regular trips down to Bernhurst, where help could be arranged. Frank tried initially heroically to soldier on in their Chelsea flat, but collapsed on 21 June and was taken to hospital. When he was discharged he reluctantly agreed to join Elizabeth in the nursing home in the room next to hers. He continued to go to the Lords, speaking in debates on prison policy and working on collecting his *Catholic Herald* columns in book form, but those around him noticed that the loss of his independent life with Elizabeth had sapped his *joie de vivre*.

Death held few fears for him. His faith was solid to the very end. He believed in heaven 'but only after a long spell in Purgatory. I see Purgatory as a purification period. I can't picture it, but I can't believe that you go straight to heaven.'[36] This was not false modesty or fishing for compliments. He recognized his own flaws, though perhaps overstated them.

He was in later years haunted by nightmares. Some he made into a joke. In one he was wrestling with Hartley Shawcross, his colleague from the Attlee years. In another he suffered a stroke like his brother Edward. But the one that caused him most angst took him back to his lowest moment – his military failure of 1940. He described the dream to Elizabeth. 'We had just been married and were walking together down the aisle, a very long one. He said to me: "I foresee a terrible war in the future but I shall go out and win a medal and give it to you". But then he paused "Perhaps they won't give me a medal." I said "I know you will win one". How amazing that Frank's failure to fight in the war still disturbs his inner life.'[37] One of the few unmovable dates in his calendar each year was to attend the Remembrance Sunday service in the church nearest to Bernhurst. He was also for many years chairman of the local British Legion there.

On 29 July 2001, he collapsed again and pneumonia was diagnosed. He was admitted again to hospital. Such had been his vigour that few could believe he was nearing the end. When his family and a few old friends came to visit, they read to him from St Matthew's Gospel. He remarked that the verse where all the beggars come to the feast was the most beautiful in the New Testament. He also asked them to read the newspapers to him. He was concerned by the fate of yet another disgraced public figure, the Conservative politician, Jeffrey Archer, who had been convicted of perjury and sent to prison. He even managed to submit a letter which the *Daily Telegraph* published, defending Archer's right to continue to be a member of the House of Lords. When a copy of the *Catholic Herald* arrived with his final column – his interview with his old friend, the broadcaster Jon Snow – he listened as Snow's account of his early years in Uganda was read aloud to him. 'Amazing, amazing,' he said, full to the end of wonder at other people's lives. His mind was alive, but his body was shutting down. Soon afterwards he lapsed into unconsciousness and with his family around him and his beloved wife at his side, he died peacefully on Friday 3 August.

His daughter Judith wrote a poem, The prince in his sleep, about his last hours.

> I sat by you all day,
> a most unfamiliar behaviour,
> you deep asleep, the sleeping prince
> returned to his beauty, my mother
> would have said. Love in the mist,
> poor thing, she could hardly see you.

Sometimes she stood and bent and kissed
your narrowing forehead and
called out loudly in her strong
deaf voice, 'My darling, I want to
keep you but I think God may want you.'
You narrowed and sank all day.

I saw your golden eyelids,
fragile, unwritten speech, smooth
as they hadn't been – Remembering
the months and years of a sad haste . . .
Ten seconds to spare, you'd open
your blue eyes lazily and wide,

your blue eyes, good as a good child,
shy, sly at your chosen curious day,
your deeds; proud, modest. The space
of your life was wide. I rattled, fell
into your space regularly, but
we, or you, or I, smoothed out,

filled in, planted a sprig, a flag,
departed smiling. It never stopped,
your switch back and my small career
colliding and keeping up, laughing,
sometimes besides myself. Your eyelids,
closed, transparent, authoritative.

Epilogue: Bernhurst, December 2002

My memories of Frank at Bernhurst are of Sundays afternoons, just as darkness is falling, the South Downs on the skyline seemingly covered in dark chocolate. We are sitting in his cold, uninviting study, to the right of the front door. The room is illuminated by a single overhead light. Perhaps I'm just imagining that it doesn't have a shade. Frank, dressed in something incongruous like jodhpurs and trainers, is at his small antique desk with a mound of muddled-up papers in front of him. I'm on the old green sofa in the window. It's squidgy and uncomfortable, with scratchy nylon covers. Just across the corridor is the warm, pretty, pink and yellow sitting room where an immaculately dressed Elizabeth is sitting working on a manuscript or a review in her armchair next to the blazing fire. Further down the corridor is the noise of what the family call Backstairs – the rear of this long, rectangular house which has been converted into a self-contained weekend home for children and grandchildren.

Frank and I are talking over some new project he's keen to rope me in on, probably involving one of the many prisoners he visits. We are slurping the sort of medium sweet sherry I always associate with dons. It was what they gave you if your tutorial ended at six o'clock. Frank will often stretch a point to allow a glass before six, especially at the weekend. His enthusiasm for the plan under discussion and his interest in my often sceptical reactions are such that any fleeting thoughts of escaping to Elizabeth's cosy world to warm up are banished. I settle back on the settee and take another sip as we get down to what needs to happen next if we are to succeed, or at least, as he urges, to make an impact on decision-makers.

This is, of course, an idealized picture. Like all such memories, it is a compilation of past visits, abiding impressions and unfulfilled schemes. I can picture him just as easily in the House of Lords, walking along its book-lined corridors, constantly being stopped by colleagues and congratulated on his latest intervention in the Upper Chamber. Or at his favourite London restaurant, a Polish café with inedible food where he was always accorded a downstairs berth of his own, paint-stripper wine and the same chicken dish. I have visited the Lords and the café since his death and they go on as if he had existed only in my head. At Bernhurst enough of him is left to help me collect some final thoughts about this colourful man and the achievements and failures of his long life.

In contrast to my memories of the place, Bernhurst today looks uninviting. As I wander up the drive, past the ancient oak trees that survived the 1987 hurricane and the newer saplings that Elizabeth planted to take the place of those that didn't, I know there will be no one to welcome me. Elizabeth survived for almost fifteen months without Frank. Though her health was failing at the time of his death, she certainly did not give up on life – Frank wouldn't want me to, she said as she organized her annual birthday party on the lawn that lies ahead of me now. She made a triumphant appearance on BBC Radio 4's *Desert Island Discs*, attended launch parties for the latest of her children's books, saw her own abridged version of her life of Wellington published, gave lectures and attended the inaugural Longford Memorial Lecture by Cherie Booth QC. The wife of Prime Minister Tony Blair described the admiration she had had, as a young woman training for the Bar in the 1970s, for Frank's work as a social reformer and the principles that lay behind it. As she spoke from the platform, his face looked down on her, an old photograph projected on to the screen behind the lectern. The ends of his mouth, so often slightly turned down, seemed in my mind's eye to lift gently into a smile as Cherie Booth praised him.

Public compliments had been few and far between after he took up the issues of Myra Hindley and pornography. He was not, as sometimes suggested, unfeeling in the face of criticism. He liked to be liked – but was never afraid like lesser mortals to be hated. The important thing was to be listened to.

For Elizabeth, after Frank's death, there were six new great-grandchildren to delight in. She remained as awe-struck as ever by new life. She spent the summer of 2002 at Bernhurst, with her children and grandchildren on hand to support her. When it was time to return to London to the nursing home, she told them that she wanted to see out her days at the home she had shared with Frank for so many years. The monuments and memories to their life together would be all around her and bring her comfort. She died, aged ninety-five, peacefully in her sleep on 23 October in their bedroom at Bernhurst which looks out over her beloved garden. In her last days, she would repeatedly reach over to Frank's side of the bed as if she felt his presence next to her. She shared his firm belief in an after-life and reunion with loved ones. It is hard not to imagine them in heaven, although as Antonia pointed out, since her father had spent his life on earth voluntarily among sinners, trying to succour them, 'he might find heaven on the dull side and therefore apply for transfer down below, to continue the good work'.

The house and its estate have now passed to Thomas Pakenham. He never used his courtesy title of Lord Silchester and doesn't wish now to be known as the Earl of Longford. Frank was probably an impossible act to follow. Thomas is in the process of moving in, but is away today, so Frank's faithful old secretary is there to let me in. I go first to his study, little changed from my memories of it. He could just have gone out on one of his visits to the Muggeridges, but on closer inspection the House of Lords order papers lying on the floor next to the desk are two years out of date.

I sink back on the sofa with my memories. On the chimney breast in front of me is a picture of Frank's mother, painted when she was a child. It has always been there, I know as soon as I think back, but its prominence has never struck me before. Here, in the place of honour, is the woman who was so unmaternal to Frank when he was a child and whose failure to love him had knock-on consequences throughout his life. The portrait itself is undistinguished, so it was perhaps a form of denial for him to hang it there, a last attempt to turn her into the mother he wanted her to be. Uninterested as he was by possessions – after some valuable antique chairs were stolen from Bernhurst, he dismissed any expressions of sympathy saying 'we can always sit on the floor' – there is something very definite about its positioning. The eighteenth-century prints of Dublin street scenes, displayed above the desk, could easily have taken its place and emphasized his attachment to Ireland. Or a more modern portrait of Catherine, the daughter whose death he mourned so privately, that is next to the bookcase. Or a scene from the Bernhurst garden, painted by his daughter, Judith, that is near the door. He was eighty-four, Elizabeth recorded in her diary, when he bought his first ever painting at an exhibition of Judith's work.

Piled up on the twin window ledges and mantelpiece is an eclectic collection of books and videos. Charles Bronson's exercise tape sits on top of one stack, a souvenir no doubt of one of Frank's trips to see the fitness fanatic (who took the movie star's name by deed poll) in jail. Perhaps Frank had been hoping to build up to a few more press-ups for the next time he visited him. Then there are biographies of his old colleagues and foes – Ernest Bevin who curtailed his deputy's mission to preach forgiveness to the Germans, Harold Macmillan who ruthlessly rose to the top of his party while Frank failed to capture the heights once he had converted to Labour. And cheek by jowl with these heavy political tomes are the smaller books that made up his daily diet of spiritual reading. A yellowing copy of Mary Craig's *Blessings*, a personal story of coping with suffering, sits on top of Frank's own book on *Forgiveness of Man by Man*. He was of his time on inclusive language.

That mix of religion, politics and prisoners was the essence of Frank's very public career. He was a maverick who combined the world of Westminster with a missionary's commitment to penal and social reform and, in the process, staked a claim to the moral high ground without precedent among his peers. A cabinet minister who simultaneously befriended notorious inmates, a pillar of Labour's front bench for twenty-two years who ran London's first centre for young, homeless, drug abusers, a member of Hugh Gaitskell's inner circle who later spearheaded a lampooned crusade against pornography, Frank attempted a unique synthesis of politics and reforming zeal.

It came at a price. The impression of failure is hard to dispel. On one wall of the study there may be the certificate that came when he received a papal knighthood from Paul VI and another to record his honorary degree at Central London Polytechnic (the Garter paraphernalia had to be returned), but despite his long front-bench service, his first-class mind, his gifts as a speaker and his connections with the most influential figures of his generation, he failed to make it into the first rank of politicians. There was, of course, the problem of him being in the Lords, but it went deeper. To his Labour colleagues there was always something unworldly about him that made him a very unpolitical politician. Conscience came before party loyalty once too often for them entirely to trust him. Instead they marginalized him. Even Attlee, his great supporter, kept him out of the cabinet when he had grounds to expect promotion to top table.

To religious leaders, by contrast, he could at times appear too worldly, too wrapped up with papers, publicity, politicians and the political process. It could never have been said of Frank, as it was, for example, of Cardinal Basil Hume, whom he greatly admired, that he backed humbly into the limelight. As a consequence they treated his own spiritual writings – particularly in the relatively uncharted waters of humility and forgiveness – too lightly. And latterly the prison reform lobby, that grew up as a result of his efforts, regarded him with affection as a Don Quixote figure, too idealistic, too interested in individual inmates, to be effective in bringing about the structural reform they so fervently desired.

He hovered in a no-man's land somewhere between all three constituencies. He was arguably out of place too in the twentieth century and belonged more to the philanthropic tradition of such figures as William Wilberforce and Lord Shaftesbury. Like them born into privilege, like them a devout Christian determined to translate faith into action, Frank attempted, as they did, to use his political savvy to win over a hostile Establishment and instigate far-reaching social reform. All three men fall into the category of archetypal do-gooders, combining a principled, almost naïve clear-sightedness with a shrewdness in playing their political cards to achieve their ends. Frank was, you could plausibly suggest, an early exponent (though not a master) of the art of political spin, using his own familiar face to attract a great deal of publicity to neglected causes.

Wilberforce tackled the slave trade, Shaftesbury conditions in the factories and mines, and Frank the penal system. Where the first two succeeded, though, Frank only aspired. He never got to be a reforming Home Secretary. There was no great piece of legislation to which he put his name, though the parole system was set up as a result of the inquiry he chaired in 1963. He did set up New Bridge in 1955, the first organization dedicated to the welfare of ex-prisoners. In 1968 he founded New Horizon for vulnerable young people. Both continue to thrive. He played a bigger than credited part in the landmark Beveridge inquiry. Moreover he awakened the conscience of Westminster to the question of penal reform. Where once he was a lone voice campaigning for change, opening the first ever debate on the subject in the House of Lords, today there is a well-organized lobby of MPs and peers with the Home Office firmly in their sights.

Most politicians leave little behind. Their achievements are as enduring as the impression left by a hand in a bucket of water. Frank may only have made a start on the penal system but his monuments at least are growing and developing. Moreover, the thousands of individual prisoners whose lives he touched never forgot him. Some owed him their freedom; others their second chance at finding a job, a home and happiness; for others again he was simply the person who was prepared to visit them when all the world shunned them, who spoke up for them when they were being denied medical treatment or access to books by the prison authorities. He mortgaged his good name to help each and every individual whose grievances he took up with the Home Office. It was a fine and noble thing to do and was too often decried as an unhealthy fascination with the infamous. The 'names' made up only a tiny section of his address book.

Back in the hallway, just to the left of the front door, is a cartoon by Peter Brookes. Hovering above Frank's benign bishop's pate is a pleasingly ambiguous symbol. It could be taken as a set of keys – to heaven? to prison? – of which the central ring doubles as a halo. Yet Frank was certainly no saint and would have laughed at the very notion. Yet neither was he – as is suggested by a *Daily Mail* cartoon, framed further down the hallway, and dating back to the pornography inquiry – a joke. He may have become a figure of fun in the tabloids and has a claim on the dubious honour of being the first in a long line of tabloid anti-heroes, set up by them to be mocked at every turn. Yet there was a sense in which this clever, contradictory man was always one step ahead of the pack. After all, he had their cartoons ridiculing him up in his hallway. He sent out as Christmas presents copies of Cecil King's diaries where he was described by Harold Wilson as having the mental age of a twelve-year-old.

The satirists may have laughed at him, but he laughed at himself first – and best. The pick of the jokes they used against him – asking for his book on humility to be in the book-shop window – were usually the ones he had first told against himself. If he played the clown, he believed, he might get away with more and achieve more. Like too many of his judgements, it proved a miscalculation, but by the time he realized it he was incapable of changing what had become instinctive behaviour. His sister Mary suggested that the habit dated back to his childhood. So he was not taken seriously enough when he had serious things to say. The medium swamped the message.

All tags that might be attached to him are too simplistic. Frank was a paradox *par excellence*. Here I am standing in the country house that was his home for half a century, but he had no interest in the countryside. He was a monkish person with eight children who enjoyed the life of a socialite and could make people laugh with him more surely than anyone I have ever met (except perhaps his son, Paddy). He was a socialist and an aristocrat, a high-minded reformer and a party-goer, an Irish patriot who lived all his life in England, a politician who called himself a social worker in his little-used passport. He valued success in his children and celebrated their achievements on the walls of his home, but he believed passionately in humility. He was patrician in some of his attitudes, often scornful of public opinion in its prejudices about prisoners, and unable to convey his concern for the victims of crime (which, it should be said, came a close second, but still second, to his concern for prisoners). Yet he was also a convinced democrat who stood above all else for human decency in its broadest, most compassionate and attractive form.

If his flaw was his judgement – 'the basic problem about Frank', Denis Healey once complained affectionately, 'is that he always takes things a bit far' – then perhaps time will give us a different perspective on some of the judgements that drove him to the margins. With his prisoners, of course, judgement is not the issue. He did not seek to judge them, or to determine guilt or innocence, but mainly concentrated on showing them friendship, solidarity and support, whatever they had done. He wanted, he often remarked, to have the words 'The Outcasts' Outcast' on his tombstone.

Back in the political arena where the judgement issue was more acute, he was sidelined because he preached reconciliation with Germany. He was just ahead of his time. Now we are all partners in the EC project of which he was one of the earliest British champions. The warnings that he sounded in the pornography inquiry in the seventies to such a chorus of scorn were with hindsight not perhaps as wide of the mark as was once imagined. Indeed, the conclusions of his report later became mainstream political wisdom. Again he was ahead of his time. Even in the case of Myra Hindley, many liberally minded public figures in the aftermath of her death in prison in November 2002 suddenly revealed themselves as converts to the notion that the parole system had failed in her case and to the concept that redemption was possible for all offenders, however serious their crimes. Perhaps, then, Frank was not so much the figure from the past – like Wilberforce and Shaftesbury – but the figure from the future. It is the final paradox about him that both can be true simultaneously.

Notes

Preface

1. *Spectator*, 4 June, 1994.
2. Longford, F., *Lord Longford's Prison Diary* (Oxford, 2000).

Chapter One

1. Brendan Behan, *Hostage* (1958).
2. Frank Pakenham, *Peace By Ordeal* (London, 1935).
3. Daisy, Countess of Fingall, *Seventy Years Young* (London, 1937).
4. Lady Mary Clive's unpublished memoir of her childhood.
5. Ibid.
6. Ibid.
7. In conversation with the author.
8. Mentioned in documents held in the Longford archive at Tullynally.
9. Lady Mary Clive's unpublished memoir of her childhood.
10. Lady Violet Powell, *Five Out of Six* (London, 1960).
11. Lady Mary Clive, *Brought Up and Brought Out* (London, 1938).
12. Powell, *Five Out of Six*.
13. Clive, *Brought Up*.
14. In conversation with the author.
15. Ibid.
16. Ibid.
17. Lady Mary Clive's unpublished memoir of her childhood.
18. Ibid.
19. Powell, *Five Out of Six*.
20. In conversation with the author.
21. From papers in the Tullynally archive.
22. In conversation with the author.
23. *The Change Makers* (London, 1987).
24. Clive, *Brought Up*.
25. Ibid.
26. Ibid.
27. In conversation with the author.
28. Frank Pakenham, *Born to Believe* (London, 1953).
29. Elizabeth Londford, *The Pebbled Shore* (London, 1986).
30. Clive, *Brought Up*.
31. Lady Mary Clive's unpublished memoir of her childhood.
32. Pakenham, *Born to Believe*.
33. Sir Roger Keyes (1865–1945), Admiral of the Fleet.
34. Longford, *The Pebbled Shore*.
35. Lady Mary Clive's unpublished memoir of her childhood.
36. From Mary Longford's diary in the Tullynally archive.
37. Clive, *Brought Up*.
38. Ibid.
39. Michael Davie (ed.), *Evelyn Waugh's Diaries* (London, 1976).
40. Clive, *Brought Up*.
41. Ibid.
42. Powell, *Five Out of Six*.
43. Pakenham, *Born to Believe*.
44. In conversation with author.
45. Ibid.
46. Peter Somerville-Large, *The Irish Country House* (London, 1995).
47. Somerville-Large, *Irish Country House*.
48. Valerie Pakenham, *The Big House in Ireland* (London, 2000).
49. Powell, *Five Out of Six*.

Chapter Two

1. Sir Alec Spearman (1906–64), Conservative MP for Bournemouth.
2. Pakenham, *Born to Believe*.
3. Dom Bede Griffiths (1906–94), India-based Catholic monk and spiritual writer.
4. Longford, *The Pebbled Shore*.
5. Cyril Alington (1872–1955), teacher and senior Anglican churchman.
6. Powell, *Five Out of Six*.
7. Recalled in a draft article for the *Catholic Herald* among Frank Longford's papers.
8. John Christie (1882–1962), founder of Glyndebourne Opera.
9. Pakenham, *Born to Believe*.
10. In conversation with author.
11. Elizabeth Longford's unpublished diaries.
12. Powell, *Five Out of Six*.
13. Pakenham, *Born to Believe*.
14. Sir Pelham Warner (1873–1963) cricketer, captain of England and Middlesex.
15. In conversation with author.
16. Pakenham, *Born to Believe*.
17. Recalled in a draft article for the *Catholic Herald* among Frank Longford's papers.
18. Anthony Powell, *To Keep the Ball Rolling* (London, 1980).
19. Unpublished, undated letter from Christine, Lady Longford, among Frank Longford's papers.
20. Lady Ottoline Morrell (1873–1938), society hostess and Bloomsbury figure.
21. Interview with Mary Craig in 1977.
22. Evelyn Waugh, *Decline and Fall* (London, 1928).
23. Hugh Gaitskell (1906–63), politician and leader of the Labour Party.
24. Quoted in Philip Williams, *Hugh Gaitskell* (London, 1979).
25. Sir John Betjeman (1906–84), Poet Laureate.
26. From essay by Betjeman in *My Oxford* (London, 1977).
27. Lord David Cecil (1902–86), literary critic and biographer.
28. Interview with Mary Craig in 1978.
29. Sir Maurice Bowra (1898–1971), classical scholar.
30. From essay by Betjeman in *My Oxford* (London, 1977).
31. Douglas (Lord) Jay (1907–95), Labour cabinet minister.
32. In conversation with author.
33. Richard Crossman (1908–74), Labour cabinet minister.
34. Quoted in Douglas Jay, *Change and Fortune* (London, 1980)
35. Quoted in Elizabeth Longford's unpublished diaries.
36. Tom Driberg (1905–76), colourful Labour politician.
37. Francis Wheen, *Tom Driberg* (London, 1990).
38. Evelyn Waugh (1903–66), English novelist.
39. Evelyn Waugh, *Decline and Fall* (London, 1928).
40. In conversation with author.
41. Evan Durbin (1906–48), Labour politician.
42. Pakenham, *Born to Believe*.
43. Ibid.
44. Ibid.
45. Lionel (Lord) Robbins (1898–1984), academic and economist.
46. Pakenham, *Born to Believe*.
47. Ibid.
48. Quoted in Philip Williams, *Hugh Gaitskell* (London, 1979).
49. Longford, *The Pebbled Shore*.
50. John Buchan, Lord Tweedsmuir (1875–1940), administrator and author. His works include *The Thirty Nine Steps*.
51. Longford, *The Pebbled Shore*.

Chapter Three

1. H.A.L. Fisher (1893–1932), historian and academic.
2. Evelyn Waugh, *Vile Bodies* (London, 1930).
3. Quoted in Selina Hastings, *Nancy Mitford* (London, 1985).
4. Freddy Furneaux, 2nd Earl of Birkenhead (1907–75), author.
5. Basil Dufferin, 4th Marquess of Dufferin and Ava (1910–45), Conservative minister.
6. Caroline Blackwood, *Great Granny Webster* (London, 1977).
7. Quoted in Bevis Hillier, *Young Betjeman* (London, 1988).
8. Longford, *The Pebbled Shore*.

9. Maureen, Marchioness of Dufferin and Ava (1907–98), 1920s 'It Girl' and society hostess.
10. In conversation with the author.
11. Pakenham, *Born to Believe*.
12. Ibid.
13. George Dangerfield, *The Strange Death of Liberal England* (London, 1966).
14. Pakenham, *Born to Believe*.
15. In conversation with the author.
16. Interviewed by Mary Craig.
17. 'Bill' Astor, 3rd Viscount Astor (1907–66), Conservative MP and philanthropist.
18. Pakenham, *Born to Believe*.
19. Bronwen, Viscountess Astor, in conversation with the author.
20. The Hon. David Astor (1912–2001), newspaper editor and social reformer.
21. In conversation with the author.
22. Quoted in Lucy Kavaler, *The Astors* (1966).
23. Hilaire Belloc (1870–1953), Catholic writer.
24. In conversation with the author.
25. John Maynard Keynes (1883–1946), economist whose *The General Theory of Employment, Money and Interest* (1936) became the set text of post-Second World War capitalism.
26. Quoted in Williams, *Hugh Gaitskell*.
27. George Lansbury (1859–1940), Christian pacifist and leader of the Labour Party.
28. Longford, *The Pebbled Shore*.
29. In conversation with the author.
30. Ibid.
31. Henry Brooke, Lord Cumnor (1903–84), Conservative politician and Home Secretary.
32. Pakenham, *Born to Believe*.
33. In conversation with the author.
34. Longford, *The Pebbled Shore*.
35. Ibid.
36. Quintin Hogg, Lord Hailsham (1907–2001), Conservative politician and Lord Chancellor.
37. Quintin Hogg, *A Sparrow's Flight* (London, 1990).
38. Sir Isaiah Berlin (1909–97), philosopher and patron saint of liberalism.
39. Elizabeth Longford's unpublished diaries.
40. Ibid.
41. Pakenham, *The Big House in Ireland*.
42. Dora Carrington (1893–1932), artist.

43. Davie (ed.), *Waugh's Diaries*.
44. Longford, *The Pebbled Shore*.
45. Ibid.
46. In conversation with the author.
47. Longford, *The Pebbled Shore*.
48. Ibid.
49. Ibid.
50. Ibid.
51. Ibid.
52. Ibid.
53. Ibid.
54. Elizabeth Longford's unpublished diaries.
55. Naomi Mitchison (1897–1999), author and social reformer.

Chapter Four

1. Oliver St John Gogarty (1878–1957), Irish author, senator and wit, the model for Buck Mulligan in James Joyce's *Ulysses*.
2. Elizabeth Longford's unpublished diaries.
3. Ibid.
4. Ibid.
5. Anthony Powell CH (1905–2000), novelist, best remembered for his *Dance to the Music of Time* series.
6. Quoted in Longford, *The Pebbled Shore*.
7. Sir Oswald Mosley (1896–1980), politician and founder of the British Union of Fascists.
8. Neville Chamberlain (1869–1940), Conservative Prime Minister.
9. Elizabeth Longford's unpublished diaries.
10. Pakenham, *Born to Believe*.
11. This story was told each year by Frank Longford at the Catherine Pakenham Award ceremony.
12. In conversation with the author.
13. Quoted in Longford, *The Pebbled Shore*.
14. Ibid.
15. In conversation with the author.
16. Pakenham, *Born to Believe*.
17. In conversation with the author.
18. Pakenham, *Born to Believe*.
19. In his preface to 1992 reissue of *Peace by Ordeal*
20. Sir William Beveridge (1879–1963), economist and author of landmark report.
21. Elizabeth Longford's unpublished diaries.
22. Desmond FitzGerald (1889–1947), Irish politician.

23. Sir Austen Chamberlain (1863–1937), Conservative Foreign Secretary and Nobel Peace Prize winner.
24. In conversation with the author.
25. Pakenham, *Born to Believe*.
26. Ibid.
27. Quoted in Longford, *The Pebbled Shore*.
28. In conversation with the author.
29. In document among Frank Longford's papers.
30. Randolph Churchill (1911–68), Conservative politician and author.
31. Sir Alan Herbert (1890–1971), writer, *Punch* contributor and Independent MP.
32. Frederick Lindemann, Viscount Cherwell (1886–1957), scientist and minister under Churchill.
33. Pakenham, *Born to Believe*.
34. Elizabeth Longford's unpublished diaries.
35. Philip Toynbee (1916–81), writer and journalist.
36. Interview with Mary Craig.
37. Ibid.
38. Patrick Gordon Walker (1907–80), Labour politician and Foreign Secretary.
39. Hugh Dalton (1887–1962), Labour politician and Chancellor of the Exchequer.
40. Sir Stafford Cripps (1889–1952), Labour politician and Chancellor of the Exchequer.
41. Ernest Bevin (1881–1951), trade union leader and Labour Foreign Secretary.
42. Pakenham, *Born to Believe*.
43. Ibid.
44. Ibid.
45. Sir John Simon (1873–1954), Liberal politician who held all three great offices of state.
46. Interview with Mary Craig.
47. Pakenham, *Born to Believe*.

Chapter Five

1. Recalled in a draft article for the *Catholic Herald* among Frank Longford's papers.
2. Samuel Johnson (1709–84), English poet, critic and lexicographer.
3. In conversation with the author.
4. Longford, *Prison Diary*.
5. Longford, *The Pebbled Shore*.
6. In conversation with the author.
7. Alexander Solzhenitsyn (1918–), Russian author and dissident.
8. Robert Pearce (ed.), Patrick Gordon Walker, *Political Diaries 1932–1971* (London, 1980).
9. In conversation with the author.
10. Anthony Eden, Earl of Avon (1897–1977), Conservative Prime Minister.
11. Pakenham, *Born to Believe*.
12. Hogg, *A Sparrow's Flight*.
13. In conversation with the author.
14. Longford, *The Pebbled Shore*.
15. Ibid.
16. Ibid.
17. In conversation with the author.
18. A.J.P. Taylor (1906–90), English historian.
19. Elizabeth Longford's unpublished diaries.
20. Ibid.
21. Ibid.
22. Longford, *The Pebbled Shore*.
23. In conversation with the author.
24. Claud Cockburn (1904–81), British writer and journalist.
25. Pakenham, *Born to Believe*.
26. P.G. Wodehouse (1881–1975), author.
27. Pakenham, *Born to Believe*.
28. W.H. Auden (1907–73), poet.
29. Pakenham, *Born to Believe*.
30. Longford, *The Pebbled Shore*.
31. A.J. Ayer (1910–89), philosopher.
32. Antonia Fraser, in conversation with the author.
33. Ibid.
34. Father Martin D'Arcy (1888–1976), Jesuit priest.
35. Patrick O'Donovan (1918–81), journalist and writer.
36. Patrick O'Donovan, *A Journalist's Odyssey* (London, 1985).
37. Longford, *The Pebbled Shore*.
38. Pakenham, *Born to Believe*.
39. Ibid.
40. Ibid.

Chapter Six

1. Denis (Lord) Healey (1917–), Deputy Leader of the Labour Party and Chancellor of the Exchequer.
2. Pakenham, *Born to Believe*.

3. In conversation with the author.
4. Longford, *The Pebbled Shore*.
5. Michael Davie (ed.), *Waugh's Diaries*.
6. In conversation with the author.
7. Longford, *The Pebbled Shore*.
8. Elizabeth Longford's unpublished diaries.
9. Longford, *The Pebbled Shore*.
10. Pakenham, *Born to Believe*.
11. Michael Davie (ed.), *Waugh's Diaries*.
12. Auberon Waugh, in conversation with the author.
13. Michael Davie (ed.), *Waugh's Diaries*.
14. Longford, *The Pebbled Shore*.
15. Longford, *The Pebbled Shore*.
16. In conversation with the author.
17. By the 1968 papal encyclical, *Humanae Vitae*.
18. In conversation with the author.
19. Cardinal Basil Hume (1923–99), leader of the Catholic Church in England and Wales.
20. Frank Longford's papers.
21. In conversation with the author.
22. Michael Davie (ed.), *Waugh's Diaries*.
23. In conversation with the author.
24. Ibid.
25. Cyril Connolly (1903–74) English writer.
26. Sir Stephen Spender (1909–95), English poet.
27. In conversation with the author.

Chapter Seven

1. Cardinal Arthur Hinsley (1868–1943), leader of the Catholic Church in England and Wales.
2. Cardinal Bernard Griffin (1899–1956), leader of the Catholic Church in England and Wales.
3. Richard Stokes (1897–1957), Labour MP for Ipswich.
4. Pakenham, *Born to Believe*.
5. Ibid.
6. In conversation with the author.
7. Harold (Lord) Wilson (1916–94), four times Labour Prime Minister.
8. Arthur Greenwood (1880–1954), Labour politician.
9. In conversation with the author.
10. Ibid.
11. Ibid.

12. Ibid.
13. Longford, *The Pebbled Shore*.
14. Janet Beveridge, *Beveridge and His Plan* (London, 1954).
15. Longford, *The Pebbled Shore*.
16. Esmond, 2nd Viscount Rothermere (1925–98), newspaper proprietor.
17. Pakenham, *Born to Believe*.
18. In conversation with the author.
19. Pakenham, *Born to Believe*.
20. Brendan (Lord) Bracken (1901–58), Conservative MP and wartime cabinet minister.
21. Emmanuel (Lord) Shinwell (1884–1986), Labour politician.
22. Pakenham, *Born to Believe*.
23. Arthur Jenkins (died 1946), Welsh miner and Labour politician, father of Roy Jenkins.
24. Pakenham, *Born to Believe*.
25. Pakenham, *Born to Believe*.
26. In conversation with the author.
27. Fritz Schumacher (1911–77), German-born economist, author of *Small is Beautiful* (1973).
28. Barbara (Baroness) Wootton (1897–1988), English social scientist, economist and writer.
29. Robert Kee (1919–), author and broadcaster.
30. Pakenham, *Born to Believe*.
31. Ibid.
32. Longford, *The Pebbled Shore*.
33. In conversation with the author.

Chapter Eight

1. Mark Amory (ed.), *Letters of Evelyn Waugh* (London, 1980).
2. Hogg, *A Sparrow's Flight*.
3. In conversation with the author.
4. Christopher (Lord) Mayhew (1915–97), Labour minister, then Liberal MP.
5. Frank Longford's papers.
6. Herbert (Lord) Morrison (1888–1965), Labour Deputy Prime Minister.
7. (Lord) George Brown (1914–85), Labour Deputy Prime Minister.
8. Longford, *The Pebbled Shore*.
9. Ibid.
10. In conversation with the author.
11. Ibid.

12. Pakenham, *Born to Believe*.
13. Mark Amory (ed.), *Letters of Evelyn Waugh* (London, 1980).
14. In conversation with the author.
15. Interview with Mary Craig.
16. Pakenham, *Born to Believe*.
17. Sir Nicholas Henderson (1919–), British diplomat and author.
18. Nicholas Henderson, *Old Friends and Modern Instances* (London, 2000).
19. Jacques Maritain (1882–1973), French Catholic priest and theologian.
20. Pakenham, *Born to Believe*.
21. In conversation with the author.
22. Ibid.
23. Leslie (Lord) Hore-Belisha (1895–1957), Liberal politician who introduced pedestrian crossings.
24. Pakenham, *Born to Believe*.
25. Ibid.
26. Frank Longford, *Eleven at No. 10* (London, 1984).
27. Ibid.
28. Kenneth Harris, *Attlee* (London, 1986).
29. John Freeman (1915–), broadcaster, Labour politician and British diplomat.
30. Viscount Montgomery of Alamein (1887–1976), British soldier and chairman of NATO forces in Europe.
31. Sir Victor Gollancz (1893–1967), publisher and humanitarian.
32. Pakenham, *Born to Believe*.
33. Bishop George Bell of Chichester (1883–1958), Anglican churchman and peace campaigner.

Chapter Nine

1. Henry Morgenthau (1881–1967), US statesman and financier.
2. In conversation with the author.
3. Ruth Dudley Edwards, *Victor Gollancz* (London, 1987).
4. George Catlett Marshall (1880–1959), US soldier, Secretary of State and Nobel Peace Prize winner.
5. Pakenham, *Born to Believe*.
6. In conversation with the author.
7. Pakenham, *Born to Believe*.
8. Given to the author by Elisa Boness.

9. Pakenham, *Born to Believe*.
10. Douglas Woodruff, editor of the *Tablet* (1936–67).
11. Pakenham, *Born to Believe*.
12. Ibid.
13. Sir Frank Roberts (1910–95), Foreign Office mandarin.
14. Count Michael de la Bedoyère (1900–73), editor and publisher.
15. Amory (ed.), *Letters of Evelyn Waugh*.
16. Pakenham, *Born to Believe*.
17. Elizabeth Longford's unpublished diaries.
18. Jimmy (James) Thomas (1874–1949), trade unionist and Labour politician who remained in National Government as Dominions Secretary.
19. In conversation with the author.
20. Ibid.
21. Longford, *The Pebbled Shore*.
22. Pakenham, *Born to Believe*.
23. Ibid.
24. In conversation with the author.
25. Aneurin Bevan (1897–1960), Deputy Leader of the Labour Party.
26. Konrad Adenauer (1867–1967), first Chancellor and prime architect of West Germany.
27. Pakenham, *Born to Believe*.
28. Sir Robert Birley (1903–82), educationalist.
29. Michael Foot (1913–), Leader of the Labour Party.
30. Pakenham, *Born to Believe*.
31. Peter (Lord) Carrington (1919–), Conservative politician and Foreign Secretary.
32. In conversation with the author.
33. Canon John Collins (1905–82), radical British churchman.
34. Jon Snow (1947–), British journalist and broadcaster.

Chapter Ten

1. Elizabeth Longford's unpublished diaries.
2. Quoted in Williams, *Hugh Gaitskell*.
3. Pakenham, *Born to Believe*.
4. Ibid.
5. Ibid.
6. Ibid.
7. Elizabeth Longford's unpublished diaries.

8. John Costello (1891–1976), Irish statesman.
9. Sean MacBride (1904–88), Irish statesman and lawyer, Nobel Peace Prize winner.
10. Pakenham, *Born to Believe*.
11. Henderson, *Old Friends*.
12. In conversation with the author.
13. Philip Williams (ed.), *The Diary of Hugh Gaitskell (1945–56)* (London, 1983).
14. Longford, *The Pebbled Shore*.
15. Duff Cooper, Viscount Norwich (1890–1954), Conservative politician and author, and his wife Lady Diana Cooper (1892–1986), celebrated beauty and actress.
16. Interview with the author.
17. Elizabeth Longford's unpublished diaries.
18. Kenneth Rose (1924–), biographer and writer.
19. James (Lord) Callaghan (1912–), Labour Prime Minister.
20. James Callaghan, *Time and Change* (London, 1987).

Chapter Eleven

NB: all quotations from the Longford children in conversation with the author.

1. Longford, *The Pebbled Shore*.
2. Hogg, *A Sparrow's Flight*.
3. R.A. (Lord) Butler (1902–82), Conservative politician who held all three great offices of state but failed to be chosen as Prime Minister.
4. Elizabeth Longford's unpublished diaries.
5. Recalled in a draft article for the *Catholic Herald* among Frank Longford's papers.
6. Vita Sackville-West (1892–1962), English poet, novelist and gardener.
7. Henderson, *Old Friends*.
8. Longford, *The Pebbled Shore*.
9. In conversation with the author.
10. Longford, *The Pebbled Shore*.
11. George (Lord) Weidenfeld 1919–), publisher.
12. Sir James Spooner (1932–), businessman and philanthropist.
13. From a tribute to Frank Longford in the *Christ Church Magazine* (2001).
14. Elizabeth Longford's unpublished diaries.
15. Manuscript among Frank Longford's papers.

Chapter Twelve

1. Frank Longford, *Five Lives* (London, 1964).
2. Robert (Lord) Blake (1916–), historian and academic.
3. From a tribute to Frank Longford in the *Christ Church Magazine* (2001).
4. Ibid.
5. Elizabeth Longford's unpublished diaries.
6. Interview with the author.
7. Ibid.
8. Davie (ed.), *Waugh's Diaries*.
9. A.L. Rowse (1903–77), historian and biographer.
10. Pakenham, *Born to Believe*.
11. Ibid.
12. Amory (ed.), *Letters of Evelyn Waugh*.
13. Longford, *Five Lives*.
14. Ibid.
15. Frank Pakenham with Roger Opie, *Causes of Crime* (London, 1958).
16. Interview with the author.
17. Longford, *Five Lives*.
18. Sonia Orwell (1918–80), widow of George Orwell.
19. Pakenham and Opie, *Causes of Crime*.
20. Ibid.
21. Ibid.
22. Among Frank Longford's papers.
23. In conversation with the author.

Chapter Thirteen

1. Daniel O'Connell (1775–1847) Irish patriot, tried by the British authorities for sedition.
2. Longford, *Five Lives*.
3. Ibid.
4. In documents among Frank Longford's papers.
5. In conversation with the author.
6. Sean Lemass (1899–1971), Irish Prime Minister.
7. Longford, *Five Lives*.
8. Ibid.
9. Ibid.
10. Interview with Mary Craig.
11. Frank Cousins (1904–86), miner and trade union leader.

12. Peter (Lord) Thorneycroft (1909–94), Conservative politician and Chancellor of the Exchequer.
13. Lord Edward Montagu of Beaulieu (1926–), motor car enthusiast.
14. Peter Wildeblood, *Against the Law* (London, 1955).
15. Robert (Lord) Boothby (1902–86), Scottish politician and Unionist MP.
16. Longford, *Five Lives*.
17. New Bridge archives.
18. Longford, *Five Lives*.
19. New Bridge archives.
20. Longford, *The Pebbled Shore*.
21. New Bridge archives.
22. Longford, *Five Lives*.
23. Ibid.
24. Gerald (Lord) Gardiner (1900–90), Labour politician and Lord Chancellor.
25. Peter (Lord) Rawlinson (1916–), Conservative politician and Attorney General.
26. Robert (Lord) Mellish (1913–92), Labour politician and Chief Whip.
27. Jack (Lord) Donaldson (1920–), English lawyer and Lord Justice of Appeal.
28. Longford, *Five Lives*.
29. Frank Pakenham, *The Idea of Punishment* (London, 1961).
30. Longford, *Five Lives*.
31. Pakenham, *Punishment*.
32. Ibid.

Chapter Fourteen

1. Longford, *The Pebbled Shore*.
2. Anthony Crosland (1918–77), Labour politician and Foreign Secretary.
3. Jay, *Change and Fortune*.
4. Sir Hugh Lane (1875–1915), Irish art connoisseur.
5. William Butler Yeats (1895–1939), Irish poet and patriot.
6. Augusta, Lady Gregory (1852–1932), Irish playwright and patriot.
7. Sir Anthony O'Reilly (1936–), Irish rugby international, industrialist and newspaper proprietor.
8. Recalled in message sent to first Longford Lecture, July 2002.
9. Documents among Frank Longford's papers.
10. Cardinal John d'Alton (1882–1963), Catholic primate of Ireland.
11. Longford, *Five Lives*.
12. Jennie (Baroness) Lee (1904–88), Labour minister and founder of the Open University.
13. Anthony Howard (ed.), *The Crossman Diaries* (London, 1975).
14. Alec Douglas-Home (Lord Home) (1903–95), Conservative Prime Minister.
15. Anthony Wedgwood-Benn (Tony Benn) (1925–), Labour politician, cabinet minister and diarist.
16. William Wedgwood-Benn, 1st Viscount Stansgate (1877–1960), Labour cabinet minister.
17. Amory (ed.), Letters of Evelyn Waugh.
18. Longford, *The Pebbled Shore*.
19. Longford, *Five Lives*.
20. Robert Maxwell (d. 1991), Labour MP, publisher and fraudster.
21. Group Captain Leonard Cheshire (1917–92), war hero and charity worker.
22. Sir Peter Ustinov (1921–), Russian-born actor and film star.
23. Longford, *Five Lives*.
24. Williams, *Hugh Gaitskell*.
25. Elizabeth Longford's unpublished diaries.
26. In conversation with the author.
27. Ibid.
28. Christopher Mayhew, *A Time to Explain* (London, 1987).
29. Kenneth Younger (1908–76), Labour politician.
30. Ben Pimlott, *Harold Wilson* (London, 1993).
31. Longford, *Five Lives*.
32. Sir Dingle Foot (1905–78), Liberal then Labour politician and Solicitor-General.
33. Angela Lambert (1940–), English novelist and journalist.
34. Interview with Mary Craig.
35. Roy (Lord) Jenkins (1920–2003), Labour, Social Democrat then Liberal Democrat politician, Home Secretary and author.
36. Unpublished essay given to author by Lord Jenkins.
37. John Profumo (1915–), Conservative politician and charity worker.
38. Bronwen, Viscountess Astor (1930–), psychotherapist and widow of Bill Astor.
39. In conversation with the author.

40. Longford, *Five Lives*.
41. In conversation with the author.
42. Ibid.
43. Ibid.
44. Peter (Lord) Shore (1924–2001), Labour politician and cabinet minister.
45. Alice (Baroness) Bacon (1909–93), Labour politician.
46. Beatrice, Baroness Serota (1919–2002), Labour Deputy Leader of the House of Lords.
47. In conversation with the author.

Chapter Fifteen

1. Frank Longford, *The Grain of Wheat* (London, 1974).
2. In conversation with the author.
3. Ibid.
4. Ibid.
5. Barbara Castle, *Diaries* (London, 1974).
6. Longford, *Grain of Wheat*.
7. Castle, *Diaries*.
8. Edward (Lord) Shackleton (1915–94), Labour politician and son of explorer.
9. Professor Bernard Crick (1929–), writer and academic.
10. *New Statesman*, 17 June 1994.
11. Howard (ed.), *Crossman Diaries*.
12. Ibid.
13. Sir Hugh Fraser (1936–84), Conservative politician.
14. Enoch Powell (1912–97), Conservative then Ulster Unionist politician.
15. Sir David Steel (1938–), Scottish politician and Liberal, then Liberal Democrat leader.
16. Douglas (Lord) Houghton (1898–1995), Labour cabinet minister and party chairman.
17. Interview with Mary Craig.
18. Ibid.
19. Ibid.
20. Ibid.
21. Interview with the author.
22. Among Frank Longford's papers.
23. Laurens van der Post (1906–96), South African writer.
24. In conversation with the author.
25. Ibid.
26. Ibid.
27. Ibid.

28. Burke (Lord) Trend (d. 1987), cabinet secretary.
29. Elizabeth Longford's unpublished diaries.
30. Marcia Williams (Lady Falkender) (1932–), political adviser.
31. Gerald Kaufmann (1930–), Labour politician and minister.
32. Joe Haines (1928–), journalist and press advisor.
33. In conversation with the author.
34. Ibid.
35. In conversation with the author.
36. Longford, *Grain of Wheat*.
37. In conversation with the author.
38. Longford, *Grain of Wheat*.
39. Tony Benn, *Office Without Power* (London, 1988).
40. Longford, *Grain of Wheat*.
41. Robert Pearce (ed.), *Patrick Gordon Walker – Political Diaries 1932–1971* (London, 1980).
42. David Marquand, *The Progressive Dilemma* (London, 1991).
43. Elizabeth Longford's unpublished diary.
44. Pearce (ed.), *Patrick Gordon Walker*.
45. Cecil (Lord) King (1901–87), scion of the Northcliffes and newspaperman.
46. Cecil King, *The Cecil King Diaries 1965–1970* (London, 1975).
47. Interview with Mary Craig.
48. In conversation with the author.
49. Ibid.
50. Longford, *Grain of Wheat*.
51. Castle, *Diaries*.
52. Davie (ed.), *Waugh's Diaries*.
53. Lady Violet Bonham-Carter (1887–1969), Liberal politician and daughter of Herbert Asquith.
54. Longford, *Grain of Wheat*.

Chapter Sixteen

1. Malcolm Muggeridge (1903–90), writer, broadcaster and Catholic convert.
2. Interview with Mary Craig.
3. Powell, *To Keep the Ball Rolling*.
4. *Spectator*, 4 June 1994.
5. Bishop William Ullathorne (d. 1889), first Catholic archbishop of Birmingham after the restoration of the hierarchy in 1850.

6. In conversation with the author.
7. Interview with Mary Craig.
8. Frank Longford, *Humility* (London, 1969).
9. In conversation with the author.
10. Charles (Lord) Forte (1908–), businessman.
11. Sir Edward Heath (1916–), Conservative Prime Minister.
12. Elizabeth Longford's unpublished diaries.
13. John Grigg (1924–2003), journalist and prize-winning historian.
14. Diana, Lady Mosley (1911–), Mitford sister and widow of fascist leader
15. Shirley Conran (1931–), writer and campaigner.
16. In conversation with the author.
17. Ibid.
18. Longford, *Grain of Wheat*.
19. In conversation with the author.
20. Interview with Mary Craig.
21. Elizabeth Longford's unpublished diaries.
22. In conversation with the author.
23. Kenneth Tynan (1927–80), theatre critic and producer.
24. In conversation with the author.
25. Ibid.
26. Ibid.
27. Ibid.
28. John Gummer (1939–), Conservative cabinet minister.
29. Mary Whitehouse (1910–2002), campaigner.
30. In conversation with the author.
31. Ibid.
32. Ibid.
33. Archbishop Trevor Huddleston (1913–98), Anglican churchman and anti-apartheid campaigner.
34. Susan (Baroness) Masham (1935–), life peer and disability campaigner.
35. Sir Peregrine Worsthorne (1923–), newspaper editor and writer.
36. Hartley (Lord) Shawcross (1924–), chief UK prosecutor at Nuremburg trials and Labour MP.
37. Sir Kingsley Amis (1922–95), novelist.
38. Elizabeth Jane Howard (1923–), novelist.
39. Frank Longford, *Pornography: The Longford Report* (London, 1972).
40. In conversation with the author.
41. Sir Larry Lamb (1929–), newspaper editor.
42. In conversation with the author.
43. Longford, *Pornography*.
44. Interview with Mary Craig.
45. Longford, *Grain of Wheat*.
46. Ibid.
47. Gyles Brandreth, *Breaking the Westminster Code* (London, 2001).
48. Ibid.
49. In conversation with the author.
50. Ibid.
51. Longford, *Pornography*.
52. In conversation with the author.
53. Ibid.
54. Diana Dors (1931–84), actress.
55. Interview by Mary Craig.
56. Robert (Lord) Carr, Conservative politician and Home Secretary.
57. In conversation with the author.
58. Brandreth, *Westminster Code*.

Chapter Seventeen

NB: *all quotations from the Longford children in conversation with the author.*

1. Longford, *The Pebbled Shore*.
2. Ibid.
3. Anthony Powell, *Journals 1982–1986* (London, 1995).
4. In conversation with the author.
5. Longford, *Grain of Wheat*.
6. In conversation with the author.
7. Longford, *The Pebbled Shore*.
8. Harold Pinter (1930–), playwright, writer and humanitarian.
9. Longford, *The Pebbled Shore*.

Chapter Eighteen

1. Emlyn Williams, *Beyond Belief* (London, 1967).
2. Interviewed by Jean Rook.
3. Elizabeth Longford's unpublished diary.
4. Harold Evans (1928–), newspaper editor and publisher.
5. Frank Longford, *Diary of a Year* (London, 1982).
6. In conversation with the author.
7. Ibid.
8. Sir Leon Brittan (1939–), Conservative Home Secretary and European Commissioner.

9. In conversation with the author.
10. Ibid.
11. Ibid.
12. Ibid.
13. Elizabeth Longford's unpublished diary.
14. Longford, *Prison Diary*.
15. Elizabeth Longford's unpublished diaries.
16. Longford, *Diary of a Year*.
17. Longford, *Prison Diary*.
18. In conversation with the author.
19. Ibid.
20. Ibid.
21. Ibid.
22. Ibid.
23. Bernard Levin (1928–), author and journalist.
24. Elizabeth Longford's unpublished diaries.
25. In conversation with the author.
26. Ibid.

Chapter Nineteen

NB: *all quotations from the Longford children in conversation with the author.*

1. Richard Ingrams (1937–), journalist, satirist and biographer.
2. A.N. Wilson (1950–), journalist and writer.
3. Elizabeth Longford's unpublished diaries.
4. Ibid.
5. Ibid.
6. Ibid.
7. Ibid.
8. Ibid.
9. Ibid.
10. Ibid.

11. Patrick (Earl of) Lichfield (1939–), society photographer.
12. Elizabeth Longford's unpublished diaries.
13. Ibid.
14. Ernie Wise (Ernest Wiseman) (1925–99), comedian and TV star.
15. Elizabeth Longford's unpublished diaries.
16. Harriet Harman (1950–), daughter of Elizabeth Longford's brother and Labour cabinet minister.
17. Elizabeth Longford's unpublished diaries.
18. Alan Clark (1928–2001), Conservative minister and diarist.
19. Elizabeth Longford's unpublished diaries.
20. In conversation with the author.
21. Roy (Lord) Hattersley (1932–), Labour Deputy Leader and writer.
22. Elizabeth Longford's unpublished diaries.
23. Longford, *Prison Diary*.
24. Longford, *Eleven at No. 10*.
25. William (Viscount) Whitelaw (1918–99), Conservative Deputy Prime Minister.
26. Elizabeth Longford's unpublished diaries.
27. Osbert Lancaster (1908–86), English writer and cartoonist.
28. Elizabeth Longford's unpublished diaries.
29. Ibid.
30. Interview with the author.
31. Ibid.
32. Michael Howard (1941–), Conservative politician and Home Secretary.
33. Patricia (Baroness) Scotland (1956–), barrister and Labour minister.
34. Paul Johnson (1928–), editor, journalist and author.
35. In conversation with the author.
36. Ibid.
37. Elizabeth Longford's unpublished diaries.

Bibliography

CHILDHOOD AND YOUTH

Acton, Harold, *Memoirs of an Aesthete* (Hamish Hamilton, 1948)
Becket, J.C., *The Anglo-Irish Tradition* (Faber, 1976)
Betjeman, John, essay in *My Oxford* (Robson Books, 1977)
Blackwood, Caroline, *Great Granny Webster* (Picador, 1977)
Hastings, Selina, *Nancy Mitford* (Jonathan Cape, 1985)
Hillier, Bevis, *Young Betjeman* (John Murray, 1988)
Norman, Diana, *Terrible Beauty* (Hodder and Stoughton, 1987)
Pakenham, Valerie, *The Big House in Ireland* (Cassell, 2000)
Palmer, Alan, *The East End* (John Murray, 1989)
Powell, Lady Violet, *Margaret, Countess of Jersey* (Heinemann, 1978)
Somerville-Large, Peter, *The Irish Country House* (Sinclair Stevenson, 1995)
Waugh, Evelyn, *Decline and Fall* (Chapman and Hall, 1928)
——, *Vile Bodies* (Chapman and Hall, 1930)
Wheen, Francis, *Tom Driberg* (Chatto and Windus, 1990)

POLITICAL LIFE

Benn, Tony, *Office Without Power* (Hutchinson, 1988)
Birkenhead, Lord, *Frederick Edwin, Earl of Birkenhead* (Butterworth, 1935)
Callaghan, James, *Time and Change* (Collins, 1987)
Castle, Barbara, *The Castle Diaries* (Weidenfeld, 1974)
Cook, Chris and Ramsden, John (eds), *By-Elections in British Politics* (Macmillan, 1973)
Foot, Michael, *Aneurin Bevan*, vols I and II (Davis Poynter, 1973)
Grigg, John, *Nancy Astor* (Sidgwick, 1980)
Hailsham, Lord, *A Sparrow's Flight: The Memoirs of Lord Hailsham* (Collins, 1990)
Harris, Kenneth, *Attlee* (Weidenfeld, 1976)
Healey, Denis, *The Time of My Life* (Michael Joseph, 1989)
Howard, Anthony, *RAB: The Life of R. A. Butler* (Jonathan Cape, 1987)
—— (ed.), *The Crossman Diaries* (Hamish Hamilton, 1975)
Jay, Douglas, *Change and Fortune* (Heinemann, 1980)
Kavaler, Lucy, *The Astors* (Harrap, 1966)
King, Cecil, *The Cecil King Diaries 1965–1970* (Jonathan Cape, 1975)
Marquand, David, *The Progressive Dilemma* (Heinemann, 1991)
Mayhew, Christopher, *A Time to Explain* (Hutchinson, 1987)
Mikardo, Ian, *Back-bencher* (Weidenfeld, 1988)
Morgan, Janet, *The House of Lords and the Labour Government 1964–1970* (Oxford, 1975)

Bibliography

Pearce, Robert (ed.), *Patrick Gordon Walker: Political Diaries 1932–1971* (The Historian's Press, 1991)
Pimlott, Ben, *Hugh Dalton* (Jonathan Cape, 1985)
——, *Harold Wilson* (HarperCollins, 1993)
Rose, Norman, *The Cliveden Set* (Jonathan Cape, 2000)
Williams, Philip, *Hugh Gaitskell* (Jonathan Cape, 1979)
—— (ed.), *The Diary of Hugh Gaitskell* (Jonathan Cape, 1983)
Wilson, Harold, *The Labour Government 1964–1970* (Weidenfeld, 1971)
Ziegler, Philip, *Wilson: The Authorised Life* (Weidenfeld, 1993)

GERMANY
Balfour, Michael, *West Germany: A Contemporary History* (Croom Helm, 1982)
Cairncross, Sir Alec, *The Price of War* (Blackwell, 1986)
Collins, Canon John, *Faith under Fire* (Leslie Frewin, 1966)
Dudley Edwards, Ruth, *Victor Gollancz* (Gollancz, 1987)
Roberts, Frank, *Dealing with Dictators* (Weidenfeld, 1991)

SOCIAL CONCERNS
Beveridge, Janet, *Beveridge and His Plan* (Hodder, 1954)
West, Ann, *For the Love of Lesley* (W.H. Allen, 1989)
Williams, Emlyn, *Beyond Belief: The Moors Murders* (Hamish Hamilton, 1967)

BY THE LONGFORDS
Clive, Lady Mary, *Brought Up and Brought Out* (Cobden-Sanderson, 1938)
Longford, Elizabeth, *The Pebbled Shore* (Weidenfeld, 1986)
Longford, Frank, *Five Lives* (Hutchinson, 1964)
——, *Humility* (Collins, 1969)
——, *Pornography: The Longford Report* (Coronet, 1972)
——, *Abraham Lincoln* (Weidenfeld, 1974)
——, *The Grain of Wheat* (Collins, 1974)
——, *The Life of Jesus Christ* (Weidenfeld, 1974)
——, *Kennedy* (Weidenfeld, 1976)
——, *Francis of Assisi* (Weidenfeld, 1978)
——, *Nixon: A Study of Extremes of Fortune* (Weidenfeld, 1980)
——, *Diary of a Year* (Weidenfeld, 1982)
——, *Pope John Paul II* (Collins, 1982)
——, *Eleven at No. 10* (Harrap, 1984)
——, *One Man's Faith* (Hodder, 1984)
——, *The Bishops* (Sidgwick, 1986)
——, *Saints* (Hutchinson, 1987)
——, *A History of the House of Lords* (Collins, 1988)
——, *Forgiveness of Man by Man* (Buchebroc, 1989)
——, *Punishment and the Punished* (Chapmans, 1991)
——, *Prisoner or Patient* (Chapmans, 1992)
——, *Young Offenders* (Chapmans, 1993)
——, *Avowed Intent* (Little Brown, 1995)
——, *Lord Longford's Prison Diary* (Oxford, 2000)
—— and McHardy, Anne, *Ulster* (Weidenfeld, 1981)

—— and O'Neill, Tim, *Eamon de Valera* (Hutchinson, 1970)
Pakenham, Elizabeth (ed.), *Catholic Approaches* (Weidenfeld, 1953)
Pakenham, Frank, *Peace by Ordeal* (Jonathan Cape, 1935)
——, *Born to Believe* (Jonathan Cape, 1953)
——, *The Idea of Punishment* (Geoffrey Chapman, 1961)
—— with Opie, Roger, *Causes of Crime* (Weidenfeld, 1958)
Powell, Lady Violet, *Five Out of Six* (Heinemann, 1960)
——, *Within the Family Circle* (Heinemann, 1976)

FRIENDS AND FOES
Amory, Mark (ed.), *Letters of Evelyn Waugh* (Weidenfeld, 1980)
Craig, Mary, *Longford: A Biographical Portrait* (Hodder, 1978)
Davie, Michael (ed.), *Evelyn Waugh's Diaries* (Weidenfeld 1976)
Henderson, Nicholas, *Old Friends and Modern Instances* (Profile, 2000)
O'Donovan, Patrick, *A Journalist's Odyssey* (Esmonde, 1985)
Powell, Anthony, *Journals 1982–1986* (Heinemann, 1995)
——, *Journals 1990–1992* (Heinemann, 1997)
Wildeblood, Peter, *Against the Law* (Weidenfeld, 1955)

Index

Index